W9-CEF-970

QuickBooks® Desktop 2020

Comprehensive

Trish Conlon

MA, Point Loma Nazarene University

LABYRINTH

LEARNING™

QuickBooks Desktop 2020: Comprehensive
Copyright © 2020 by Labyrinth Learning

LABYRINTH
LEARNING™

Labyrinth Learning
PO Box 2669
Danville, CA 94526
800.522.9746
On the web at lablearning.com

President
Brian Favro

Product Manager
Jason Favro

Development Manager
Laura Popelka

Production Manager
Debra Grose

Senior Editor
Alexandra Mummery

Editor
Alexandria Henderson

Editorial Team
Donna Bacidore, Maddy
Gessford, Cindy Brown,
Diana D'Abruzzo

Composition
Happenstance Type-O-Rama

Indexing
Valerie Haynes Perry

Cover Design
Sam Anderson Design

All rights reserved. Printed in the United States of America. No part of this material protected by this copyright notice may be reproduced or utilized in any form or by any means, electronic or mechanical, including photocopying, recording, scanning, or by information storage and retrieval systems without written permission from the copyright holder.

Labyrinth Learning™ and the Labyrinth Learning logo are trademarks of Labyrinth Learning. Intuit® and QuickBooks® are registered trademarks of Intuit, Inc. Microsoft® is a registered trademark of Microsoft Corporation in the United States and/or other countries and is used by Labyrinth Learning under license from owner. This title is an independent publication not affiliated with Intuit, Inc., or Microsoft Corporation. Other product and company names mentioned herein may be the trademarks of their respective owners.

The example companies, organizations, products, people, and events depicted herein are fictitious. No association with any real company, organization, product, person, or event is intended or should be inferred.

Screenshots reprinted with permission.

PRINT ITEM: 1-64061-209-2
ISBN-13:   978-1-64061-209-9

Manufactured in the United States of America

GPP   10 9 8 7 6 5 4 3 2 1

Contents in Brief

Table of Contents

Chapter 6
Bringing It All Together:
Service Project

Chapter 7
Managing Physical Inventory

Chapter 8
Working with Balance Sheet
Accounts and Budgets

Chapter 9

Using QuickBooks for Payroll — 311

Chapter 10

Job Costing, Creating Estimates, and Time Tracking — 355

Preface

QuickBooks® Desktop 2020: Comprehensive provides essential overage of the latest version of Intuit's popular bookkeeping program. QuickBooks topics covered include backing up files, creating new company files, vendors and customers, banking with QuickBooks, classes, physical inventory, payroll, estimates and time tracking, balance sheet accounts, budgets, closing the books, and more. Also covered are the basic accounting principles (GAAP) and a discussion of the accounting cycle.

New to this edition: The text now teaches QuickBooks using the Premier Accountant edition. We've expanded our Behind the Scenes feature to show the accounts affected in each transaction as well as which accounts increase/decrease and by how much. We also added more Check Figure lines to help students stay on track. And this edition features two chapter-length projects, one covering Chapters 1–5 (service-based project) and the other covering Chapters 7–11 (merchandising-based project). Both work with Quick Grader!

Resources & Tools

Every textbook purchase comes with elements designed to support both educators and students.

- The interactive ebook delivers learning content in an engaging manner. Features may include elements such as videos or animations, self-assessments, slide shows, and more. Our ebooks support highlighting, note-taking, and searching.

- eLab, our course management tool, provides additional learning content such as chapter overviews and automatically graded reports and tests. eLab can be fully integrated with a school's LMS, making course management even easier.

- The Learning Resource Center is for classrooms not using eLab. Here students can download the needed exercise files and chapter overviews: labyrinthelab.com/lrc

- Instructors can register on our site and then download a comprehensive support package that includes lesson plans and editable overview presentations, answer keys, a course syllabus, test banks, additional exercises, and more: lablearning.com

Certification and This Text

This textbook has been certified by and carries the ProCert logo, distinguishing this courseware as a trusted and critical part of preparing for a certification exam. This solution meets all course objectives to prepare students to take the QuickBooks Certified User (QBCU) exam.

About the Author

Trish Conlon (BS, Biology; MA, Education) has been a QuickBooks educator since 1998 and has authored QuickBooks texts for Labyrinth Learning since 2004. She earned her BS from Washington State University and her MA from Point Loma Nazarene University. She has a Teaching License in Finance & Business and Management & Administration from Oregon, a Teaching Credential in Finance & Business from California, and a Certificate in Online Teaching from the University of California San Diego (Extension) and is a QuickBooks Pro Advisor. Currently, she is pursuing her law degree at Willamette University.

Acknowledgements

Many individuals contribute to the development and completion of a textbook. The following individuals provided invaluable feedback for this edition:

Gerald Childs, *Waukesha County Technical College*
Mark Gershman, *Oakton Community College*
Kathy Marquette, *North Dakota State College of Science*
Margaret Pond, *Front Range Community College*
Howard Randall, *Mission College*
Jaye Simpson, *Tarrant County Community College*

This learning solution has also benefited from the feedback and suggestions from these individuals:

Pete Bada, *NVCC*
Lisa Briggs, *Columbus State Community College*
Dwayne Briscoe, *Bookkeeping-Results, LLC*
Hoa Burrows, *Miami Dade College*
Kathy Camp, *Conway Adult Education Center*
David Campbell, *Northern Virginia Community College*
Amy Chataginer, *William Carey University*
Janine Clover, *Southeastern Community College*
Paul Croitoru, *Wilbur Wright College*
Sarah Dixon-Hackey, *North Dakota State College of Science*
Kerry Dolan, *Great Falls College Montana State University*
Doris Donovan, *Dodge City Community College*
Valorie Duvall, *South Plains College*
Jesse Fink, *Touro College*
Shmuel Fink, *Touro College*
Debbra Finney, *Turlock Adult School*
Roger Fulk, *Upper Valley Career Center – Adult Workforce Division*
Helen Hall, *Quik-help.com*
Diann Hammon, *JF Drake State Community and Technical College*

Maggie Hilgart, *Mid-State Technical College*
Pam Hillman, *Gateway Technical College*
Nancy Howard, *Mt. Hood Community College*
Jenny Jones, *Bluegrass Community and Technical College*
Ruby Kowaney, *Venice Skills Center*
Myles Lambert, *Brookdale Community College*
Vicki Maheu, *San Diego Community Colleges, Continuing Education*
Steven Manske, *Mission College*
Giselinda Mathieu, *Goodwill Workplace Training and Assistance Center*
Deb Niedermeyer, *Montana State University*
Patti Norris, *Central Oregon Community College*
Veronica Paz, *Indiana University of Pennsylvania*
Roxanne Phillips, *CCCOnline*
Karla Robinson, *Kellogg Community College*
Philip Slater, *Forsyth Technical Community College*
Randy Watkins, *Contra Costa College*
Sheree White, *Palm Beach County School District*
Peter Young, *San Jose State University*

1 | Introducing QuickBooks Desktop

QuickBooks has become the software of choice for many owners of small- to medium-sized businesses. No doubt, this is due to the ease of use and helpful features the software offers. In this chapter, you will explore the various editions of QuickBooks and determine which is right for you. You will also discover what goes on behind the scenes and why it is important to have a basic understanding of accounting. Finally, you will be introduced to a few QuickBooks basics that are vital to your success as a QuickBooks user.

LEARNING OBJECTIVES

▸ Explain basic accounting concepts

▸ Describe the attributes of QuickBooks editions

▸ Identify features of the QuickBooks window

▸ Restore a portable company file

▸ Back up and restore a company file

📁 Project: Parrot's Paradise Resort

Throughout this book you will learn about QuickBooks by working with the company file for Parrot's Paradise Resort, an ocean resort in Key West, Florida, owned by Jimmy Parrot. The resort not only provides lodging but also features equipment rentals, an event venue, and a gift shop. In this chapter, you will work with the company file as you're introduced to the QuickBooks software and some accounting basics.

Getting to Know QuickBooks

QuickBooks is a software program that allows companies to:

- Keep track of customers, vendors, employees, and other important entities

- Process sales transactions and cash receipts

- Process purchase transactions and payments to vendors

- Run payroll

- Track and sell inventory

- Run end-of-period financial reports

- Track assets (what you own) and liabilities (what you owe)

- Keep track of bank accounts

- Collaborate with accountants easily and efficiently

Each year, Intuit introduces a version of QuickBooks with new and improved features. As you work through this book, notice that new aspects are called out with a special icon.

 This is how you'll be able to identify new or improved QuickBooks features.

Editions of QuickBooks

There are two main varieties of QuickBooks—Desktop and Online—and within each, there are several editions. Careful evaluation is required to select the edition that best suits your business. Every edition performs basic tasks required for small-business bookkeeping but will differ in terms of capabilities. For example, the Premier and Enterprise editions of QuickBooks Desktop are better suited than Pro for the manufacturing industry. QuickBooks Enterprise Solutions is aimed at larger companies, allows for more users, and has more advanced inventory capabilities.

Desktop editions include QuickBooks Pro, multiple QuickBooks Premier editions, and QuickBooks Enterprise. An advantage to choosing one of the industry-specific QuickBooks Premier editions is that it will provide more industry-specific functionality, for example, running a donor contribution report for a nonprofit business or tracking profitability by product. QuickBooks Pro works well, and can be customized, for companies in a variety of industries, including nonprofit organizations. Ideally, your company should have fewer than twenty employees and less than $1 million in annual revenue to use Pro (these are not strict rules but rather guidelines). This book, including the trial software provided, is based on the *Premier Accountant* edition. The similarities between Pro and Premier will make it easy for you to adapt to switching between them, just as once you learn to drive a Honda, it is easy to switch to driving a Ford.

Note! Intuit also supports a QuickBooks edition for Mac users. It's similar to the Windows-based version in function, though not in look. The downloadable files associated with this book are *not* compatible with the Mac or international versions of QuickBooks.

You can determine the version and edition you are running from the Help menu.

 Help→About QuickBooks Accountant Desktop 2020

QuickBooks Online

Intuit provides a desktop and an online variety of QuickBooks to provide users with flexibility to choose the one that best suits their needs.

COMPARING QUICKBOOKS DESKTOP AND ONLINE		
	QuickBooks Desktop (QBD)	**QuickBooks Online (QBO)**
Location of company file	On a computer's hard drive, cloud storage, private company network, or other location controlled by the company	Hosted online by Intuit
Access to company file	Through the use of a computer on which the software is installed or via a mobile device app	Remotely by an Internet browser on a computer or mobile device
Cost	One-time purchase; price is determined by the edition, and you can use a version for multiple years without incurring an additional cost	Monthly subscription fee; price is determined by the edition
Editions available	Pro, Premier, and Enterprise	Self-Employed, Simple Start, Essentials, and Plus
Features	It's been around longer and has more features	Apps are available for purchase to fill in the "gaps" between the two programs
Miscellaneous	Better at managing large amounts of inventory and job costing	Intuit is investing a lot in QBO and makes improvements on a regular basis

For more detailed information about QuickBooks Desktop or QuickBooks Online, visit the company's website at: intuit.com

Types of Tasks

There are many tasks you can perform with QuickBooks. They can be broken down into two main categories: those that affect the accounting behind the scenes (activities and company setup) and those that do not (lists and reporting).

QUICKBOOKS TASKS AND THEIR FUNCTIONS

Task	Function
Lists (database)	Lists store information about customers, vendors, employees, services, products, payment methods, and more.
Activities	Activities affect what happens behind the scenes and are entered on forms, such as invoices or bills.
Company Setup	This task walks you through the basic steps to set up a new company in QuickBooks.
Reports	QuickBooks provides many preset reports and graphs that are customizable.

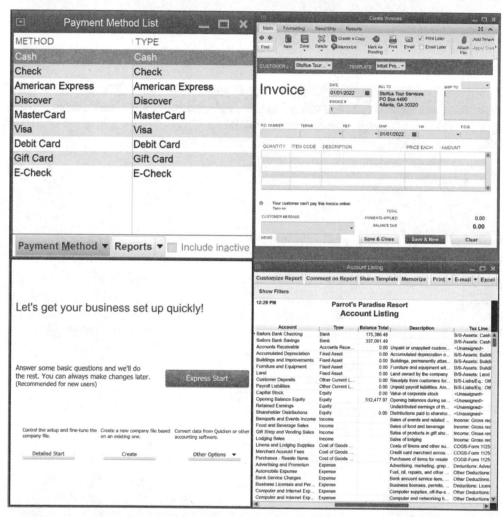

The four types of tasks, clockwise from top left: the Payment Method List used to store information, the Create Invoices window used to enter an activity, the Account Listing report to display all accounts in a company's Chart of Accounts, and the QuickBooks Desktop Setup window.

Accounting Basics

QuickBooks is quite intuitive, but you could find yourself running into problems if you don't understand the accounting basics on which QuickBooks is based. Having the basic knowledge as explained in this book will help you set up your company more effectively and provide a better picture of the health of the business.

What Is GAAP?

GAAP stands for Generally Accepted Accounting Principles (GAAP). These principles are accounting rules used in the United States to prepare, present, and report financial statements for a variety of entities. The organization that creates the rules is called the Financial Accounting Standards Board (FASB). Publicly owned companies follow these rules unless they can show that doing so would produce information that is misleading. It's wise for small-business owners to adhere to GAAP as well.

As GAAP attempt to achieve basic objectives, they have several assumptions, principles, and constraints. Throughout the book you will see reminders of how GAAP apply to tasks you're completing in QuickBooks via the Flashback to GAAP feature.

GENERALY ACCEPTED ACCOUNTING PRINCIPLES (GAAP)	
Principle	**Description**
Business entity principle	The business is separate from the owners and from other businesses. Business revenues and expenses should be kept separate from the business owner's personal expenses.
The assumption of the going concern	The business will be in operation indefinitely.
Monetary unit principle	A stable currency will be the unit of record.
Time-period principle	The activities of the business can be divided into time periods.
Cost principle	When a company purchases assets, it should record them at cost. An item worth $750 bought for $100 is recorded at $100.
Revenue principle	Publicly traded companies must record when the revenue is realized and earned (accrual basis of accounting), not when cash is received (cash basis of accounting).
Matching principle	Expenses are matched with revenues during the same accounting period. This allows for better evaluation of profitability and performance (how much did you spend to earn the revenue?).
Objectivity principle	A company's statements should be based on objectivity.
Materiality principle	When an item is reported, its significance is considered. An item is considered significant when it would affect the decision made regarding its use.
Consistency principle	The company uses the same accounting principles and methods from year to year.
Prudence principle	When choosing between two solutions, the one that is least likely to overstate assets and income should be selected.

An Accountant's Worst Nightmare (or Greatest Dream?)

Picture yourself as an accountant who just received a QuickBooks file from a client. The client has no idea how accounting works and, to him, debit and credit are just types of plastic cards he carries in his wallet. In his file you find duplicate accounts in the Chart of Accounts, accounts created as the wrong type, items posted to incorrect accounts, accounts payable inaccuracies, payroll inaccuracies, and more. As an accountant, you might consider this a nightmare because you'd have to run numerous diagnostics to find all the mistakes (which could have been easily avoided if your client had learned how to use QuickBooks properly in the first place) or a dream because your billable hours would increase rapidly.

This scenario is exactly why you, as the client, need to learn what happens behind the scenes in QuickBooks, as well as how to use the day-to-day functions of the software. Knowing basic accounting and how to use QuickBooks properly translates to less time your accountant spends cleaning up your company file. Appendix A, "Need-To-Know Accounting," provides a good overview of fundamental accounting principles, including an explanation of T-accounts (also called T-charts).

Throughout each chapter you'll see elements such as Behind the Scenes, BTS Brief, and Flashback to GAAP to provide you with just-in-time (JIT) accounting information directly related to what you're doing in QuickBooks. If you want to delve even deeper, Labyrinth's *Accounting Basics: An Introduction for Non-Accounting Majors* provides all the accounting fundamentals you might need.

Accrual vs. Cash Basis Accounting

Companies can choose to implement one of two methods for keeping their books. QuickBooks makes it easy for you to produce reports using either method, and your data entry will be the same regardless of which method you choose. The two main types of accounting methods are:

- Accrual basis: Income is recorded when cash is earned, and expenses are recorded when incurred.

- Cash basis: Income is recorded when cash is actually received, and expenses are recorded when paid.

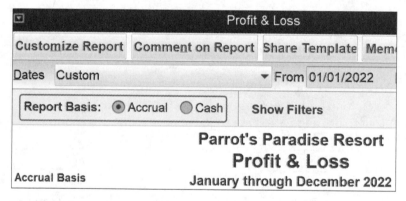

QuickBooks makes it very easy to change the report basis right from the window of a report.

Jimmy's business is growing, and he plans to open a retail store on site in the near future, so his accountant has recommended he use the accrual basis of accounting. He will enter the information into QuickBooks the same regardless, with the big difference being seen in the reports he generates.

The Accounting Equation and Behind the Scenes

If you haven't taken a basic bookkeeping or accounting class yet, the concept of debits and credits may be very confusing. This is not an intuitive concept, and individuals with postgraduate degrees may not even understand it, so don't beat yourself up if you have trouble! Generally, when people "get" how debits and credits work, it's like a lightbulb turns on and the concept is understood from that point forward. This text will look at both the concept of increases and decreases as well as debits and credits to balance the scales when working with transactions. Think of an old-fashioned scale: to balance, each side must have the same weight. Accounting works similarly. If there's an amount in one account, there eventually has to be the same amount in another account.

At the foundation of accounting is the accounting equation. Just as math equations must be equivalent on either side of the equals sign, so does this fundamental equation. Behind the Scenes sections appear whenever you are learning about an activity performed within QuickBooks, such as creating an invoice or entering a bill. This section explains the accounting that Quick-Books performs when you record a transaction and includes the accounting equation as well as T-accounts showing the relevant debits and credits.

> **Note!** The account names used in Behind the Scenes use QuickBooks, rather than traditional accounting, nomenclature. For instance, QuickBooks considers all funds received as *income*, whereas traditional accounting uses the term *revenue*, with *income* being used to describe net profit, the amount remaining after expenses and taxes are subtracted from revenue.

BEHIND THE SCENES: *Invoice*

Accounts Receivable
INCREASE to Assets

Sales
INCREASE to Revenue

$$\text{Assets} = \text{Liabilities} + (\text{Capital} + \overset{\text{Equity}}{\text{Revenue}} - \text{Expenses})$$

$$\$2{,}000.00 = \$0.00 + \$0.00 + \$2{,}000.00 - \$0.00$$

Accounts Receivable		Sales	
Debit	Credit	Debit	Credit
$2,000.00			$2,000.00

Managing Basic QuickBooks Files

Before you begin working with a QuickBooks file, you need to understand some basic file-management operations. This section covers the different types of QuickBooks files and how to open and restore QuickBooks portable company files.

Types of QuickBooks Files

There are three different types of files in which you can store your QuickBooks data: company files, backup files, and portable company files.

- The working file is the **company file** (**.QBW** extension). It's not compressed and contains all your company data.

- A **portable company file** (**.QBM**) is a compressed company file that must be decompressed, or restored, before it can be used. This is a convenient way to send company information by email. It is not a backup (does not validate the integrity of the file before compressing it)!

- A **backup file** (**.QBB**) is created when you select the Backup option. It's used to store a copy of your data in case your main file becomes corrupted. A backup file is a compressed file that must be restored before it can be used. File integrity is validated during a backup.

Two other QuickBooks file types play important support roles for your company data. A network data file (**.ND** extension) contains important configuration data. A transaction log (**.TLG** extension) can help you recover any data entered after your last backup operation.

Your company file can be stored anywhere on your computer. The QuickBooks default storage location is the QuickBooks folder for the current version you are using.

Warning! Even though .ND and .TLG files do not allow you to work with your company information, do not delete them. Doing so can affect the integrity of your company data.

Opening and Restoring QuickBooks Files

Through the File menu, you can open a QuickBooks company file or restore a backup or portable file. The last company file that was open when you exited QuickBooks is the file that will open automatically when you next start QuickBooks, although this isn't always the case if you're working on a shared computer. When you save a transaction, it's saved automatically to the QuickBooks working company file, and you don't have to issue a separate save command, as you would do in a program such as Microsoft Word or Excel.

The company file should be backed up periodically. You can also create a portable file for easy transport via email or USB drive. You cannot "open" a backup or portable company file for use; it must be restored.

Warning! When opening or restoring older file versions, you'll be asked to update the file to the newer version. QuickBooks will make a copy of the file first. After updating, you won't be able to open this file in an older version of QuickBooks.

File→Open or Restore Company

No Company Open

If a company file is not open, the No Company Open screen will display. From this screen, you can create a new file, open or restore a file, open a sample file, or locate a company file. In this book, you will be directed to use the menu bar to open or restore files; just realize that if a company file is not open, you can also use this screen.

The No Company Open screen offers options for displaying a company file. Sample files are provided by Intuit for you to practice using QuickBooks before you start working with your own company file or to explore features you may be considering using for your own company.

Find a Company File

A new feature in QuickBooks 2020 helps you locate a recently used QuickBooks file more easily. Click the Find a Company File button to search a variety of storage locations for the file you wish to work with. The Find a Company File feature is available only from the No Company Open screen.

Search for files using keywords.

Company, Backup, and Portable files will all appear here.

Choose where to search for files.

NEW! 2020 ▶ The Find a Company File feature in QuickBooks 2020 allows you to easily search for company, backup, and portable company files.

How to Use This Book and the Student Files

You may be curious about the large number of student exercise files that come with this book and how using this book as a learning tool compares to working with your own company file. This Q&A section should help set you in the right direction!

Why is there a different company file for each exercise?

When learning QuickBooks, it's much easier to follow the instructions if your screen matches the illustrations in the book (or your instructor's screen). Having a fresh file at the beginning of each chapter helps ensure that mistakes naturally made by students learning new material don't compound and cause a disconnect between student files and the example illustrations. This is why we don't provide one file that continues from chapter to chapter.

Is this how I will work in QuickBooks in "real life"?

No, using a separate file for each type of task (e.g., working with vendors, customers, inventory, etc.) is *not* how you will operate in "real life." In the real world, you will have *one* company file only. The multiple company files are for training purposes only.

Do I have to complete the chapters in the order presented in the book?

No, you can approach the chapters in any order you choose. For instance, some people prefer the discussion of how to create a company to come after learning the basics (i.e., after Chapter 5).

> **Tip!** A fresh company file for each chapter also means that the chapters in this book can be completed in any order.

Why do portable company files take so long to restore? What can I do while waiting for a file to restore?

Portable company files are compressed files that QuickBooks "inflates" before you use them. Think of the space bags you may have seen on an infomercial. Using a vacuum to remove all the air from a space bag, you can fit some thirty sweaters into a shoebox. (Okay, this is a stretch, but you get the idea!) This is akin to QuickBooks creating a portable company file. Opening the seal and letting the air back in is like what happens when you restore a portable company file.

It takes time for QuickBooks to prepare the portable company files just as it takes time for air to seep back into a space bag so the sweaters can return to their normal volume. If you're using an old computer system or a USB drive, the process will take longer than it will if you have a newer system. Many users are not happy about waiting for the restore process to occur, but it is a necessity if you have chosen this file option. You may want to begin a chapter by restoring the portable company file first so you can read the concepts discussions while it restores.

Are company files better than portable company files?

You can use either company files or portable company files for this course. For every portable company file there is also a regular company file—except for the first exercise in this chapter, which has everyone restore a portable company file to learn the process. Company files take longer to download than the portable files and use more space on your storage drive, which is not as much of an issue now that computer hard drives are larger and cloud storage is the norm. On the plus side, you can simply open a company file from your file storage location, and you don't have to worry about restoring or saving it with a different name, which is required for portable company files. Follow the exercise directions based on the file type you are using.

How do I create a PDF file?

Your instructor may ask you to save reports as PDF files, as they're easy to submit and save paper. To save a report as a PDF, first create and display the report. Next, click the Print button on the report toolbar and choose to Save As PDF.

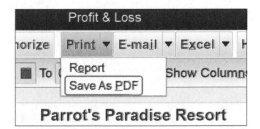

It's easy to save a report in PDF format right from the report toolbar.

Tip! You may be tempted to try to complete tasks as you're reading through the topics. Only complete the steps as outlined in the Develop Your Skills exercises (the first follows this tip). They're carefully designed to lead you through tasks step by step to help ensure your success and avoid frustration and confusion while you're learning QuickBooks.

DEVELOP YOUR SKILLS 1-1

In this exercise, you will restore a QuickBooks portable company file. Even if you download the company files, you will use a portable company file for this exercise.

Before You Begin: *Visit the Learning Resource Center at labyrinthelab.com/lrc to retrieve the exercise files for this course. Two versions of the files are available—portable company files and company files. The password for all files unless otherwise stated is Password1.*

1. Start QuickBooks 2020.

   A splash screen displays the version of QuickBooks you're launching and opens the program window. If this is the first time you've used the QuickBooks installation on this computer, the QuickBooks Setup window will appear.

2. Choose **File** and then choose the **Open or Restore Company** command.

Note! In the future, menu bar commands like this will be written as *Choose File→Open or Restore Company*.

3. Choose **Restore a Portable File** and click **Next**.
4. Navigate to your file storage location, click **DYS_Chapter01 (Portable)**, and click **Open**.
5. Click **Next** and save the file as: **DYS_Chapter01 Parrot's Paradise Resort**

6. Type **Password1** and click **OK**.

   It may take up to a few minutes for the portable company file to open.

   If asked to update the file, click Update Now. Click Done in the update window when the process is complete. (Intuit provides maintenance releases throughout the lifetime of the product, and this may require you to update your exercise files before working with them.)

7. Close all windows that QuickBooks launched for you, such as the New Feature Tour and Assisted Payroll information windows.

   For the rest of the Develop Your Skills exercises in this book, you can either restore a portable company file or open a company file.

Note! Unless otherwise instructed, leave the company file open at the end of the exercises.

The QuickBooks Window

The QuickBooks window features many components designed to help you complete all the tasks necessary to manage your business effectively.

Click a menu bar item to open a
drop-down menu of related options.

The title bar shows the company name
and the QuickBooks version/edition.

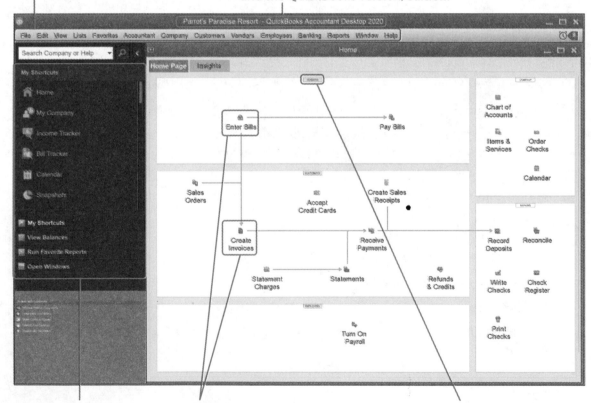

The icon bar is docked at
left by default. Use the
icons to access centers,
personal shortcuts,
apps, and services.

Click the task icons
to launch windows
that allow you to
complete tasks.

Click the button at the top of a
Home Page section to go to that
center (e.g., clicking Vendors takes
you to the Vendor Center).

Flowing Through the Home Page

The workflow diagram on the Home Page is indicated by arrows going from one task icon to another. Follow the diagram so you don't run into trouble. Here are two examples of potential trouble spots:

- If you choose Write Checks rather than Pay Bills (for a bill that's been entered), the accounting behind the scenes will still show the bill as not paid, and expenses will be overstated. However, you might need to use Write Checks occasionally, such as when you handwrite a paper check to pay for something unbilled or make any payment not entered as a bill.

- If you choose Record Deposits rather than Receive Payments (for an invoiced amount), the accounting behind the scenes will still show the invoice as unpaid, and income will be overstated. However, you might use Record Deposits on its own occasionally, such as when you receive a tax refund.

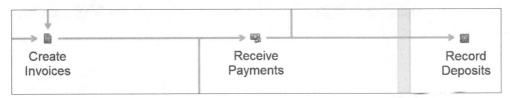

The QuickBooks Icon Bar

The icon bar provides a quick way to access QuickBooks centers, snapshots, shortcuts, apps, and services. It's docked on the left side of the QuickBooks window by default but can be moved to the top or hidden altogether using the View menu.

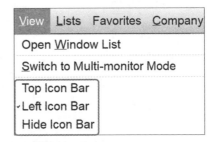

> **Note!** All commands accessible on the icon bar and Home Page can be found through the menu bar, but the opposite is not true.

QuickBooks Calendar

The QuickBooks Calendar allows you to keep up with deadlines. It also integrates a To-Do list so you can keep track of your calendar and tasks in one handy place. The Calendar can be accessed via the Company menu or the icon bar.

The Open Windows List and Working with Multiple Monitors

You may wish to display the Open Windows List at the top of the icon bar to keep track of open windows. The active window always appears at the top of the list. This list is not open by default.

If you need to keep one window active (such as a report) while performing other tasks or viewing other reports, you can extend the QuickBooks screen over as many as three monitors! You can have a report display on one monitor, an invoice on the second monitor, and a customer's record on the third monitor. An icon will appear on the title bar of each window to move the window to another monitor.

View→Switch to Multi-Monitor Mode | Ctrl + Alt + M

The Insights Tab

The Insights tab on the Home Page offers a comprehensive and easy-to-understand overview of your business. With the Insights tab:

- You always know how your business is doing, as you're provided quick access to real-time data.

- You can customize your Home Page with your company logo and information.

- You can compare data from multiple years.

- You can view your best customers.

- You can view several quick charts.

The Insights tab provides a colorful, informative display of your company's data.

DEVELOP YOUR SKILLS 1-2

In this exercise, you will explore the QuickBooks window.

1. Click the **Vendors** [VENDORS] button in the Vendors area of the Home Page.

The Vendor Center opens, from where you can work with the vendors on your list, manage various vendor transactions, and create new vendors.

2. Choose **Lists→Chart of Accounts** from the menu bar to see the list of accounts for this company.

3. Click **Snapshots** from the icon bar, scrolling down if necessary, to open the Company Snapshot window.

4. Choose **View→Open Window List** from the menu bar and then click **Chart of Accounts** from the Open Windows List on the left of your screen.

   The Chart of Accounts window becomes active and is pulled to the front of the other windows.

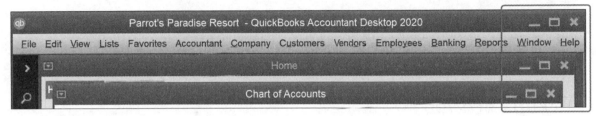

   All windows have their own set of quick-sizing buttons (Minimize, Restore/Maximize, Close), which you use to control the display. Be sure to use the buttons for the correct window!

5. Click the **Close** button for the Chart of Accounts window.

6. Choose **Window→Close All**.

   This command closes all open windows, including the Home Page because it is a window. The Open Window List/icon bar remains open.

7. Open the Home Page by choosing **My Shortcuts** from the icon bar and then clicking **Home**.

8. Choose **View→Hide Icon Bar**.

Exit and Reopen QuickBooks

9. Choose **File→Exit**; if necessary, click **No** on the Automatic Backup window.

10. Open QuickBooks, following the directions for the version of Windows you are using.

11. Type the password **Password1** and click **OK**. Close any windows that QuickBooks opens for you except for the Home Page and then maximize the QuickBooks window.

    Notice that QuickBooks opens the file you were last working on and that the icon bar is not visible.

12. Choose **View→Left Icon Bar** to display the icon bar.

13. Mouse over the Pay Bills task icon to display the ToolTip for that icon.

    Leave QuickBooks open with the Home Page displayed.

Backing Up and Updating Your Company File

Because the company file contains all your company's transactions and financial data, it's important to do timely backups. This process also verifies the integrity of the file. QuickBooks saves all activities and actions automatically. There is no need to perform a save command, and there isn't even an option to do so! The backup operation backs up the entire file.

 File→Back Up Company→Create Local Backup→Local Backup→Options

 File→Open or Restore Company→Restore a Backup Copy

Backup Location

Don't back up your company file to the same location as where the company file is stored. Choose an alternate backup location such as a network drive, external hard drive, USB drive, cloud storage, or the QuickBooks' online backup option. If you back up your file to a USB drive or some other removable media, make sure to store the backup drive in another physical location. Store the backup drive off site in the event of a fire or water damage at the place of business.

 Best Practice

You should back up daily if you enter a lot of transactions each day; do it weekly at a minimum. Having a current backup to restore in the event of a serious crash could get you back up and running quickly.

Backing Up Your Data Online

To ensure the security of your QuickBooks data in the event of human error, a natural disaster, or a computer crash, you may wish to use Intuit Data Protect. This online subscription service encrypts and backs up automatically each day to secure servers, for a monthly fee. It allows you to recover your data in the event you lose your working company file. You can also use the service to back up any of your other important files.

 File→Back Up Company→Setup/Activate Online Backup

When to Save a Backup Copy

QuickBooks allows you to choose among three options when backing up your company file:

- Save it now.

- Save it now and schedule future backups.

- Schedule only future backups.

The future backup options make it easy to back up your company file on a regular basis without having to remember to issue the command every time. You can select a specific day of the week and time to have the backup run automatically.

If you choose scheduled backups, make sure the backup location is available to QuickBooks at the scheduled times. For instance, make sure your USB flash drive is attached if that's your backup location. Once a backup has been created, you can restore it, if necessary. It will restore back to the date that the backup was created.

Updating Your QuickBooks Company File

Earlier in this chapter you learned about the different versions of QuickBooks available for purchase each year. Intuit releases free QuickBooks updates throughout the life of the version. These updates are available for download and may include such things as a new service, maintenance release, new feature, or something else relevant to your company. Eventually, Intuit will announce that it will no longer support an older version of QuickBooks. The easiest way to stay abreast of these updates is to have QuickBooks automatically check for and download them for you through the Help menu.

 Help→Update QuickBooks Desktop: Options tab

Determining the Release Number

You can find the release number for your version of QuickBooks by tapping the F2 key. This will launch the Product Information window that displays the release number and additional information such as the license and product numbers.

DEVELOP YOUR SKILLS 1-3

In this exercise, you will create a backup copy of your company file.

1. Choose **File→Back Up Company→Create Local Backup**.
2. Verify that Local Backup is selected and then click **Options**.
3. Click **Browse** and navigate to your file storage location in the Browse for Folder window; click **OK**.
4. Click **OK** and then click **Use This Location**, if necessary.

   If you are saving the file to the same drive on which the company file is stored, QuickBooks will display a warning.
5. Click **Next**, choose **Save It Now**, and then click **Next** again.
6. Ensure the correct file storage location is displayed and then click **Save**.
7. Click **OK** to acknowledge the information window that tells you a backup file has been created.
8. Choose **File→Exit** to close QuickBooks and the company file.

Self-Assessment

Check your knowledge of this chapter's key concepts and skills using the Self-Assessment quiz here, in your ebook, or in your eLab course.

1. QuickBooks Pro would be a good software program for a company with 100 employees.   *True*   *False*

2. Performing an activity within QuickBooks affects what happens behind the scenes in the program.   *True*   *False*

3. In the cash basis of accounting, you record the expenses when they are accrued.   *True*   *False*

4. A portable company file is the same as a backup file.   *True*   *False*

5. You must store your QuickBooks company file on a cloud drive.   *True*   *False*

6. To use a QuickBooks backup file, you must restore it first.   *True*   *False*

7. All commands accessible on the Home Page can be found through the menu bar as well.   *True*   *False*

8. The icon bar can be either displayed or hidden in your QuickBooks window.   *True*   *False*

9. Updates or maintenance releases are available for QuickBooks for a small fee.   *True*   *False*

10. Where should you NOT back up your company file?
    A. A USB flash drive
    B. Intuit's Online Backup service
    C. A drive where your main company file is stored
    D. An external hard drive

11. In the event of a data loss, what type of file helps you recover any data entered after the last backup operation?
    A. A transaction log
    B. A backup
    C. A portable company
    D. A network

12. To use QuickBooks portable company files, you first _____ the files.
    A. restore
    B. replace
    C. reuse
    D. open

13. Which account is increased when an invoice is created?
    A. Opening Balance Equity
    B. Checking
    C. Selling Expense
    D. Accounts Receivable

Reinforce Your Skills

In most *Reinforce Your Skills* exercises, you will work with the company Donnell Construction, for which Colleen Donnell is the president. This limited liability company (LLC) provides general contracting services to residential and commercial customers, and you will assist Colleen in a variety of QuickBooks tasks. The password for all files unless otherwise stated is Password1.

REINFORCE YOUR SKILLS 1-1

Find Your Way Around QuickBooks

In this exercise, you will take a look at Donnell Construction's QuickBooks company file. You will begin by restoring a portable company file.

1. Start QuickBooks 2020.
2. Choose **File→Open or Restore Company**.
3. Choose to **Restore a Portable File** and then click **Next**.
4. Navigate to your file storage location and double-click **RYS_Chapter01 (Portable)**.
5. Click **Next** and save the file as: `RYS_Chapter01 Donnell Construction`
6. Type **Password1** and click **OK**. Click **OK** in the QuickBooks Desktop Information window and close any windows QuickBooks opened for you except the Home Page.

   The company file opens with the Home Page displayed.

Navigate in the Company File

7. Click the **Items & Services** task icon in the Company area of the Home Page to display the Item List window.
8. Click **Calendar** on the icon bar to display the Calendar window.
9. Choose **Vendors→Enter Bills** from the menu bar to prepare for entering a bill.
10. Choose **Company→Lead Center** to review any active, hot, converted, etc., leads.
11. Choose **Customers→Customer Center** to see any outstanding balances or run a QuickReport.
12. Choose **View→Open Window List**.

    All open windows are listed. Clicking one will make that window active. Alternatively, you can click the Window menu to see a list of open windows.

13. Choose **Window→Close All**.
14. Click **My Shortcuts** on the icon bar and then click **Home** to display the Home Page.

REINFORCE YOUR SKILLS 1-2

Create a Backup File and Schedule Future Backups

In this exercise, you will back up Colleen's QuickBooks company file and schedule future backups.

1. Choose **File→Back Up Company→Create Local Backup**.
2. Click **Options** and then, in the Backup Options window, navigate to your file storage location.

3. Ensure Complete Verification is selected and click **OK**.

4. Click **Use This Location**, if necessary.

5. Click **Next**, choose **Save It Now and Schedule Future Backups**, click **Next**, and then click **New** to set up the schedule.

6. Follow these steps to schedule a backup:

   • Type **Weekly Backup** in the Description field.

   • Navigate to where you want to store your backup. (Reminder: This shouldn't be where your company file is stored.)

   • Choose **7:00 PM**.

   • Select **Friday** and click **OK**. If prompted for a Windows username and password, enter them here. If unknown, click **Cancel**, and your backup will not be scheduled.

   Performing a backup requires a Windows Administrator password. If you're not signed on as Administrator, you won't be able to complete this task. Click OK if you get the warning message.

7. Click **Finish** and then click **OK**. Click **OK** again to acknowledge the creation of a backup file.

8. Choose **File→Exit** to exit QuickBooks.

REINFORCE YOUR SKILLS 1-3

Work with the Accounting Equation

In this exercise, you will use your accounting knowledge. Refer back to the chapter or Appendix A if you need assistance.

1. Open and complete the **CH01_RYS_Work with the Accounting Equation** worksheet in your file storage location.

2. Open and complete the **CH01_RYS_Work with T-Accounts** worksheet in your file storage location.

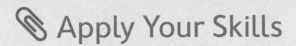# Apply Your Skills

In the Apply Your Skills exercises, you will work with a company called Wet Noses Veterinary Clinic. It's run by Dr. Sadie James, DVM, a small-animal veterinarian specializing in dogs and cats. The password for all files unless otherwise stated is Password1.

APPLY YOUR SKILLS 1-1

Explore QuickBooks and Create a Backup File

In this exercise, you will explore QuickBooks, back up a QuickBooks company file, and schedule future backups.

1. Start QuickBooks 2020.

2. Either open **AYS_Chapter01 (Company)** *or* restore **AYS_Chapter01 (Portable)** and save it as: `AYS_Chapter01 Wet Noses Clinic`

   You only need to save the file with a different name if you're using a portable company file. If you're using a company file, you can simply open it from your file storage location and begin working.

3. Open **CH01_A1_Explore QuickBooks Worksheet** from your file storage location.

   You will be capturing screenshots and pasting them in the worksheet. There's a quick primer on how to do that in the file.

4. Enter the version and edition of QuickBooks you are using on the worksheet.

5. Display the Insights tab and change the view to display expenses for this fiscal quarter. Capture your work and paste it under the Insights Tab Expenses title on the worksheet.

6. Customize the Insights tab to add the Income and Expense Trend panel. Click the arrows to display this new panel and then capture your work and paste it under the Insights Tab Expenses Trend title.

7. Open these windows using any method described in this chapter:

   • Receive Payments

   • Company Snapshot

   • Income Tracker

   • Chart of Accounts

8. Switch back to the Receive Payments window.

9. Capture the screen with the Open Windows List displayed and paste it under the Windows title on the worksheet.

10. Close all windows.

11. Back up the company file and schedule daily backups to occur every Monday through Thursday at 7:00 PM. Capture the Schedule Backup window before clicking OK and paste it under the Backup title in the Excel worksheet.

12. Save the worksheet file to your storage location as: `CH01_A1 Explore QuickBooks`

13. Close the company file.

Get a Grasp on Accounting Principles

In this exercise, you will use your accounting knowledge, first to brainstorm the accounts that would be required of a veterinary business and then to use the accounting equation.

1. Open and complete the **CH01_A2_Get a Grasp on Accounting Principles** worksheet in your file storage location.

2. Open and complete the **CH01_A2_Keep it in Balance** worksheet in your file storage location.

◢ Extend Your Skills

You've been hired by Arlaine Cervantes to help her with her organization's books. She is the founder of Niños del Lago, a nonprofit organization that provides impoverished Guatemalan children with an engaging educational camp experience. In each chapter, you will sit down at your desk and open a large envelope with a variety of documents as well as emails from Arlaine. It's your job to sort through the papers and emails and make sense of what you find, entering information into QuickBooks as appropriate and answering any questions posed. Remember, you're dealing with random papers dumped out of an envelope and various emails, so part of your challenge is determining the order in which to complete the tasks.

In this first chapter, you will determine which QuickBooks edition is best for Niños del Lago and make other decisions regarding how to use QuickBooks, including devising a backup plan. Think of the preliminary steps necessary to create and start using QuickBooks to track your new company. Open **CH01_EYS_Preliminary Steps Worksheet** and complete all fields.

2 | Creating a Company File

Before we jump into working with customers, vendors, and banking tasks, we'll go through the process of creating and setting up a company file. By taking the knowledge you gain from this chapter and coupling it with what you will learn in the rest of the book, you will be ready at the end of your QuickBooks studies to create a file for your own company. In this chapter, you will create a new company file as well as set up the Chart of Accounts and new users.

LEARNING OBJECTIVES

▸ Plan and create a company

▸ Edit your QuickBooks preferences and customize a company file

▸ Enter opening balances and historical transactions

▸ Run list reports and find help for QuickBooks

▸ Set up QuickBooks users

▸ Explain the benefits of the QuickBooks Ecosystem

📁 Project: Parrot's Paradise Resort

You've already had a chance to review the QuickBooks company file for Parrot's Paradise Resort, an ocean resort in Key West, Florida, owned by Jimmy Parrot. Now you will go back in time and create the file. There are many things to take into consideration when creating a new company file in QuickBooks. For instance, you need to know how your business is formed, when your fiscal year begins, what your federal identification number is, and whether you will be operating under a cash or accrual basis. You also need to think about what you want to get out of your QuickBooks file and what type of questions you want to be able to answer with your data. As you work through this chapter, creating and customizing the company file for Jimmy Parrot, you will gain an understanding of what information you need to gather before ever sitting down in front of a computer.

Parrot's Paradise Resort
Checklist for New QuickBooks Company

Company Name	Parrot's Paradise Resort
Address	730 Panama Street
	Key West, FL 33040
Office Phone	(305) 555-1435
Start Date	12/31/2021
Start of Fiscal Year	January
EIN	94-4555555
Income Tax Form	Form 1120S (S Corporation)
Need from Accountant	Chart of Accounts, how should I set up my items?
Customers	Need names and contact information, payment terms, and account numbering system
Vendors	Need names, addresses, account numbers, and payment terms for each
Accounting Basis	Accrual
Email	parrotsparadiseresort@outlook.com
Website	Parrotsparadiseresort.wordpress.com

Note! Remember to wait until you get to a Develop Your Skills exercise to start working in QuickBooks on your computer!

Planning and Creating a Company File

Before setting up your QuickBooks company, it's important to do some careful planning. Take the time to think about the information you want to get from QuickBooks. As with many situations, garbage in will equal garbage out!

Choosing Your Start Date

Choosing the start date that is right for you is important. Very ambitious people may think they want to start their QuickBooks file the day they started their company. This is a nice idea, but it isn't very practical for a busy or cost-conscious entrepreneur. Keep in mind that you must enter all transactions for your company (invoices, checks, bills paid, etc.) from the start date forward. If you choose a date too far in the past, this process will take a long time to complete.

Start your QuickBooks company file at the beginning of a month, a quarter, or your fiscal year. You may want to discuss this matter with your accountant to help determine the best and most practical starting date for your business. The actual start date should be the last day of the prior period rather than the first day of the current period; for example, we will use 12/31/2021 rather than 1/1/2022. This is important because you can run reports showing your opening balances before any new transactions are added. You will then be able to analyze and, if necessary, make changes to opening balances much more easily.

The Five Ps

Sit down and figure out what you want QuickBooks to do for you. It's difficult to go back and add a new field for every customer or change every transaction! A little planning at the beginning can save you a lot of time in the future. Think about the five Ps (Prior Planning Prevents Poor Performance) as you get ready to start your company and consider the needs of all the stakeholders involved. What type of information will each stakeholder need to be able to interact efficiently with your business? Potential stakeholders may include your accountant, customers, vendors, employees, stockholders, partners, etc.

How Many QuickBooks Company Files Should You Create?

Generally, the best guideline is to set up a separate QuickBooks company file for each tax return you will file.

FLASHBACK TO GAAP: BUSINESS ENTITY

Remember, the business is separate from the owners and from other businesses. Revenues and expenses of the business should be kept separate from the personal expenses of the business owner. Also, revenues and expenses for other companies operated by the same owner must be kept separate from one another.

Creating a New QuickBooks File

There are several ways to create a new QuickBooks file:

- Create a company from scratch.
- Upgrade from a previous version of QuickBooks.
- Convert from a different QuickBooks edition.
- Convert a Quicken file.
- Convert a file from other accounting software.

Intuit Accounts

To access connected services in QuickBooks, or even just use your software, you must log in to an Intuit account. As a part of the setup process, QuickBooks will work to sign in to the account for you, although you will have to enter your Intuit username or email and your password. QuickBooks allows you to work with your company file for up to 28 days before requiring the login.

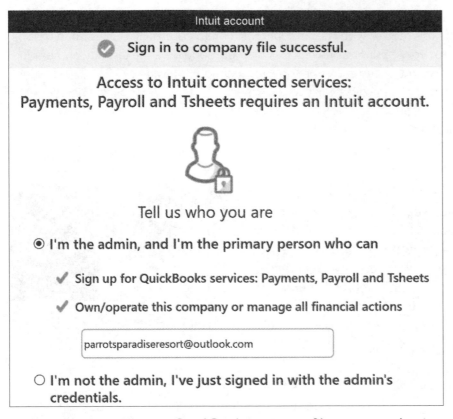

To keep working with your QuickBooks company file, you must log in to your Intuit account.

Choosing a Setup Path

When you create a new company, QuickBooks makes it easy to select from a variety of options. The first decision you must make is who the company is being created for. When working with your own company (or a company for which you're an administrator), you will choose the first option. If you're creating it for someone else (for instance, if you work as a QuickBooks consultant or bookkeeper and are setting up QuickBooks for a client), you will choose the second option, which allows you to create the file without logging in.

Start Setup

The Start Setup option allows you to provide a minimal amount of information and get started with QuickBooks right away. Once you've entered the Start Setup information and your company file is created, you will need to set up the rest of the information required to run your business.

Detailed Start/EasyStep Interview

Choosing the Detailed Start option takes you to the EasyStep Interview window. Here you provide more information when creating your company file.

Using an Existing QuickBooks File as a Template for a New File

If you wish to create your new company file based on an older one, QuickBooks will allow you to keep the lists and preferences from the old file while removing the unneeded transactions. Some QuickBooks users prefer to keep a separate company file for each fiscal year of the business, and being able to keep preferences and list data while removing transactions makes this easy.

To complete this task, you must clean up your company data from the old file using the Clean Up Company Wizard. Be sure you have a large window of time available before you start this process, as it can take a while to clean up a large file. QuickBooks will create a backup and archive a copy of your file as a part of this process, as well as verify file integrity.

Converting Data to Start a New Company File

An additional option available to you when creating a new company file is to convert an existing file from Quicken or other accounting software.

A Setup Checklist

At the beginning of the chapter, you can see the list Jimmy prepared before he set up his new company file. A checklist with this information, along with the additional information you will need to have after setup, is provided for you in your student exercise files folder (QuickBooks Company Setup Checklist). The good news is that most of the information can be changed after you set up your company. The one item you can't change later is the industry type because your entire starter Chart of Accounts will be based on it, so make sure you have it correct for the initial setup. You will work more with the Chart of Accounts later in this chapter.

A Quick Payroll Primer

Although we don't discuss payroll in this chapter, you do need to know a tad about it if you choose to create your new company using the Advanced Setup method. To include an addition or deduction on an employee's paycheck, you must first set it up as a payroll item. During the EasyStep interview you will have an opportunity to create payroll items. If you will be using QuickBooks for payroll and wish to set it up during the setup process (you can also set it up later), you will need to have:

- Information for each employee: name, address, social security number, and withholding information (from the employee's W-4)

- All "additions" that will be found on a paycheck, such as salaries, hourly wages, and bonuses

- All payroll taxes the employees are required to pay

- All payroll taxes you, as the employer, are required to pay

- Any additional deductions you will be withholding from paychecks, such as investment plan contributions or child support payments

Choosing the Correct Industry

During the setup process, QuickBooks will ask you to search for the industry that your company most closely resembles. QuickBooks will use your choice to create a Chart of Accounts close to what you need. (It will take you less time to edit it to fit your unique business than to start from scratch.) QuickBooks will also create profile list entries based on your selection. Choose carefully here, as you *cannot* go back and change the industry type option.

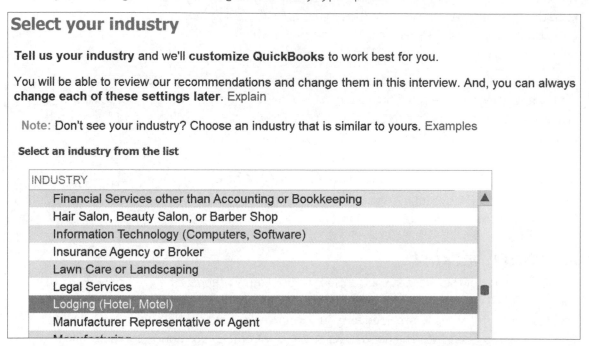

QuickBooks has several predefined industry templates that will help users in those or similar industries streamline their setup processes.

DEVELOP YOUR SKILLS 2-1

In this exercise, you will begin the first steps of setting up Parrot's Paradise Resort's QuickBooks company file using the Detailed Start process.

1. Start QuickBooks 2020.
2. Choose **File→New Company**.
3. Click to the left of *For myself (I'm the admin)*.

> ◉ For myself (I'm the admin)
>
> My email will be used to create an Intuit account, which will be used to access all Intuit products.

4. Click **Detailed Start**.

5. Complete the Enter Your Company Information step:

Company Name	**Parrot's Paradise Resort**
Legal Name	**Parrot's Paradise Resort, Inc.** The legal name depends on the company type being set up and is usually the name associated with the tax ID used in filing taxes. It's used on payroll tax forms.
Tax ID	**94-4555555**
Street Address	**730 Panama Street**
City	**Key West**
State	**FL**
Zip	**33040**
Phone	**(305)555-1435**
Email	**parrotsparadiseresort@outlook.com**
Web Site	**parrotsparadiseresort.wordpress.com**

This information will appear on forms such as invoices and bills, so ensure that punctuation, capitalization, and spelling are correct.

6. Click **Next**.

7. Complete the Initial setup process, clicking **Next** after each selection:

Select your industry	**Lodging (Hotel, Motel)**
How is your company organized?	**S Corp**
Select the first month of your fiscal year	**January**
Set up your administrator password	Type **Password1** and then tap Tab and type it again.

Although including a password is marked as optional, the next time you sign on, you will be required to enter one. The administrator has full control over all areas of QuickBooks.

8. In the Create Your Company File window, click **Next** again and save the company file to your file storage location as: **DYS_Chapter02 Parrot's Paradise Resort**

QuickBooks automatically suggests the name of the business as the company file name.

9. Click **Next** to continue customizing your business and then, clicking **Next** as needed, fill in this information:

What do you sell?	Services only
Sales tax	No
Estimates	No
Statements	No
Invoices	Yes
Progress invoicing	No
Manage bills you owe	Yes
Do you want to track time in QuickBooks?	No
Do you have employees?	Yes, W-2 employees

All these preferences can be changed later as your company changes.

Set the Start Date and Starter Chart of Accounts

In the next steps, you will set the date on which you will start tracking the company's finances in QuickBooks and ensure the desired accounts are included in your starter Chart of Accounts.

10. Click **Next** on the Using accounts in QuickBooks window; choose **Use today's date or the first day of the quarter or month**, tap Tab, and then type **123121** and click **Next**.

11. Click **Banquets and Events Income**, scroll down and click **Janitorial Expense** to include both accounts in the Chart of Accounts, and then click **Next**.

    The Chart of Accounts list is grouped by type, not account name. From this window, you can also get answers and explanations on accounts or restore recommendations.

Adding People, Items, and Bank Accounts

As a part of the setup process, you have the option of adding the people with whom you do business, the products and services you sell, and your bank accounts. It's up to you whether you enter the information here or in the individual lists later. The beginning balances of accounts can be entered during this process as well.

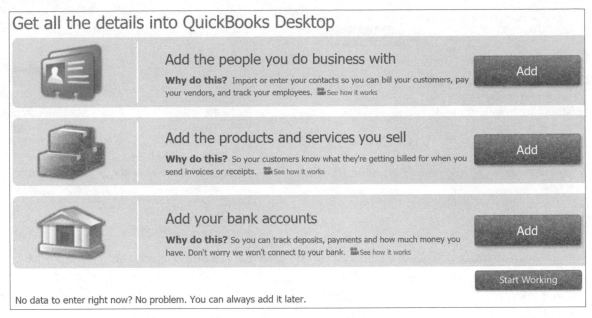

Get all the details into QuickBooks Desktop

Add the people you do business with

Why do this? Import or enter your contacts so you can bill your customers, pay your vendors, and track your employees. 🎥 See how it works

[Add]

Add the products and services you sell

Why do this? So your customers know what they're getting billed for when you send invoices or receipts. 🎥 See how it works

[Add]

Add your bank accounts

Why do this? So you can track deposits, payments and how much money you have. Don't worry we won't connect to your bank. 🎥 See how it works

[Add]

[Start Working]

No data to enter right now? No problem. You can always add it later.

At the end of the setup process, the QuickBooks Desktop Setup window displays. You can choose to add the information through this window or later via the various QuickBooks lists.

You can access the QuickBooks Desktop Setup window again later from the Company menu by choosing to bulk-enter business details.

 Company→Bulk Enter Business Details

Double-Entry Accounting and the Opening Balance Equity Account

If you have an existing company for which you are setting up QuickBooks, you should enter the balances of all asset and liability accounts during the setup process (although you can enter them in the registers later). These account beginning balances are termed "opening balances" in QuickBooks.

When you add the asset and liability accounts with an opening balance to your company file, the accounting equation will not be in balance unless at least one other account is involved. Therefore, after you create your first balance sheet account, QuickBooks will create an Opening Balance Equity account, in which the account beginning balances you enter will be placed. Asset beginning balances credit (or increase) the account, while liability beginning balances debit (or decrease) it. This account is created so you have an accurate balance sheet from the start even if you haven't entered all assets and liabilities for your company.

NAME	TYPE	BALANCE TOTAL
Sailors Bank Checking	Bank	175,368.48
Sailors Bank Savings	Bank	337,091.49
Accumulated Depreciation	Fixed Asset	0.00
Buildings and Improvements	Fixed Asset	0.00
Furniture and Equipment	Fixed Asset	0.00
Land	Fixed Asset	0.00
Customer Deposits	Other Current Liability	0.00
Payroll Liabilities	Other Current Liability	0.00
Capital Stock	Equity	0.00
Opening Balance Equity	Equity	512,459.97
Retained Earnings	Equity	
Shareholder Distributions	Equity	0.00

The balance sheet accounts are displayed in the Chart of Accounts. Note that the accounting equation is in balance: Assets ($175,368.48 + $337,091.49) = Liabilities ($0.00) + Equity ($512,459.97)

Note! To ensure your books are set up properly from the beginning, ask your accountant to confirm that your Chart of Accounts is set up correctly. A quick conversation and small bill now can prevent a large bill in the future.

Going Behind the Scenes

Behind the Scenes is a special feature in this book that shows you the accounting that QuickBooks does for you when you enter information into forms. Remember that the names used in this feature are the account names QuickBooks uses, not traditional accounting nomenclature. If you'd like to learn more about basic accounting principles and what the "behind the scenes stuff" is all about, check out Appendix A, "Need-To-Know Accounting."

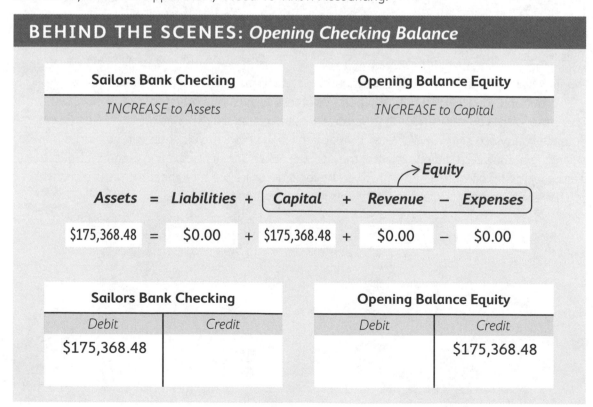

BEHIND THE SCENES: *Opening Checking Balance*

Sailors Bank Checking	Opening Balance Equity
INCREASE to Assets	*INCREASE to Capital*

Equity

Assets = Liabilities + (Capital + Revenue − Expenses)

$175,368.48 = $0.00 + $175,368.48 + $0.00 − $0.00

Sailors Bank Checking		Opening Balance Equity	
Debit	Credit	Debit	Credit
$175,368.48			$175,368.48

In this exercise, you will finalize the setup by using the QuickBooks Desktop Setup Window to create list entries for a customer, a vendor, and a bank account.

1. Click **Go to Setup** and click the top **Add** button to move to the **Add the people you do business with** screen.

   If you can't see the Add button, you will need to click and drag the title bar of the window so it is centered on your screen.

2. Click to choose to **paste from Excel or enter manually** and then click **Continue**.

   Notice that you can import people you do business with from a variety of sources.

3. Enter the new customer and vendor, tapping Tab to move from one field to the next, and then click **Continue**.

Type	Customer	Vendor
Name/Company Name	**Stolfus Tour Services**	**Evergreen Janitorial**
Name	**Elena Stolfus**	**Todd Tsai**
Phone	**(404) 555-6100**	**(305) 555-8000**
Address	**PO Box 4490**	**235 Sealth St.**
City, State, Zip	**Atlanta, GA 30320**	**Key West, FL 33040**

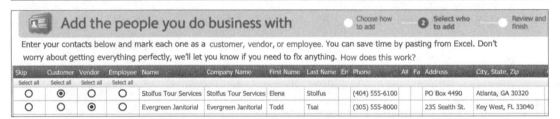

Notice how the sizes of some fields were adjusted so all the relevant fields could be displayed.

4. Click **Continue** again and then click **Add** to add your bank accounts.

5. Create the new bank account:

Account Name	**Sailors Bank Checking**
Account Number	**5493-2223**
Opening Balance	**175368.48**
Opening Balance Date	Click the calendar icon, navigate to December 2021, and click the **31st**.

In most date fields you can simply type the date, but in this screen you must choose it by navigating to the correct month/year first.

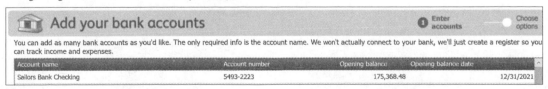

6. Click **Continue**, click to choose **No Thanks**, and then click **Continue** again.

7. Click the **Start Working** button at the bottom of the window.

   You need an Intuit account to use QuickBooks. Remember that you set one up when you accessed your trial software.

   Dismiss any windows that QuickBooks may have launched, such as the New Feature Tour or an unnamed window featuring an advertisement for an assisted payroll service.

8. Click in the checkbox to choose not to view the QuickBooks Assisted Payroll window again and then close the window, if necessary.

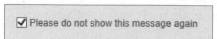

9. Click to the left of *I'm the admin* and then enter the email address you used when you signed up for your Intuit account; click **Continue**.

   In the next window, you'll either sign in with your Intuit username or email and password or choose to be reminded to do so in either 7 or 14 days.

10. Complete the appropriate step:

    • Enter your Intuit user ID or email and your password and then click **Sign In**.

    • Click the **Remind Me** button and choose **In 14 Days**. Click **OK** in the Sign In Reminder window.

    If you didn't log in to your Intuit account, you'll have 28 days in which to do so. Since you're using the company file in this chapter only, you shouldn't have a problem with this timeline.

11. Choose **Window→Close All**.

    This command closes all open windows, including those that QuickBooks launched for you.

QuickBooks Preferences

You can control many options and features in QuickBooks. When you created the new company in the previous exercises, you set many preferences such as whether the company has employees or collects sales tax, and those can be changed through the Preferences window as your business changes. So, basically, the way you interact with QuickBooks is controlled by the preferences you select. The Preferences window has twenty-three categories of preferences you can set or modify so QuickBooks can work more efficiently for your company.

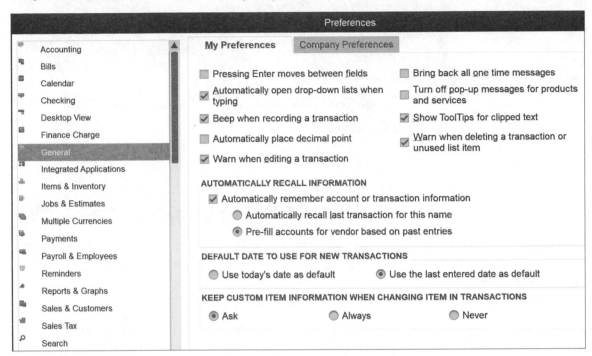

The Preferences window lets you control how you interact with QuickBooks, and the company administrator can make changes on the Company Preferences tab for how all users interact with it.

Company vs. Personal Preferences

Each category has two tabs on which changes to preferences can be set: the Company Preferences tab and the My Preferences (personal) tab. Company preferences are controlled by the administrator. They determine how the entire company interacts with QuickBooks. Personal preferences are controlled by each individual user. They dictate interactions between QuickBooks and that one user only.

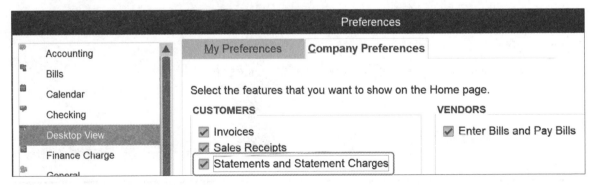

Changes made by an administrator affect all users. Here, an administrator turned on the preference to include task icons for Statements and Statement Charges on the Home Page.

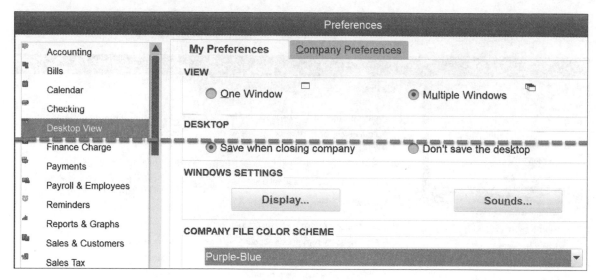

Individual users can change general settings on the My Preferences tab that affect only their individual QuickBooks user login, including the program's color scheme. This is a good place for you to look if QuickBooks is not acting "normal," as a preference may have been changed.

Company Preference: Customize the Home Page and Set Report Basis

The administrator sets all the company preferences for a QuickBooks file. This person makes decisions such as what is displayed on the Home Page, the default basis for reports, whether sales tax is assessed, and whether to use account numbers. In the next exercise, you will customize the task icons that appear on the Home Page and ensure the default report basis is accrual. Since you will likely be working with this book outside of the date range used for the company file, you will also turn off date warnings for the file.

> *Note!* Many companies still use account numbers with their Chart of Accounts, though a current trend shows fewer companies doing so. This preference is found on the Company tab in the Accounting category.

Personal Preference: Set the Color Scheme and Refresh Reports Automatically

In many Preferences categories, an individual user can choose from a variety of options. In the next exercise, for example, you will change the color scheme for your QuickBooks file and choose to refresh your reports automatically.

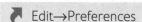 Edit→Preferences

DEVELOP YOUR SKILLS 2-3

In this exercise, you will first act as administrator as you customize the Home Page, set the report basis to accrual, and turn off date warnings. You will then set a personal color scheme and a personal report preference.

1. Choose **Edit→Preferences**.
2. Click the **Desktop View** category and then click the **Company Preferences** tab.

3. Click the **Statements and Statement Charges** checkbox and then click the **Reports & Graphs** category, choosing **Yes** in the Save Changes window and **OK** in the warning window, if necessary.

4. On the **Company Preferences** tab, make sure **Accrual** is the Summary Report Basis selected.

5. Click the **My Preferences** tab and choose **Refresh Automatically** for the Reports and Graphs option.

6. Click the **Desktop View** category and then click **Yes** in the Save Changes window.

7. Click the **My Preferences** tab, if necessary, and then click the drop-down arrow ▼ in the Company File Color Scheme area and choose the company file color scheme of your choice.

8. Click the **Accounting** category, click **Yes** in the Save Changes window, and then click the **Company Preferences** tab.

9. Click both checkboxes to turn off date warnings for past and future transactions.

10. Click **OK** in the Preferences window and then choose **Company→Home Page**.

Modifying the Lists in a New File

During the setup process you chose the industry type that was the most similar to your own. Now it's up to you to customize the QuickBooks file to fit your company. You will need to look at several lists after you set up your new QuickBooks company to ensure they are correct. If any of these lists is incorrect or incomplete, you will need to edit, delete, or add entries to them:

- Chart of Accounts
- Customers & Jobs List
- Vendor List
- Item List
- Customer & Vendor Profile Lists
- Fixed Asset Item List
- Employees List
- Payroll Items List
- Price Level List

Basic entries in these lists are populated during the setup process, and you may have added list entries in the QuickBooks Desktop Setup window during setup. It's up to you to continue adding and modifying entries in this list once the company has been created. You will begin this process by working with the Chart of Accounts.

Customizing the Chart of Accounts

The Chart of Accounts is comprised of all the asset, liability, equity, income, and expense accounts your company uses. You use the Chart of Accounts list window to create new accounts, edit existing accounts, and delete unused accounts.

If you're using QuickBooks for an existing business, you'll want to talk to your accountant and get a copy of your current Chart of Accounts. If you're starting a new business, you may also want to contact your accountant for guidance on how best to set up your Chart of Accounts for your unique company.

FIVE MAIN ACCOUNT TYPES	
Accounts Associated with the Balance Sheet	
Account Type	Description
Asset	What the company owns (cars, supplies, inventory, buildings, bank accounts)
Liability	What the company owes (loans, wages, interest, vendor purchases, collected taxes)
Equity	Funds contributed by owners or stockholders plus the retained earnings (or loss)
Accounts Associated with the Income Statement/Profit & Loss Report	
Income (Revenue)	Service fees or product sales (rentals, souvenirs, food, beverages)
Expense	What the company spends to generate revenue (rent, salaries, supplies, display fixtures, uniforms)

In QuickBooks, you will choose from a variety of account types that are all based on accounting's five main account types. The next table shows the account types available in QuickBooks:

ANATOMY OF A QUICKBOOKS CHART OF ACCOUNTS			
Type	**Example**	**Normal Balance**	**Account Type**
Bank	Checking Account	Debit	Asset
Accounts Receivable	Accounts Receivable	Debit	Asset
Other Current Asset	Prepaid Rent	Debit	Asset
Fixed Asset	Machinery	Debit	Asset
Other Asset	Long Term Notes Receivable	Debit	Asset
Accounts Payable	Accounts Payable	Credit	Liability
Credit Card	American Express	Credit	Liability
Other Current Liability	Short Term Loan	Credit	Liability
Long Term Liability	Auto Loan	Credit	Liability
Equity	Opening Balance Equity	Credit	Equity
Income	Sales	Credit	Income
Cost of Goods Sold	Cost of Goods Sold	Debit	Expense
Expense	Telephone Expense	Debit	Expense
Other Income	Interest Income	Credit	Income
Other Expense	Corporate Taxes	Debit	Expense

Adding Accounts

When you add an account to the Chart of Accounts, make sure to select the correct account type, as this is one of the most prevalent errors accountants find in their clients' QuickBooks files. Keep in mind that your "behind the scenes" action will be incorrect if the wrong account type is selected.

To Edit or Delete—That Is the Question...

The generic Chart of Accounts that QuickBooks provides will have some accounts you probably won't need for your unique business. You can choose to rename (edit) these accounts or delete them. Renaming an account is appropriate if you're working with the same account type. Deleting is appropriate if you no longer need additional accounts of the same type.

Moving and Sorting Accounts

You can change the order in which accounts appear within your Chart of Accounts. By default, QuickBooks alphabetizes accounts by type. The Chart of Accounts is structured so assets are listed first, liabilities second, equity accounts third, income accounts fourth, cost of goods sold accounts fifth, and expense accounts last. This structure must remain intact; you can move accounts around only within their own type.

Moving list items works the same way in the various lists in QuickBooks—by clicking and dragging the diamond to the left of the list entry. If you move your accounts and later decide you want them alphabetized by type once again, QuickBooks allows you to re-sort the list. Re-sorting the list restores the QuickBooks default.

Tying Accounts to Tax Forms

Having a properly set up QuickBooks file will make filing your taxes much easier. To set up your file to track information for taxes, you will need to tie the accounts in your Chart of Accounts to the correct tax lines.

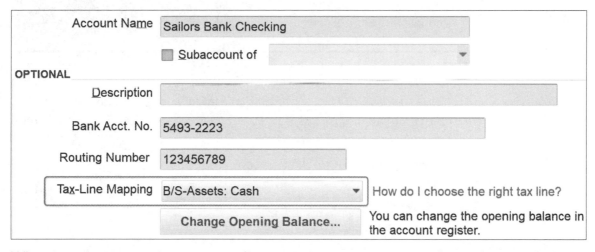

When you create a new account or edit an existing one, you can set the tax line to which it aligns.

Subaccounts

To keep precise records, you may wish to use QuickBooks subaccounts. For instance, to keep the number of expense accounts within reason, you are likely to use only one expense account for all your computer and Internet expenses. To track expenses more closely, though, you may want separate accounts for your hardware, software, and Internet service. Subaccounts are a great way to track these separate expenses while keeping the number of expense accounts down.

Computer and Internet Expenses	Expense
Hardware	Expense
Internet Service	Expense
Software	Expense

When you run profit & loss reports and budgets, you have the option to expand the report (display subaccounts) to show details or collapse the report (display only main accounts) for brevity.

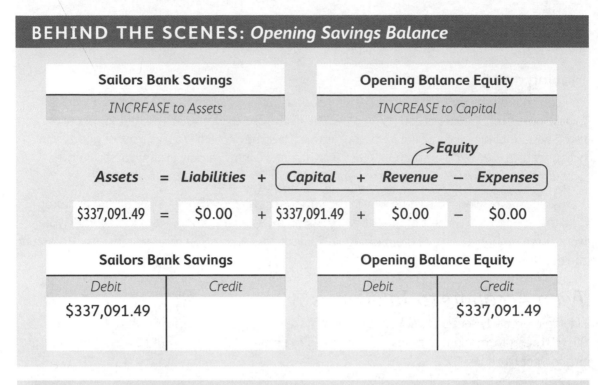

BEHIND THE SCENES: *Opening Savings Balance*

Sailors Bank Savings	Opening Balance Equity
INCRFASE to Assets	*INCREASE to Capital*

→**Equity**

Assets	**=**	**Liabilities**	**+**	**Capital**	**+**	**Revenue**	**−**	**Expenses**
$337,091.49	=	$0.00	+	$337,091.49	+	$0.00	−	$0.00

Sailors Bank Savings		Opening Balance Equity	
Debit	*Credit*	*Debit*	*Credit*
$337,091.49			$337,091.49

Lists→Chart of Accounts

DEVELOP YOUR SKILLS 2-4

In this exercise, you will take the generic Chart of Accounts created for Parrot's Paradise Resort and make it fit the needs of the company. The first task is to add an additional bank account that Jimmy needs but that was not created during the setup process.

1. Click the **Chart of Accounts** task icon in the Company area of the Home Page and then resize the window.

   Chart of Accounts

   QuickBooks opens the generic Chart of Accounts created for you. Notice the Sailors Bank Checking account created during setup. The color of your title bars may be different based on the color scheme chosen in the last exercise.

2. Click the **Account menu** button `Account ▾` at the bottom left of the window and choose **New**.

3. Click in the circle to the left of **Bank** and then click **Continue**.

4. Use this information for the new account:

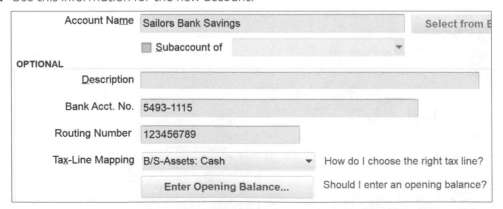

Account Name	Sailors Bank Savings Select from E
	☐ Subaccount of ▾
OPTIONAL	
Description	
Bank Acct. No.	5493-1115
Routing Number	123456789
Tax-Line Mapping	B/S-Assets: Cash ▾ How do I choose the right tax line?
	Enter Opening Balance... Should I enter an opening balance?

The Tax-Line Mapping field is filled in for you based on the account type chosen. If the wrong tax line is filled in, you can always override it and choose the correct one.

5. Click the **Enter Opening Balance** button and then use this screen to enter the opening balance:

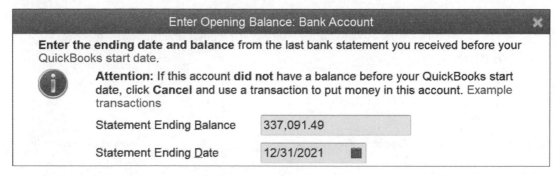

6. Click **OK** and then click **Save & Close**. Click **No** in the Set Up Bank Feed window.

   The new bank account will be debited (increased) by $337,091.49 and the Opening Balance Equity account that QuickBooks automatically created for you will be credited (increased) by the same amount.

Edit and Delete Accounts

When you created the checking account during the setup process, you did not have the option to enter a routing number and tax-line mapping information, so you will edit the account to include that information.

7. Right-click the **Sailors Bank Checking** account and choose **Edit Account**.

8. Edit the account as indicated:

   • Routing Number: **123456789**

   • Tax-Line Mapping: Click the drop-down arrow ▾, scroll down, and choose **B/S-Assets: Cash**.

9. Click **Save & Close**.

   Note that you can change the account's opening balance in this window. You also have the option of editing it in the account register.

   You realize you don't need a Janitorial Expense account after all, so you will delete that account.

10. Right-click the **Janitorial Expense** account, scrolling down if necessary, and choose **Delete Account**.

11. Click **OK** in the Delete Account window.

Create Subaccounts

Jimmy wants to track his computer and Internet expenses more carefully, so he has decided to use subaccounts.

12. Single-click **Computer and Internet Expenses** in the Chart of Accounts.

    You don't have to click the parent account first, but it can be helpful to visualize where you're adding the subaccounts by selecting it first.

13. Click the **Account menu** Account ▾ button at the bottom left of the window and choose **New**.

14. Click in the circle to the left of **Expense** and then click **Continue**.

15. Use this image to complete the new subaccount:

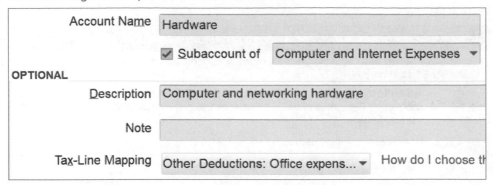

16. Click **Save & New** to save your new account and leave the window open to add another one.

17. Create additional subaccounts for Computer and Internet Expenses, clicking **Save & New** after creating the first subaccount:

Subaccount Name	Description	Tax-Line Mapping
Software	Computer and device software	Other Deductions: Office Expense
Internet Service	Internet service	Other Deductions: Office Expense

18. Click **Save & Close** to create the last new subaccount and close the Chart of Accounts window.

The top Close button is for the QuickBooks program. If you accidentally click it, QuickBooks will ask you to confirm that you want to exit the program; cancel the command.

Customer & Vendor Profile Lists

Now that you've learned how to work a bit more with the Chart of Accounts, it's time to learn about Customer & Vendor Profile Lists. These lists contain data you will use throughout Quick-Books in forms such as invoices and bills and as fields in other lists such as the Vendor List. When Jimmy created his new QuickBooks company and chose the company type on which to base it, QuickBooks created a generic Chart of Accounts and populated the Customer & Vendor Profile Lists with entries relevant to that company type.

Look at the profile lists that QuickBooks provides to track customer and vendor information, as well as the examples of forms and lists in which you may find them appearing as fields.

PROFILE LISTS AND WHERE THEY APPEAR	
Name of List	**You may find this list as a field on the...**
Sales Rep List	Customer & Job List (Additional Info tab) or Create Invoices form
Customer Type List	Customer & Job List (Additional Info tab)
Vendor Type List	Vendor List (Additional Info tab)
Job Type List	Customer & Job List (Additional Info tab)

(cont.)

PROFILE LISTS AND WHERE THEY APPEAR (cont.)	
Name of List	**You may find this list as a field on the...**
Terms List	Vendor List or Create Invoices and Enter Bills forms
Customer Message List	Enter Sales Receipt and Create Invoices forms
Payment Method List	Customer & Job List (Payment Settings tab) or Receive Payments form
Ship Via List	Create Invoices form (product or custom template)
Vehicle List	Enter Vehicle Mileage window

Making the Lists Work for You

Using the Customer & Vendor Profile Lists can help you in many ways. You can even use a list for a purpose other than that for which it was intended. For instance, if your company doesn't ship products, you have no need for the Ship Via field so you can use that field to track a different additional aspect of your company. You can't create new profile lists, so you need to maximize the lists QuickBooks provides by modifying them to track all information needed by your company.

There are two main benefits of fully using these lists:

- They can be included on reports and used to filter the reports. For example, you can use the Customer Type to display only residential customers on your Profit & Loss or Customer reports to conduct a focused marketing effort.

- They can be used to customize form templates such as a custom invoice.

Using Classes in QuickBooks

In this chapter we don't go into using classes in QuickBooks in detail. Classes allow you to track income and expenses for one specific aspect of your company, and they are not tied to any particular customer, job, vendor, or item. For right now, understand that if you choose to use classes for your own business (after you've learned more about them!), the best option is to set them up when you create your new company file.

 Lists→Customer & Vendor Profile Lists

DEVELOP YOUR SKILLS 2-5

In this exercise, you will work with the Customer Message, Vendor Type, and Customer Type lists. You can use these procedures with any other profile list as well. You will begin by editing a profile list entry.

1. Choose **Lists→Customer & Vendor Profile Lists→Customer Message List**.
2. Double-click **Thank you for your business.**
3. Replace the current message with: **We truly appreciate your business.**
4. Click **OK** to save the edited message.

   Now you can select this message on the Create Invoices and Enter Sales Receipt forms that you create for your customers.

5. Close the Customer Message List window.

Create a New Profile List Entry and Delete Another

You will now add a new entry to the Customer Type List.

6. Choose **Lists→Customer & Vendor Profile Lists→Customer Type List**.

7. Click the **Customer Type menu** button ▼ and choose **New**.

8. Enter `From Website` as the new type, click **OK**, and then close the Customer Type List.

   You don't really need both Suppliers and Supplies on the Vendor Type List, so you will delete one.

9. Choose **Lists→Customer & Vendor Profile Lists→Vendor Type List**.

10. Single-click **Supplies**.

11. Click the **Vendor Type** drop-down arrow ▼ and choose **Delete Vendor Type**; click **OK** to confirm the deletion.

    In this case you were able to delete the vendor type. If an entry in any list has been used in at least one transaction, you will not be able to delete it; you should make it inactive instead.

12. Close the Vendor Type List.

Opening Balances and Historical Transactions

If you chose a start date for your company that was not the first day you were in business, it's important to enter all the historical transactions and opening balances in your file.

Entering and Editing Account Opening Balances

You need to make sure you have the correct opening balances in QuickBooks for all your accounts. There are five methods by which you can enter opening balances. The type of account you're dealing with determines which method, or combination of methods, will work the best. The five methods available are:

- EasyStep Interview (for bank accounts only)

- Journal entries

- Forms (for individual transactions)

- Registers

- Lists (lump sums can be entered when creating entries)

Editing a Beginning Balance

If you need to correct a beginning balance, you have three options: via the Edit Account window (which provides a link to the account register), the account register, or a journal entry. For example, if you incorrectly entered $15,000 as the opening balance for a bank account when you created it, you could open the account register by double-clicking the account in the Chart of Accounts and change the amount in that window.

Entering Historical Transactions for an Account

There are two ways to enter historical transactions into your QuickBooks file. Transactions can be entered either individually or in a summary journal entry.

Entering Historical Transactions Individually

To enter transactions individually, you must have all the data for each one. This can be very time-consuming to gather if you're already a few months into the year, but you will have all the details for every transaction in QuickBooks if you decide to use this method. It's very important to enter the transactions in the correct order.

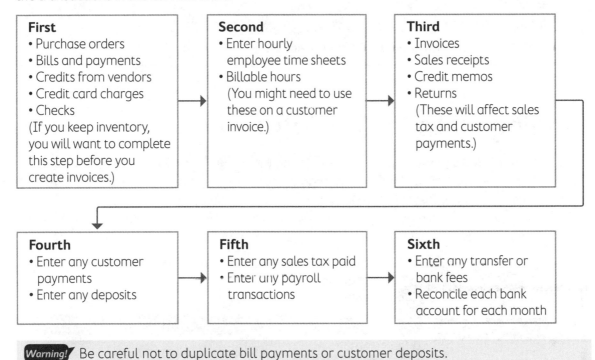

First
- Purchase orders
- Bills and payments
- Credits from vendors
- Credit card charges
- Checks
(If you keep inventory, you will want to complete this step before you create invoices.)

Second
- Enter hourly employee time sheets
- Billable hours
(You might need to use these on a customer invoice.)

Third
- Invoices
- Sales receipts
- Credit memos
- Returns
(These will affect sales tax and customer payments.)

Fourth
- Enter any customer payments
- Enter any deposits

Fifth
- Enter any sales tax paid
- Enter any payroll transactions

Sixth
- Enter any transfer or bank fees
- Reconcile each bank account for each month

Warning! Be careful not to duplicate bill payments or customer deposits.

Making a Summary Journal Entry

In a summary journal entry, you don't enter the details of individual transactions; you enter only the total amounts. If you aren't an experienced QuickBooks user, general journal entries should be made only under the guidance of a bookkeeper or accountant, so we will not use them. Rather, you will have an opportunity to edit an opening balance in a register.

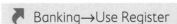 Banking→Use Register

---

DEVELOP YOUR SKILLS 2-6

In this exercise, you will work with a register to deal with an adjustment to the opening balance for the Checking account. The account you will credit in this transaction is 30000•Open Balance Equity.

1. Click the **Check Register** task icon in the Banking area of the Home Page.
2. Click **OK** to choose Sailors Bank Checking as the account.

Check Register

3. Change the amount of the opening balance to **175,386.48** and then click the **Record** button.

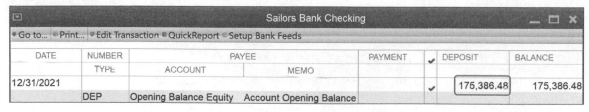

4. Click **Yes** in the Transaction Reconciled window.

   Because it was an opening balance, QuickBooks automatically marked it as reconciled. In most instances, it is not *recommended to edit a reconciled transaction!*

5. Close the Sailors Bank Checking register window.

Finding Help in QuickBooks

When you're starting a new company file, you'll likely have questions. QuickBooks has a built-in help feature as well as a "coaching" feature that can come to your rescue. Through the Help menu you can get a New Business Checklist guide, Year End Guides, Add Services, and other useful tools. There are two main ways to get help. You can use the Search field on the icon bar to search through the company file, or you can use the Help menu.

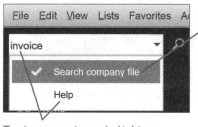

Choose this option to search through customers, invoices, and other areas of the company file.

Typing a topic and clicking Help opens the Have a Question? window with help on that topic.

Choosing Help→QuickBooks Desktop Help launches the Have a Question? window. (The [F1] key also launches this window.)

The "Have a Question?" Window

The *Have a Question?* window is a separate window you can launch to search for help. This window is contextual, which means its contents change depending on the active window. For instance, if you choose to launch it while the Chart of Accounts window is open, the results will relate to that window. When you choose to get help from QuickBooks, a separate Help Article window will also launch and appear to the right of the *Have a Question?* window.

When you launch the *Have a Question?* window, topics related to the active window appear. Don't worry, though! You can type keywords in the search field related to any aspect of QuickBooks to find help.

Help Articles

You click a result in the *Have a Question?* window to launch the Help Article window, which displays the information. And remember, this window launches with the *Have a Question?* window automatically if you issue the Help command.

 Help→QuickBooks Desktop Help

DEVELOP YOUR SKILLS 2-7

In this exercise, you will use the contextual help feature in QuickBooks to look for help on invoices and then use the search field to search the company.

Note! As of the time of publication, the Have a Question? window does not display properly. Do your best to work through steps 1–5 or skip to step 6.

1. Choose **Lists→Chart of Accounts**.
2. Choose **Help→QuickBooks Desktop Help**.

   The Have a Question? *window displays with information about the active window, Chart of Accounts. You can click on a link to read more about the topic.*

3. Type **invoice** in the blank search field at the top of the window and tap [Enter].
4. Click one of the articles and read through it.
5. Close the *Have a Question?* window and then click in the **Search Company or Help** field at the top of the icon bar.

   You may need to choose to view your icon bar to the left to see the search field (View→Left Icon Bar).

6. Type **invoice** and choose **Search Company File** and then click the magnifying glass. Resize the Search window to view all the contents.

7. Tap ⎡Enter⎤ to use the recent search and then click **Update Search Information** to search for the newest transactions.

   The search will return with results. You can choose any of the links in the various sections.

8. Take some time to click the links and explore the Search window and then close the Search and Chart of Accounts windows.

Setting Up Users

As your company grows and you hire additional employees, you may decide to allow certain employees access to your QuickBooks file. You can define different roles by creating users and granting them access to specific areas or functions. The use of passwords is required to ensure protection of your company data. The administrator can allow users to stay logged in for up to 90 days.

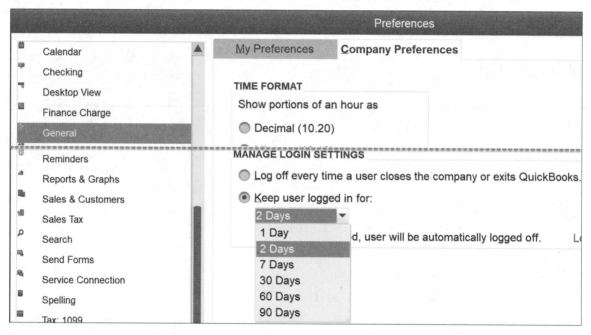

There are things to consider when enabling the option to keep users logged in, though. For instance, this feature is not available in a hosted environment that uses roaming profiles. If multiple users are accessing the same company file on the same computer, you still must log off. (Talk to your IT professional.)

Administrators and Users

During the setup process, the Administrator account is created. The administrator ("admin user") controls access for all users and determines the company's preferences. If you're the sole user of the company file, you can continue to use that account.

Limiting access is sometimes done according to a role the employee plays. For example, you can hire an employee to do accounts payable and receivable, giving that user access only to those areas. You can further restrict access to not allow the printing of checks. It's a good idea to have a plan as to which users or roles have access to which areas of QuickBooks. A written guide in a table format might be a good approach. Keep in mind that the administrator controls all company preferences in the Preferences window; users can change only their own personal preferences. QuickBooks allows you to set up unlimited users for your company file, although the number that can access the file at any one time depends on your QuickBooks license agreement.

Note! A user set up as an external accountant has access to all areas of QuickBooks except those that contain confidential customer information. An external accountant can review your file and make changes separate from those of other users. Only an administrator can create an external accountant user.

The number of areas for which you can give access rights to a user depends on the preferences turned on for the company. Jimmy has a bookkeeper for the resort, Marlene, who needs access to all areas of sales and accounts receivable and purchases and accounts payable (creating new transactions, printing forms, and running reports), as well as the ability to create new checking and credit card transactions.

Passwords

It's important to make sure you have a password that is not easy for others to guess and yet is easy for you to remember. Once you set your username and password, the Change QuickBooks Password window allows you to change your password whenever you wish and to set or change your secret "challenge question" that will allow you to retrieve a forgotten password. This challenge question should not have an answer with which others are familiar.

Note! Minimum password requirements are seven characters with one uppercase letter and one numeral. Include a symbol such as $ or % for more security. Usernames are not case-sensitive, but passwords are.

When you set up new users, you should set them up with a generic password, such as 123abc, as it's temporary and QuickBooks will force them to change it when they first log in.

Working with QuickBooks in a Multi-User Environment

QuickBooks provides a way for more than one user to access a company file at the same time. In QuickBooks Pro and Premier, up to five users can have simultaneous access to the file. Most tasks that you usually do can be completed in multi-user mode, but there are some that must be performed in single-user mode. These tasks cannot be completed while in multi-user mode:

- Create a new company file
- Set or edit a closing date
- Rebuild, clean up, or verify the file
- Create or work with accountant's copies
- Merge, delete, and sort list information
- Change company preferences
- Export and import data

↗ Company→Set Up Users and Passwords→Set Up Users

↗ File→Switch to Single-user Mode *or* Switch to Multi-user Mode

In this exercise, you will help Jimmy set up Marlene Hernandez, his bookkeeper, as a user for the Parrot's Paradise Resort company file.

1. Choose **Company→Set Up Users and Passwords→Set Up Users**.

2. Type **Password1** as the Admin password and click **OK**.

3. Click the **Add User** button in the User List window and add Marlene:
   - User Name: **Marlene**
   - Password: **Password1**
   - Confirm Password: **Password1**

   The first time users log in, they will be prompted to change their passwords.

4. Click **Next** twice.

   Each time you click Next as you move through the password setup screens, you can change the access for the user in one of nine areas.

5. Click to choose **Full Access** for the Sales and Accounts Receivable option and click **Next**.

6. Click the circle to the left of **Full Access** for Purchases and Accounts Payable and click **Next**.

7. Click the **Selective Access** circle for Checking and Credit Cards.

   The Create Transactions Only *option will automatically be selected.*

8. Click **Next** and view the permissions information for Payroll and Employees. Continue clicking **Next**, viewing the details on each screen for the remainder of the nine areas.

   A summary of Marlene's user access rights appears on the last screen. If time tracking was turned on for the company, you would see it listed as an area as well.

Access for user: Marlene
You have finished setting this user's access rights and password. Below is a summary of this user's access rights. Click the Finish button to complete this task.

AREA	CREATE	PRINT	REPORTS
Sales and Accounts Receivable	Y	Y	Y
Purchases and Accounts Payable	Y	Y	Y
Checking and Credit Cards	Y	N	n/a
Payroll and Employees	N	N	N
Sensitive Accounting Activities	N	N	N
Sensitive Financial Reports	N	N	n/a
Changing or Deleting Transactions	Y	n/a	n/a
Changing Closed Transactions	N	n/a	n/a

9. Click **Finish**.

   Marlene has been added to the User List.

10. Close the User List.

The QuickBooks Ecosystem

In the olden days of QuickBooks, it was pretty much a standalone product that didn't have to play nicely in the sandbox with any other programs (other than integrating with Microsoft Office applications). This has changed, though, and the apps that are available to you are a key aspect in QuickBooks functionality. For instance, you may choose to use Method CRM to manage relationships with your customers, SmartVault to securely manage your documents online, or Qvinci for actionable financial reporting. Collectively, QuickBooks and all the apps that work with it to help users increase productivity are termed the QuickBooks Ecosystem.

The Importance of QuickBooks Apps

QuickBooks is an amazing program, but it can't be everything to everybody, and that's where the apps come in. Intuit has embraced this ecosystem and provides support for the independent, third-party developers, including having a contest each year called the Apps Showdown with a $100,000 prize! In fact, at the time of this writing, on the QuickBooks Desktop Apps website (desktop.apps.com/home), there are three apps developed by Intuit and 215 by third-party developers! The ones you use will be determined by how you use QuickBooks for your company.

Identifying the Right App

Some apps are useful for companies from a variety of industries, while others are created for a specific industry. On the QuickBooks Desktop Apps website, you can search by industry, business function, QuickBooks version, or a combination of these. You can then expand or narrow your search, compare the apps, and research them by exploring customer reviews, case studies, demos, tours, and more.

The cost for an app is determined by the developer and may be free, a one-time fee, or a monthly subscription. Many of the apps also provide a trial or demo copy so you can try before you buy. Once you've chosen an app, follow the instructions on the developer's website to purchase and download it.

 Help→App Center:Find More Business Solutions

DEVELOP YOUR SKILLS 2-9

In this exercise, you will search the QuickBooks Desktop ecosystem for apps designed for the hospitality industry. You'll also explore the full selection of apps available to you.

1. Choose **Help→App Center:Find More Business Solutions**.

   Your default Internet browser launches, and the Apps for QuickBooks Desktop Marketplace displays.

   Note! You will be viewing a website that may have been edited since this book was published, so options may be located in different places on the page.

2. Click the **Industry** category on the left and then click **Hospitality**.

   QuickBooks Desktop apps specially designed for the hospitality industry are displayed.

3. Click one of the apps and explore how it can help Jimmy run his resort business.

   Note the tabs across the top that aid you in learning more about the app, as well as the Details panel on the right that provides information in a nutshell: Rating, QuickBooks Compatibility, Business Function, Industry, Developer, and Pricing.

4. Click the **Back** button at the top of the browser.

5. Spend some time searching for apps that may help you in running the business of your dreams; when you're finished exploring, close the browser window.

The Report Center and Running List Reports

To view the information in your QuickBooks file in a meaningful way, you need to become skilled at producing reports. You'll need to produce list reports early on in your QuickBooks experience. For instance, your accountant may wish to see a list of the accounts you've set up for your business to ensure all is well before you get too far down the road.

The Report Center

The Report Center allows you to learn about different types of reports without having to create them by trial and error. It includes sample reports and descriptions of the type of information each report provides. It also provides a search feature to aid you in finding the right report.

Tabs provide access to a variety of report selection options.

There are three main views available in the Report Center: Carousel, List, and Grid.

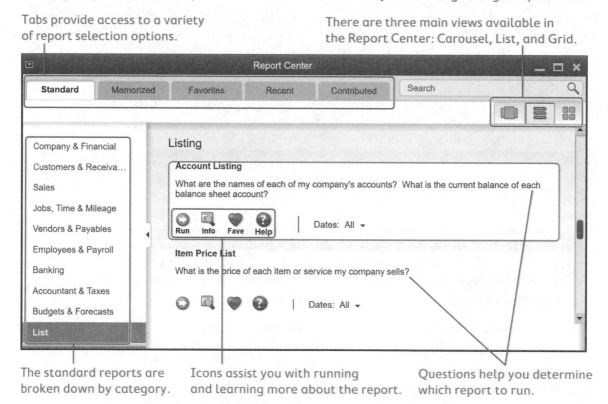

The standard reports are broken down by category.

Icons assist you with running and learning more about the report.

Questions help you determine which report to run.

Reports Menu

Once you're familiar with the reports in QuickBooks, you might find using the Reports menu a quicker way to access them. The menu is divided into the same categories seen in the Report Center and provides additional options, such as Scheduled Reports, Commented Reports, and Process Multiple Reports.

List Reports in QuickBooks

One category of reports you can access contains list reports. They simply display the information found in your various QuickBooks lists in an easy-to-read format.

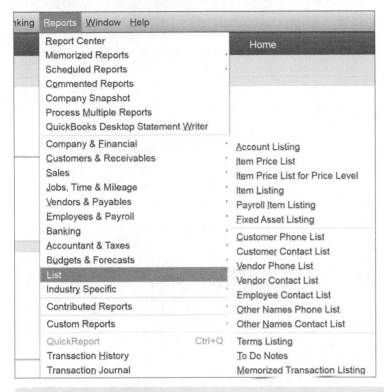

The Reports menu options are similar to those found in the Report Center but with more available. Each small arrow signifies a submenu; the List one is displayed here.

 Reports→Report Center

 Reports→List→[desired list report]

DEVELOP YOUR SKILLS 2-10

In this exercise, you will create a report for Jimmy's accountant that displays the accounts in his Chart of Accounts. You'll also review the contact information for the customer you created during setup.

1. Choose **Reports→Report Center**.

2. Follow these steps to display the report:

   • Click the **List View** button in the top-right portion of the window.

   • Click the **List** category on the left side of the Report Center.

   • Scroll down and then click the **Run** button for the Account Listing report.

   A report displaying all the accounts in the Chart of Accounts is displayed.

3. Close the Account Listing report and the Report Center window.

4. Choose **Reports→List→Customer Contact List**.

   The customer you added during company setup is displayed.

5. Close the Customer Contact List report. Either exit QuickBooks or leave it and the company file open to complete the Tackle the Tasks section.

Tackle the Tasks

Now is your chance to work a little more with Parrot's Paradise Resort and apply the skills you've just learned to accomplish additional tasks. Continue with the same company file you've been using in this chapter so far. If you need to reopen the company file, the password is *Password1*.

Add Accounts	Bank account: Money Market
	Income accounts: Rental Income, Excursion Income, and Camp Income
	Expense accounts: Event Entertainment, Event Rentals, and Boat Fuel
Add Subaccounts	To the Utilities account: Gas & Electric, Water
Enter Account Opening Balance	Money Market: $37,382.35, as of 12/31/2021
Search for Help	Use the QuickBooks Help feature to learn how to enter a customer
Change Preferences	Turn off pop-up messages for products and services (Hint: General category, My Preferences tab)
	Show the Sales Orders task icon on the Home Page (Hint: Sales & Customers category, Company Preferences tab)
Create a List Report	Show all the Terms available (these list entries were automatically added when you created the company)

Self-Assessment

Check your knowledge of this chapter's key concepts and skills using the Self-Assessment in your ebook or eLab course.

1. Always set your QuickBooks start date to be the first day you start your business.   *True   False*

2. The normal balance of an income account is a debit balance.   *True   False*

3. By default, liabilities are listed first in the Chart of Accounts.   *True   False*

4. Preferences control the way you interact with the QuickBooks program.   *True   False*

5. Create a separate QuickBooks company file for each tax return you file.   *True   False*

6. The Report Center lets you see what a report will look like without having to produce it.   *True   False*

7. The QuickBooks Ecosystem is comprised of free apps for you to use.   *True   False*

8. You can create multiple users and give each user different access rights.   *True   False*

9. Passwords are required in QuickBooks.   *True   False*

10. Subaccounts are always displayed on a report.   *True   False*

11. Which account has a credit normal balance?
    A. Auto Loan
    B. Accounts Receivable
    C. Checking
    D. Rent Expense

12. What can you NOT do when the company file is in multi-user mode?
    A. Enter an invoice
    B. Change company preferences
    C. Enter a new customer
    D. Enter a bill from a vendor

13. Which of these is NOT a customer and vendor profile list?
    A. Chart of Accounts
    B. Sales Rep List
    C. Terms List
    D. Ship Via List

14. Which of these is an asset account?
    A. Checking
    B. Accounts Payable
    C. Sales
    D. Credit Card

Reinforce Your Skills

Colleen Donnell has decided to use QuickBooks to manage the finances for her growing business, Donnell Construction. You will create the new company file for her as well as set up the Chart of Accounts and set preferences. The password for all files unless otherwise stated is Password1.

REINFORCE YOUR SKILLS 2-1

Set Up a New QuickBooks Company

In this exercise, you will use the Detailed Start method to create the company file for Donnell Construction.

1. Launch QuickBooks 2020.
2. Choose **File→New Company**.
3. Choose **For myself (I'm the admin)** and then click **Detailed Start**.

   The EasyStep Interview window is displayed.
4. Complete the EasyStep Interview:

Company Name	`Donnell Construction`
Legal Name	`Donnell Construction, LLC`
Tax ID (Employer Identification Number or Social Security Number)	`99-9999999`
Address	`2794 Mt. Pleasant Ave.`
City/State/Zip	`Oak Park IL 60302`
Phone	`(872) 555-3759`
Email	`DonnellConstruction@email.com`

5. Click **Next** to continue the interview and then click **Next** after each of these steps:

Select Your Industry	**Construction General Contractor**
Company Organization	**Single-Member LLC**
Fiscal Year	**January**
Administrator Password	`Password1`
QuickBooks Filename	`RYS_Chapter02 Donnell Construction`
What Do You Sell?	**Services only**
Sales Tax	**No**
Estimates	**Yes**
Billing Statements	**Yes**
Progress Invoicing	**No**
Bill Tracking	**Yes**
Time Tracking	**Yes**
Employees	**No**
Start Date	Choose **Use today's date or the first day of the quarter or month** and then enter: **123121**
Income & Expense Accounts	**Start with the accounts provided**

6. Click **Go to Setup** to complete the interview.

The QuickBooks Desktop Setup window appears.

7. Click **Start Working** and close the window promoting QuickBooks assisted payroll, choosing not to have this window shown again.

8. Choose the **For myself (I'm the admin)** option and then enter the email address associated with your Intuit account; click **Continue**.

9. Complete the step for your situation:

- Sign in by entering your Intuit user ID or email and password.

- Click **Remind Me** and choose **In 14 Days**.

10. Choose **Window→Close All**.

REINFORCE YOUR SKILLS 2-2

Change Company Preferences

In this exercise, you will set two preferences for Donnell Construction.

1. Choose **Edit→Preferences**.

2. Choose the **Accounting** category.

3. Click the **Company Preferences** tab.

4. Click in the boxes to turn off both the **Date Warnings** preferences.

Display Additional Task Icons on the Home Page

You've decided to create sales receipts in QuickBooks, so you will change the company preferences to reflect this.

5. Choose the **Desktop View** category and click **Yes** to save your changes.
6. Click the **Company Preferences** tab.
7. Click the checkbox to the left of **Sales Receipts** in the Customers section of the window.
   Notice the related preferences section shows which features are turned on and off for your company.
8. Click **OK** to change the preference.
9. Choose **Company→Home Page**.

   The Create Sales Receipts task icon has been added to the Customers section, making it easier to create sales receipts.

REINFORCE YOUR SKILLS 2-3

Work with the Chart of Accounts

In this exercise, you will add accounts to the Chart of Accounts and edit an account.

1. Choose **Lists→Chart of Accounts** and then resize the window.
2. Click the **Account** button and choose **New**.
3. Choose **Bank** and click **Continue**.
4. Complete the account creation:

Account Name	`Checking`
Description	`Company checking account`
Bank Acct. No.	`456-456-4444`
Routing Number	`333000333`
Opening Balance	`378,290.45 on 12/31/2021`

5. Click **Save & Close** and then close the Set Up Bank Feed window.
6. Click the **Account** button and choose **New**.
7. Choose **Income** and click **Continue**.
8. Complete the account creation:

Account Name	`Remodel Income`
Description	`Remodeling project income`

9. Right-click the **Construction Income** account and choose **Edit Account**.
10. Change the name of the account to: `New Construction Income`
11. Click **Save & Close** and then close the Chart of Accounts.

Create List Reports

In this exercise, you will create an Account Listing report to review the work you've completed on the Chart of Accounts.

1. Choose **Reports→List→Account Listing**.
2. Review the report to ensure you entered the accounts from the previous exercise correctly.
3. Close the Account Listing report and then close your company file.

Apply Your Skills

Dr. Sadie James has decided to use QuickBooks for her practice, so you will assist her in creating a new QuickBooks company file and getting it set up for her unique business. The password for all files unless otherwise stated is Password1.

APPLY YOUR SKILLS 2-1 QG

Create a New Company File

In this exercise, you will create the QuickBooks company file for Dr. Sadie James, DVM, using the Detailed Start method.

1. Set up a new company file for Dr. James:

Company/Legal Name	Wet Noses Veterinary Clinic
Tax ID Number	99-9999999
Address	589 Retriever Drive, Bothell, WA 98011
Phone	(425) 555-2939
E-mail address	Dr.James@email.com
Industry	**Medical, Dental, or Health Service**
Company Type	**LLP**
Fiscal Year first month	**January**
Password	Password1

2. Save the file to your file storage location as: **AYS_Chapter02 Wet Noses Veterinary Clinic**

3. Use this information for the remainder of the setup; accept defaults where not stated:

   - You sell services and products
   - Charge sales tax
   - Don't use estimates
   - Don't use sales orders
   - Use billing statements
   - Use invoices
   - No progress invoicing

   - Track bills
   - Track inventory for products you sell
   - No time tracking
   - Employees: You have 1099 contractors
   - Start Date: 12/31/2022
   - Select Subaccounts: **Medical Records Supplies** and **Medical Supplies**

4. Choose to **Start Working** and close all windows except for the Home Page.

5. Choose the *I'm the admin* option, enter your email address (the one you used for your Intuit account), and click **Continue**.

6. Sign in or choose to be reminded to do so in two weeks.

7. Close all windows with one command.

8. Create the **Account Listing** report to ensure you completed the initial setup properly.

9. Click the **Excel** Excel ▾ button and export the report to a new workbook saved to your file storage location as: **CH2_A1 Account List Report**

   See the installation guide if you need additional directions on how to export a file to Excel.

10. Close Excel and then close the Account Listing report window.

APPLY YOUR SKILLS 2-2

Set Company and User Preferences

In this exercise, you will set preferences for Wet Noses as a company and yourself as a user. The categories are provided for you, but you will have to determine if they are company or individual user preferences.

1. Open the **Preferences** window.

2. Display the **Desktop View** category and change the **Company File Color Scheme** to your favorite color.

3. Display the **General** category and choose to bring back all one-time messages.

4. Display the **Reminders** category and choose to have QuickBooks show To Do Notes in list format when the company file is opened.

5. Display the **Accounting** category and choose to turn off date warnings.

6. Close the **Preferences** window.

APPLY YOUR SKILLS 2-3 QG

Modify the Chart of Accounts

In this exercise, you will modify the Chart of Accounts for Wet Noses.

1. Open the **Chart of Accounts**.

2. Add two new bank accounts: Checking and Savings

3. Add a new income account: Boarding Income

4. Add two new expense accounts: Boarding Food, Lab Supplies

5. Change the Vaccines and Medicines account name to Pharmaceuticals.

6. Add two subaccounts for Pharmaceuticals: Vaccines and Medicines.

7. Delete the **Uniforms** account.

8. Create the **Account Listing** report to ensure you set up the Chart of Accounts correctly.

9. Click the **Excel** button and export the report to a new workbook saved to your file storage location as: **CH2_A3 Account List Report**

10. Close Excel and then close the Account Listing report window.

Enter Opening Balances in a Register

In this exercise, you will enter the opening balances for the Wet Noses Checking and Savings accounts.

1. Open the **Checking** register.
2. Enter the opening balance of $126,791.80 as a deposit to the account on **12/31/2022**, crediting **Opening Balance Equity**.
3. Open the **Savings** register.
4. Enter the opening balance of $57,921.34 as a deposit to the account on **12/31/2022**, crediting **Opening Balance Equity**.
5. Create the **Account Listing** report to ensure you entered the opening balances correctly.
6. Click the **Excel** button and export the report to a new workbook saved to your file storage location as: **CH2_A4 Account List Report**
7. Close Excel and then close the Account Listing report window; close your company file.

Extend Your Skills

You've been hired by Arlaine Cervantes to help her with her organization's books. She is the founder of Niños del Lago, a nonprofit organization that provides impoverished Guatemalan children with an engaging educational camp experience. You just sat down at your desk and opened a large envelope from Arlaine that contains a variety of documents; you also have several emails from her. It's your job to sort through the papers and emails and make sense of what you find, entering information into QuickBooks as appropriate and answering any other questions in a word-processing document saved as: CH02_EYS_[LastnameFirstinitial]

Remember, you're dealing with random papers dumped out of an envelope and various emails, so part of your challenge is determining the order in which to complete the tasks.

- Forwarded email from Arlaine's accountant: Set up the Chart of Accounts, use Non-Profit as the industry type, and add Grant Revenue as an income account.

- Bank statement from Salem First National Bank dated 05/31/2020. Checking account #21375-01, ending balance $25,462.11. Savings account #21375-20, ending balance $118,203.54.

- Handwritten sticky note: Need to give three volunteers (Bill, Karel, and Chris) access to entering donor revenue. How can I make sure they can do this but don't have access to other areas in QuickBooks?

- Scrap of paper that reads: Fiscal year June–May.

- Scribbled phone message from Arlaine's accountant: Do not use account numbers when you set up in QuickBooks.

- Sticky note: Is there a reminders list to keep me on track???

- Another email from Arlaine's accountant: Make sure to not have the starting date the day you started the organization...would be too much information to enter. How about 5/31/2020 instead, since it's the end of the fiscal year?

- Copy of last year's taxes: Form 990, Federal EIN 99-9999999.

- Torn piece of company letterhead:

niños del lago

1013 Kiddos Way
Salem, OR 97301
ninosdellago.org
(503) 555-1013

3 | Working with Customers

One of the best parts of being in business is creating and developing relationships with customers. After all, who doesn't enjoy receiving payment for a job well done? Intuit describes a customer as "any person, business, or group that buys or pays for the services or products that your business or organization sells or provides." When working with QuickBooks, consider a customer anyone who pays you funds. This simple definition will help if you have a unique business, such as a not-for-profit organization that doesn't normally use the term "customer." The job feature is an optional aspect of QuickBooks, but it can be extremely helpful if you have more than one project for a customer. In this chapter, you will examine QuickBooks' lists, activities, and reports that allow you to effectively deal with customers.

LEARNING OBJECTIVES

▸ Identify Customer Center features and create new customers and jobs

▸ Create service and non-inventory items

▸ Create invoices and sales receipts

▸ Receive payments on invoices

▸ Correct errors in customer transactions

▸ Create customer-related reports

Project: Parrot's Paradise Resort

Now that Jimmy's company file has been created, the next step is for you to set up the company to track customers. You will begin by working with the Customers & Jobs List, which is accessed through the Customer Center. Services need to be added to the Item List so that sales transactions such as invoices and sales receipts can be entered. Information in the Item List allows you to tie the service that is offered to an income account. Finally, you will create reports that will tell the story about customer-related transactions.

The Customer Center

The Customer Center is where you will set up all aspects of doing business with each customer. This includes payment terms, sales tax, credit card information, and the ability to track the customer type. In addition, you can track the sales representative who made the sale, if appropriate. Selecting a customer from the Customer Center will give you access to a lot of information on that customer.

Tip! The Customers & Jobs List can be exported to contact management software such as Microsoft Outlook.

The Customer Center icon bar provides access for creating new customers, jobs, and transactions; print options; Excel and Word integration; and the Income Tracker tool.

Apply a filter such as limiting the view to customers with open balances.

Click the pencil to edit the customer information.

Pinned notes added through the Notes tab will display here.

Use these column headers to sort.

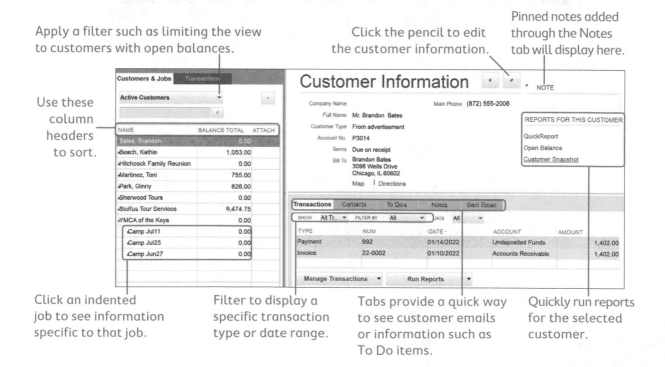

Click an indented job to see information specific to that job.

Filter to display a specific transaction type or date range.

Tabs provide a quick way to see customer emails or information such as To Do items.

Quickly run reports for the selected customer.

The more information you enter for each customer, the more flexibility you will have later when you customize and run reports. If you use all the fields, you can sort, group, and filter your reports using those fields.

Managing the Customers:Jobs List

Customers must be entered into the Customers & Jobs List, which is integrated into the Customer Center, before an invoice can be created. In QuickBooks, jobs provide you with a way to separate individual projects, events, or other distinguishing characteristics for a customer.

A new customer or job can be added any time, and the Quick Add feature allows you to add a customer right from an invoice or sales receipt. If you Quick Add just a name, you can go back later to edit the customer record, adding all the pertinent information.

Best Practice

An excellent way of organizing multiple jobs for a customer is to create each job separately under that customer. When an invoice is created, you then apply it to the specific job, making it easy to track job costs.

Many times, you will have repeat customers. In some cases, you may want to set up separate jobs if there will be many projects, or trips in the case of a resort, for that customer. An example is a customer who requests an estimate on an entirely new vacation package that includes lodging, excursions, dining, and more. In this case, creating a job for the customer would allow you to track that job separately as well as enable job costing for analyzing costs per job, providing a more accurate picture on your profit/loss reports.

Creating a New Customer

The more information you enter for each customer, the better your reports will be. For example, if you track how you acquired the customer (referral, website, or print ad), you can pull a report by this field to determine how most of your customers find you. This could be a potential money saver if you see that the print ads are giving you a low customer acquisition rate. Perhaps you'd stop doing print ads! You can also set defaults for specific information for each customer, such as the sales tax rate and preferred method of payment.

Best Practice

To have your customer list display in alphabetic order by last name, type entries as "last name, first name" in the Customer Name field when there is an individual rather than a company as a customer.

Edit an Existing Customer

You can edit a customer record at any time. Any changes made to a customer record will be reflected in future and past transactions.

Tip! To adjust an opening balance for a customer, right-click the customer name or job and choose Use Register. The change will be reflected in future and past transactions.

Delete or Make a Customer Inactive

On occasion, it's appropriate to delete a customer. An example would be a customer for whom you did an estimate and more than six months have passed with no order. You can delete a customer or job from the Customers & Jobs List as long *as you have not used that customer or job in a transaction.* If you have, you can make the customer or job inactive, but you cannot delete until after you close the books for a period and clean up your company's data.

Add a Job for a Customer

It's not always necessary to create jobs for customers. An example is a resort that creates a separate job for each visit by a return customer. In a case like this, you can create multiple jobs under the customer so you can track each job individually and also provide this information to the customer.

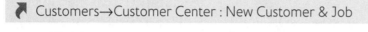 Customers→Customer Center : New Customer & Job

Customers→Customer Center : [select customer]→Edit *or* Delete *or* Make Inactive

---

DEVELOP YOUR SKILLS 3-1

In this exercise, you will add a new customer and edit, delete, and add jobs. Unless otherwise instructed, keep the Customer Center open. The password for all files unless otherwise stated is Password1. *Leave the company file open unless otherwise instructed.*

1. Start QuickBooks 2020 and choose **File→Open or Restore Company**.

2. Open **DYS_Chapter03 (Company)** *or* restore **DYS_Chapter03 (Portable)** and save it as: **DYS_Chapter03 Parrot's Paradise Resort**

   You need to save the file with a different name only if you're using a portable company file. If you're using a company file, just open it and begin working.

   It will take a few moments for the portable company file to open. You may have to update the file to the latest QuickBooks release after it opens.

3. Type **Password1** and click **OK**. Close all open windows except for the Home Page.

   Now you will create a new customer.

4. Click **Customers** [CUSTOMERS] on the Home Page and then click the **New Customer & Job** button and choose **New Customer**.

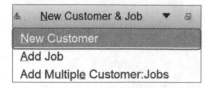

5. Enter this information in the Address Info tab:

Customer Name	**Sherwood Tours** Because you're not entering an opening balance, you don't need to change the date for the As Of field.
Company Name	**Sherwood Tours** You can use keyboard shortcuts to copy/paste if it's faster for you.
Full Name	**Ms. Cheri Romaine**
Job Title	**Owner**
Main Phone	**(503) 555-9962**

Tip! Use the [Tab] key to move from field to field.

6. Address Details Invoice/Bill To: **21192 Langer Farms Pkwy**[Enter]**Sherwood, OR 97140**

Before typing the address, click at the end of the last line of text, in this case the name Cheri Romaine, *and press* [Enter].

7. Click **Copy>>** to copy the address to the Ship To field, which saves it as the default shipping address, and click **OK** in the Add Shipping Address Information window.

8. Click the **Payment Settings** tab and use this image to fill in the information:

9. Click the **Additional Info** tab and select **Referral** from the Customer Type list.

Tip! Tracking how customers were acquired can serve as a valuable marketing tool.

10. Click **OK** to complete the New Customer record.

Edit a Customer

Ginny Sinclair got married and changed her name, so you need to edit the entry in the Customers & Jobs List.

11. Locate and then double-click **Sinclair, Ginny** in the Customers & Jobs List to open the Edit Customer window.

12. Correct the name to read: `Park, Ginny`

You will need to correct this in four separate places in the Edit Customer window.

13. Click the **Additional Info** tab and select **From advertisement** as the Customer Type.

14. Click **OK** to accept the change and leave the Customer Center open.

Delete a Customer

Willamette Tour Enterprises has gone out of business without booking a tour, so you will delete the company from the Customers & Jobs List. And since you don't anticipate Jose Hernandez returning as a customer, you will mark him as inactive.

15. Locate and right-click **Willamette Tour Enterprises**, choose **Delete Customer:Job**, and click **OK** to confirm.

16. Right-click **Hernandez, Jose** and choose **Make Customer:Job Inactive**; leave the Customer Center open.

Jose Hernandez will no longer appear on the Customers & Jobs List, as it's filtered to show only active customers. If you choose the Active Customers drop-down arrow ▼ and select All Customers, you will see the inactive customers listed with an "X" next to their names and jobs. Switch back to Active Customers to hide the Inactive Customers.

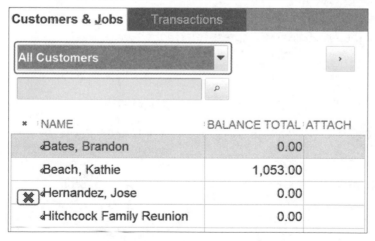

Add Jobs to a Customer

The YMCA has submitted its summer camp schedule, so you will create a separate job for each camp session it will be running.

17. From the Customers & Jobs List, select **YMCA of the Keys**, click the **New Customer & Job** button, and choose **Add Job**.

18. Type **Camp Mar28** in the Job Name field and click **OK**.

 Notice the right side of the window says Job Information *rather than* Customer Information.

19. Using the procedure in steps 17–18, create these additional jobs for the YMCA:

 - **Camp Jun27**
 - **Camp Jul11**
 - **Camp Jul25**

20. Close the Customer Center window.

Note! Unless otherwise directed, always leave the company file open at the end of an exercise.

The QuickBooks Lead Center

The QuickBooks Lead Center provides you with a tool to track potential sales leads. Within the Lead Center, you can create tasks and track them, input contact and location information, and keep notes. This feature helps you manage potential customers and allows you to easily convert a lead into a customer once you have landed its or their business.

Right-clicking a lead in the Lead Center allows you to easily convert that lead into a customer.

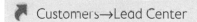 Customers→Lead Center

The To Do List

QuickBooks allows you to track all your tasks or "to dos" in one place: the To Do List. You can enter and view items on this list from the various centers or the To Do List window itself. You can even run the To Do Notes report to display all your tasks. If you wish to view a list of to dos every time you open QuickBooks, you can set a preference.

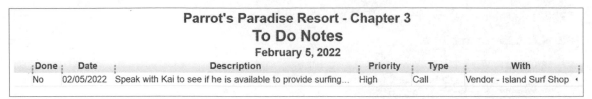

Done	Date	Description	Priority	Type	With
No	02/05/2022	Speak with Kai to see if he is available to provide surfing...	High	Call	Vendor - Island Surf Shop ◀

Parrot's Paradise Resort - Chapter 3
To Do Notes
February 5, 2022

After creating to dos through the Lead Center, you can view them in the To Do Notes report.

Company→To Do List

Reports→List→To Do Notes

DEVELOP YOUR SKILLS 3-2

In this exercise, you will explore the Lead Center and add Lucy Ricardo as a customer lead. You will add a task to contact the owner of a surf shop in town on Lucy's behalf to see whether Lucy's request for lessons for her family can be fulfilled. Finally, you will view the task in the To Do List and run a To Do Notes report.

1. Choose **Customers→Lead Center**.
2. Click **New Lead**.

3. Create the lead:

Name	**Ricardo, Lucy**
Main Phone	**(203) 555-9991**
Main Email	**LucyR@email.com**

4. Click **OK** and then click **To Do** at the bottom of the window.

5. Enter the task:

Type	**Call**
Priority	**High**
With	**Vendor: Island Surf Shop**
Due Date	**2/5/2022**
Details	**Speak with Kai to see if he is available to provide surfing lessons for Lucy and her family 3/17/22 - 3/19/22.**

6. Click **OK** to close the Add To Do window.

The task will not be displayed because the To Do item is linked to the vendor and not directly to this lead. It will be displayed in the Vendor Center, To Do List, and To Do Notes report.

Add a Second Task and Run the To Do Report

7. Ensure **Ricardo, Lucy** is selected, click **To Do**, and enter the task details:

Type	**Call**
Priority	**High**
With	**Lead**
Due Date	**2/10/2022**
Details	**Call Lucy with status update of surf lessons**

8. Click **OK** to close the Add To Do window.

The call will be displayed because the To Do item was associated directly with the lead.

9. Click **Reports** at the bottom of the window to launch the To Do Notes report.

You can also see a To Do list by going to the Company menu or viewing the calendar.

10. Choose **Window→Close All** and then click **Home** on the icon bar.

The Item List

As you saw from your work with the Customers & Jobs List, Chart of Accounts, and others, lists are the way QuickBooks stores the data necessary for many of the behind-the-scenes activities to occur. There are lists that store the services and products you sell, accepted payment methods, price levels, sales tax, and even the messages that appear on a customer's invoice. You might say that lists are the backbone of QuickBooks. Accessing and managing these lists will differ slightly depending on whether the list is integrated into a QuickBooks center (Customers & Jobs, Vendors, and Employees) or is accessible via the Lists menu.

Creating Items

Before you can create an invoice, the services or products you sell must be entered into the Item List. Although there are other types of items, in this section we will cover how to create items for service and non-inventory parts. An item is defined in QuickBooks as something a company buys, sells, or resells in the course of business. Keep in mind that if an item is not in the Item List, it can't be bought or sold through an invoice or bill.

When creating an item, you will select the income account to which it should be assigned. When an invoice is created with that item selected, it will automatically affect the proper income account.

TYPES OF ITEMS

Item Type	Description
Service	Services you charge for or purchase (e.g., a sunset cruise, parasailing, specialized labor, consulting hours, or professional fees)
Non-inventory Part	A product you purchase but don't resell, sell but do not purchase, or purchase and resell but don't stock or track as inventory
Inventory Part	Goods you purchase, track as inventory, and resell
Other Charge	Used for things like shipping charges, markups, and other line items that appear on invoices
Subtotal	Totals all items above it on a form up to the last subtotal; use it to apply a percentage discount or surcharge to many items
Group	Quickly enters a group of individual items on an invoice
Discount	Subtracts a percentage or fixed amount from a total or subtotal; don't use for an early payment discount
Payment	Records a partial payment at time of sale; reduces the amount owed on an invoice
Sales Tax Item	Calculates a single sales tax at a specific rate that you pay to a single tax agency (may not appear in all businesses)
Sales Tax Group	Calculates and individually tracks two or more sales tax items that apply to the same sale; customer sees only the total sales tax (may not appear in all businesses)

Service Items

Service items are used in QuickBooks to track services that you both sell to customers and purchase from vendors. Service items can also be used on timesheets and paychecks to track time. Jimmy's accountant likes to organize items based on broad categories, so he's helped him to set up the service items in his Item List. There's more than one right way to set up an item list; choose the one that makes the most sense for your business and you.

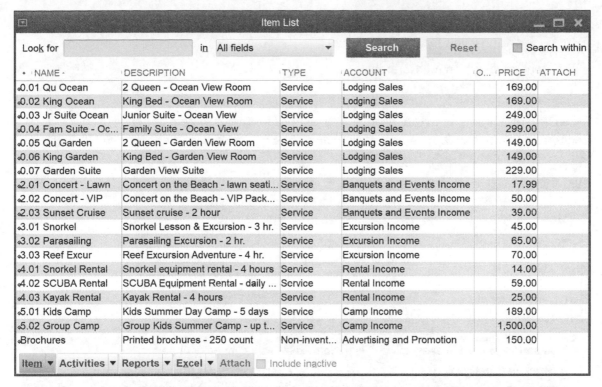

The service items for Parrot's Paradise Resort are arranged in five main categories, with corresponding income accounts: 0-lodging, 1-retail, 2-events, 3-excursions, 4-rentals, 5-camps, 6-restaurant, and 7-spa services. The retail, restaurant, and spa service operations have not opened, so there are no items set up for them yet.

Non-Inventory Items

Non-inventory part items are things that a business buys but doesn't stock as inventory. Some companies will use purchase orders to obtain non-inventory items to track items that are used in their businesses but not resold to customers, such as paper and printer ink. You can also purchase non-inventory items through the Enter Bills window by using the Items tab.

Items Both Purchased and Sold

To track both purchase and sales information for an item, you need to identify that the item is "used in assemblies, purchased for a specific customer:job, or performed by a subcontractor or partner" in the New or Edit Item window. While inventory items are the most common type to fall into this category, it can also be used for service and non-inventory items. Service items may be set up for both purchase and sale if the work is done by subcontractors. Non-inventory items may be set up this way if items are drop-shipped from a supplier and never physically stored in inventory.

Subitems

To track your items in a more detailed fashion, you can use subitems. They can be created for any item on your Item List and can be useful on reports to determine aspects of your business such as profitability. You might use subitems in your company file to:

- Differentiate between broad categories of products/services and individual items within them

- Manage pricing levels for volume discounts

- Differentiate between measurements

- Track multiple vendors for an item

When using subitems, you state an item with no price for the main item and then list prices for the subitems beneath it or leave them blank to apply pricing directly on sales forms. You will work with subitems in the Reinforce Your Skills exercise.

When you choose this option, you'll see a place to enter purchase and sales information.

Indicate the parent item here if you are creating a subitem.

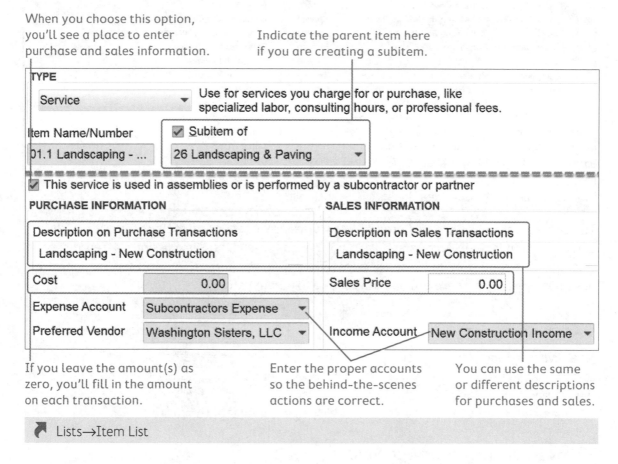

If you leave the amount(s) as zero, you'll fill in the amount on each transaction.

Enter the proper accounts so the behind-the-scenes actions are correct.

You can use the same or different descriptions for purchases and sales.

Lists→Item List

DEVELOP YOUR SKILLS 3-3

In this exercise, you will create three new items for Jimmy. Parrot's Paradise Resort (PPR) is now offering surfboards for rent, so you will set this up as a service item. In addition, Jimmy hired a massage therapist who is offering massage-by-the-sea services, another service item. Jimmy is also adding beach towels as a non-inventory item, as they're provided to guests. You will start by creating the service items.

1. Click the **Items & Services** task icon in the Company area of the Home Page.

Items & Services

2. Follow these steps to create the surfboard rental item:

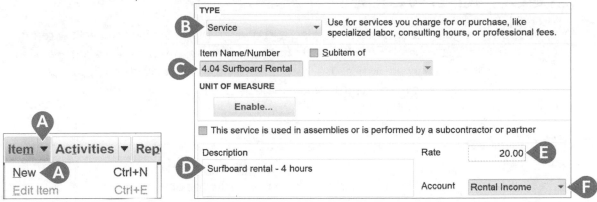

Ⓐ Choose **Item→New**.

Ⓑ Tap `Tab` to select the default item type, **Service**.

Ⓒ Type: **4.04 Surfboard Rental**

Ⓓ Tap `Tab` four times and type: **Surfboard rental - 4 hours**

Ⓔ Tap `Tab` and type: **20**

Ⓕ Tap `Tab` and then type **r** and tap `Tab`.

When you type "r," QuickBooks fills in Rental Income for you as it is the first list entry that starts with "r" in that field. It's imperative that you enter the correct account here! An item directs the flow of dollars from the sales input form to the account indicated here.

3. Click **Next** and create the next service item.

Item Name/Number	**7.01 Massage - 1 hr**
Description	**One-hour massage-by-the-sea**
Rate	**65**
Account	Type **Spa Income** and then tap `Tab` and click **Set Up**. Click **Save & Close** in the Add New Account window.

The previous account, Rental Income, will automatically fill in, so you will need to replace it with Spa Income.

4. Click **OK** and leave the Item List open.

Create a Non-Inventory Part

5. Choose **Item→New** and create a new **Non-inventory Part** with this information:

Item Name/Number	**Beach towels**
Description	**Beach towels for customer use, one dozen**
Rate	**72**
Expense Account	**Service Supplies**

6. Click **OK** and then close the Item List.

Creating Invoices

Once you've set up your initial Customers & Jobs List and the Item List, you can begin entering sales transactions. In this section, you will learn to create invoices, which use Accounts Receivable, the account debited when invoices are created. When you create an invoice, you *must* specify a customer because Accounts Receivable (along with the customer's individual subregister) will be debited by the transaction.

> **Tip!** Invoicing a customer is also known as a customer making a purchase "on account."

After you select your customer from the drop-down list at the top of the form, all the relevant information you entered in that customer's record will fill into the appropriate fields on the Create Invoices window. Even though the description fills in from the Item List, you can always change it on individual invoices.

From the Main tab, you can email, print, and delete invoices; attach files; receive payments; and more.

Additional tools are available on the Formatting, Send/Ship, and Reports tabs.

When a Customer:Job is selected, the information is filled in from the underlying list.

The default template is Intuit Service Invoice, but other templates are available or can be created.

Change or set the payment terms for a customer.

Select items and enter descriptions and quantities here. The amount is automatically calculated.

This message is pulled from the Customer Message List.

Memo is a searchable field, which can aid in finding transactions.

Summary and transaction information is shown here for the active customer.

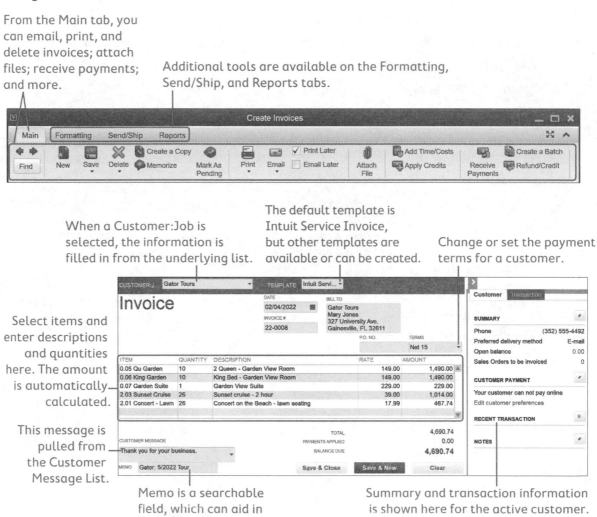

Entering Customers Not on the Customers & Jobs List

When you type a new entry into a field that draws from a list, QuickBooks gives you the opportunity to add the record to the list. You can choose to Quick Add the new record (the name will be entered into the list without accompanying information, which you can add at a later date) or to complete a full setup (a New Customer window appears in which you can type all of the relevant information).

Form Templates

When you first install QuickBooks, Intuit provides you with various templates, such as the Intuit Service Invoice, Intuit Product Invoice, and Intuit Professional Invoice. You can use these templates as they are, create custom templates to meet your specific needs, or download templates from the QuickBooks website. In this section, you will work with one of the default templates—the Intuit Service Invoice.

Payment Terms

Payment terms dictate an agreement between buyer and seller as to when and how much is to be paid for a product or service. In the case of "Net 30" payment terms, the net (or entire) amount of the invoice is due in thirty days. By default, if payment terms are not stated for a customer or on an invoice, QuickBooks will set the payment due date to be ten days from the date of sale.

Invoice Status Tracker

One of the most helpful recent features in QuickBooks Desktop (in my humble opinion...) is the ability to track the status of your invoices right from the Create Invoices window. You can click the See History link to the right of Invoice to open a window that shows the invoice's history.

The dates that are tracked with this feature are:

- Date created

- Due Date and Past Due Status

- If it has been emailed and whether it has been viewed by the recipient

- The date payment was received

- The date the funds were deposited in your account

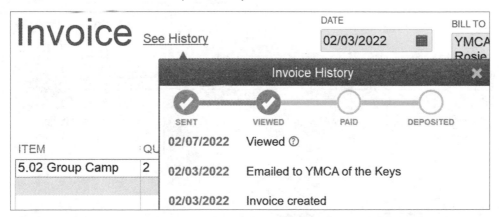

When you click the See History link in the Create Invoices window, you can see the current status of the invoice to aid you in managing your receivables.

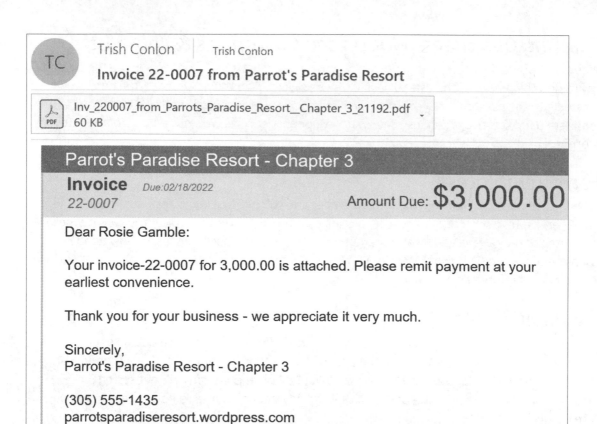

Trish Conlon | Trish Conlon

Invoice 22-0007 from Parrot's Paradise Resort

PDF Inv_220007_from_Parrots_Paradise_Resort__Chapter_3_21192.pdf
60 KB

Parrot's Paradise Resort - Chapter 3

Invoice *Due:02/18/2022*
22-0007   Amount Due: **$3,000.00**

Dear Rosie Gamble:

Your invoice-22-0007 for 3,000.00 is attached. Please remit payment at your earliest convenience.

Thank you for your business - we appreciate it very much.

Sincerely,
Parrot's Paradise Resort - Chapter 3

(305) 555-1435
parrotsparadiseresort.wordpress.com

Invoices can be mailed directly from the Create Invoices window. If you are set up to collect credit card payments through QuickBooks, there will be a link in the email to make it easy for the customer to click and pay the invoice.

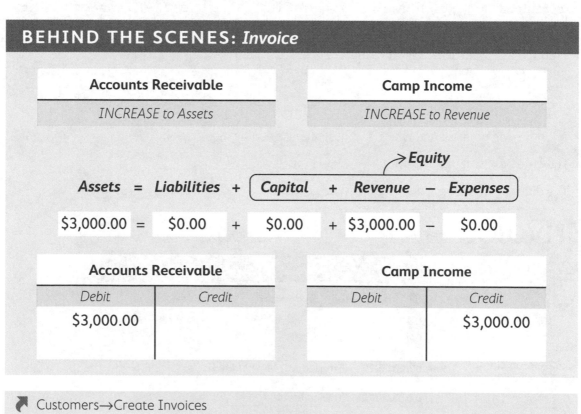

BEHIND THE SCENES: *Invoice*

Accounts Receivable	Camp Income
INCREASE to Assets	*INCREASE to Revenue*

→Equity

Assets = Liabilities + (Capital + Revenue − Expenses)

$3,000.00 = $0.00 + $0.00 + $3,000.00 − $0.00

Accounts Receivable		Camp Income	
Debit	*Credit*	*Debit*	*Credit*
$3,000.00			$3,000.00

Customers→Create Invoices

In this exercise, you will create invoices for customers. The YMCA spring break camp (for which you set up the job in Develop Your Skills 3-1) is coming up soon and they need to be invoiced for twenty campers.

1. Click the **Create Invoices** task icon in the Customers area of the Home Page.

2. Click the **Customer:Job** drop-down arrow ▼ at the top of the window and choose **YMCA of the Keys:Camp Mar28**.

Create Invoices

Notice that the customer's address and terms fill in for you from the underlying list.

3. Follow these steps to complete the invoice:

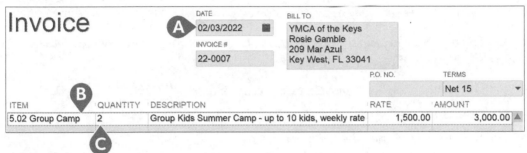

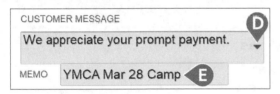

Ⓐ Tap [Tab] two times and type: **020322**

Tip! When you type in a date field, you don't need to include the slash marks. QuickBooks will format the date properly once you move to the next field.

The next invoice number, 22-0007, will automatically fill in for you.

Ⓑ Click the **Item** drop-down arrow ▼, scroll down, and choose **5.02 Group Camp**.

The drop-down arrow will not be displayed until you click in the field or [Tab] to it.

Ⓒ Tap [Tab] and then type **2** and tap [Tab] again.

QuickBooks automatically calculates the total amount when you move to another field.

Ⓓ Click the drop-down arrow ▼ and choose **We appreciate your prompt payment.**

Ⓔ Tap [Tab] and type: **YMCA Mar 28 Camp**

Notice the Customer and Transaction tabs that appear to the right of the Invoice. You can edit the customer record or see any prior transactions using these tabs. If this pane is not displayed to the right of the invoice, click Show History ◄ to display it.

4. Click **Save & New**.

BEHIND THE SCENES BRIEF
Accounts Receivable DR 3,000.00; **Camp Income CR 3,000.00**
Accounts Receivable has **increased**; Camp Income has **increased**
Check Figure: Accounts Receivable $15,108.75

Tip! You can easily compare the check figures to those in your Chart of Accounts.

Create an Invoice for a Customer "On the Fly"

A new customer, Mary Jones, is the owner of Gator Tours out of Gainesville, Florida. She called to book a block of rooms, tickets for a concert on the beach, and a sunset cruise for an upcoming tour she's hosting. You will add her company as a new customer "on the fly" while creating the invoice for her.

Your insertion point should be in the Customer:Job field at the top of a new invoice. If it's not, choose Customers→Create Invoices.

5. In the Customer:Job field, type **Gator Tours** and tap ⌧Tab⌧.
6. Click **Set Up** in the Customer:Job Not Found window.
7. Add these details to the new customer record:

Company Name	**Gator Tours**
Full Name	**Ms. Mary Jones**
Job Title	**Owner**
Main Phone	**(352) 555-4492**
Address (copy to the Ship To field)	**327 University Ave., Gainesville, FL 32611**
Account Number	**T154**
Terms	**Net 15**
Customer Type	**Tour Company**

If you chose Quick Add, you would have to edit the customer record later to fill in this information.

8. Click **OK** and then tap ⌧Tab⌧ to go to the Date field and type: **020422**

You can also tap the ⊞ or ⊟ keys to move the date forward or backward one day at a time.

9. Use this screen to enter the items, leaving the invoice number as 22-0008 and the terms as Net 15:

ITEM	QUANTITY	DESCRIPTION	RATE	AMOUNT
0.05 Qu Garden	10	2 Queen - Garden View Room	149.00	1,490.00
0.06 King Garden	10	King Bed - Garden View Room	149.00	1,490.00
0.07 Garden Suite	1	Garden View Suite	229.00	229.00
2.03 Sunset Cruise	26	Sunset cruise - 2 hour	39.00	1,014.00
2.01 Concert - Lawn	26	Concert on the Beach - lawn seating	17.99	467.74

10. Choose **Thank you for your business.** as the Customer Message and type **Gator: 5/2022 Tour** as the Memo.

Memos are searchable fields and can be displayed on reports. It's a good idea to use them and be consistent in how you enter the memo.

BEHIND THE SCENES BRIEF

Accounts Receivable DR 4,690.74; **Lodging Sales CR 3,209.00 | Banquets and Events Income CR 1,481.74**

Accounts Receivable has **increased**; Lodging Sales and Banquets and Events Income have **increased**

Check Figure: Accounts Receivable 19,799.49

---

11. Click **Save & Close** and close the Check Spelling window, if necessary.

Receiving Payments

After you've created an invoice and received the payment, entering that payment through the Receive Payments window is the next step. Using the Receive Payments window will credit accounts receivable and the appropriate customer subregister. The other half of the equation (the account to be debited) depends on how you treat the payments received. The Payment Method List keeps track of the different methods of receiving payments. You can also add additional methods such as gift cards.

The Undeposited Funds Account

By default, when you receive payments on invoices or from cash sales, the funds are grouped into the Undeposited Funds asset account. QuickBooks automatically creates this Other Current Asset account (it's a Cash and Cash Equivalent account). As long as you don't change the default, payments received through the Receive Payments and Make Deposits windows will be directed to the Undeposited Funds account behind the scenes.

Tip! Use the Receive Payments window! If you don't, the invoices will remain open and your income and amount in accounts receivable will be overstated. After you receive payments, there will be a number notification on the Record Deposits task icon. This is a reminder to deposit the payment(s) in the bank, moving them out of Undeposited Funds.

Record Deposits

The Income Tracker

The Income Tracker gives you an at-a-glance picture of customer activity. Use this tool to help manage your incoming cash flow.

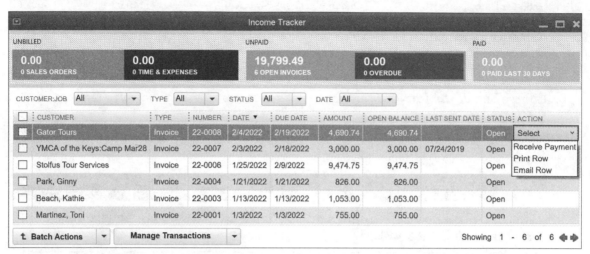

The Income Tracker allows you to easily keep track of customer transactions. You can choose to perform actions on an individual row, as displayed by the drop-down list for invoice #22-0008, or for multiple rows by selecting them and then choosing an option from the Batch Actions menu.

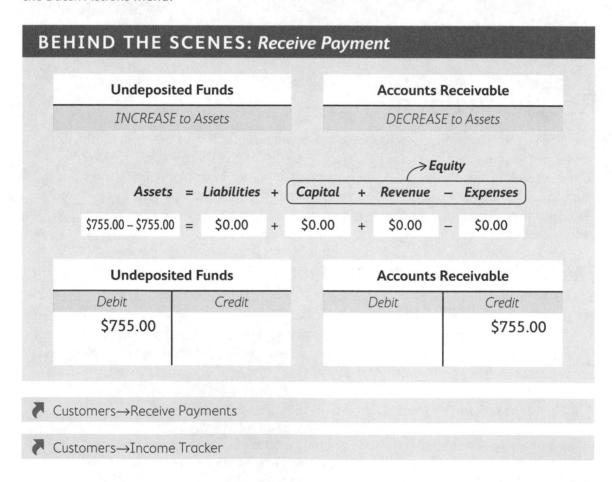

BEHIND THE SCENES: *Receive Payment*

Undeposited Funds	Accounts Receivable
INCREASE to Assets	*DECREASE to Assets*

Equity

Assets = Liabilities + (Capital + Revenue − Expenses)

$755.00 − $755.00 = $0.00 + $0.00 + $0.00 − $0.00

Undeposited Funds		Accounts Receivable	
Debit	*Credit*	*Debit*	*Credit*
$755.00			$755.00

Customers→Receive Payments

Customers→Income Tracker

In this exercise, you will record payments received from invoiced customers. You have just received a credit card payment from Toni Martinez for invoice #22-0001.

1. Click the **Receive Payments** task icon in the Customers area of the Home Page.

Receive Payments

2. Follow these steps to complete the payment:

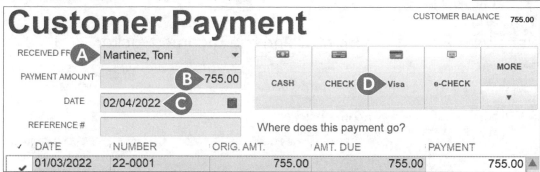

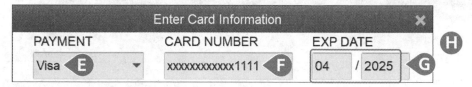

Ⓐ Type **m** and tap `Tab`.

Ⓑ Type **755** and tap `Tab`.

Ⓒ Type: **020422**

Ⓓ Choose the **Credit/Debit** card option (it will be displayed with the last payment type used; here, Visa).

Ⓔ Choose **Visa**.

Ⓕ Tap `Tab` and type: **4444333322221111**

Ⓖ Tap `Tab`, type **04** and tap `Tab`, and then type: **25**

Ⓗ Click **Done**.

Notice that when you typed the amount, it was automatically applied to the invoice listed with the same amount. If no invoices match the amount, it would be applied to invoice(s) beginning with the oldest one.

Note! The Card Security Code (CSC) can't be saved, as that would violate the Payment Applications Best Practices guidelines by the Payment Card Industry (PCI) for software providers.

3. Enter **`Martinez Inv 22-0001 payment`** as the memo text in the bottom-left corner and click **Save & Close**.

> **BEHIND THE SCENES BRIEF**
>
> Undeposited Funds DR 755.00; **Accounts Receivable CR 755.00**
>
> Undeposited Funds has **increased**; Accounts Receivable has **decreased**
>
> **Check Figure:** Accounts Receivable $19,044.49

Receive a Partial Payment Using the Income Tracker

Jimmy just received a check from Kathie Beach for a portion of the amount she owes on invoice #22-0003. You will view the Income Tracker and initiate this partial payment from it.

4. Choose **Customers→Income Tracker**.

5. Click anywhere in the line for Kathie Beach's invoice #22-0003, click the **Action** drop-down arrow ▾, and choose **Receive Payment**.

Notice that the customer and the payment amount are automatically filled in for you.

6. Tap Tab and then type **553** and tap Tab again.

7. Type **020722** as the date and click **Check** as the payment type.

8. Tap Tab and then type **3392** for the check number.

9. Tap Tab and then type **`Beach Inv 22-0003 partial payment`** in the **Memo** field.

By choosing to leave this as an underpayment, when you receive the next payment from this customer, the Receive Payments window will show that there is a balance due of $500.00 for invoice #22-0003.

> **BEHIND THE SCENES BRIEF**
>
> Undeposited Funds DR 553.00; **Accounts Receivable CR 553.00**
>
> Undeposited Funds has **increased**; Accounts Receivable has **decreased**
>
> **Check Figure:** Accounts Receivable $18,491.49

10. Click **Save & Close** and close the Income Tracker window.

Sales Receipts

When a customer pays at the time of sale and there's no need to create an invoice, you can generate a Sales Receipt for the customer. A Sales Receipt does not affect Accounts Receivable but will still affect Undeposited Funds.

Selecting the Correct Form for Customer Sales

There are three main ways of recording customer sales and charges. Choosing the appropriate form depends on the circumstances.

COMPARING CUSTOMER FORMS	
Form	**When to Use**
Invoices	Use this when a customer doesn't make a payment at the time of service and/or receipt of product. The invoice amount is held in Accounts Receivable.
Sales Receipts	Use this when a customer makes a payment at the time of service and/or receipt of product. Accounts Receivable is not affected. This form is a combination of the Create Invoices and Receive Payments windows.
Statements	If you have a customer for whom you do multiple jobs throughout the month, you can gather the charges and send one statement for all of them. The statement will show previous account balances, new charges, and payments for a specific time period.

Duplicating a Transaction

There are many times when you may need to create a duplicate transaction, and QuickBooks has a command that allows you to do just that! The duplicated transaction can be used for the same or a different customer; in fact, you can modify anything on it before saving it. While duplicating a transaction can save you time, if you anticipate that you need to duplicate the same transaction many times, you may wish to memorize it instead.

> **QuickBooks Desktop Information**
>
> A duplicate Sales Receipt has been created. Make any changes you need and save the Sales Receipt.
>
> If you want to duplicate this Sales Receipt regularly, you may want to use Memorized Transactions instead. Click here for more information on Memorized Transactions.

Depositing Payments

After you've received payments for both sales on account and cash sales, you will need to deposit them. We will not go through this activity in this chapter, but just be aware that the next step is to empty Undeposited Funds and move the amount to a bank account.

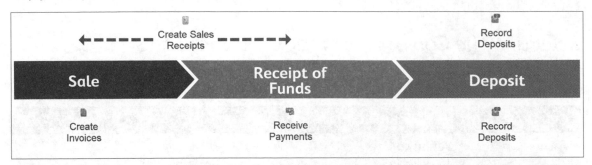

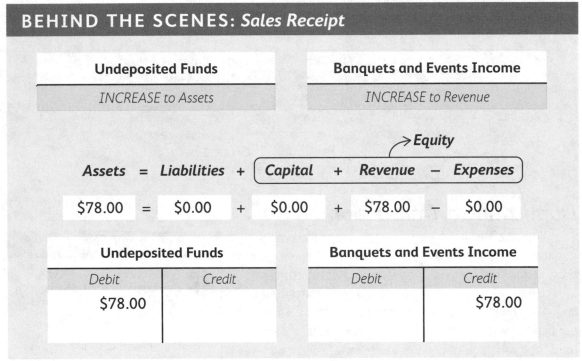

BEHIND THE SCENES: *Sales Receipt*

Undeposited Funds	Banquets and Events Income
INCREASE to Assets	*INCREASE to Revenue*

→ *Equity*

$$Assets = Liabilities + (Capital + Revenue - Expenses)$$

$$\$78.00 = \$0.00 + \$0.00 + \$78.00 - \$0.00$$

Undeposited Funds		Banquets and Events Income	
Debit	*Credit*	*Debit*	*Credit*
$78.00			$78.00

↰ Customers→Enter Sales Receipts

↰ Edit→Duplicate Sales Receipt

DEVELOP YOUR SKILLS 3-6

In this exercise, you will receive payment at the time of the sale. You will sell a sunset cruise to an existing customer, and then you will create a sales receipt without entering a customer. Finally, you will duplicate an existing invoice to enter a new sale.

1. Click the **Create Sales Receipts** task icon in the Customers area of the Home Page.

   The Enter Sales Receipts window opens with the insertion point in the Customer:Job field.

Create Sales Receipts

2. Type **b** and tap Tab to select **Bates, Brandon** as the customer.

3. Follow these steps to complete the sales receipt:

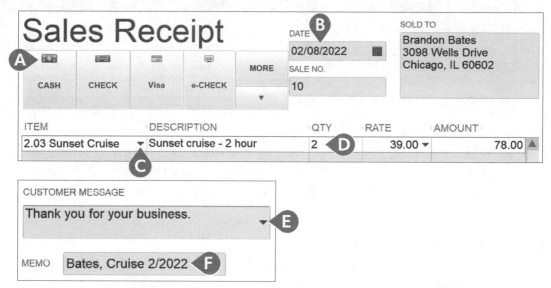

(A) Click **Cash** and tap `Tab`.

(B) Type: **020822**

(C) Click the **Item** drop-down arrow ▼ and choose **2.03 Sunset Cruise**.

(D) Tap `Tab` twice and type: **2**

(E) Click the **Customer Message** drop-down arrow ▼ and choose **Thank you for your business.**

(F) Tap `Tab` and type: **Bates, Cruise 2/2022**

BEHIND THE SCENES BRIEF
Undeposited Funds DR 78.00; **Banquets and Events Income CR 78.00**
Undeposited Funds has **increased**; Banquets and Events Income has **increased**
Check Figure: Undeposited Funds $1,386.00

4. Click **Save & New**.

Your insertion point should be in the Customer:Job field of a new Enter Sales Receipt window.

Record a Sales Receipt Without a Specified Customer

Because Accounts Receivable is not affected when you enter a cash sale, you can create a sales receipt without choosing a customer. This may come in handy if you sell something to someone just once and don't need that customer listed in your Customers & Jobs List or if you provide services in a different capacity. In this case, Jimmy sold tickets to a concert to someone who just stopped in the office.

5. Complete the sales receipt on 02/10/2022:

Payment Type	**Cash**
Item	**2.01 Concert Lawn**
Quantity	**3**
Memo	**Concert, 2/2022**

BEHIND THE SCENES BRIEF

Undeposited Funds DR 53.97; **Banquets and Events Income CR 53.97**

Undeposited Funds has **increased**; Banquets and Events Income has **increased**

Check Figure: Undeposited Funds $1,439.97

6. Click **Save & Close**.

This transaction debits Undeposited Funds and credits Banquets and Events Income, but no customer is tracked. The purpose of selecting a customer for a sales receipt is to ensure you can produce meaningful customer reports, such as Sales by Customer Summary, if they are important to your business.

Duplicate a Transaction

Mary Jones from Gator Tours called to book another tour for a different group in April. You will duplicate the invoice you created for her previously and edit it to save time.

7. Click the **Create Invoices** task icon in the Customers area of the Home Page.

8. Click the **Previous** ⬅ button on the Main tab of the ribbon to display the invoice for **Gator Tours**.

Create Invoices

9. Choose **Edit→Duplicate Invoice** and click **OK** in the QuickBooks Desktop Information window.

A copy of the invoice you created for Gator Tours will be displayed with the next invoice number entered. You can now edit it for the April tour group.

10. Use the ⊞ key to change the date to **02/14/2022** and then change the terms to **Net 30**.

11. Change the quantity of the items as indicated (if an item isn't listed, the quantity isn't changed):

Item	Previous Qty	New Qty
0.05 Qu Garden	10	**7**
0.06 King Garden	10	**15**
2.03 Sunset Cruise	26	**32**
2.01 Concert – Lawn	26	**29**

12. Change the memo to: `Gator: 4/2022 Tour`

BEHIND THE SCENES BRIEF
Accounts Receivable DR 5,276.71; **Lodging Sales CR 3,507.00 | Banquets and Events Income CR 1,769.71**
Accounts Receivable has **increased**; Lodging Sales and Banquets and Events Income have **increased**
Check Figure: Accounts Receivable $23,768.20

13. Click **Save & Close**, choosing **No** in the Information Changed window. Close the Check Spelling window, if necessary.

The change in terms for this invoice was only for the one transaction; you don't want to make it permanent.

Adjusting Customer Transactions

It's inevitable that you will need to deal with errors or modifications to transactions. It is very important to do this properly to ensure that everything behind the scenes is correct.

Editing Existing Transactions

To edit an existing transaction, you simply open the window where the transaction is recorded and make the changes. You do need to think about the implications of any modifications you make, though. Many transactions are tied to others, and a change to one can affect another. For instance, if an invoice has been paid, both the invoice and the payment are linked in QuickBooks.

 **Best Practice**

After a transaction has been cleared during the reconciliation process, it should not be changed. Because each situation may require a different solution, you may want to check with an accountant.

Voiding vs. Deleting Transactions

QuickBooks allows you to either void or delete a transaction you no longer need recorded. In most cases, you will want to void a transaction so you can keep a record of it. This will remove everything from behind the scenes and yet leave evidence that the transaction existed.

Locating Transactions in QuickBooks

QuickBooks provides two methods for locating transactions in your company file: Find and Search.

The Find Feature

The Find feature helps you locate a transaction if you don't know all the information about it from within the form itself. There are two options within Find:

- **Simple** to perform basic searches

- **Advanced** to perform more complex searches, using filters to help to sort through your data

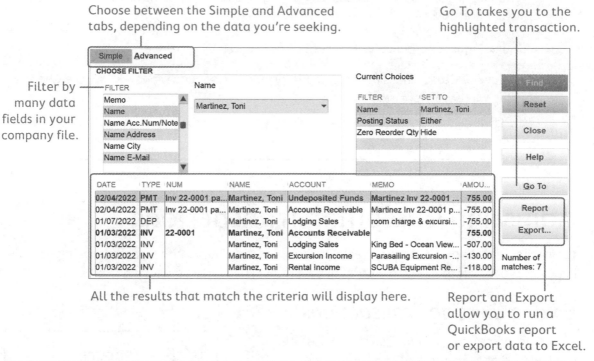

Choose between the Simple and Advanced tabs, depending on the data you're seeking.

Go To takes you to the highlighted transaction.

Filter by many data fields in your company file.

All the results that match the criteria will display here.

Report and Export allow you to run a QuickBooks report or export data to Excel.

> ↱ Edit→Find : Simple tab *or* Advanced tab

The Search Feature

Search is more powerful than Find. Accessed above the icon bar or through the menu bar, it allows you to search the entire company file for the following types of information:

- Forms/transactions (invoices, estimates, etc.)

- People and companies (customers, vendors, employees, and other names)

- List entries (items, tax items, etc.)

- Amounts and dates

- Menu commands (QuickBooks opens the menu and highlights the command for you.)

- Specific text within notes, descriptions, memos, and transactions

Fixing Errors

Many errors are simple to fix, such as correcting the number of items sold on an invoice, as long as the payment has not been received. However, once you add an additional transaction, addressing the error is more complicated. The following table outlines a common customer-related error, the effect of the error behind the scenes, and how to correct it.

A COMMON ERROR AND ITS FIX

Error	Effect Behind the Scenes	The Fix
An invoice is entered but the Receive Payments window is not used when the payment is deposited.	Your income will be double-stated and Accounts Receivable for the customer is not "cleared out."	Delete the deposit and then enter the transaction properly using the Receive Payments window.

FLASHBACK TO GAAP: PRUDENCE

Remember, if you need to choose between two solutions, pick the one that is less likely to overstate assets and income.

 Edit→Search

DEVELOP YOUR SKILLS 3-7

Jimmy forgot to tell you that he offered a discounted price to Mary Jones for the cruise and concert when she booked the second tour. In this exercise, you will first find and then edit the Gator Tours invoice.

1. Choose **Edit→Find**.

2. Ensure the Transaction Type option is set to *Invoice* and then click the **Customer:Jobs** drop-down arrow ▼ and choose **Gator Tours**.

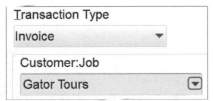

3. Click **Find**.

   Both invoices for Gator Tours will be displayed in the bottom portion of the window.

4. Select the invoice dated **02/14/2022** and click **Go To**.

   Invoice 22-0009 will be displayed.

5. Change the rate to **35** for **2.03 Sunset Cruise** and to **15** for **2.01 Concert – Lawn**; click **OK** in the Price Level/Billing Rate Level window.

ITEM	QUANTITY	DESCRIPTION	RATE	AMOUNT
0.05 Qu Garden	7	2 Queen - Garden View Room	149.00	1,043.00
0.06 King Garden	15	King Bed - Garden View Room	149.00	2,235.00
0.07 Garden Suite	1	Garden View Suite	229.00	229.00
2.03 Sunset Cruise	32	Sunset cruise - 2 hour	35.00	1,120.00
2.01 Concert - Lawn	29	Concert on the Beach - lawn seating	15.00	435.00

BEHIND THE SCENES BRIEF

Banquets and Events Income DR 214.71; **Accounts Receivable CR 214.71**

Banquets and Events Income has **decreased**; Accounts Receivable has **decreased**

Check Figure: Accounts Receivable $23,553.49

6. Click **Save & Close** and then click **Yes** to record the transaction with the changes; close the Find window.

Correct an Error

On 1/7/2022, a temp worker Jimmy hired saw a check for $755 from Toni Martinez and entered it as a deposit in QuickBooks. The check was set aside and never deposited in the bank. Earlier in this chapter, you received this payment for Jimmy in QuickBooks. Now the income and assets are both overstated by $755. You will now correct this error.

7. Choose **Edit→Find** and display the **Advanced** tab.

8. Follow these steps to find the transaction:

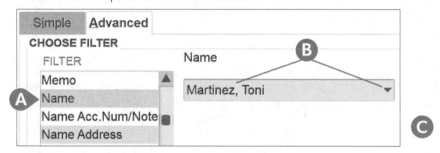

Ⓐ Scroll down the Filter list and select **Name**.

Ⓑ Click the **Name** drop-down arrow ▼ and choose **Martinez, Toni**.

Ⓒ Click **Find**.

Ⓓ Click the **01/07/2022** deposit transaction.

Ⓔ Click **Go To**.

The Make Deposits window opens, displaying the deposit entered for Toni.

9. Choose **Edit→Delete Deposit** and click **OK** to confirm.

Since you've already entered the payment correctly, you are finished correcting this error.

BEHIND THE SCENES BRIEF
Lodging Sales DR 755.00; **Sailors Bank Checking CR 755.00**
Lodging Sales has **decreased**; Sailors Bank Checking has **decreased**
Check Figure: Sailors Bank Checking $180,204.32

10. Close the Make Deposits and Find windows.

Customer-Related Reports

Once you've entered transactions affecting your customers, it's time to run reports to display and analyze your data.

Types of Reports

While there are many preset reports in QuickBooks and thousands of contributed ones, there are three main types of reports into which they are classified. They are:

- List reports

- Summary reports that subtotal data and provide a summary

- Transaction reports that show each transaction that makes up the subtotal in a summary report

To see reports based on customer transactions, there are different reports you can run depending on the specific information you are seeking. The Customer Balance reports (both summary and detail, found in the Customers & Receivables category) show only the open transactions affecting Accounts Receivable (transactions entered and paid as invoices). The Income by Customer reports (both summary and detail, found in the Company & Financial category) show all customer transactions that have resulted in income for the company, not just those affecting Accounts Receivable.

QuickReport

A QuickReport can be run from the various center and list windows. QuickReports show all transactions recorded in QuickBooks for a particular center list entry or account. You will use this report to get a quick snapshot of all customer transactions for Brandon Bates.

QuickZoom

QuickBooks has a great feature called QuickZoom. It allows you to drill down (or "zoom") through underlying subreports until you reach the form where the data was originally entered. This can be extremely useful if you have questions as to where a figure in a report comes from. You can even edit the source transaction once you have navigated to it.

Parrot's Paradise Resort - Chapter 3
Customer Balance Detail
All Transactions

Type	Date	Num	Account	Amount	Balance
Gator Tours					
Invoice	02/04/2022	22-0008	Accounts Receivable	4,690.74	4,690.74
Invoice	02/14/2022	22-0009	Accounts Receivable	5,062.00	9,752.74
Total Gator Tours				9,752.74	9,752.74
TOTAL				**9,752.74**	**9,752.74**

The zoom pointer indicates that you can double-click to dive deeper into your data. The number of layers to zoom through depends on the report (or graph) type you started with. Here, double-clicking opens the Create Invoices window with the invoice #22-0009 for Gator Tours displayed.

FLASHBACK TO GAAP: TIME PERIOD

Remember, it's implied that the activities of the business can be divided into time periods.

 Customers→Customer Center : [Select Customer]→Quick Report

 Reports→Customers & Receivables→Customer Balance Summary

DEVELOP YOUR SKILLS 3-8

In this exercise, you will run customer-related reports for Parrot's Paradise Resort, beginning with a QuickReport.

1. Click the **Customers** CUSTOMERS button on the Home Page to open the Customer Center and choose **Bates, Brandon**.

   You must always select the list item on which you wish to run a QuickReport.

2. Click the **QuickReport** link at the right of the Customer Center window.

REPORTS FOR THIS CUSTOMER
QuickReport
Open Balance
Customer Snapshot

3. Type **a** to set the date range to All. Resize the window so you can see all transactions, if necessary.

A customer QuickReport can also display all transactions for a selected customer within a designated date range. This report shows transactions for Brandon that both did and did not affect Accounts Receivable.

4. Close the QuickReport and the Customer Center windows.

Create a Customer Summary Report and Use QuickZoom

Next you will create a summary report and then use QuickZoom to drill down to the transaction where the data originated.

5. Choose **Reports→Customers & Receivables→Customer Balance Summary**.

6. Place the mouse pointer over or next to the **Gator Tours** amount (9,752.74) and double-click.

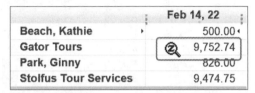

A Customer Balance Detail report will open with all the transactions that make up the balance for Gator Tours displayed.

7. Place the mouse (zoom) pointer over or next to the **invoice 22-0008** amount (4,690.74) and double-click.

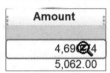

The Create Invoices window opens with invoice #22-0008 displayed. It doesn't matter if the zoom pointer is next to or on top of the amount you are drilling down to.

8. Choose **Window→Close All**, choosing not to memorize the report.

Create an Open Invoices Report

Another report you may wish to create as you work with customers is the Open Invoices report, which shows all outstanding invoices for the company.

9. Choose **Reports→Report Center**.

10. Select the **Customers & Receivables** category and then scroll down to **Open Invoices**.

11. Click the **Dates** drop-down arrow ▼, choose **All**, and click **Run**

QuickBooks displays the Open Invoices report, which shows all unpaid invoices.

12. Choose **Window→Close All**.

Sales Reports

Running sales reports will help you to stay on top of your company's revenue. Sales reports can be grouped by customer, item, or sales rep (if set up). You can also view sales information by job if you have jobs set up for your company. To see all sales for the company, you will want to view the sales by item report.

Parrot's Paradise Resort - Chapter 3
Sales by Item Summary
All Transactions

	Qty	Amount	% of Sales	Avg Price
Service				
0.01 Qu Ocean (2 Queen - Ocean View Room)	5	845.00	2.8%	169.00
0.02 King Ocean (King Bed - Ocean View Room)	33	5,577.00	18.5%	169.00
0.03 Jr Suite Ocean (Junior Suite - Ocean View)	4	996.00	3.3%	249.00
0.04 Fam Suite - Ocean (Family Suite - Ocean View)	6	1,794.00	5.9%	299.00
0.05 Qu Garden (2 Queen - Garden View Room)	17	2,533.00	8.4%	149.00
0.	49	7,301.00	24.2%	149.00
0.	2	458.00	1.5%	229.00
2.	99	1,694.30	5.6%	17.11
2.	8	400.00	1.3%	50.00
2.	94	3,538.00	11.7%	37.64
3.	7	315.00	1%	45.00
3.	17	1,105.00	3.7%	65.00
3.	2	140.00	0.5%	70.00
4.	2	28.00	0.1%	14.00
4.	4	236.00	0.8%	59.00
4.	10	250.00	0.8%	25.00
5.	2	3,000.00	9.9%	1,500.00
To	361.00	30,210.30	100.0%	83.69
TO	361	30,210.30	100.0%	83.69

Parrot's Paradise Resort - Chapter 3
Sales by Customer Summary
All Transactions

	Feb 14, 22
Bates, Brandon	1,480.00
Beach, Kathie	1,053.00
Gator Tours	9,752.74
Hernandez, Jose	2,389.00
Martinez, Toni	755.00
Park, Ginny	826.00
Stolfus Tour Services	9,474.75
YMCA of the Keys	
Camp Mar28	3,000.00
Total YMCA of the K...	3,000.00
TOTAL	**28,730.49**

To see the total sales for the company, run a report based on the items sold, rather than one based on customer sales, if you ever enter sales receipts without specifying a customer. Note the difference between the totals on these two reports: $1,479.81. It's the amount of sales that doesn't have a customer identified.

Basic Report Modifications

Many times, you will run a report and the columns are so narrow that you can't see all your data. Or, you may have columns displayed that you don't wish to view. These dilemmas are easily solved without having to travel deep into the jungle of the Modify Report window; in fact, you can adjust them in the regular report window.

To change the width of columns, simply drag the little dashed line dividing the column headers when you see the double arrow (similar to how you adjust column width in Microsoft Excel). To eliminate a column, drag one side of a column divider across the entire column and across the divider on the other side. Not all columns can be deleted, however. When you try to delete a column that must remain, it will simply be resized instead.

		Parrot's Paradise Resort - Chapter 3						
		Sales by Item Detail						
		All Transactions						
Type	Date	Num	Memo	Name	Qty	Sales Price	Amount	Balance
Service								
0.01 Qu Ocean (2 Queen - Ocean View Room)								
Invoice	01/13/2022	22-0003	2 Queen - Oc...	Beach, Kathie	5	169.00	845.00	845.00
Total 0.01 Qu Ocean (2 Queen - Ocean View Room)					5		845.00	845.00

When you place your mouse pointer over a column divider, a double arrow appears. You can then drag to resize the column. Or, if you drag all the way across the column and pass the next divider, you can delete the column from the report in many cases.

 Reports→Sales→[select specific sales report]

DEVELOP YOUR SKILLS 3-9

In this exercise, you will run a report displaying the details of item sales and modify its structure by dragging column dividers.

1. Choose **Reports→Sales→Sales by Item Detail**.

2. Type **a** to set All as the date range for the report and then resize it to view the data.

   The data in the Num field that you wish to see is not visible, and you have decided not to display the memos on this report, so you will make a couple changes to the report structure.

3. Place the mouse pointer over the column divider to the right of Num and drag to the right until you can see the numbers fully displayed in the column.

Num	Memo
w Room)	
22-0003	2 Queen - Oc.

4. Place the mouse pointer over the column divider to the right of Memo and drag to the left until you cross the column divider to the left of Memo.

   The Memo column is no longer displayed on the report.

5. Close the Sales by Item Detail report, choosing not to memorize it.

Tackle the Tasks

Now is your chance to work a little more with Parrot's Paradise Resort and apply the skills you've just learned to accomplish additional tasks. Continue with the same company file you've been using in this chapter so far. If you need to reopen the company file, the password is *Password1*.

Add Customers	York, Olivia, 1021 Miller St., Medford, OR 97504; (541) 555-8921; Referral; Due on Receipt
	Humboldt Tour Company, James McDonald, 575 Industrial Way, Eureka, CA 95501; (707) 555-6722; From Advertisement; Net 15
	Laughlin, Tim; 8 College Drive, Cambridge, MA 02138; (617) 555-4419; Referral; Due on Receipt
Create Items	Service item: 2.04 Dinner Cruise; Dinner Cruise - 3 hr.; $65; Banquets and Events Income
	Service item: 5.03 Kids Day Camp; Kids Summer Day Camp - 1 day; $40; Camp Income
	Service item: 7.02 Couples Massage; Couple one-hour massage-by-the-sea; $120; Spa Income
	Non-inventory item: Logo Marketing Pens; Printed logo pens - 500 count; $175; Advertising and Promotion
Create Invoices	Olivia York; 2/23/2022; 2 Dinner Cruises; Thank you for your business.; York: Dinner Cruises 2/2022
	Humboldt Tour Company; 2/26/2022; 12 King Bed - Ocean View rooms, 5 King Bed - Garden View rooms, 24 Reef Excursion Adventures; Thank you for your business.; Humboldt: 4/2022 Tour
	Laughlin, Tim; 2/27/2022; 3 Kids Day Camp - 1 day; Thank you for your business.; Laughlin: Kids Camp 3/2022
Create Sales Receipts	Angeles, Kyra (Quick Add new customer); 2/25/2022; Check #4420; 2 Dinner Cruises; Thank you for your business.; Angeles: Dinner Cruises 2/2022
	[No Customer]; 2/28/2022; Cash; 5 VIP concert packages; Enjoy the concert! (Add as a new customer message); Cash: VIP Concert 2/2022
Receive Payments	Receive full payment for invoice #22-0007 from the YMCA of the Keys:Camp Mar28 (select the specific job!); check #1632; 2/27/2022; YMCA Inv 22-0007 payment
	Receive full payment for invoice #22-0008 from Gator Tours; check #872; 2/27/2022; Gator Inv 22-0008 payment

Correct a Customer Transaction Error	On 1/29/2022, Jimmy deposited check #233 for $826 from Ginny Park rather than receiving it as payment on invoice #22-0004; correct this error
Generate Reports	Create reports that answer these questions: • What is the contact information for all your customers? • What is the total amount of sales for each customer? • How many open invoices are there for Parrot's Paradise Resort? • Can you create a report that just shows the transactions for Kathie Beach?

Self-Assessment

Check your knowledge of this chapter's key concepts and skills using the Self-Assessment in your ebook or eLab course.

1. A customer is a person or a company to whom or which you issue funds. *True   False*

2. You can delete a customer from the Customers & Jobs List as long as that customer hasn't been used in a transaction. *True   False*

3. If you want to invoice a customer for a service, the service must first be set up as an item. *True   False*

4. When you use a sales receipt to bill a customer, Accounts Receivable is debited. *True   False*

5. Invoicing a customer is also known as a customer making a purchase on account. *True   False*

6. You can enter customers "on the fly" in the Create Invoices window. *True   False*

7. When you void a transaction, every trace of it is removed from behind the scenes, but evidence that the transaction existed remains in QuickBooks. *True   False*

8. QuickZoom allows you to drill down to where data was originally entered. *True   False*

9. If an invoice is entered but the Receive Payments window is not used when the payment is recevied, your income will be double stated. *True   False*

10. The Invoice Status Tracker shows you if an invoice is overdue. *True   False*

11. Which account is debited when invoices are created?
    A. Accounts Payable
    B. Accounts Receivable
    C. Checking
    D. Income Account

12. What type of account is Undeposited Funds?
    A. Asset
    B. Liability
    C. Equity
    D. Income

13. Which QuickBooks form do you use when a customer is making a purchase on account?
    A. Enter Sales Receipts
    B. Create Sales Form
    C. Enter Invoice Receipt
    D. Create Invoices

14. Which report do you produce to see total sales for the company?
    A. Open Invoices
    B. Sales by Item Summary
    C. Customer Summary Report
    D. Company QuickReport

Reinforce Your Skills

Colleen Donnell's company, Donnell Construction, is growing rapidly and she's hired you to manage the books. Your first tasks will involve working with her customers and item list. The password for all files unless otherwise stated is Password1.

Manage Your Customers & Jobs List

In this exercise, you will create and edit Customers & Jobs List entries for Colleen.

1. Choose **File→Open or Restore Company**.
2. Open **RYS_Chapter03 (Company)** *or* restore **RYS_Chapter03 (Portable)** and save it as:
   RYS_Chapter03 Donnell Construction
3. Choose **Customers→Customer Center**.
4. Double-click **Archive Coffee & Wine** to open it for editing.
5. Change the customer's full name to: **Ms. Janice Bing**

   You will have to change the name in three locations. This customer's name will change in all the transactions that Archive was involved in, as well as in all of the future transactions.

6. Click **OK** to accept the change and leave the Customer Center open.

Add a New Customer

7. Click the **New Customer & Job** button and choose **New Customer**.
8. Set up the new customer:

Customer Name	**Unity Temple**
First	**Felix**
Last	**Alexander**
Main Phone	**(872) 555-4433**
Mailing Address	**875 Lake Street** Enter **Oak Park, IL 60301**
Type	**Referral**
Terms	**Net 15**

9. Click **OK** to accept the new record and leave the Customer Center open.

Add a Job to a Customer

10. Click the customer you just created, **Unity Temple**, to select it.
11. Choose **New Customer & Job→Add Job**.
12. Type **Parking Lot** as the name of the job and click **OK**.
13. Close the Customer Center window.

Create Service Subitems

In this exercise, you will create four service subitems for Donnell Construction.

1. Choose **Lists→Item List** and then choose **Item→New**.

2. Create a new service subitem for **26 Landscaping & Paving**:

Item Name/Number	`01.1 Landscaping - New`
Subitem	**26 Landscaping & Paving**
Click the Checkbox For	**This service is used in assemblies or is performed by a subcontractor or partner.**
Description	`Landscaping - New Construction`
Cost or Sales Price	Don't enter a cost or sales price, as they'll be entered for each transaction.
Expense Account	**Subcontractors Expense**
Preferred Vendor	**Washington Sisters, LLC**
Income Account	**New Construction Income**

3. Click **Next** to accept the new item and prepare to enter the next one.

4. Create a new service subitem for **26 Landscaping & Paving**:

Item Name/Number	`01.2 Asphalt - New`
Subitem	**26 Landscaping & Paving**
Click the Checkbox For	**This service is used in assemblies or is performed by a subcontractor or partner.**
Description	`Asphalt Paving - New Construction`
Cost or Sales Price	Don't enter a cost or sales price, as they'll be entered for each transaction.
Expense Account	**Subcontractors Expense**
Preferred Vendor	**Cusak Paving, Inc.**
Income Account	**New Construction Income**

5. Click **OK** to accept the new item and close the window.

6. Using the preceding information as reference, create two additional subitems:

- **01.3 Landscaping – Remodel**
- **01.4 Asphalt - Remodel**

7. Close the Item List.

Enter Sales Transactions

In this exercise, you will create an invoice and a sales receipt for Donnell Construction.

1. Choose **Customers→Create Invoices**.
2. Choose **Unity Temple:Parking Lot** as the Customer:Job.
3. Complete the invoice:

Date	**020522**
Template	**Intuit Service Invoice Template**
Invoice #	Leave 22-0005 as the invoice #.
First Item	**26.01.4 Asphalt - Remodel**
Description	**Repave rear parking lot**
Rate	**16,890**
Second Item	**26.01.3 Landscaping - Remodel**
Description	**Landscape - perimeter rear parking lot**
Rate	**2,500**
Customer Message	**We appreciate your prompt payment.**
Memo	**Unity: Repave/landscape back lot**

4. Click **Save & Close** to record the transaction and then close the Check Spelling on Form window.

Enter a Sales Receipt

5. Choose **Customers→Enter Sales Receipts**.

6. Complete the cash sale:

Add a new job for Finn, Bodhi	**Ext Paint**
Customer:Job	**Finn, Bodhi:Ext Paint**
Date	**020722**
Item	**24 Paint**
Rate	**2,580**
Customer Message	**Thank you for your business.**
Memo	**Bodhi: exterior paint job**

Accept the next sale number that fills in for you.

7. Click **Save & Close** to record the transaction.

Receive Payments

In this exercise, you will receive the payment for the invoice you created earlier.

1. Choose **Customers→Receive Payments**.

2. Choose **Unity Temple:Parking Lot** from the Received From field and complete the payment:

Make sure to apply the payment to the job, not just the customer!

Amount	**19,390**
Date	**021522**
Payment Method	**Check**
Check Number	**1574**
Memo	**Unity: 22-0005 payment**

3. Click **Save & Close**.

Find and Edit a Transaction

In this exercise, you will use the Find feature to locate a transaction that was entered incorrectly and then correct it.

1. Choose **Edit→Find**, display the **Simple** tab, and use this information to complete the Find:
   - Leave the Transaction Type as Invoice
   - Customer:Job: **Burning Sparrow Tattoo** (click **Find**)

   The invoice for the customer will be displayed in the bottom of the window.

2. Double-click the invoice dated **01/19/2022** in the bottom portion of the window.

   The Invoice window opens.

3. Change the amount to **1450** and tap Tab to recalculate.

4. Click **Save & Close** and click **Yes** to record the changes; close the Find window.

Run Customer-Related Reports

In this exercise, you will run three reports for Colleen, beginning with a QuickReport.

1. Choose **Customers→Customer Center**.

2. Click **Popelka, Hayden** to select it.

3. Click the **QuickReport** link at the far-right side of the window.

4. Set the date range to **All**.

   You will see a report that shows the transaction for Hayden Popelka.

5. Choose **Window→Close All** and leave the company file open.

6. Choose **Reports→Customers & Receivables→Customer Phone List**.

7. Double-click **DeMaira Dance Studios, Inc**.

   QuickBooks opens an Edit Customer window, from where you can make any changes to the customer's information.

8. Add Sun's Mobile number as **(872) 555-5124** and click **OK**.

9. Choose **Reports→Company & Financial→Income by Customer Summary**.

10. Change the dates to **All**.

    You will see all the customers that currently have outstanding balances.

11. Choose **Window→Close All**, do not memorize the report, and close the company file.

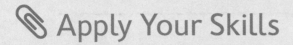 Apply Your Skills

The Wet Noses Veterinary Clinic advertising campaign was a success, and Dr. James has acquired new customers and added new services. In this exercise, you will be creating new customers and adding services. You will also perform daily tasks such as creating invoices, receiving payments, and running reports. The password for all files unless otherwise stated is Password1.

APPLY YOUR SKILLS 3-1 `QG`

Set Up Customers and Jobs

In this exercise, you will create new customers and jobs.

1. Choose **File→Open or Restore Company**.
2. Open **AYS_A1_Chapter03 (Company)** *or* restore **AYS_A1_Chapter03 (Portable)** and save it as: **AYS_A1_Chapter03 Wet Noses Clinic**
3. Open the Customer Center.
4. Set up three customers for Wet Noses Veterinary Clinic:

	Customer 1	**Customer 2**	**Customer 3**
Customer Name	York, Edison	Reeves, LaShonda	Sanders, Ellie
Main Phone	(425) 555-4401	(425) 555-3953	(425) 555-7731
Address	7931 NE 176th St. Enter Bothell, WA 98011	11908 100th Pl. NE Enter Kirkland, WA 98034	302 Northshore Blvd. Enter Bothell, WA 98011
Terms	**Due on Receipt**	**Due on Receipt**	**Due on Receipt**
Account Number	D22	C94	D34
Type	**From Advertisement**	**Referral**	**From Advertisement**
Job	Dog-Scruffy	Dog-Nicky	Cat-Josie

5. Run the **Customer Contact List** report, which should include these new customers and any open balances.
6. Click the **Excel** `Excel ▾` button and export this list to a new workbook saved as: **CH3_A1 Customer Contacts**
7. Close Excel and the Customer Contact List report.

Set Up Service and Non-inventory Items

In this exercise, you will create new items for the company to sell.

1. Set up two service items:

	First Item	**Second Item**
Item Name	Boarding	Dental
Description	Overnight Boarding	Dental Cleaning
Rate	35.00	45.00
Account	**Nonmedical Income**	**Fee for Service Income**

2. Set up a non-inventory part:

Item Name	Treats
Description	Treats for patients - by the box
Rate	18.43
Account	**Nonmedical Income**

3. Run an **Item Price List** report to include the new items and their prices.

4. Click the **Excel** button and export this list to a new workbook saved as:
   CH3_A2 Item Price List

5. Close Excel and the Item Price List report.

APPLY YOUR SKILLS 3-3

Record Sales Transactions and Receive Payments

In this exercise, you will help Dr. James record invoices and cash sales. You will enter the sales information and update the customer's record to capture the custom field information for each pet.

1. On 06/01/2023, Emily Dallas brought in her dog, Cowboy, for an Exam, Vaccine, and Rabies Vaccine. She also bought two boxes of treats. Create an invoice for these services and items. Terms are Net 30; choose to save the new terms for the customer. Choose a customer message and enter this memo: Dallas: Dog-Cowboy, Exam & Vaccines

2. On 06/02/2023, Ellie Sanders brought in her cat, Josie, for a New Patient Exam, Feline DHC, and FIV/FeLV, and one box of treats. She paid cash, so create a sales receipt for her. Choose a customer message and enter this memo: Sanders: Cat-Josie, New Patient

3. On 06/03/2023, Becky Todd brought in her dog, Jedi, for an ACTH Stimulation Test, CBC Chem, and Boarding for three nights. Create an invoice for her. Choose a customer message and enter this memo: Todd: Dog-Jedi, Boarding & Tests

4. On 06/04/2023, Edison York brought in his dog, Scruffy, for Dental and Boarding for two nights. He paid cash, so create a sales receipt for him. Choose a customer message and enter this memo: York: Dog-Scruffy, Dental & Boarding

---

APPLY YOUR SKILLS 3-4 QG

Accept Customer Payments for Invoices

In this exercise, you will receive payments from customers.

1. On 06/07/2023, you received check #773 for $93.76 from Emily Dallas as payment for invoice #176. Use the memo: Dallas: Inv. 176

2. On 06/08/2023, you received check #2310 for $284.21 from the County Animal Shelter as payment for invoice #163. Use the memo: County Animal - Inv. 163

3. Run a **Sales by Customer Summary** report for your customers, from 04/01/2023 through 06/30/2023 (the second quarter).

4. Click the **Excel** button and export this report to a new workbook saved as:
`CH3_A4 Sales by Customer Summary`

5. Close Excel and close the Sales by Customer Summary report.

6. Run the **Open Invoices** report for the date of 06/30/2023 to determine if there are any outstanding invoices for the month.

7. Click the **Excel** button and export this report to a new workbook saved as:
`CH3_A4 Open Invoices`

8. Close Excel, the Open Invoices report, and the company file.

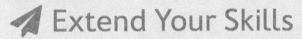

Extend Your Skills

Before You Begin: Open **EYS_Chapter03 (Company)** *or* restore **EYS_Chapter03 (Portable)**. The password is *Password1*.

You've been hired by Arlaine Cervantes to help her with her organization's books. She is the founder of Niños del Lago, a nonprofit organization that provides impoverished Guatemalan children with an engaging educational camp experience. You just sat down at your desk and opened a large envelope from Arlaine that contains a variety of documents; you also have several emails from her. It's your job to sort through the papers and emails and make sense of what you find, entering information into QuickBooks as appropriate and answering any questions in a word-processing document saved as: CH03_EYS_[LastnameFirstinitial]

Remember, you're dealing with random papers dumped out of an envelope and various emails, so part of your challenge is determining the order in which to complete the tasks.

- Sticky note: We now also receive donations from Hanson Family Trust. Do we set them up as a customer? The info for the trust is 900 SE Commercial St., Salem, OR 97306; (503) 555-9331; contact, Richard Hanson.

- Handwritten note: We'll be providing cultural competency training to schools and organizations to raise additional funds. Can we set up a service item directed to Service to Outside Orgs? (You'll need to set up this account as a subaccount for Program Income.) Set the amount to zero as it will be entered at the time of "sale."

- Handwritten note: How do we set up the students who participate in our program? They don't pay us money, so are they customers or is there another list? When you find the answer, enter Diego Margarita, Maria Prentice, Felipe Valdez, and Rosa Batres.

- Scrap of paper that reads: Provided a Cultural Competency 3-day workshop on 7/9/2020 at St. Martin's Catholic School, received check #3821 for $4,500. Can we enter this receipt of cash into QuickBooks?

- Letter from the House Foundation: They will be providing a $5,000 grant (not yet received) to the organization to complete construction of the dormitories. Set up the new customer, located at 552 Sheridan Avenue, Macon, GA 31205.

- Handwritten invoice dated 7/10/2020: Cultural competency workshop to be held at Lakeside Christian School on 7/27/2020 for $1,500. Due Net 15. (They agreed to pay 50% up front.)

- Scribbled note from Arlaine: Can you produce a report that shows all donors and customers for Niños del Lago?

- Photocopy: Check #1826 from Lakeside Christian School for $750 (50% deposit for upcoming training), with a note of "deposited into checking account on 7/15/2020."

- Handwritten note: I don't have customers, but I do have donors and grants.... How do I set them up if QuickBooks just has customers?

4 | Working with Vendors

Tracking expenses properly is very important for your financial statements as well as for keeping your vendors happy! A vendor is essentially anyone to whom you pay money, excluding employees. A vendor could be the electric company, the organization to which you pay taxes, a merchandise supplier, or subcontractors you pay to do work for you or your customers. QuickBooks allows you to produce 1099 tax forms for subcontractors at the end of the year. In this chapter, you will examine the QuickBooks lists, activities, and reports that allow you to effectively deal with vendors.

LEARNING OBJECTIVES

▸ Identify features of the Vendor Center and Vendor List

▸ Enter and pay bills

▸ Write and print checks

▸ Correct errors in vendor transactions

▸ Produce vendor and profit & loss reports

Project: Parrot's Paradise Resort

Now that you've set up Jimmy's customers and entered the transactions related to them, it's time to set up the Vendor List so you can enter transactions to track expenses. These transactions include entering and paying bills and writing checks. You will also produce reports that will provide relevant vendor information for Jimmy as well as a profit & loss report.

The Vendor Center

You can access the Vendor List and activities (entering and paying bills) from the Vendor Center. When you select a vendor from the Vendor Center, it provides an all-in-one look at that vendor's information, bills, and payments.

The Vendor List

An integrated part of the Vendor Center, the Vendor List contains list entries that are used in various forms and reports. Each vendor's record in the list is organized into five tabs: Address Info, Payment Settings, Tax Settings, Account Settings, and Additional Info, where you can create custom fields to store additional data. This list can even be exported to contact management software such as Microsoft® Outlook.

The Vendor List is integrated into the Vendor Center.

Create transactions for the selected vendor here.

This is the information about the selected vendor.

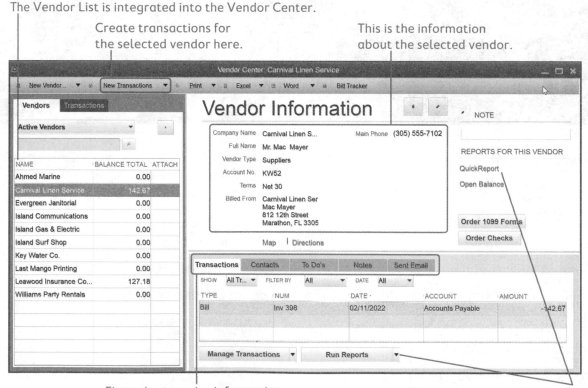

Five tabs organize information related to the selected vendor.

Various reports can be issued right from the Vendor Center.

Creating and Editing Vendors

New vendors are created from the Vendor Center or "on the fly" when you're entering them on a bill or check. Keep in mind that the more information you enter for each vendor, the better your customized reports will be because you can sort, group, and filter your reports using information pulled from the vendor records.

Once created, a vendor can always be edited through the Vendor Center. The only item that can't be edited after you've created and saved a new vendor is the opening balance (it must be adjusted through the accounts payable register). When you change the information for a vendor, including the vendor's name, it will be reflected in both future and past transactions.

Deleting or Making a Vendor Inactive

You can delete a vendor from the Vendor List *as long as you haven't used it in a transaction*. If you have used it in a transaction, you can make it inactive, but you can't delete it until after you close the books for a period. After making it inactive, you can reactivate it if you find you need it again.

Setting Up Default Expense Accounts for a Vendor

In QuickBooks, when you add a new vendor, you have the option to associate up to three expense accounts with that vendor. These accounts will automatically fill in when you enter a bill for this vendor. By setting up expense account information to be prefilled, tracking expenses is easier and faster. Once set up, when that vendor is entered in the Enter Bills, Write Checks, or Enter Credit Card Charges windows, QuickBooks will automatically fill in the expense account names for you. You can always choose to override the default accounts that are filled in by changing them in the individual transaction window. If there are fewer than three expense accounts for a vendor, just leave the additional account prefill fields blank.

Vendors vs. Employees

It's important to understand the difference between vendors and employees. Even though you pay money to employees (which is the basic definition of a vendor), you set up employees in the Employee List, as the information you must track and the records you must keep when dealing with payroll are of utmost importance. On the other hand, you set up subcontractors or independent contractors as vendors, not employees. The laws that govern these non-employee relationships can be complex and change with new legislation, so make sure you know the laws for your jurisdiction.

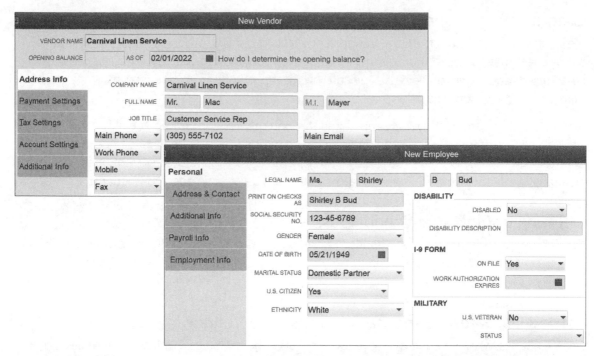

Look at the different fields and types of data collected and tracked for vendors and employees. Make sure you understand the difference between the two and enter them correctly in QuickBooks for everything to be correct behind the scenes and for your payroll to operate within the legal guidelines.

Merge Duplicate List Entries

Occasionally, you may find that you have two records created for the same list entry. QuickBooks allows you to merge these duplicate entries. You perform the merge by editing one of the entries and changing its name to match the other exactly. The two entries will permanently become one, and all prior transactions with the merged list entry will reflect the change in name. You must be logged in as an Admin user to merge list entries.

MERGING RULES FOR CUSTOMERS AND VENDORS

Customers	Vendors	Applies to Both Lists
• You can merge only two customers at one time. • If there are jobs under both customers, you must either delete the jobs from one name or move the jobs from one name to the other name first.	• You can merge up to four vendors at a time. • You cannot merge vendors with online transactions or direct deposits.	• You cannot merge a customer and a vendor because they are on different lists. • You can merge list entries only when you are logged in as a QuickBooks "Admin" user.

Warning! Merging list entries cannot be undone!

Designating Sales Reps in QuickBooks

For many businesses, being able to track sales by a representative (or "rep") is important, and QuickBooks provides a way to track this information by including Sales Rep List as one of the Customer & Vendor Profile Lists. Sales reps may be employees, partners in the business, or independent contractors to whom you issue 1099s. You will manage this list the same as you do other lists in QuickBooks, and you can choose to display this field on forms and reports. There are even pre-set reports that allow you to determine sales by rep.

 Vendors→Vendor Center : New Vendor→New Vendor

DEVELOP YOUR SKILLS 4-1

In this exercise, you will manage the Vendor List for Parrot's Paradise Resort by adding, editing, merging, and deleting vendors. The password for all files unless otherwise stated is Password1. *Leave the company file open unless otherwise instructed.*

1. Start QuickBooks 2020 and choose **File→Open or Restore Company**.

2. Open **DYS_Chapter04 (Company)** *or* restore **DYS_Chapter04 (Portable)** and save it as:
   DYS_Chapter04 Parrot's Paradise Resort

   Last Mango Printing was Quick Added "on the fly," so you will edit it now to include the important information.

3. Click the **Vendors** VENDORS button in the Vendors area of the Home Page.

4. From the list of vendors, double-click **Last Mango Printing** to open it for editing.

Tip! When you double-click a record on the Vendor List, QuickBooks opens it for editing. You could also single-click the vendor and then click the Edit button.

5. Edit the vendor:

Company Name	**Last Mango Printing**
Full Name	**Ms. Tina Shakoor**
Job Title	**Sales Manager**
Main Phone	**(305) 555-1974**
Address Details Billed From	**2019 Vacado Blvd.** Enter **Key West, FL 33040** Click **Copy>>** to copy the Billed From address to the Shipped From field and click **OK**.
Vendor Type (on the Additional Info tab)	**Suppliers**

6. Click **OK** to complete the change to the vendor record.

Add a New Vendor

Next you will add a new vendor to the list.

7. Click the **New Vendor** button on the toolbar of the Vendor Center and choose **New Vendor**.

8. Complete the vendor record:

Vendor Name	**Carnival Linen Service**
Company Name	**Carnival Linen Service**
Full Name	**Mr. Mac Mayer**
Job Title	**Customer Service Rep**
Main Phone	**(305) 555-7102**
Address Details Billed From	**812 12th Street** [Enter] **Marathon, FL 33050** Copy the address to Shipped From.

9. From the New Vendor window, click the **Payment Settings** tab and enter the payment information:
   - Account No: **KW52**
   - Payment Terms: **Net 30**

10. Click the **Additional Info** tab and choose **Suppliers** from the Vendor Type list.

11. Click **OK** to create the new vendor record.

Delete a Vendor

Jimmy's never done a job with John's SCUBA Shop, and the company has just gone out of business. You will now delete this company from the Vendor List.

12. Click the **John's SCUBA Shop** record in the Vendor List to select it.

13. Choose **Edit→Delete Vendor** from the QuickBooks menu bar.

   You're asked to confirm the deletion. QuickBooks wants to ensure you don't delete anything by accident; it will always ask you to confirm deletions.

14. Click **OK** to confirm the deletion.

Merge Two Vendors

You just realized that the phone company, Island Communications, was entered twice on the Vendor List. You will now merge Island Comm with Island Communications.

15. Double-click **Island Comm** (the vendor name you don't wish to keep).

16. Type **Island Communications** as the Vendor Name.

   The name must be typed exactly as it appears in the vendor record it will be merged with.

17. Click **OK**.

QuickBooks prompts you to confirm the merging of list entries. Remember, clicking Yes is a permanent action!

18. Click **Yes** to permanently merge the two entries and then close the Vendor Center window.

Entering Bills

After you have set up your initial Vendor List, you can begin to enter purchase transactions. In this section, you will learn to enter bills and use accounts payable, which is the account credited when bills are entered. When you enter a bill, you *must* specify a vendor because accounts payable, and the vendor's subregister, will be credited by the transaction.

When entering bills, you need to decide if the expenditure is for an expense or for items you will add to your inventory (if you're tracking inventory) and enter it on the correct tab at the bottom.

The Main tab of the ribbon links to tasks such as Memorize or Pay Bills.

The right pane shows a snapshot of the selected vendor or specific transaction, depending on the tab displayed.

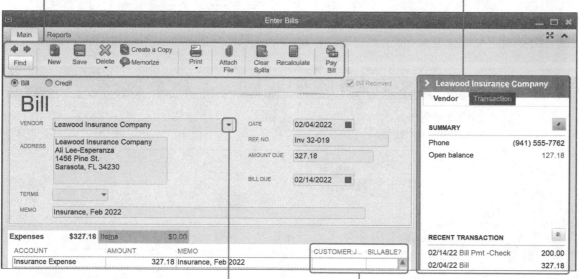

Use the Vendor menu button to select an existing vendor and fill in stored information.

To pass on an expense to a customer, select the Customer:Job and check the Billable? column.

The Reports tab (Enter Bills window) provides links to vendor-related reports that can provide information you need before entering the bill, such as whether it's already been entered or which item to select if you're entering a purchase on the Items tab.

The Importance of Entering Reference Numbers and Memos

When entering a bill, it's critical to enter reference information or the bill number in the Ref. No. field and notes in the Memo fields. The first memo field is for information that will print on a check created when you pay this bill. The second memo field is for internal use and can include any information that you want to track. The memo information displays in reports, is searchable, and can aid you if you are looking for a transaction.

Passing on Expenses to Customers

When you enter a bill, you may be purchasing equipment or supplies or incurring a consultant's fee that you want to pass on to the customer. QuickBooks allows you to easily indicate which expenses are to be billed to a customer by providing a "Billable?" column in the Enter Bills window. When you make an item billable to a specific customer, the next time you invoice that customer you will be asked if you'd like to add the outstanding billable time and costs to the invoice.

FLASHBACK TO GAAP: COST

Remember that when a company purchases assets, it should record them at cost, not fair market value. For example, if you bought an item worth $750 for $100, the item should be recorded at $100.

BEHIND THE SCENES: *Enter Bills*

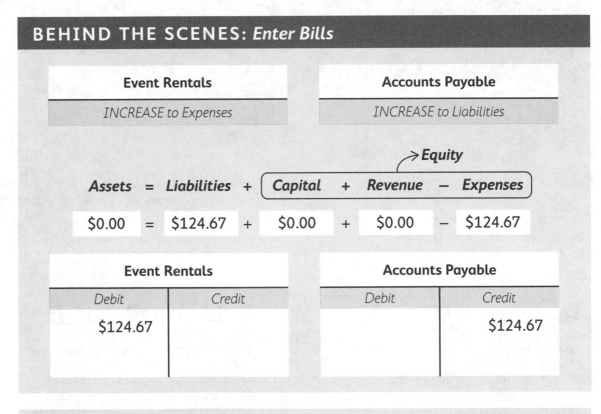

Event Rentals	
INCREASE to Expenses	

Accounts Payable	
INCREASE to Liabilities	

→ Equity

$$Assets = Liabilities + (Capital + Revenue - Expenses)$$

$$\$0.00 = \$124.67 + \$0.00 + \$0.00 - \$124.67$$

Event Rentals		Accounts Payable	
Debit	Credit	Debit	Credit
$124.67			$124.67

Vendors→Enter Bills

DEVELOP YOUR SKILLS 4-2

In this exercise, you will enter bills, track expenses, and enter a vendor "on the fly." You just received a bill for linen service that you will enter into QuickBooks.

1. Click the **Enter Bills** task icon in the Vendors area of the Home Page.

2. Follow these steps to complete the bill:

(A) Click the **Vendor** drop-down arrow ▼ and choose **Carnival Linen Service**.

(B) Tap [Tab] and type: **021122**

(C) Tap [Tab] and type: **Inv 398**

(D) Tap [Tab] and type: **124.67**

(E) Tap [Tab] three times and type: **Linens for 2/3/2022 event**

Look at the form and notice that the vendor's address and terms fill in for you from the underlying list and that the due date is calculated.

(F) Click the **Account** drop-down arrow ▼ and choose **Event Rentals**.

(G) Tap [Tab] two times and type: **Linens for 2/3/2022 event**

Set Default Accounts for a Vendor

You know that the majority of, if not all, bills for Carnival Linen Service will use the same expense account, so you will now edit the vendor and set the account prefills right from the Enter Bills window.

3. Click the **Edit** [✎] button in the history pane of the Enter Bills window to display the Edit Vendor window.

4. Click the **Account Settings** tab and choose **Event Rentals** from the first drop-down list.

Since you're already in the process of entering the bill, you will need to enter Event Rentals this time, but it will fill in whenever you choose to enter a bill for this vendor in the future.

5. Click **OK** to save the changes to the vendor record and return to the bill.

6. Change the Terms field on the bill to **Net 15**.

Whenever you make a change to a vendor's information on a form such as the Enter Bills window, QuickBooks asks whether you want to make that change permanent when you save. Otherwise, the new information will appear only on the current form.

BEHIND THE SCENES BRIEF

Event Rentals DR 124.67; **Accounts Payable CR 124.67**

Event Rentals has **increased**; Accounts Payable has **increased**

Check Figure: Accounts Payable $2,228.96

7. Click **Save & New** to enter the bill and then click **Yes** to change the default terms for the vendor. Leave the Enter Bills window open.

Enter a Bill for a Vendor Not on the Vendor List

When you enter a vendor name that is not on the Vendor List, QuickBooks allows you to add it to the Vendor List "on the fly."

8. In the Vendor field at the top of a new bill, type **Leawood Insurance Company** and tap ⌈Tab⌋.

    A Vendor Not Found window will appear.

9. Click **Set Up**.

    You could have chosen to Quick Add the vendor, in which case you could proceed with the bill; however, you would have to return to the Vendor List at a later time and edit the entry to enter all the vendor information in your company file.

10. Create the new vendor:

Company Name	**Leawood Insurance Company**
Full Name	**Ms. Ali Lee-Esperanza**
Job Title	**Owner/Agent**
Main Phone	**(941) 555-7762**
Address Details Billed From	**1456 Pine St.** ⌈Enter⌋**Sarasota, FL 34230** Copy the address to the Shipped From field.

11. Click **OK** to accept the information for the new vendor.

12. Create the bill:

Date	**020422**
Ref. No	**Inv 32-019**
Amount Due	**327.18**
Memo	**Insurance, Feb 2022**
Account	Type **in** and tap ⌈Tab⌋ to choose **Insurance Expense**.

A good practice is to fill in both memo fields; if it's faster for you, you can copy the memo from the first memo field and paste it into the memo field on the expense line.

BEHIND THE SCENES BRIEF

Insurance Expense DR 327.18; **Accounts Payable CR 327.18**

Insurance Expense has **increased**; Accounts Payable has **increased**

Check Figure: Accounts Payable $2,556.14

13. Click **Save & Close** to record the bill.

Paying Bills

When you have entered your bills, you will need to pay them in a timely manner. In QuickBooks, you use the Pay Bills window to debit accounts payable. The other half of the equation (the account that will be credited) depends on the account from which you withdraw funds (or charge, in the case of bill payment by credit card).

Warning! When you've used the Enter Bills window, be sure to use the Pay Bills window to issue the payment—*not* the Write Checks window! Using the Write Checks window will not pay off the bill, thus you will expense the purchase twice and not "clear out" the entry in the accounts payable account.

Payment Details

At the bottom of the Pay Bills window, you must make three important choices regarding your payment: Payment Date, Payment Method, and Payment Account.

- **Payment Date**—Make sure you select the date you want the payment to be reflected in your bank and accounts payable account.

- **Payment Method**—You can choose how you will pay the bill. If you choose to pay by check, you must select whether you will print the check later in a batch, or assign it a check number immediately after choosing to pay selected bills. If you choose to pay by credit card, you must have a credit card account set up prior to selecting it from the Payment Method drop-down list.

- **Payment Account**—You can select to pay the bill from any bank account you have set up. When you select an account, QuickBooks will show you the ending balance for the account so you can ensure you have enough money to pay the bill. Make sure to select the proper account, as it will be credited behind the scenes!

If you have many bills listed, you can filter or sort them to easily find the one(s) you wish to pay.

Once a bill has been selected, the amount due will display here.

Select the bills to pay here.

If you need to review the details of a bill, click Go to Bill.

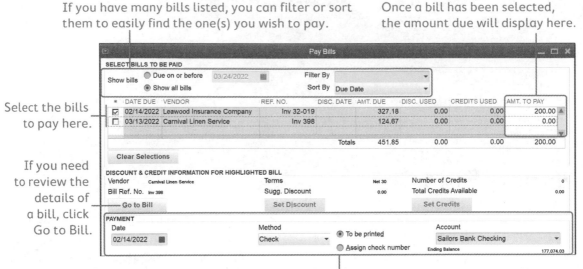

Be sure to confirm the payment details.

The Payment Summary Window

Once you have completed the task of paying your bills, QuickBooks will display a Payment Summary window. There are three options available to you from this window: pay another bill, print checks, or close the window.

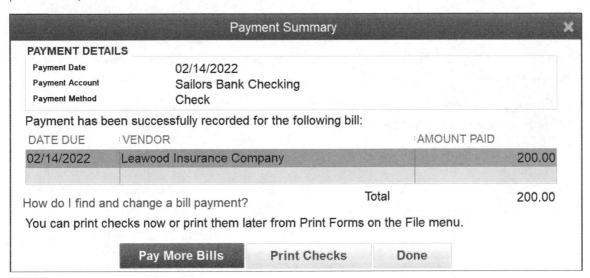

The Payment Summary window appears after bills have been paid, providing links to help you take the next step of paying more bills, printing checks, or finishing the bill paying task.

BEHIND THE SCENES: *Pay Bills*

Accounts Payable
DECREASE to Liabilities

Sailors Bank Checking
DECREASE to Assets

→ **Equity**

$$Assets = Liabilities + \boxed{Capital + Revenue - Expenses}$$

$$-\$1,529.29 = -\$1,529.29 + \$0.00 + \$0.00 - \$0.00$$

Accounts Payable	
Debit	Credit
$1,529.29	

Sailors Bank Checking	
Debit	Credit
	$1,529.29

Vendors→Pay Bills

DEVELOP YOUR SKILLS 4-3

In this exercise, you will pay an overdue bill and then enter a partial payment for another bill. You will complete this task for Jimmy via the Pay Bills window because the bills were originally entered in the Enter Bills window and, therefore, are "sitting" in Accounts Payable.

1. Click the **Pay Bills** task icon in the Vendor area of the Home Page.

2. Click in the checkbox beside the bill due for **Island Gas & Electric**.

Pay Bills

*	DATE DUE	VENDOR	REF. NO.	DISC. DATE	AMT. DUE	DISC. USED	CREDITS USED	AMT. TO PAY
☐	01/22/2022	Williams Party Rentals	Inv. 345, 1/7/22		575.00	0.00	0.00	0.00
☑	01/27/2022	Island Gas & Electric	2022-01-93789		1,529.29	0.00	0.00	1,529.29
☐	02/14/2022	Leawood Insurance Company	Inv 32-019		327.18	0.00	0.00	0.00
☐	02/26/2022	Carnival Linen Service	Inv 398		124.67	0.00	0.00	0.00
				Totals	2,556.14	0.00	0.00	1,529.29

Notice that when you click to select the bill, the amount due fills into the Amt. to Pay column.

3. Enter this in the Payment section at the bottom of window:

   • Date: **020722**

   • Method: **Check**, marked **To Be Printed**.

   • Account: **Sailors Bank Checking**

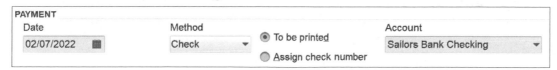

PAYMENT			
Date	Method		Account
02/07/2022 📅	Check ▾	⦿ To be printed ○ Assign check number	Sailors Bank Checking ▾

BEHIND THE SCENES BRIEF

Accounts Payable DR 1,529.29; **Sailors Bank Checking CR 1,529.29**

Accounts Payable has **decreased**; Sailors Bank Checking has **decreased**

Check Figure: Accounts Payable $1,026.85

4. Click the **Pay Selected Bills** button.

5. Click **Pay More Bills** in the Payment Summary window.

Make a Partial Bill Payment

Now you'll help Jimmy pay a partial amount of the bill for Leawood Insurance Company.

6. Click in the checkbox beside the bill due for **Leawood Insurance Company** to select it.

7. Double-click **327.18** in the Amt. To Pay column to select it for the Leawood Insurance Company bill and then type **200** and tap ⌈Tab⌉.

8. Set the payment date to: **2/14/2022**

BEHIND THE SCENES BRIEF

Accounts Payable DR 200.00; **Sailors Bank Checking CR 200.00**

Accounts Payable has **decreased**; Sailors Bank Checking has **decreased**

Check Figure: Accounts Payable $826.85

9. Click the **Pay Selected Bills** button to complete the transaction.

10. Click **Pay More Bills** in the Payment Summary window.

    Look at the current bills to be paid in the Pay Bills window. The bill for Leawood Insurance Company is still on the list, but only for the remaining amount due of $127.18.

11. Close the Pay Bills window.

Writing and Printing Checks

If you're using the cash basis of accounting, you don't have to use the QuickBooks enter bills and pay bills features—even though they're useful for managing cash flow. Instead, you can simply write a check to pay for your expenditures when they're due and expense them properly. Unlike the Enter Bills window, you can choose to create a check from any of the names lists (Vendor, Customer:Job, Employee, and Other) as doing so does not affect Accounts Payable.

Warning! If you use the Enter Bills feature, you must use the Pay Bills feature for the bills you've entered! If you don't, your expenses will be overstated, funds will remain in Accounts Payable, and your reports will not reflect accurate amounts.

The Print Later option sets
the check number as TO PRINT.

Use the menu to fill in names from any of your name
lists: Vendor, Customer:Job, Employee, or Other.

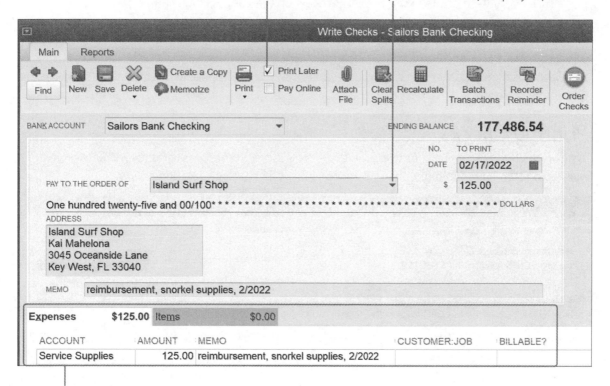

The bottom of the window has the same tabs and functions the same as the Enter Bills window.

As with the Pay Bills window, you must decide from which account to issue the check and whether to print the check or add it to a batch for later printing.

Check to Pay Bills

When you open the Write Checks window and try to pay a vendor for whom there is an outstanding bill, QuickBooks will display a Check for Bills window. The default in this window is the "Go to Pay Bills" button, meaning if you tap [Enter] when you see the window appear, it will assume you want to pay a bill rather than write a check not associated with an outstanding bill.

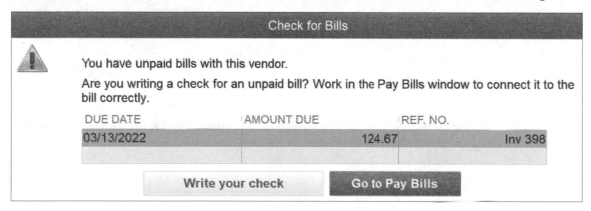

When you try to write a check for a vendor for whom there is an outstanding bill, the Check for Bills window displays to help you make sure you don't get yourself in trouble!

Print Checks Setup

To be sure every item prints in the proper location on the checks, you will need to align the checks to your printer. If you change your printer, remember to realign your checks. It's important to select the check style that matches the checks you've purchased and to print a sample check to ensure proper alignment. Uploading a signature graphic file instead of manually signing each check is a great time-saver, although caution should be applied if others have access to the Write Checks feature.

Printing Checks

When you choose to print your checks in the Pay Bills and Write Checks windows, QuickBooks will "hold" all of them in a queue until you're ready to print a batch of them.

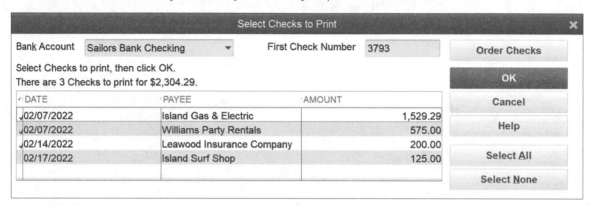

Choose which checks from your batch to print, which account to print from, and enter the first check number.

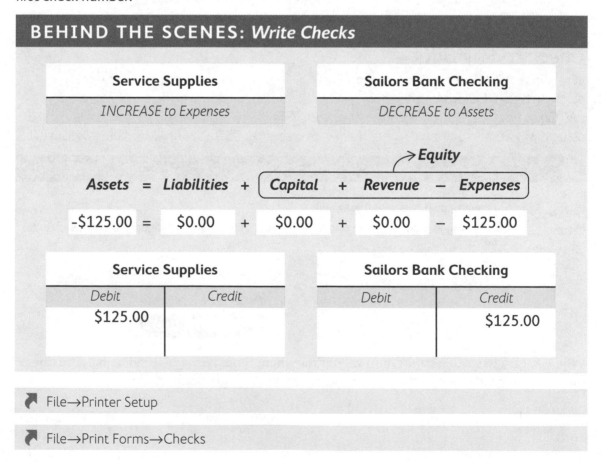

File→Printer Setup

File→Print Forms→Checks

Kai picked up some supplies for Jimmy when he was in Miami, and you need to reimburse him. In this exercise, you will pay for expenses with both printed and handwritten checks.

1. Click the **Write Checks** task icon in the Banking area of the Home Page.

2. Follow these steps to complete the check:

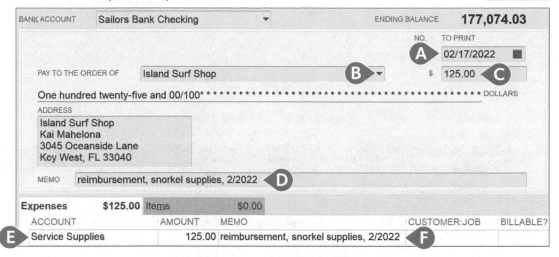

Ⓐ Tap Tab and type: **021722**

Ⓑ Click the drop-down arrow ▼ and choose **Island Surf Shop**.

Ⓒ Tap Tab and type: **125**

Ⓓ Tap Tab twice and type: **reimbursement, snorkel supplies, 2/2022**

Ⓔ Tap Tab and type: **se**

Ⓕ Tap Tab twice and type the memo displayed.

BEHIND THE SCENES BRIEF
Service Supplies DR 125.00; **Sailors Bank Checking CR 125.00**
Service Supplies has **increased**; Sailors Bank Checking has **decreased**
Check Figure: Sailors Bank Checking $177,479.03

3. Click **Save & New** to record this check and leave the Write Checks window open.

Record a Handwritten Check

There may be occasions when you need to handwrite a check. In this exercise, you will record a check that Jimmy wrote for oil for the boat.

4. Click to remove the checkmark from the **Print Later** box, so the check number field can be edited.

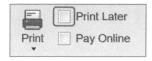

5. Record the handwritten check:

No	**3793**
Date	**022122**
Pay to the Order of	**Ahmed Marine** Then tap Tab and choose **Quick Add**, choose **Vendor**, and click **OK**.
Amount	**37.49**
Memo	**Boat oil, 2/2022**
Account	**Repairs and Maintenance**

BEHIND THE SCENES BRIEF

Repairs and Maintenance DR 37.49; **Sailors Bank Checking CR 37.49**

Repairs and Maintenance has **increased**; Sailors Bank Checking has **decreased**

Check Figure: Sailors Bank Checking $177,441.54

6. Click **Save & Close** to complete the transaction.

Print a Batch of Checks

After you have indicated that checks are to be printed, you need to issue a separate command to print them.

7. Click the **Print Checks** task icon in the Banking area of the Home Page.

> **Print Checks**

> **Note!** If you don't see the Print Checks task icon, use the sizing arrow to make the Home Page larger or choose File→Print Forms→Checks.

8. Enter **3794** as the first check number.

By default, all the checks will be selected.

9. Click the checkmark to the left of **Island Surf Shop** to deselect it and then click **OK**.

10. Click the **Printer Name** drop-down arrow ▾ and choose a PDF driver (or a printer for physical checks), ensuring that **Voucher** is chosen as the check style.

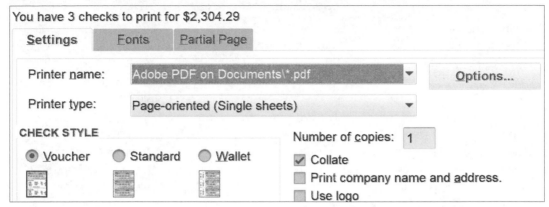

At this point you can verify that the correct printer is selected. By choosing a PDF driver and saving these practice checks as a file, you can avoid wasting paper and ink while still processing the checks and assigning numbers to them. When you are working with your own company, you will make sure the printer you're using is selected.

11. Click **Print** and then click **Save** to save the PDF file in your default file location.

    When complete, QuickBooks will display a Print Checks - Confirmation window. Here you can choose to reprint any checks that did not print correctly or to troubleshoot the order in which your checks printed.

12. Click **OK** in the Print Checks - Confirmation window.

    Notice that there are links to help you if your checks do not print correctly.

Editing Vendor Transactions

QuickBooks tries very hard to make sure you don't make errors that will affect what happens behind the scenes, as shown by the Check for Bills window that we discussed earlier. However, sometimes users still end up making mistakes that need to be corrected!

Fixing Errors

The following table outlines a common vendor-related error as well as an error that occurs in the Write Checks window, the effects of the errors behind the scenes, and how to correct them.

 *Best Practice*

After a transaction has been cleared during the reconciliation process, it should not be changed. Because each situation may require a different solution, you may want to check with an accountant.

COMMON ERRORS AND FIXES

Error	Effect Behind the Scenes	The Fix
A bill is entered but the Pay Bills window is not used when the payment is made.	Expenses are double-stated and Accounts Payable for the vendor is not "cleared out."	Void the check or credit card payment and then enter the transaction properly via the Pay Bills window.
A "regular" check was cut to pay payroll or sales tax liabilities.	The liability accounts are not cleared out; QuickBooks payroll essentially has a second set of books that are affected only when you pay the liabilities through the proper method.	Void the "regular" check and then process the payment through the proper method (Pay Payroll Liabilities or Pay Sales Tax).

FLASHBACK TO GAAP: PRUDENCE

Remember that if you need to choose between two solutions, pick the one that is less likely to overstate assets and income.

 Edit→Void Check

DEVELOP YOUR SKILLS 4-5

In this exercise, you will find and edit a bill. You will start by editing the bill for Carnival Linen Service, as it should have been for $142.67 rather than $124.67.

1. Choose **Edit→Find**.
2. Be sure the **Simple** tab is selected and then enter this information:
   - Transaction Type: **Bill**
   - Vendor: **Carnival Linen Service**
3. Click the **Find** button, single-click the bill for **Inv 398** in the results list, and then click **Go To**.
4. Change the **Amount Due** on the bill to: **142.67**

BEHIND THE SCENES BRIEF

Event Rentals DR 18.00; **Accounts Payable CR 18.00**

Event Rentals has **increased**; Accounts Payable has **increased**

Check Figure: Accounts Payable $844.85

5. Click **Save & Close**; click **Yes** to record the transaction with the changes.
6. Close the Find window.

Void a Check and Pay a Bill with a Check

Unfortunately, Jimmy went straight to the Write Checks window to pay the Williams Party Rentals bill, which means he stated the expense twice and the amount was not cleared from Accounts Payable. You will fix this mistake by voiding the original check and reissuing it using the Pay Bills window.

7. Choose **Banking→Write Checks**.

8. Click the **Previous** button (above Find) until check #3791 paid to Williams Party Rentals dated 1/24/2022 is displayed.

    You can look for a transaction by using the Previous and Next buttons if you believe the transaction to be easy to locate. If not, use Find or Search.

9. Choose **Edit→Void Check**.

10. Set the check number to: **VOID 3791**

11. In the Memo field (after *VOID:*), type: **incorrectly entered, reprocessed through pay bills**

12. Click **Save & Close** to close the Write Checks window and click **No, Just Void the Check** in the QuickBooks window, if necessary.

    You would click Yes if the check was written in the prior period. Because this check was written in the same period, no journal entry is necessary. Since Jimmy has already sent this check to the vendor, you want the date and number of the bill payment check to match what he originally entered.

13. Choose **Vendors→Pay Bills**.

14. Click the checkbox for **Williams Party Rentals** and correctly enter this payment information:

Payment Date	**012422**
Payment Method	**Check**
Check No.	Click in the **Assign Account Number** checkbox
Account	**Sailors Bank Checking**

15. Click **Pay Selected Bills**, enter **3791** in the Assign Check Numbers window, and click **OK**.

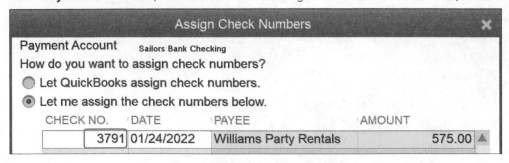

16. Click **Done** in the Payment Summary window.

Before moving on, think about what you've just completed and make sure you understand the why behind it. You have deleted the overstated expenses by voiding the check and have cleared out Accounts Payable for Williams Party Rentals by processing the payment correctly.

Vendor and Profit & Loss Reports

After you have recorded your vendor-related transactions, QuickBooks has many reports you can produce to view your data. To see all transactions grouped by vendor, there are two reports you can run. The Vendor Balance Detail report (in the Vendors & Payables category) shows only those transactions affecting Accounts Payable (transactions entered and paid as "bills"). The Expense by Vendor reports (both summary and detail, found in the Company & Financial category) show transactions made by all payment methods.

A Deep-Dive into the Report Center

You've already learned about the basics of the Report Center. Now we'll travel through the other tabs to see what this center can really do for you.

Memorized Reports

Once you've modified a report so it meets your needs, you can memorize it so you can easily reproduce it in the future. This tab of the Report Center groups all your memorized reports for easy access.

Favorite Reports

Just as you can mark web pages as favorites, QuickBooks allows you to mark the reports you use regularly as favorites. These favored reports are easily accessed via the Favorites tab in the Report Center.

Recent Reports

Sometimes you may not remember the name of a report you just used that worked brilliantly for you. Have no fear because QuickBooks has a solution for that! The Recent tab in the Report Center shows the reports you've accessed recently so you can easily produce them again.

Different day ranges are displayed in this pane to help you choose a report based on when it was last produced.

Grid View, the default Report Center view, is selected.

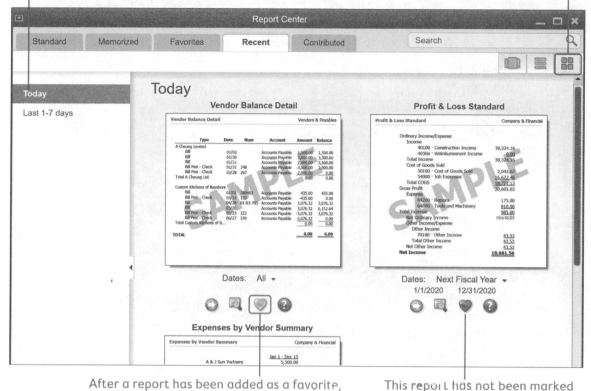

After a report has been added as a favorite, the Fav heart icon is no longer red.

This report has not been marked as a favorite.

Contributed Reports

Contributed reports are specialized reports submitted by users and integrated into the Report Center. You can search for specialized reports by your industry type, and you can even rate a report for other users to show how valuable it is to you. If you are feeling ambitious, you can submit a custom report that you've created for others to use!

The Profit & Loss (P&L) Report

Now that you have recorded both income and expenses, you will be able to run a meaningful profit & loss (P&L) report. It's important to enter all income and expense transactions so income is matched to expenses for the period you are reporting. The P&L report will reflect all transactions that have affected income and expense accounts.

Tip! The profit & loss report is also called an income statement. These terms can be used interchangeably.

FLASHBACK TO GAAP: MATCHING

Remember that expenses need to be matched with revenues from the same accounting period.

Reports→Report Center : Company & Financial→Profit & Loss | Reports→Company & Financial→Profit & Loss

In this exercise, you will produce a vendor summary report, a vendor detail report, and a profit & loss report. You will start by creating a report that shows what you owe all vendors. Then you will use QuickZoom to see the details of where a balance originated.

1. Choose **Reports→Report Center.**
2. Click the **Vendors & Payables** category on the left and scroll down to the Vendor Balance Detail report.

   Notice that the date range All is selected, as it is the default for this report.
3. Click the **Run** button to display the report.

   You believe this is a report that will be useful to Jimmy, so you'll mark it as a favorite for him.
4. Close the report and, in the Report Center, click the **Fav** button for the Vendor Balance Detail report.

   The heart turns white after you click it, indicating that it has been added as a favorite.
5. Click the **Favorites** tab.

   The Vendor Balance Detail report is displayed. Leave the Report Center open.

Display a Vendor Summary Report

Now you will create a report that shows a summary of all expenses by vendor for the company.

6. Click to display the **Standard** tab.

   By default, the Company & Financial category will be displayed.
7. Scroll down and click the **Run** button for the Expenses by Vendor Summary report.
8. Type **a** to set the date range to All and then resize the report window to see all the data, if necessary.

   If you don't set a date range before creating the report in the Report Center, you can do it once the report is displayed. This report lists the total amount ever paid or accrued for each active vendor.
9. Close the report, clicking **No** when asked to memorize it.

Create a Profit & Loss Report and Open a Recent Report

Jimmy wants to see whether the company had a net income or loss for February 2022, based on the transactions you have entered.

10. With the Company & Financial category still displayed, scroll up to the Profit & Loss Standard report and click its **Run** button.
11. Tap Tab, type **020122** and tap Tab again, and then type: **022822**

12. Click **Refresh** on the Report toolbar and then resize the report window to see all data, if necessary.

Parrot's Paradise Resort - Chapter 4
Profit & Loss
February 2022

	Feb 22
▾ **Ordinary Income/Expense**	
▾ **Income**	
Banquets and Events Inco...	3,678.71
Camp Income	3,120.00
Excursion Income	1,680.00
Lodging Sales	9,489.00
Total Income	17,967.71
Gross Profit	17,967.71
▾ **Expense**	
Event Rentals	142.67
Insurance Expense	327.18
Repairs and Maintenance	37.49
Service Supplies	125.00
Total Expense	632.34
Net Ordinary Income	17,335.37
Net Income	**17,335.37**

The report shows the total income and expenses for the time period along with the resulting net income (or loss). The date range was set to Custom on the toolbar when you entered the dates. QuickBooks lets you set exact date ranges in your reports.

13. Close the Profit & Loss report, choosing not to memorize it.

After reviewing the Profit & Loss report, you decide to take a look at the Expenses by Vendor Summary report again.

14. Click the **Recent** tab.

Notice that the reports you just ran are displayed, ready for you to quickly reproduce them.

15. Choose to **Run** ◉ the Expenses by Vendor Summary report and then tap ⓐ to set the date range to All.

16. Choose **Window→Close All**, choosing not to memorize the report.

QuickBooks Graphs

In addition to the preset reports, QuickBooks provides six graphs:

- Income and Expense
- Net Worth
- Accounts Receivable
- Sales
- Accounts Payable
- Budget vs. Actual

Graphs are accessible through the Reports option on the menu bar or via the Report Center. If you can't find a graph that suits your needs, you always have the option of exporting a report to Microsoft Excel and using the more advanced charting features offered there to analyze your data.

The Graph Toolbar

The Graph toolbar displays different buttons depending on the graph created. Once you have created your graph, you can use the Graph toolbar to complete a variety of tasks, such as customizing your graph by date, choosing how to view your data, or printing your graph. Some graphs also have buttons below the pie chart that allow you to choose how to view the data at the bottom of the window (e.g., by Income or by Expense).

QuickZooming with Graphs

The QuickZoom feature is also available with graphs. You simply double-click on a portion of a graph (when you see the QuickZoom pointer) to zoom in and see where the data comes from.

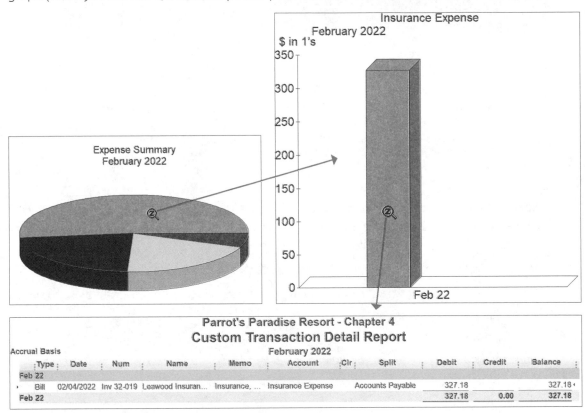

When you QuickZoom on a pie chart, you see a bar graph. When you QuickZoom on a bar graph, you see the report from where the data originated.

DEVELOP YOUR SKILLS 4-7

In this exercise, you will display an Income and Expense Graph for the month of February 2022.

1. Choose **Reports→Company & Financial→Income & Expense Graph**.

   Remember that you can access all reports from either the menu bar or the Report Center.

2. Click the **Dates** button on the toolbar, tap Tab, type **020122** and tap Tab, and then type **022822** and click **OK** to set the date range.

   You will see a bar chart at the top of the window showing both income and expenses. At the bottom you will see a pie chart of the expenses.

   Next you will change the pie chart to display the income.

3. Click the **Income** button at the bottom of the window.

    The pie chart shows the distribution of income between accounts. Now you will use QuickZoom to drill down to see where a piece of the expenses pie originated.

4. Click the **Expense** button at the bottom of the window and then double-click the green **Insurance Expense** piece of the pie chart.

5. Double-click on the resulting green column of the Insurance Expense chart.

    A Custom Transaction Detail report displays, showing where the amount for the Insurance Expense originated. Note that it shows the debits and credits affecting the account as well as the current balance. Expenses have a debit normal balance, so a debit increases the account balance.

6. Choose **Window→Close All**.

Tackle the Tasks

Now is your chance to work a little more with Parrot's Paradise Resort and apply the skills you've just learned to accomplish additional tasks. Continue with the same company file you've been using in this chapter so far. If you need to reopen the company file, the password is *Password1*.

Add Vendors	Professional Software Distributors; 6439 Washington Square, Wausau, WI 54401; Contact: Abby Gibbs, Manager, (715) 555-9922; Acct #: PR203X; Vendor Type: Supplies; Net 15; Account Settings: Computer and Internet Expenses:Software
	Handyman by the Bay; 16 Spruce Street, Key West, FL 33040; Contact: Bryan Duffy, Manager, (305) 555-1212; Acct #: 20944; Vendor Type: Service Providers; Due Upon Receipt; Account Settings: Repairs and Maintenance
	Star Office Supplies; 40 Noor Ave., S. San Francisco, CA 94080; Contact: Jim Nadiera, Manager, (650) 555-9999; Acct#: 87340; Vendor Type: Supplies; Due Upon Receipt; Account Settings: Office Supplies
Enter Bills	Professional Software Distributors; Dated: 02/20/2022; Amt. $563.27; Ref. No.: Inv 17-222; Memo: Hospitality software; Acct: Computer and Internet Expenses:Software
	Handyman by the Bay; Dated: 2/22/2022; Amt. $245; Ref. No.: Inv 16-001; Memo: Monthly maintenance fee; Acct: Repairs and Maintenance
	Star Office Supplies; Dated: 2/25/2022; Amt. $82.37; Ref. No. Inv. 1223-73642; Memo: March Event Supplies; Acct: Office Supplies
Pay Bills	On 2/28/2022, pay all bills due on or before 2/28/2022; Acct.: Sailors Bank Checking; checks to be printed

Write and Print Checks	Write a check on 2/25/2022 to Last Mango Printing for $36.21 for business cards; Advertising & Promotion; check #3796 Print all checks waiting in the queue; first check #3797
Generate Reports	Create reports that answer these questions: • Which bills are due as of 03/20/2022? • What is the company's current balance with each vendor? • What is the contact information and current balance for each vendor? • Did the business have a profit or a loss during January and February 2022?

Self-Assessment

Check your knowledge of this chapter's key concepts and skills using the Self-Assessment in your ebook or eLab course.

1. Vendors must be entered into the Vendor List before you can enter a bill for them. *True   False*

2. You can delete a vendor from the Vendor List if it has been used fewer than ten times in transactions. *True   False*

3. When you use the Enter Bills window in QuickBooks, you MUST specify a vendor. *True   False*

4. You can choose a payment method from the Pay Bills window. *True   False*

5. You must use the Enter Bills and Pay Bills features to account for expenses when using the cash basis of accounting. *True   False*

6. If using the cash basis of accounting, you MUST use the Write Checks (not Enter Bills) window when paying bills. *True   False*

7. QuickZoom allows you to view a report displaying the data a graph is based on. *True   False*

8. If you accidently merge two list entries, you can choose to undo the action. *True   False*

9. You must enter only your income transactions to create an accurate Profit & Loss report. *True   False*

10. When you pay a bill, which account is debited?
    A. Accounts Payable
    B. Checking
    C. Accounts Receivable
    D. Telephone Expense

11. Which is NOT one of the five tabs shown when editing a vendor's record?
    A. Payment Settings
    B. Report Settings
    C. Tax Settings
    D. Account Settings

12. What will prevent you from deleting a vendor record from the Vendor List?
    A. You have previously edited the vendor's information.
    B. You entered an account number for the vendor.
    C. You used the vendor in a transaction.
    D. All of these options

13. In QuickBooks, subcontractors are considered:
    A. Vendors
    B. Employees
    C. Customers
    D. Contacts

📌 Reinforce Your Skills

Donnell Construction has accumulated bills that you will help Colleen to manage by entering vendors, entering and paying bills, and writing checks. The password for all files unless otherwise stated is Password1.

REINFORCE YOUR SKILLS 4-1

Manage the Vendor List

In this exercise, you will work with the Vendor List. You will edit an existing vendor, create a new vendor, and delete a vendor. To begin, IT&T has changed its name to Midwest Telephone. You will make that change in QuickBooks.

1. Choose **File→Open or Restore Company**.
2. Open **RYS_Chapter04 (Company)** *or restore* **RYS_Chapter04 (Portable)** and save it as: **RYS_Chapter04 Donnell Construction**
3. Choose **Vendors→Vendor Center** and double-click **IT&T** to open it for editing.
4. Change the vendor's name to: **Midwest Telephone**

    You will have to change the name in five separate places, including the Vendor Name, Company Name, both addresses on the Address Info tab, and on the Payment Settings tab in the Print Name on Check As field. This new name will be reflected in all transactions that deal with this vendor—past and present.

5. Click **OK** to accept the change.

Add a New Vendor

Colleen has begun to purchase job supplies from a new vendor in Chicago. You will set up the company as a vendor.

6. Click the **New Vendor** button and choose **New Vendor**.
7. Create a new vendor:

Company Name	**Michigan Building Supply**
Contact Name	**Ms. Aimee Nguyen**
Job Title	**Owner**
Phone	**(773) 555-9438**
Email	**anguyen@email.com**
Address	**256 Main Street** Enter **Chicago, IL 60616**
Account #	**84-976**
Terms	**Net 15**

8. Click **OK** to accept the new vendor record.

Delete a Vendor

9. Click **The Pipe Gal** to select it.

10. Choose **Edit→Delete Vendor**.

11. Click **OK** to confirm the deletion and then close the Vendor Center window.

Enter and Pay Bills

In this exercise, you will enter a bill Colleen just received. You will also pay a bill.

1. Choose **Vendors→Enter Bills** and complete the bill:

Vendor	**Midwest Telephone Company**
Date	**020322**
Ref. No.	**8725553759-02**
Amount	**$274.39**
Memo	**Phone bill, 2/2022**
Account	**Telephone Expense**

2. Click **Save & Close** to enter the transaction and close the window.

Pay a Bill

3. Choose **Vendors→Pay Bills** and select the bill for **Rhimes Hardware Co.**

4. Set the date to **020322** and set the check to be printed from the **Checking** account.

5. Click **Pay Selected Bills** to record the payment and close the window.

6. Click **Done** in the Payment Summary Window.

Write and Print Checks

In this exercise, you will write a check for an expense and print the checks you have created.

1. Choose **Banking→Write Checks**.

2. Set the check to print later and enter this information:

Date	020622
Pay to the Order of	**Cook County** (Quick Add it as a Vendor)
Amount	**$250**
Memo	**Business License, 2022**
Account	**Business License and Permits**

3. Click **Save & Close** to accept the transaction and close the window.

Print a Batch of Checks

4. Choose **File→Print Forms→Checks**.

   Notice that, by default, QuickBooks selects all checks; you can change this if you need to.

5. Ensure that **Checking** is the bank account, enter **3501** as the first check number, and click **OK** to move to the Print Checks window.

   At this point you can verify that the correct printer and check style are selected. You can choose to print to PDF to send the checks to a file in order to not waste paper and ink on practice checks.

6. Click **Print**; if you are creating a PDF file, click **Save** after choosing where to save the checks.

7. Click **OK** in the Print Checks - Confirmation window.

REINFORCE YOUR SKILLS 4-4

Find and Edit a Transaction

You are checking to make sure bills have been entered correctly and discover that an incorrect amount was entered for the bill from R&C Powers Interior Design. In this exercise, you will use the Find feature to locate the bill and then edit it in the Enter Bills window.

1. Choose **Vendors→Enter Bills** and then choose **Edit→Find Bills**.

   Notice that when a window is open where transactions are entered (Enter Bills, Create Invoices, etc.), the find option from the Edit menu is specific to the transaction type.

2. Choose **R&C Powers Interior Design** as the Vendor and click **Find**.

   You could enter additional information in the Find window to narrow down the results if many will be displayed. Because there is only one bill for the vendor, the details automatically fill in the Enter Bills window.

3. Change the amount of the bill to **425** and then tap Tab.

   When you change the amount due, QuickBooks will automatically enter the new amount on the Expenses tab.

4. Click **Save & Close**, choosing **Yes** to record the change, and then close the Find window.

Run Vendor and Profit & Loss Reports

In this exercise, you will run vendor and P&L reports for Donnell Construction.

1. Choose **Reports→Vendors & Payables→Vendor Balance Summary**.

2. Review the Vendor Balance Summary report and then close it.

3. Choose **Reports→Company & Financial→Expenses by Vendor Detail**.

4. Type **a** to set the date range to All.

5. Choose **Reports →Company & Financial→Profit & Loss Standard** and then set a date range of 01/01/2022 to 02/28/2022.

6. Click the **Reports** menu and look at the options.

    You can't run favorite or recent reports from here; they must be accessed through the Report Center.

7. Choose **Window→Close All**, choosing not to memorize any reports, and then close the company file.

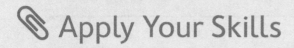 # Apply Your Skills

Wet Noses Veterinary Clinic hasn't had time to maintain its vendor records, so it's up to you to get them caught up. You will manage the vendor list, enter and pay bills, write checks, and edit transactions to bring the company QuickBooks file up to date. The password for all files unless otherwise stated is Password1.

APPLY YOUR SKILLS 4-1 QG

Work with the Vendor List

In this exercise, you will manage the Vendor List and create a report of vendors with contact information for Wet Noses Veterinary Clinic.

1. Open **AYS_Chapter04 (Company)** or restore **AYS_Chapter04 (Portable)** and save it as: **AYS_Chapter04 Wet Noses Clinic**

2. Create three new Vendor List entries.

	Vendor 1	Vendor 2	Vendor 3
Name	Casey's Consulting	Take a Walk	Billy's Van Service
Contact Name	Ms. Casey Scripps	Ms. Shannon High	Mr. Billy Ranch
Job Title	Owner	Walker	President
Main Phone	425-555-9569	206-555-9433	425-555-4477
Address	902 Creekview Dr. Enter Kirkland, WA 98034	13602 75th Ave. NE Enter Seattle, WA 98132	9501 NE 182nd Pl. Enter Bothell, WA 98011
Account Number	JR154	VET87	BB23
Terms	**Due on Receipt**	**Net 15**	**Net 15**
Type	**Consultant**	**Service Providers**	**Service Providers**

3. Edit the **Puget Sound Power Company** vendor record to display Shaunda Jones as the contact.

4. Add these vendor types to the existing vendor records, adding a new entry to the **Vendor Type List** when necessary:
   - Wyland Broadband: **Service Providers**
   - Northshore Water Company: **Utilities**
   - Oberg Property Management: **Service Providers**
   - Puget Sound Power Company: **Utilities**
   - Seattle Vet Supply: **Suppliers**
   - Whoville Office Supplies: **Supplies**
   - Brian's Pet Taxi: **Service Providers**

5. Run the **Vendor Contact List** report to display your list of vendors with contact information.

6. Click the **Excel** Excel ▾ button and export this list to a new workbook saved as:
   `CH4_A1 Vendor Contact List`

APPLY YOUR SKILLS 4-2 QG

Enter and Pay Bills

In this exercise, you will first manage expenses incurred by Wet Noses Veterinary Clinic and then run a report showing all unpaid bills and pay the bills.

1. On 07/02/2023, Dr. James received a bill from Seattle Vet Supply for $3,813.58 that is broken down by account as $1,773.25 for medical supplies, $1,056.92 for vaccines, and $983.41 for medicines. The Ref. No. is Inv 77-9-56 and the memo is: Seattle Vet, Inv 77-9-56, 07/2023

2. Enter a bill for $210.67 received on 07/08/2023 from Northshore Water Company. The Ref. No. is Water Bill, 07/2023 and the memo is: Northshore Water, Water Bill 07/2023

3. On 07/18/2023, a bill for $241.33 was received from Puget Sound Power Company. The Ref. No. is Power Bill, 07/2023 and the memo is: Puget Sound Power, Power Bill 07/2023

4. Enter a bill received on 07/21/2023 from Wyland Broadband for $159.44 that is broken down by account as $55.99 for Internet service and $103.45 for telephone service. The Ref. No. is Int/Phone 07/2023 and the memo is: Wyland, Int/Phone, 07/2023

5. Run the **Unpaid Bills Detail** report for all dates to determine which bills are outstanding and to see the total amount payable.

6. Click the **Excel** button and export this list to a new workbook saved as:
   `CH4_A2 Unpaid Bills`

7. On 07/22/2023, Sadie decided to sit down and pay her bills. Pay all the bills due on or before 07/22/2023. You will print the checks later.

APPLY YOUR SKILLS 4-3 QG

Write Checks, Find and Adjust a Bill, and Print Checks

In this exercise, you will write checks for Dr. James. You will also record an adjusted amount for the bill from Wyland Broadband, using the Find feature to locate the transaction. Finally, you will print checks.

1. Dr. James took her employees to Rose's Cafe on 07/24/2023 for a working lunch. She wrote check 1418 at the restaurant for $84.35 using the **Meals and Entertainment** expense account. Memo: Working lunch for staff 7/2023

2. On 07/25/2023 Sadie received a bill from Animal Lovers for $135.00 for an advertisement. Because she just paid her bills, she decides to write a check for the expense and print it later. Memo: Animal Lovers: Advertisement

3. Locate the **Wyland Broadband** bill dated **07/21/2023** and increase the Computer and Internet Expenses portion of the bill by $40.00, to $95.99 (the revised total due is $199.44).

4. Run the **Expenses by Vendor Detail** report for July 1 through 31, 2023.

5. Click the **Excel** button and export this list to a new workbook saved as:
   CH4_A3 Expenses by Vendor Detail

6. Print to PDF all checks in the queue using 1419 as the first check number.

7. Close the company file.

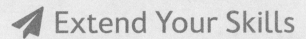

Extend Your Skills

Before You Begin: Open **EYS_Chapter04 (Company)** *or* restore **EYS_Chapter04 (Portable)**. The password is *Password1*.

You've been hired by Arlaine Cervantes to help her with her organization's books. She is the founder of Niños del Lago, a nonprofit organization that provides impoverished Guatemalan children with an engaging educational camp experience. You just sat down at your desk and opened a large envelope from Arlaine that contains a variety of documents; you also have several emails from her. It's your job to sort through the papers and emails and make sense of what you find, entering information into QuickBooks as appropriate and answering any questions in a word-processing document saved as: CH04_EYS_[LastnameFirstinitial]

Remember, you're dealing with random papers dumped out of an envelope and various emails, so part of your challenge is determining the order in which to complete the tasks.

- Sticky note: New source for cultural competency books—enter Woods Publishing Company as a vendor: 921 Pamela Lake Drive, Pittsburg, KS 66762; (620) 555-2211; Terms: Net 30; Contact: Pam Woods.

- Bill: From Network Links (for website hosting), dated 7/3/2020, for $34.57, due 7/13/2020.

- Canceled check: Written to USPS for stamps on 7/2/2020 for $25.10, number 1003.

- Sticky note dated 7/15/2020: There are some checks that can be used with the printer. Would you please print checks for any bills that I didn't write a check for?

- Scribbled note from Arlaine: I need a report that shows all the bills entered into QuickBooks.

- Packing slip and bill: Materials received for a cultural competency seminar; need to enter the bill for $124.32, payable to Chandler Distributors, dated 7/1/2020, terms Net 15. (Arlaine is not tracking inventory in QuickBooks.)

- Carbon copies of checks: Used to pay Network Links (#1004, 7/7/2020, for full amount) and Hernandez Catering (#1005, 7/15/2020, for full amount).

- Bill: From Child Play, Inc., for supplies for the camp, dated 7/5/2020, for $1,212.65, due 7/15/2020.

- Printed email message from the accountant: Please send a report that shows the amount owed to each vendor as of 7/10/2020.

- Bill: From Hernandez Catering for food provided at a fundraising event in California, dated 7/8/2020, payment due on receipt, for $167.21.

5 | Banking Tasks

A ny business must be able to work with bank accounts and the funds contained within to be able to operate effectively. If you use debit and credit cards as well as online payment services such as PayPal for your business, you'll need to know how to work with them as well. In this chapter, you will deal with a variety of financial operations in QuickBooks, from entering transactions to running reports about them. Once you have performed banking tasks in QuickBooks, you will need to reconcile your books with the bank. This can be done physically or online, or you can use a combination of both, and you'll see how QuickBooks connects online with your financial institution.

LEARNING OBJECTIVES

▶ Create a credit card account

▶ Transfer funds and make deposits

▶ Manage debit and credit card transactions

▶ Reconcile accounts

▶ Create banking reports

▶ Use online banking with QuickBooks

Project: Parrot's Paradise Resort

You've been getting comfortable performing the basic vendor and customer transactions in QuickBooks for Parrot's Paradise Resort. Now you will be taking on the responsibility for ensuring money is on hand to pay bills, running timely banking reports, and reconciling both the bank and credit card accounts. In addition, you will investigate how online banking and payment services such as PayPal work with QuickBooks, as Jimmy is deciding if he wants to expand how he manages his finances online.

Moving Funds Between Accounts

Parrot's Paradise Resort has three bank accounts—one to pay bills (Sailors Bank Checking), another at the same bank where extra cash is kept (Sailors Bank Savings), and a third (Money Market) that earns a higher interest rate. These accounts are set up in QuickBooks as bank (asset) accounts. He also uses a company credit card in his business. This is set up as a credit card (liability) account in QuickBooks.

Almost every business will have a need to transfer money between its bank accounts. QuickBooks has a feature that allows you to record this transfer. If you use online banking, you may even be able to set QuickBooks to perform the transfer for you when you go online (if your financial institution allows it).

Because you're transferring funds between two asset accounts, you want to debit the account that is increasing and credit the account that is decreasing. Look at the following T-accounts to visualize this transaction:

FLASHBACK TO GAAP: MONETARY UNIT

Remember that it is assumed a stable currency will be the unit of record.

BEHIND THE SCENES: Transfer Funds

Sailors Bank Savings	Sailors Bank Checking
INCREASE to Assets	DECREASE to Assets

$$Assets = Liabilities + (Capital + Revenue - Expenses)$$
$$\$10,000.00 - \$10,000.00 = \$0.00 + \$0.00 + \$0.00 - \$0.00$$

Sailors Bank Savings		Sailors Bank Checking	
Debit	Credit	Debit	Credit
$10,000.00			$10,000.00

DEVELOP YOUR SKILLS 5-1

In this exercise, you will transfer funds from the checking to the savings account. The password for all files unless otherwise stated is Password1. *Leave the company file open unless otherwise instructed.*

1. Start QuickBooks 2020 and choose **File→Open or Restore Company**.
2. Open **DYS_Chapter05 (Company)** *or* restore **DYS_Chapter05 (Portable)** and save it as: **DYS_Chapter05 Parrot's Paradise Resort**
3. Close all windows except for the Home Page, if necessary.
4. Choose **Banking→Transfer Funds**.
5. Follow these steps to complete the funds transfer:

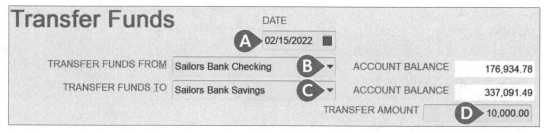

Ⓐ Type: **021522**

Ⓑ Click the **Transfer Funds From** drop-down arrow ▼ and choose **Sailors Bank Checking**.

Ⓒ Click the **Transfer Funds To** drop-down arrow ▼ and choose **Sailors Bank Savings**.

Ⓓ Tap [Tab] and type: **10000**

QuickBooks displays the account balances of the accounts involved in the transfer so you can verify sufficient funds are available. Funds transfer also appears in the Memo field.

BEHIND THE SCENES BRIEF

Sailors Bank Savings DR 10,000.00; **Sailors Bank Checking CR 10,000.00**

Sailors Bank Savings has **increased**; Sailors Bank Checking has **decreased**

Check Figure: Sailors Bank Checking $166,934.78

6. Click **Save & Close** to record the transaction.

The Chart of Accounts Revisited

In paper-based accounting, a business's accounts are listed in a Chart of Accounts. This is no different in QuickBooks, where you will see that the Chart of Accounts is a list of all the asset, liability, equity, income, and expense accounts your company uses. A company can add accounts to the Chart of Accounts according to its needs.

Note! Remember, there's an exchange of funds from one account to another that happens behind the scenes in QuickBooks as you enter transactions. This keeps your books balanced and allows you to run meaningful reports. You use the forms (Create Invoices, Receive Payments, etc.) to perform the transactions, and QuickBooks does the rest!

NAME	TYPE	BALANCE TOTAL
Money Market	Bank	37,382.35
Sailors Bank Checking	Bank	166,934.78
Sailors Bank Savings	Bank	347,091.49
Accounts Receivable	Accounts Receivable	19,739.75
Undeposited Funds	Other Current Asset	10,336.71
Accumulated Depreciation	Fixed Asset	0.00
Buildings and Improvements	Fixed Asset	0.00
Furniture and Equipment	Fixed Asset	0.00
Land	Fixed Asset	0.00
Accounts Payable	Accounts Payable	563.27
Customer Deposits	Other Current Liability	0.00
Payroll Liabilities	Other Current Liability	0.00
Capital Stock	Equity	0.00
Opening Balance Equity	Equity	549,860.32
Retained Earnings	Equity	
Shareholder Distributions	Equity	0.00

The Chart of Accounts displays all accounts for a company and shows balances for balance sheet accounts, though it doesn't show balances for income, COGS, and expense accounts. Sort columns by clicking the headings. The highlighted account is affected when a command is issued.

Searching in the Chart of Accounts

Some companies have a very large number of accounts, and QuickBooks has a search feature at the top of the Chart of Accounts window that can help you

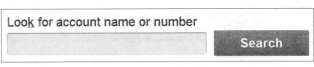

search through them to find the one you need. All you need to do is type all or part of the name of the account or account number in the search field.

Company→Chart of Accounts | Lists→Chart of Accounts

Account Registers

Each balance sheet account (except for Retained Earnings) has its own register, which is a record of all transactions pertaining to that account. A QuickBooks register looks like the check register you may already keep for your personal checking account. The running balance automatically recalculates as you record each new transaction. QuickBooks responds differently when you double-click listings in the Chart of Accounts, depending on the type of account.

DOUBLE-CLICKING ACCOUNTS AND QUICKBOOKS RESPONSES

When you double-click...	QuickBooks responds by...
Any balance sheet account (asset, liability, or equity)	Opening an account register for that account (Exception: The Retained Earnings account is a specially created account without a register. You get a QuickReport when you double-click this account.)
Any income statement account (income or expense)	Creating an account QuickReport

This checking account register image is the result of double-clicking the checking account. Double-clicking on a transaction takes you to the source of the transaction, similar to when you QuickZoom on a report.

The header, consisting of two lines, describes each field.

Edit a transaction or run a QuickReport from the toolbar.

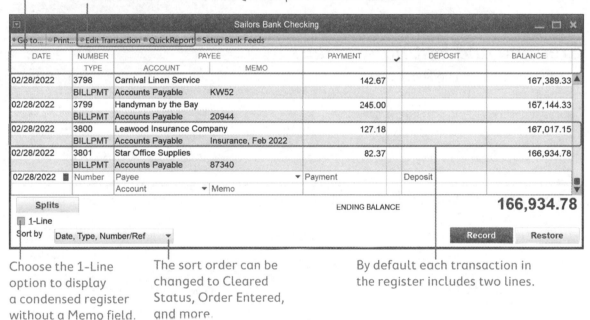

Choose the 1-Line option to display a condensed register without a Memo field.

The sort order can be changed to Cleared Status, Order Entered, and more.

By default each transaction in the register includes two lines.

DEVELOP YOUR SKILLS 5-2

In this exercise, you will view the Chart of Accounts and checking register to see the transaction you performed and how it affected the two accounts. You will also drill down to see a customer's bill.

1. Click the **Chart of Accounts** task icon in the Company area of the Home Page.

    Note the balances for the balance sheet accounts (assets, liabilities, and equity).

Chart of Accounts

2. Double-click **Sailors Bank Checking** to open the associated register.

    Scroll up, if necessary, and note that the 10,000 you transferred is in the Payment column for 2/15/2022.

3. Close the register and double-click **Sailors Bank Savings**.

   Note that the 10,000 is in the Deposit column.

4. Close the Sailors Bank Savings register and then double-click **Lodging Sales** and tap a, scrolling down if necessary.

   An Account QuickReport is displayed instead of a register because you double-clicked on an income statement account.

5. Close the Account QuickReport window and leave the Chart of Accounts open.

Open a Register and Drill Down

6. Double-click the **Sailors Bank Checking** account.

7. Locate and then double-click anywhere within the two lines of the 2/14/2022 Leawood Insurance Company **No. 3795 Bill Payment** transaction.

   It may be easier to find the transaction if you make the window larger. QuickBooks will drill down to the Bill Payments(Check) - Checking window.

8. Close the Bill Payments(Check) and Sailors Bank Checking windows; leave the Chart of Accounts open.

Creating and Editing Accounts

As you know, you can add new accounts to the Chart of Accounts as needed. When you add an account, the QuickBooks account type must be specified. You can't delete an account that has been used, though you can make it inactive.

 Company→Chart of Accounts : Account→New [or other action]

DEVELOP YOUR SKILLS 5-3

In this exercise, you will set up Jimmy's two business credit cards in QuickBooks.

1. Click the **Account** drop-down arrow ▼ and choose **New**.

2. Select **Credit Card**, click **Continue**, and create the new credit card account:

Account Name	**Visa-4545**
Description	**Sailors Bank Visa**
Credit Card Acct. No.	**4555 2222 3030 4545**

   If this card was in use before your QuickBooks start date and had a balance, you would need to put in the Opening Balance from your last statement.

   Notice that the Tax-Line Mapping field filled in for you as a current liability when you chose credit card as the account type.

3. Click **Save & New**.

4. Set up the second credit card account (with Credit Card still the account type):

Account Name	**AmEx-6902**
Description	**American Express Card**
Credit Card Acct. No.	**3000 123456 76902**

5. Click **Save & Close** and click **No** in the Set Up Bank Feed window. Close the Chart of Accounts window.

Deposits

If you use the Undeposited Funds account when you receive funds through the Receive Payments and Enter Sales Receipts windows, you'll need to take one more step to move the payment to your bank account. This is done through the Make Deposits window, which can also be used when you make a sale and don't need a sales receipt or when you want to deposit a lump sum that will credit an income account and debit your bank account.

Tip! Think of the Undeposited Funds account as a "holding tank" that stores all the funds you collect until you're ready to make a deposit to your bank.

If you have payments sitting in your Undeposited Funds account, you can empty it (make a deposit) by clicking the Record Deposits task icon on the Home Page. This opens the Payments to Deposit window, where you can choose which payments to deposit.

The Payments to Deposit window displays the type and method of payment. You can filter by payment method and sort by the payment date, method, number, name, or amount.

Tip! You can always close the Payments to Deposit window if you're not ready to deposit the payments but still need to work with the Make Deposits window.

Print a detailed report, including deposit slips, from this toolbar. Select a transaction to run a journal report.

Change the deposit account, date, or memo here.

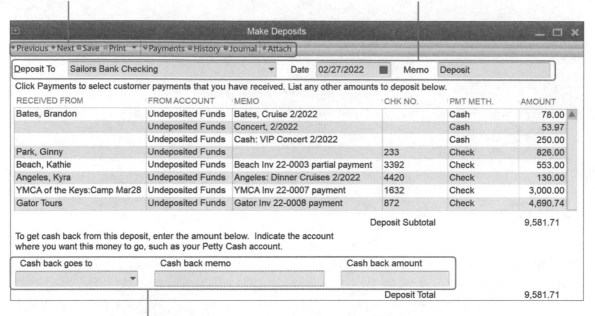

If you wish to keep cash back from a deposit (to refresh your petty cash account, for example), indicate the amount here.

BEHIND THE SCENES: *Deposit*

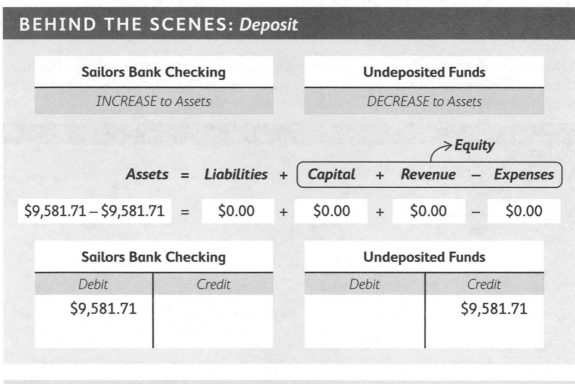

Sailors Bank Checking		Undeposited Funds	
INCREASE to Assets		*DECREASE to Assets*	

$$Assets = Liabilities + (Capital + Revenue - Expenses)$$

$$\$9{,}581.71 - \$9{,}581.71 = \$0.00 + \$0.00 + \$0.00 - \$0.00$$

Sailors Bank Checking		Undeposited Funds	
Debit	*Credit*	*Debit*	*Credit*
$9,581.71			$9,581.71

Banking→Make Deposits

DEVELOP YOUR SKILLS 5-4

In this exercise, you will work with the Make Deposits window to deposit funds from the Undeposited Funds account and to make a deposit without a sales form. The Record Deposits task icon will display a number indicating the number of deposits being held in Undeposited Funds.

Record Deposits

1. Click the **Record Deposits** task icon in the Banking area of the Home Page.
2. Click the **View Payment Method Type** drop-down arrow ▼ and choose **Cash and Check**.

    The payment made by credit card is no longer displayed.

3. Click the **Select All** button and see that QuickBooks places a checkmark to the left of all cash and check payments waiting to be deposited.

> **Note!** The payments you've selected can be printed on a deposit slip, which you can take to the bank. The total amount will be reflected on your monthly bank statement.

4. Click **OK** to accept the payments for deposit and move to the Make Deposits window.
5. Finish the deposit using this information:
    - Deposit To: **Sailors Bank Checking**
    - Date: **022722**
6. Choose the **Print** drop-down arrow ▼, choose **Deposit Slip**, and then click **Preview** to view the deposit slip.

    Only cash and checks can be printed on the deposit slip. You will need to make another deposit for the remaining payments.

7. Click **Close** and then click **Cancel**.
8. Click **Save & New** to make the deposit to your Checking account.

    The Payments to Deposit window will still be open displaying the remaining credit card payment.

9. Click **Select All** and then click **OK**.
10. Finish the deposit with this information:
    - Deposit To: **Sailors Bank Checking**
    - Date: **022722**
11. Click **Save & New** to make the deposit to your Checking account and leave the Make Deposits window open.

BEHIND THE SCENES BRIEF
Sailors Bank Checking DR 9,581.71; **Undeposited Funds CR 9,581.71**
Sailors Bank Checking has **increased**; Undeposited Funds has **decreased**
Check Figure: Sailors Bank Checking $177,271.49

Undeposited Funds has been cleared out and is no longer holding money that has been deposited. This will reflect in any balance sheet reports that are run.

Make a Deposit Without Specifying a Customer

Earlier in the month, Jimmy hosted a concert with a cover charge at the door. Because there were multiple customers whom he does not want to track individually, you will make a deposit to Checking, directly crediting Banquets and Event Income without using a specific item.

12. Complete the deposit:

Deposit To	**Sailors Bank Checking**
Date	**022222**
Memo	**2/19/22 Trop Rock Concert**
From Account	**Banquets and Event Income**
Pmt Meth	**Cash**
Amount	**1430**

There's no item entered for this transaction, but you do need to fill in the account. Remember that an item is used to direct funds to the underlying account. You can't leave the From Account field blank because you must specify the account that will be credited, as you'll be debiting a bank account with the deposit.

BEHIND THE SCENES BRIEF

Sailors Bank Checking DR 1,430.00; **Banquets and Events Income CR 1,430.00**

Sailors Bank Checking has **increased**; Banquets and Events Income has **increased**

Check Figure: Sailors Bank Checking $178,701.49

---

13. Click **Save & Close**.

Your deposit is recorded and the window closes.

Credit and Debit Card Transactions

Credit cards give business owners an easy way to track expenses and manage cash flow. Quick-Books allows you to track credit card transactions just as you do checking and savings account transactions. You can set up as many credit card accounts as you need.

> **Note!** If you occasionally use a personal credit card for business purposes, do *not* enter it in QuickBooks as a business credit card. Create accounts only for business credit cards.

Credit card transactions are classified as either a charge (when you make a purchase) or a credit (when you make a return). As you will use the same form for both types, you need to choose the correct type when entering transactions. A credit card is a liability, so its normal balance is a credit. This means you credit (increase) the account when you make a purchase and debit (decrease) the account when you make a payment.

Just like in the Write Checks window, you can choose any name in this field, not just vendors.

Click here to enter a credit or refund.

Download all charges from your bank to enter or match them.

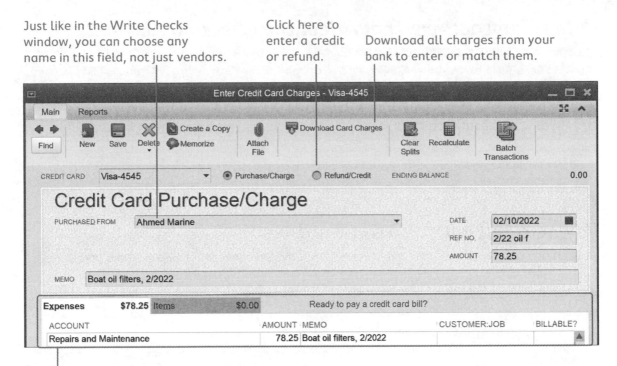

The bottom portion of the window is almost the same as the Enter Bills and Write Checks window.

Debit Card Transactions

When you make a purchase or pay a bill with a debit card, funds are taken directly from your checking account, which is different from what occurs with credit card purchases. Use the Write Checks window to handle debit card transactions. And when you enter a transaction, use a code such as "DB" in the No. field to indicate that it's a debit card transaction.

If you use the Enter/Pay Bills windows in QuickBooks, you can continue to use them when working with debit card purchases instead of the Write Checks window. This means if you enter a bill in QuickBooks and then choose a debit card to pay it, you enter that payment through the Pay Bills window—otherwise, the expenses will be overstated, and the bill will be left in Accounts Payable.

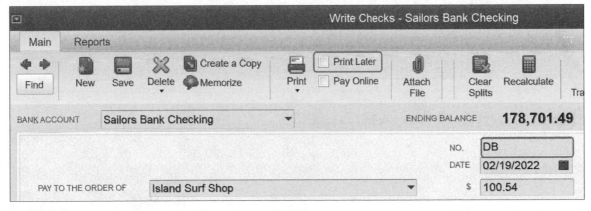

Make sure the Print Later checkbox is unchecked so you can enter your debit card code ("DB" here) in the No. field.

Other Transactions That Affect the Checking Account

In addition to debit card transactions, you'll likely have other transactions that draw funds from a checking account. For instance, ATM cards and online service such as PayPal™ can withdraw funds directly from your bank account. All these transactions will be entered using the Write Checks window; you just need to create common codes for the No. field to record each type ("ATM" for an ATM card transaction, and "PP" for a PayPal payment, for example).

> **Tip!** Use whatever codes you like, just take care to use a different code for each type of transaction and stick with it. Consistency matters!

Paying a Bill with a Credit Card

You can pay a bill with a credit card. If you entered the bill in the Enter Bills window, you'll use the Pay Bills window to pay it by credit card. Otherwise, use the Enter Credit Card Charges window to pay the bill, much as you would use the Write Checks window if you were paying by check and didn't use the Enter Bills window. Remember, if you're using the accrual basis of accounting, you *must* use the Enter Bills/Pay Bills windows.

PAYMENT		
Date	Method	Account
02/26/2022	Credit Card	Visa-4545

Once you've created a credit card account in QuickBooks, you'll be able to choose to pay bills by credit card in the Pay Bills window.

> **Warning!** If you use a credit card to pay a bill that you entered through the Enter Bills window, you *must* use the Pay Bills window when you pay it. If you use the Write Checks or Enter Credit Card Charges windows, expenses and Accounts Payable will be overstated!

BEHIND THE SCENES: *Credit Card Purchase*

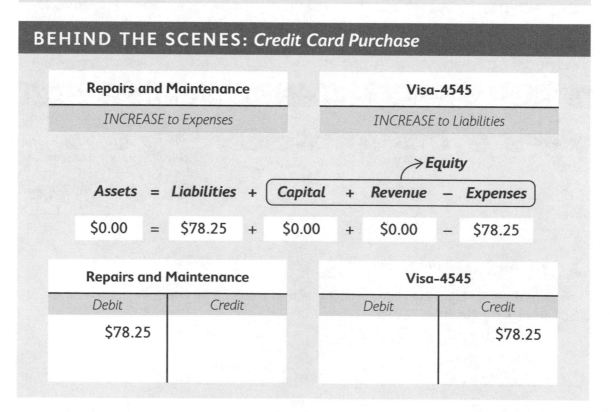

Repairs and Maintenance	Visa-4545
INCREASE to Expenses	*INCREASE to Liabilities*

Equity

Assets	=	Liabilities	+	Capital	+	Revenue	−	Expenses
$0.00	=	$78.25	+	$0.00	+	$0.00	−	$78.25

Repairs and Maintenance		Visa-4545	
Debit	*Credit*	*Debit*	*Credit*
$78.25			$78.25

	Banking→Enter Credit Card Charges
	Banking→Write Checks (for debit card transactions)
	Vendors→Pay Bills

DEVELOP YOUR SKILLS 5-5

Jimmy used a credit card to purchase oil filters for the boat and his debit card to purchase flip-flops for giveaways to promote the resort. In this exercise, you will enter the credit card and debit card purchases. You'll also enter a credit card return and pay a bill using a credit card.

1. Click the **Enter Credit Card Charges** task icon in the Banking area of the Home Page.

   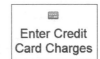

   Because you have two credit cards set up, you must choose the appropriate card before entering other information.

2. Follow these steps to enter the credit card purchase information:

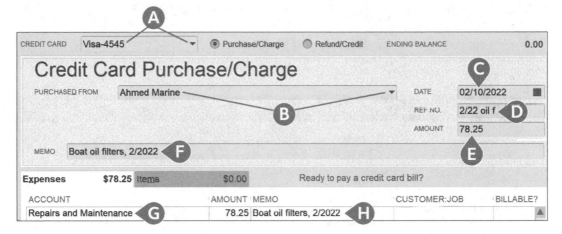

- Ⓐ Click the **Credit Card** drop-down arrow ▾ and choose **Visa-4545**.
- Ⓑ Click the **Purchased From** drop-down arrow ▾ and choose **Ahmed Marine**.
- Ⓒ Tap ⌷Tab⌷ and type: **021022**
- Ⓓ Tap ⌷Tab⌷ and type: **2/22 oil f**
- Ⓔ Tap ⌷Tab⌷ and type: **78.25**
- Ⓕ Tap ⌷Tab⌷ and type: **Boat oil filters, 2/2022**
- Ⓖ Click the drop-down arrow ▾ and choose **Repairs and Maintenance**
- Ⓗ Tap ⌷Tab⌷ twice and type: **Boat oil filters, 2/2022**

BEHIND THE SCENES BRIEF

Repairs and Maintenance DR 78.25; **Visa-4545 CR 78.25**

Repairs and Maintenance has **increased**; Visa-4545 has **increased**

Check Figure: Visa-4545 $78.25

3. Click the **Save & New** button.

Record a Credit Card Return

It ends up the oil filters were not the right fit for both of his boats, so Jimmy will return one of them.

4. Choose **Refund/Credit**.

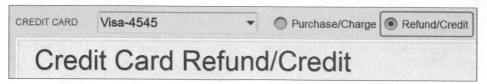

5. Complete the credit card refund:

Purchased From	**Ahmed Marine**
Date	**021722**
Ref No	**oil f ret**
Amount	**39.13**
Memo (use in both)	**oil filter return, 2/2022**
Account	**Repairs and Maintenance**

Notice that the account and amount prefill.

BEHIND THE SCENES BRIEF
Visa-4545 DR 39.13; **Repairs and Maintenance CR 39.13**
Visa-4545 has **decreased**; Repairs and Maintenance has **decreased**
Check Figure: Visa-4545 $39.12

6. Click **Save & Close**.

QuickBooks records the transaction and closes the Enter Credit Card Charges window.

Make a Debit Card Purchase

When you make a debit card purchase, you will record it in the Write Checks window. Jimmy has purchased surfing supplies from Island Surf Shop with his debit card that you will now enter.

7. Click the **Write Checks** task icon in the Banking area of the Home Page.

8. Ensure Sailors Bank Checking is the bank account and then complete the debit card purchase:

No.	**DB**
Date	**021922**
Pay to the Order of	**Island Surf Shop**
Amount	**100.54**
Memo	**surfing supplies, 2/2022**
Account	**Service Supplies**

When you pay a bill with a debit card, you're affecting the Checking account, so you will need to enter the "check number" (or code) for debit card transactions in the No. field. In this scenario, the code is DB.

BEHIND THE SCENES BRIEF

Service Supplies DR 100.54; **Sailors Bank Checking CR 100.54**

Service Supplies has **increased**; Sailors Bank Checking has **decreased**

Check Figure: Sailors Bank Checking $178,600.95

9. Click **Save & Close**.

Pay a Bill with a Credit Card

10. Click the **Pay Bills** task icon in the Vendors area of the Home Page.

Pay Bills

11. Click to select the bill for Professional Software Distributors and then complete the bill payment:

Date	**022622**
Method	**Credit Card**
Account	**Visa-4545**

After selecting Credit Card as the method, you'll be able to choose from all your credit cards in the Account field.

BEHIND THE SCENES BRIEF

Accounts Payable DR 563.27; **Visa-4545 CR 563.27**

Accounts Payable has **decreased**; Visa-4545 has **increased**

Check Figure: Visa-4545 $602.39

12. Click **Pay Selected Bills** and then click **Done**.

Alternative Types of Bank Accounts

For most businesses, the days are gone when they only use cash, checks, and credit/debit cards. Now mobile payment services, such as PayPal and Zelle, provide new ways to accept and disburse funds, which you need to be able to enter in QuickBooks.

Many mobile payment services hold funds in a separate account for you. You can then use the funds to pay for products and services, or they can be deposited in your bank account. You will need to set up these holding accounts as bank accounts in QuickBooks.

Managing PayPal Transactions in QuickBooks

The PayPal account is treated as a bank account in QuickBooks, so you will use the bank account forms with PayPal transactions.

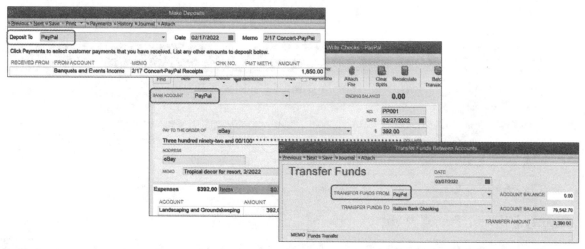

You use the same forms you've used for other bank accounts; just be sure to choose PayPal as the account!

Receiving Funds

To enter a lump amount for sales collected via PayPal, you can use the Make Deposits window. You don't have to specify a customer; this window allows you to choose just the income account that is affected. Conversely, if you wish to track individual customer information for these transactions, you can either use the Enter Sales Receipts window or divvy up the individual transactions by customer in the Make Deposits window.

Making a Purchase

When you use your PayPal balance to make a purchase, you enter the transaction through the Write Checks window or in the account register. Make sure to choose PayPal as the bank account, not your checking account, when you're spending from your PayPal balance! Conversely, if you use PayPal and it draws directly from your checking account, you would *not* record the transaction in the PayPal account—but rather in your checking account.

Transferring Funds to Checking

Just as you used the Transfer Funds window to transfer funds between your checking and savings accounts, you will use the same method to transfer funds between your PayPal and checking accounts. Of course, you must initiate the transfer from PayPal. This section just looks at how to record the transfer in QuickBooks after it has occurred.

> 🏹 Lists→Chart of Accounts : [Select Account]→Account→New

> 🏹 Banking→Make Deposits *or* Write Checks *or* Transfer Funds

DEVELOP YOUR SKILLS 5-6

Jimmy has been accepting payment for the Trop Rock concerts through PayPal. In this exercise, you will help Jimmy set up the account in QuickBooks, record the sales, make a purchase on eBay™, and then transfer the balance to his checking account.

1. Click the **Chart of Accounts** task icon in the Company area of the Home Page.
2. Press ⎡Ctrl⎤+⎡n⎤, select **Bank** as the new account type, and click **Continue**.
3. Create the new mobile payment service bank account:

   • Account Name: **PayPal**

   • Description: **PayPal Holding Account**

4. Click **Save & Close** and then click **No** in the Set Up Bank Feed window.
5. Close the Chart of Accounts window.

Chart of
Accounts

Record PayPal Sales

Jimmy hosted a special concert for which many guests paid online via PayPal. You will record the ticket sales directly in the Make Deposits window because you don't want them to be held in Undeposited Funds (they're instead being held by PayPal).

6. Click the **Record Deposits** task icon in the Banking area of the Home Page.
7. Choose **PayPal** as the Deposit To account and click **OK** in the Setting Default Accounts window, if necessary.

Record
Deposits

8. Complete the deposit:

Date	021722
First Memo	2/17 Concert-PayPal
From Account	Banquets and Events Income
Second Memo	2/17 Concert-PayPal Receipts
Amount	1850

Your screen should match this illustration:

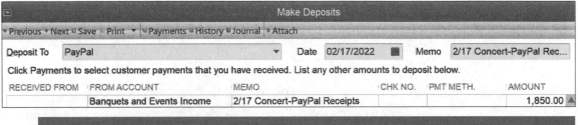

BEHIND THE SCENES BRIEF

PayPal DR 1,850.00; **Banquets and Events Income CR 1,850.00**

PayPal has **increased**; Banquets and Events Income has **increased**

Check Figure: PayPal $1,850.00

9. Click **Save & Close** to record the deposit.

Make a Purchase with PayPal

Jimmy found some outdoor décor on eBay that is perfect for the resort, and he put in a bid for it. He won the auction! You will now use the balance in his PayPal account for the purchase.

10. Click the **Write Checks** task icon in the Banking area of the Home Page.

11. Choose **PayPal** as the bank account (click **OK** in the Setting Default Accounts window, if prompted) and complete the check:

Number	PP001
Date	022722
Pay to the Order Of	**eBay** (**Quick Add** the new **Vendor**)
Amount	392
Memo	Tropical decor for resort, 2/2022
Account	**Landscaping and Groundskeeping**

BEHIND THE SCENES BRIEF
Landscaping and Groundskeeping DR 392.00; **PayPal CR 392.00**
Landscaping and Groundskeeping has **increased**; PayPal has **decreased**
Check Figure: PayPal $1,458.00

12. Click **Save & Close**.

Transfer PayPal Funds to Checking

Jimmy still has funds in his PayPal account that he now wants to transfer to his checking account. Of course, he must initiate the transfer with PayPal; all you need to do in QuickBooks is record it as a transfer between bank accounts.

13. Choose **Banking→Transfer Funds** and complete the transfer:

Date	022822
Transfer Funds From	**PayPal**
Transfer Funds To	**Sailors Bank Checking**
Transfer Amount	1458
Memo	Funds Transfer, PayPal to Checking

BEHIND THE SCENES BRIEF
Sailors Bank Checking DR 1,458.00; **PayPal CR 1,458.00**
Sailors Bank Checking has **increased**; PayPal has **decreased**
Check Figure: Sailors Bank Checking $180,058.95

14. Click **Save & Close**.

Dealing with Bounced Checks

Unfortunately, almost all business owners must deal with customers whose checks are returned for nonsufficient funds (NSF) at some time or another. These returned checks are also called bounced checks. If you've invoiced a customer and used the Receive Payments window, you can easily use the Record Bounced Check feature in the Receive Payments window to deal with a returned check. QuickBooks will create a new invoice that includes the fee you want to charge the customer, and the original invoice will be marked unpaid. You can then send the customer the new invoice along with either a statement or the original invoice.

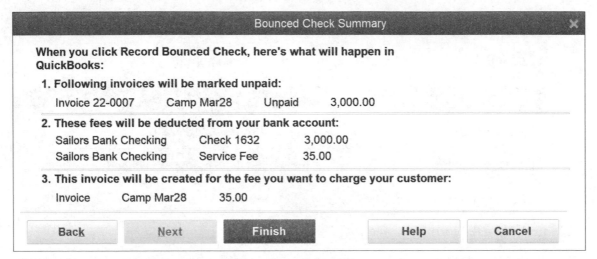

When you record a bounced check through the Receive Payments window, you will get a summary that shows exactly what happened behind the scenes.

However, if the bounced check was received on a sales receipt or directly through a deposit, you will need to account for it using this alternate method:

1. Create an Other Charge item for the service charge, directing it to the Other Income account.

2. Record the bank's fee in your bank account register (Bank Service Charges as account).

3. Record the check in your bank account register (Customer:Job as payee; Accounts Receivable as account).

4. Enter a statement charge for the customer's fee.

5. Send the customer a statement that shows the bounced check and fee.

BEHIND THE SCENES: *Bounced Check Bank Fee*

Bank Service Charges	Sailors Bank Checking
INCREASE to Expenses	*DECREASE to Assets*

→**Equity**

Assets = Liabilities + (Capital + Revenue − Expenses)

-$35.00	=	$0.00	+	$0.00	+ $0.00 − $35.00

Bank Service Charges		Sailors Bank Checking	
Debit	*Credit*	*Debit*	*Credit*
$35.00			$35.00

This example shows one part of the bounced check transaction: the assessing of the bank fee. The entire transaction will be displayed in the BTS Brief that appears in Develop Your Skills 5-7.

 Customers→Receive Payments

DEVELOP YOUR SKILLS 5-7

YMCA of the Keys wrote a check on the wrong account, and it bounced when you deposited it in the bank. The bank has charged you $35 for the returned check. In this exercise, you will account for the returned check and pass on the fee to the customer.

1. Click the **Receive Payments** task icon in the Customers area of the Home Page.

2. Click the **Previous** ◀ button two times to display the YMCA of the Keys check #1632 payment.

3. Click the **Record Bounced Check** button on the Main tab of the ribbon.

Receive Payments

4. Follow these steps to set the fees for the bounced check:

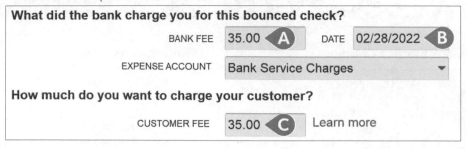

What did the bank charge you for this bounced check?

BANK FEE **35.00** 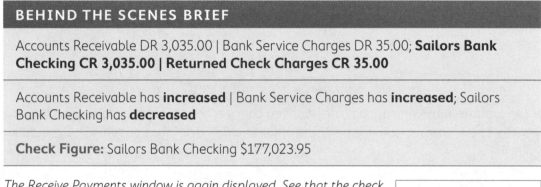 (A)   DATE **02/28/2022** (B)

EXPENSE ACCOUNT   Bank Service Charges ▾

How much do you want to charge your customer?

CUSTOMER FEE   **35.00** (C)   Learn more

(A) In the Bank Fee field, type: **35**

(B) Tap [Tab] and type: **022822**

(C) Tap [Tab] twice and type: **35**

The Expense account is prefilled with Bank Service Charges.

5. Click **Next** and then **Finish**.

BEHIND THE SCENES BRIEF

Accounts Receivable DR 3,035.00 | Bank Service Charges DR 35.00; **Sailors Bank Checking CR 3,035.00 | Returned Check Charges CR 35.00**

Accounts Receivable has **increased** | Bank Service Charges has **increased**; Sailors Bank Checking has **decreased**

Check Figure: Sailors Bank Checking $177,023.95

The Receive Payments window is again displayed. See that the check has been marked as a bounced check and a new invoice dated 02/28/2022 has been created to account for the bounced check fee.

 **⚠ BOUNCED CHECK**

6. Click **Save & Close**.

Reconciling Accounts

An important task is to ensure that your QuickBooks records match those of your bank. The process of matching transactions to your bank statement is called reconciliation. There needs to be extra attention paid to details when performing a reconciliation!

The Bank Statement

Each month you will receive a statement from the bank that shows all transactions that have cleared your account. The statement will also show any deposits or withdrawals the bank has entered, such as interest earned or a service fee, that you will need to account for in QuickBooks.

When you enter these amounts in the Begin Reconciliation window, they are automatically entered in your account register for you.

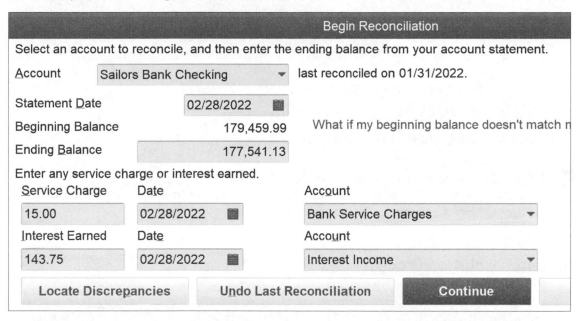

You enter the information from your bank statement in the Begin Reconciliation window.

When Your Accounts Don't Match

The goal of a reconciliation is to show a difference of $0 between the bank statement and your QuickBooks account. When the reconciliation shows a difference, you'll need to put on your detective hat and find where the discrepancy lies.

You will click to place a checkmark for all transactions found on your bank statement.

You can choose to limit the transactions to clear by hiding those after the statement's end date.

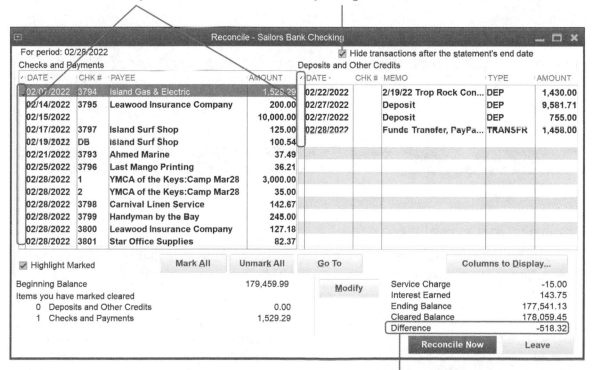

The goal is for the difference to be zero once you've marked off (reconciled) the transactions from your bank statement.

Locating Discrepancies

If reconciliation displays a difference, you can use Locate Discrepancies during the reconciliation process. You can also run a Reconciliation Discrepancy report that lists transactions affecting the reconciliation balance. The types of transactions that can affect the balance are:

- Deleted transactions

- A change to a previously cleared amount

- Transactions that were manually uncleared in the register

- Transactions for which the date was changed to a different statement period

> **Warning!** After you've cleared transactions through the reconciliation process, do *not* change them. Changes may alter your starting balance for the next reconciliation. If this does happen, run the Reconciliation Discrepancy report to find the problem(s).

Problem Resolution Process

If you finish your reconciliation without balancing, consider the following suggestions:

- Look for a transaction with the same amount as the difference and ensure whether or not it should be cleared.

- Determine whether you are missing a deposit or a payment by looking at the totals of each on the bank statement and the QuickBooks reconciliation window.

- Compare the number of transactions on the bank statement to the number of cleared transactions in QuickBooks.

- Verify the individual amount of each transaction on the bank statement and compare it to the amounts you have in QuickBooks.

- Determine whether it is a bank error (the bank may have recorded a transaction for the wrong amount, for example).

- If it is a bank error, you can create an adjustment transaction in QuickBooks, notify the bank, and then reverse the adjustment transaction after the bank corrects the error.

- Run a Reconciliation Discrepancy report to see whether any changes were made to previously cleared transactions. If so, undo the last reconciliation and redo it.

> **FLASHBACK TO GAAP: ASSUMPTION OF THE GOING CONCERN**
>
> Remember that it is assumed that the business will be in operation indefinitely.

Reconciling Credit Cards

You can reconcile your credit cards the same way as you reconcile your bank account; just choose a credit card account instead. Another way to access the reconciliation task is through the Chart of Accounts.

After you've reconciled the credit card, you have the option to pay any amount due. You can either write a check or enter a bill for the payment. QuickBooks takes the balance due on the credit card and fills it in to either the Enter Bills or the Write Checks window. If you don't plan to pay the entire amount owed, you can change the amount manually. You will reconcile the credit card in the Tackle the Tasks section of this chapter.

Banking→Reconcile

Banking→Reconcile : Locate Discrepancies

Reports→Banking

DEVELOP YOUR SKILLS 5-8

In this exercise, you will reconcile the Checking account in QuickBooks to the company's January 2022 Sailors Bank checking account statement.

Sailors Bank

75 Captain Drive
Key West, FL 33040
(305) 555-3810

Statement of Account
2/1/2022 – 2/28/2022
Checking Account #5493-2223

Total Deposits:	13,224.71	Total Payments:	15,272.32
Beginning Balance:	179,459.99	Ending Balance:	177,541.13

Date	Transaction Type	Payment	Deposit	Balance
2/1/2022	Beginning Balance			179,459.99
2/10/2022	Check #3794	1529.29		177,930.70
2/15/2022	Txfr to Savings	10,000.00		167,930.70
2/16/2022	Check #3795	200.00		167,730.70
2/19/2022	DB-Island Surf Shop	100.54		167,630.16
2/20/2022	Check #3797	125.00		167,505.16
2/22/2022	Deposit		1,430.00	168,935.16
2/24/2022	Check #3793	37.49		168,897.67
2/27/2022	Deposit		9581.71	178,479.38
2/27/2022	Deposit		755.00	179,234.38
2/28/2022	Check #3799	245.00		178,989.38
2/28/2022	NSF Check	3,000.00		175,989.38
2/28/2022	NSF Fee	35.00		175,954.38
2/28/2022	Deposit-PayPal		1,458.00	177,412.38
2/28/2022	Interest Earned		143.75	177,556.13
2/28/2022	Service Charge	15.00		177,541.13
2/28/2022	Ending Balance			177,541.13

1. Click the **Reconcile** task icon in the Banking area of the Home Page.

   QuickBooks displays the Begin Reconciliation window.

Reconcile

2. Follow these steps to begin the reconciliation by entering the information from your bank statement (some of the data may already be filled in for you):

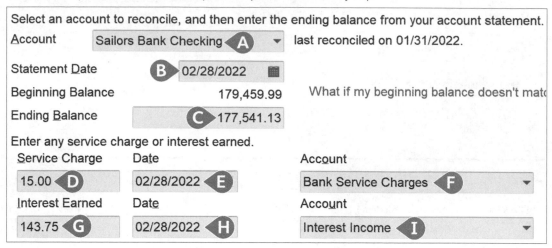

Select an account to reconcile, and then enter the ending balance from your account statement.

Account   Sailors Bank Checking **A**   last reconciled on 01/31/2022.

Statement Date   **B** 02/28/2022

Beginning Balance   179,459.99   What if my beginning balance doesn't mat

Ending Balance   **C** 177,541.13

Enter any service charge or interest earned.

Service Charge   Date   Account

15.00 **D**   02/28/2022 **E**   Bank Service Charges **F**

Interest Earned   Date   Account

143.75 **G**   02/28/2022 **H**   Interest Income **I**

Ⓐ Click the **Account** drop-down arrow ▾ and choose **Sailors Bank Checking**.

Ⓑ Tap ⸢Tab⸥ and type: **022822**

Ⓒ Tap ⸢Tab⸥ and type: **177541.13**

Ⓓ Tap ⸢Tab⸥ and type: **15**

Ⓔ Tap ⸢Tab⸥ and type: **022822**

Ⓕ Click the **Date** drop-down arrow ▾ and choose **Bank Service Charges**.

Ⓖ Tap ⸢Tab⸥ and type: **143.75**

Ⓗ Tap ⸢Tab⸥ and type: **022822**

Ⓘ Click the **Account** drop-down arrow ▾ and choose **Interest Income**.

3. Click **Continue** to move to the Reconcile–Sailors Bank Checking window.

   The Reconciliation-Checking window shows all transactions waiting to be cleared.

4. Click the checkbox for **Hide transactions after the statement's end date** to concentrate on this reconciliation period.

5. Click in the checkmark column to the left of each transaction that matches the entry on the bank checking statement provided.

Checks and Payments				Deposits and Other Credits		
✓ DATE ▾	CHK #	PAYEE	AMOUNT	✓ DATE ▾	CHK #	MEMO
✓ 02/07/2022	3794	Island Gas & Electric	1,529.29	✓ 02/22/2022		2/19/22 Trop R
✓ 02/14/2022	3795	Leawood Insurance Company	200.00	✓ 02/27/2022		Deposit

6. Look at the Difference amount at the bottom-right of the window to see whether you have successfully reconciled your account.

   The difference should be zero. If something was missed or there was some other issue, the Difference line will display the amount that it is off. The Difference is calculated by determining the variance between the transactions on the bank statement and those that you have marked cleared in QuickBooks, including any interest or other charges that you entered on the Begin Reconciliation window. If your difference is not zero, use the problem-resolution process described to troubleshoot and fix the discrepancy.

7. Click **Reconcile Now** and click **OK** in the Information window, if necessary.

   There may be a pause as QuickBooks records the marked transactions as cleared. The Select Reconciliation Report window is displayed.

8. Choose **Summary** and then click **Display** to view the Summary report.

9. Click **OK** to close the Reconciliation Report window.

Parrot's Paradise Resort - Chapter 5
Reconciliation Summary
Sailors Bank Checking, Period Ending 02/28/2022

	Feb 28, 22
Beginning Balance	179,459.99
Cleared Transactions	
Checks and Payments - 10 ite...	-15,287.32
Deposits and Credits - 5 items	13,368.46
Total Cleared Transactions	-1,918.86
Cleared Balance	177,541.13
Uncleared Transactions	
Checks and Payments - 4 items	-388.43
Total Uncleared Transactions	-388.43
Register Balance as of 02/28/2022	177,152.70
Ending Balance	177,152.70

The Cleared Balance amount will be the Beginning Balance amount for the next reconciliation. The Ending Balance amount should match the ending balance in your check register.

10. Close the Reconciliation Summary window.

Importing Banking Transactions into QuickBooks

There are two methods of bringing in transactions from a bank. One is manual, and the other is to use the automated Bank Feeds feature (Direct Connect). The Bank Feeds feature is a convenient, quick, and effective way to manage reconciliation and ensure accuracy. With Bank Feeds you can download transactions, view the transactions that have cleared your account, see your current balance, and add new transactions to QuickBooks from your financial institution. This feature can also assist in cash flow management.

You will need to check with your financial institution to determine which services are offered (or if any are offered at all). Although there is no fee to use bank feeds in QuickBooks, your financial institution may charge a fee for the automated service.

Tip! If you choose to do a manual download of transactions, you can do so through Bank Feeds, QuickBooks' online browser, or from any browser, and the downloaded file can be imported into QuickBooks. Not all banks may offer this feature.

QuickBooks provides a listing of financial institutions that participate in bank feeds for banking account access, credit/charge card account access, or payment access. Regardless of which method you use to bring your transactions into QuickBooks, you will first have to activate your banking, credit card, or other account for online service through your financial institution.

Note! Bank feeds exclusivity means if you work on your company file with others, only one person at a time can use bank feeds. The person who will be performing bank feed tasks must acquire exclusive use. This applies if you are working in multiuser mode only.

The Modes of Bank Feeds

You can choose how to work with your banking transactions through bank feeds, as there are two modes:

- **Express:** In this mode, you work within the Transactions List window to match and add transactions; renaming rules are created for you automatically.

- **Classic:** This version is the mode used in QuickBooks 2013 and earlier versions. Here, you work within account registers to match and add transactions, and you work with aliases to match names.

Bank Feeds and Reconciliation

When you use bank feeds you still must reconcile your accounts in the same way as you learned earlier in this chapter. The big advantage to using bank feeds is that the majority (if not all) of your transactions have been matched already, so reconciliation will be quicker. If you do have a discrepancy, then use the outlined problem-solving process to resolve it.

Setting Up Bank Feeds in QuickBooks

The setup process involves four steps that QuickBooks will guide you through. Setting up credit card and checking accounts are similar processes.

During the setup process, you link the account to one of your accounts in the Chart of Accounts. In this case, the Citibank credit card you've accessed online will link to the Visa-4545 account in QuickBooks. Once Bank Feeds is set up, the Bank Feeds Center will appear in the Banking menu.

Matching and Recording Bank Feeds

After you have set up Bank Feeds in QuickBooks, you will be able to download transactions from your financial institution(s), match them to transactions you've entered into QuickBooks, and properly record new transactions that are not yet entered into QuickBooks (remember, you have to get it right behind the scenes!).

After downloading, the number of transactions is displayed. The Transaction List button brings you to the next step, where you tell QuickBooks how to handle each transaction.

You will have four actions to choose from for each of the downloaded transactions. Choosing Match to Existing Transaction
will help to reconcile the credit card if you've already paid the
credit card bill with Write Checks. You can also choose multiple
transactions and then process all of them as a batch.

Note! Recording deposits and expenses often requires more than one transaction. You will
need to match the individual items in your register to the downloaded information. Avoid
creating duplicate entries or selecting the wrong type of account.

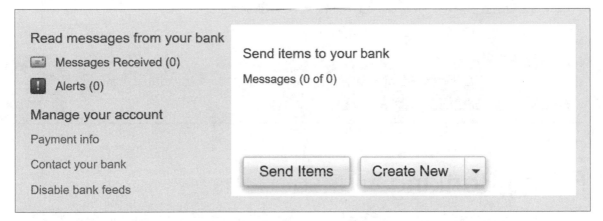

You can even send and receive messages with your bank in the Bank Feeds feature, provided
your bank offers this functionality.

Tip! Making Vendor Payments can also be done by using the QuickBooks online vendor
payment service set up through your financial institution, if they support it.

Attaching a File to a Transaction

Files can be added to QuickBooks transactions from a variety of sources, including a scanner, a
storage drive (local computer, cloud, network, or removable drive), or an Outlook message. You
can add these files to the QuickBooks Doc Center directly or use the Attach feature from within
a form such as an invoice; from bill pay; or from the customer, vendor, or employee centers.
Examples of scanned items are invoices, receipts, and packing slips.

If you use the Attach feature in one of the centers or from a
form, the documents will be listed in the Doc Center. There is no
fee for this feature.

The Attach File button
appears in forms.

Attach
File

The paper clip appears
in the Customer Center
and Vendor Center.

↱ Banking→Bank Feeds→Set Up Bank Feed for an Account

↱ Customers→Customer Center : Attach | Vendors→Vendor Center : Attach

DEVELOP YOUR SKILLS 5-9

In this exercise, you will attach a receipt to a bill.

1. Click the **Enter Bills** task icon in the Vendors area of the Home Page.

Enter Bills

2. Use the **Previous** ◀ button to locate the bill for Star Office Supplies dated 02/25/2022 for $82.37.

3. Click **Attach File**, click **Computer**, and then browse to the file location and click **Star Office Supplies 2-2002.pdf**.

4. Click **Open** and resize the Attachments window, if necessary.

   The name of the file will appear in the list. You can select it to detach it, view details, or open it.

5. Click **Done**.

   The Attach File button displays a number, referring to the number of attachments.

Attach File

6. Click **Save & Close**.

Fixing Banking Transactions

Inevitably, you will need to deal with errors or modifications to transactions in QuickBooks. It's very important to do this properly to ensure everything behind the scenes is correct. Deleted and voided transactions are recorded and become part of the overall records. This helps to create an audit trail that can be traced.

Study these examples of errors. The first is related to the Chart of Accounts, and the second occurs when dealing with a debit card transaction incorrectly.

COMMON ERRORS AND FIXES		
Error	**Effect Behind the Scenes**	**The Fix**
The wrong account type was chosen when creating a new account in the Chart of Accounts.	The types of accounts involved determine the damage behind the scenes (and there will be damage!).	Edit the account through the Chart of Accounts, choosing the correct account type.
A debit card transaction was entered in the Enter Credit Card Charges window, or vice versa.	The wrong account is credited, inflating the amount in Checking as well as the credit card account.	Delete the incorrectly entered transaction and reenter it in the proper window.

↱ Lists→Chart of Accounts

↱ Banking→Enter Credit Card Charges

DEVELOP YOUR SKILLS 5-10

The business has just received a Discover card that will be used for expenses. By mistake, it was set up as an expense and not as a credit card account. In this exercise, you will fix the error so it doesn't have huge ramifications behind the scenes.

1. Click the **Chart of Accounts** task icon in the Company area of the Home Page.

Chart of Accounts

2. Scroll down to the expenses, right-click **Discover Card** in the Chart of Accounts window, and choose **Edit Account**.

3. Edit the account:
   - Account Type: **Credit Card**
   - Account Name: `Discover-8010`
   - Description: `Company Discover Card`

4. Click **Save & Close** and then close the Chart of Accounts window.

Banking and Balance Sheet Reports

Running reports is a method of pulling information out of QuickBooks in a meaningful way. In this section, you will learn which reports to run to depict banking activities, as well as reports that display information about your balance sheet accounts (asset, liability, and equity). Snapshots are a quick way to see the status of payments, the company, and customers. Register QuickReports are a way of running a more specific report for a specific account.

Banking Reports

QuickBooks comes with preset reports to use to get answers from your data. Banking reports deal with answers to questions such as:

- Can you show all transactions involving a specific payee?
- Which checks have not cleared the bank as of the last bank statement?
- Which payments still need to be deposited?
- Where can I find a list of all transactions that affect my checking account?
- Which changes in transactions may affect my next reconciliation?

QuickReports are run right from a register window. From within a register, once you select a transaction and click the QuickReport button, you will receive a report that shows all transactions for the payee, vendor, or customer for the selected transaction.

Reconciliation reports show transactions that have cleared as well as those that have yet to clear the bank. QuickBooks allows you to save reconciliation reports in a PDF format.

Alternatives to Printing Reports

While any report can be sent to a printer, there are other options for storing or saving a report:

- **Email:** QuickBooks can convert the report to PDF. This allows viewing of the report exactly as it would print even for those who do not have QuickBooks. You have a choice of sending it as a PDF file or an Excel workbook.

- **Create an Excel Workbook:** QuickBooks can export the report to Excel so you can use Excel's powerful spreadsheet features to work with your data.

- **Saving Reports and Forms in PDF:** Save copies for your own records.

> ↱ Banking→Use Register : [select a transaction]→QuickReport

> ↱ Company→Chart of Accounts : [double-click the account]→[click the transaction]→ QuickReport

> ↱ Reports→Banking

DEVELOP YOUR SKILLS 5-11

In this exercise, you will produce two banking reports and save one of them as a PDF file.

1. Choose **Reports→Banking→Previous Reconciliation**.

2. Use this information to run the report:
   - Account: Ensure **Sailors Bank Checking** is displayed
   - Statement Ending Date: **02/28/2022**
   - Type of Report: **Detail**
   - In this report include: **Transactions Cleared at Time of Reconciliation**

   You can include cleared transactions at time of reconciliation or cleared transactions plus any changes that might have been made to those transactions.

3. Click the **Display** button to produce the report, resizing the report window as necessary.

   The report may take a few moments to display, so be patient!

4. Close the Reconciliation Detail report window.

Run a Register QuickReport

You will now create a report based on information contained within your checking account.

Check Register

5. Click the **Check Register** task icon in the Banking area of the Home Page.

6. Select **Sailors Bank Checking** as the account and click **OK**.

   The Parrot's Paradise Resort Checking register will be displayed.

7. Locate and single-click the **Island Surf Shop 2/19/2022** transaction and then click **QuickReport** from the toolbar at the top of the window.

   The report displays all the transactions from the checking register for Island Surf Shop. Notice the various buttons on the toolbar to print, email, export to Excel, and perform other tasks.

Produce a PDF Copy of a Report

8. With the Register QuickReport for Island Surf Shop window still active, choose **File→Save as PDF** from the main QuickBooks menu bar.

9. Save the file as: **CH5_D11 Island Surf Shop**

10. Choose **Window→Close All**.

Balance Sheet Reports

Many reports can be run as a summary report or a detail report. The Balance Sheet Summary report provides a look at your assets, liabilities, and equity as of a certain date. They should be in balance. Look at this report often, especially if your business handles numerous transactions on a daily or weekly basis. The detail version shows at the transaction level and can be a useful troubleshooting tool.

While the default is for a balance sheet report to display all your asset, liability, and equity accounts (hence the designation the "balance sheet accounts"), you can customize it to show only certain accounts. This report and the profit & loss report (or income statement) are two key financial reports for a business.

Company Snapshot

The Company Snapshot gives you a quick view of your company's bottom line in one convenient place. You can customize it to include at-a-glance reports that are most important to your company. The Company Snapshot will show information only within a preset date range of the current year. (If you don't see anything displayed, it's likely because the date for which you are performing the exercise is after the current year available through the snapshot.)

Switch tabs to view different snapshots.

Add content panels meaningful to your business or restore defaults.

These fields are used to customize the Company Snapshot to display date ranges or specific accounts.

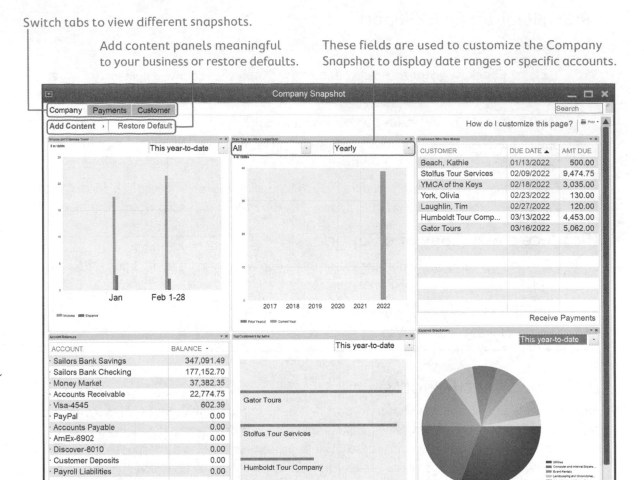

These links quickly take you to another window.

Reports→Company & Financial→Balance Sheet Standard

Reports→Company Snapshot

DEVELOP YOUR SKILLS 5-12

In this exercise, you will create both a balance sheet report and a company snapshot for Parrot's Paradise Resort. When you create a balance sheet report, it will be based as of a certain date rather than for a period of time (as is the case for a profit & loss report).

1. Choose **Reports→Company & Financial→Balance Sheet Standard**.
2. Tap ⌈Tab⌉ and then type **022822** and tap ⌈Tab⌉ again. Resize the window to see the entire report, if necessary.

   QuickBooks displays a balance sheet report showing the asset, liability, and equity account balances as of February 28, 2022. Notice that Total Assets = Total Liabilities + Equity.
3. Close the Balance Sheet window, choosing not to memorize the report.

Display and Customize the Company Snapshot

You will customize the Company Snapshot and then restore the default.

4. Choose **Reports→Company Snapshot** and then resize the window, if necessary.

   Depending on the date that you perform this exercise, you may or may not have information displayed as all the transactions entered may be for a future date. For this exercise, focus on how to manipulate the snapshots.

5. Click **Add Content**, click **Add** for Income Breakdown content, and then click **Done**.

6. Remove the Income and Expense Trend content panel from the snapshot by clicking the ☒. Click **OK** to confirm the removal.

   Notice that after you remove the Income and Expense Trend panel, another panel snaps up into the vacated space. You will now restore the default content panels to the snapshot.

7. Click the **Restore Default** link below the Payments tab at the top of the window and then click **Yes** in the Restore Default window.

8. Close the Company Snapshot window.

Tackle the Tasks

Now is your chance to work a little more with Parrot's Paradise Resort and apply the skills you've just learned to accomplish additional tasks. Continue with the same company file you've been using in this chapter so far. If you need to reopen the company file, the password is *Password1*.

Create Banking and Credit Card Accounts	Payroll Checking; Fins Left Credit Union; Account #3245645; Routing #599222043 Master Card-3928; Fins Left Credit Union; 5555 6666 2222 3928
Make a Deposit	Jimmy hosted a benefit concert (3/5/2022), and many attendees paid via PayPal; deposit the $2,390 in Banquets and Events Income from this concert to PayPal on the same day with the memo: YMCA Benefit Concert, 3/2022
Transfer Funds	3/5/2022: Transfer $100,000 from Sailors Bank Checking to Payroll Checking 3/7/2022: Transfer $2,390 from PayPal to Sailors Bank Checking

(cont.)

Enter Credit Card Transactions (Visa-4545); add new vendors as needed	3/6/2022: Purchased pizza for an employee retirement celebration from Changes in Latitudes Pizzeria; Ref No. EA-32022 for $165.11, using the Meals and Entertainment account (add as a new expense account); memo: Employee appreciation party 3/10/2022: Purchased a new wireless mouse; Ref. No. 05; from Ricky's Electric City for $49.52, using Office Supplies as the account; memo: wireless mouse 3/12/2022: Took a prospective chef out to lunch; Ref. No. HR-03; at Sauce Boss for $62.09, using Meals and Entertainment as the account; memo: Chef Lucy lunch 3/15/2022: Returned the wireless mouse for $49.52 to Ricky's Electric City; Ref. No. 05r; memo: Returned wireless mouse
Reconcile a Credit Card	Reconcile your 2/28/2022 Visa credit card statement (displayed below); then enter a bill for payment later (Quick Add Sailors Bank as a Vendor), Ref. No. 0322; memo: Visa 3/2022; create a summary reconciliation report, and pay the bill on 3/23/2022; no finance charges; check to be printed later
Generate a Report	Display a balance sheet standard report dated March 31, 2022

Sailors Bank

75 Captain Drive
Key West, FL 33040
(305) 555-3810

Statement of Account
2/1/2022 – 2/28/2022
Visa Account #5493-2223

Total Charges:	641.52	Total Payments:	39.13
Beginning Balance:	0.00	Ending Balance:	602.39
Minimum Payment Due:	25.00	Payment Due Date:	3/16/2022

Date	Details	Charge	Payment	Balance
2/1/2022	Beginning Balance			0.00
2/10/2022	Ahmed Marine	78.25		78.25
2/17/2022	Ahmed Marine		39.13	39.12
2/26/2022	Professional Software Dist	563.27	0.00	602.39
2/28/2022	Interest Paid		0.00	602.39
2/28/2022	Finance Charge	0.00		602.39
2/28/2022	Ending Balance			602.39

Self-Assessment

Check your knowledge of this chapter's key concepts and skills using the Self-Assessment in your ebook or eLab course.

1. Payments received on an invoice held in Undeposited Funds automatically appear in the checking register.   *True*   *False*

2. When you make a deposit to Checking, the amount shows on the credit side of the t-account.   *True*   *False*

3. In QuickBooks, Credit Card is a type of bank account.   *True*   *False*

4. Only bank accounts have registers that detail all account transactions.   *True*   *False*

5. When you double-click a liability in the Chart of Accounts, a QuickReport is displayed.   *True*   *False*

6. Bank feeds allow you to save time from having to type in all your transactions, help you to maintain better accuracy in your records, and assist in cash flow management.   *True*   *False*

7. Reconciliation is the process of matching your QuickBooks bank accounts to your bank statements.   *True*   *False*

8. The Chart of Accounts is a list of just your company's bank accounts.   *True*   *False*

9. The Reconciliation Discrepancy report helps you find transactions changed since your last reconciliation.   *True*   *False*

10. Reconciliation reports display only transactions cleared by the bank.   *True*   *False*

11. What's the recommended first step if your cleared QuickBooks transactions and the bank statement don't balance during reconciliation?
    A. Look for a transaction that is the same amount as the difference.
    B. Click the Unmark All button so you can start over.
    C. Go through all the deposit transactions and make sure they're all checked.
    D. Review the payment transactions and make sure they're all the correct amounts.

12. What window appears when you choose Banking→Make Deposits if there are funds in the Undeposited Funds account?
    A. Undeposited Funds Register
    B. Make Deposits
    C. Deposits in Wait
    D. Payments to Deposit

13. What account do you find on a balance sheet report?
    A. Payroll Liabilities
    B. Utilities Expense
    C. Sales
    D. Cost of Goods Sold

Reinforce Your Skills

Donnell Construction entered customer and vendor transactions in QuickBooks, and now it's time to take care of various banking tasks. You will help Colleen with tasks such as transferring funds, entering debit and credit card transactions, reconciling bank accounts, and running related reports. The password for all files unless otherwise stated is Password1.

REINFORCE YOUR SKILLS 5-1

Set Up Bank Account

In this exercise, you will take care of some banking tasks for Donnell Construction. Because the business checking account does not earn interest, Colleen has decided to open a savings account. You will set up this account in QuickBooks.

1. Choose **File→Open or Restore Company**.
2. Open **RYS_Chapter05 (Company)** *or* restore **RYS_Chapter05 (Portable)** and save it as: **RYS_Chapter05 Donnell Construction**
3. Choose **Lists→Chart of Accounts** and then click the **Account** drop-down arrow ▾ and choose **New**.
4. Choose **Bank** as the account type and click **Continue**.
5. Complete the account:
   - Account Name: **Savings**
   - Description: **Company Savings Account**
   - Bank Acct. No.: **456-456-4445**
   - Routing Number: **333000333**
6. Click **Save & Close**, choosing **No** in the Set Up Bank Feed window.
7. Close the Chart of Accounts window.

Move Funds Between Accounts

Because the savings account earns interest, you will transfer $200,000 from the checking account into it.

8. Choose **Banking→Transfer Funds**.
9. Complete the transfer:
   - Date: **021522**
   - Transfer Funds From: **Checking**
   - Transfer Funds To: **Savings**
   - Transfer amount: **200000**
10. Click **Save & Close** to record the transfer and close the window.

Make Deposits

Colleen delivered the keynote address for a local community college on the topic of women in the trades. You need to deposit the fee she earned into the checking account along with the funds that are currently in the Undeposited Funds account. You will do this in two separate steps.

11. Choose **Banking→Make Deposits**.

12. Click **Select All** in the Payments to Deposit window and then click **OK**.

13. Complete the deposit:
    - Deposit To: **Checking**
    - Deposit date: **021622**

14. Click **Save & New** and complete the next deposit to **Checking**:
    - Date: **021722**
    - Memo: **Keynote, Keizer College**
    - From Account: **Consultation Income** (click **Set Up**)

15. Choose **Income** as the account type, click **Continue**, and complete the new account:
    - Account Name: **Consultation Income**
    - Description: **Consultation income including presentations**

16. Click **Save & Close**.

17. Complete the remainder of the deposit:
    - Memo: **Keynote, 2/2022**
    - Check number: **753**
    - Payment Method: **Check**
    - Amount: **1500**

    Remember, you do not have to enter a customer, but you must enter an income account!

18. Click **Save & Close** to record the transaction.

REINFORCE YOUR SKILLS 5-2

Reconcile a Bank Account

Colleen's checking account statement has just arrived. In this exercise, you will reconcile Donnell Construction's checking account. Refer to the illustration shown after step 3.

1. Choose **Banking→Reconcile** and select **Checking** as the account.

2. Use the Ending Balance from the statement and this information to begin the reconciliation:

Statement Date	**022822**
Service Charge	**25**
Service Charge Date	**022822**
Account	**Bank Service Charges**
Interest Earned	**122.41**
Interest Earned Date	**022822**
Account	**Interest Income** (create a new Other Income account)

3. In the Reconcile-Checking window, mark only those transactions that have cleared the bank (and are on the bank statement).

Use this bank statement to reconcile the account:

Illinois State Bank

239 Lake Michigan Blvd.

Chicago, IL 60602

(773) 555-3810

Statement of Account

2/1/2022 – 2/28/2022

Checking Account #456-456-4444

Total Deposits:	23,470.00		Total Payments:	200,400.00	
Beginning Balance:	382,204.38		Ending Balance:	205,371.79	

Date	Transaction Type	Payment	Deposit	Balance
2/1/2022	Beginning Balance			382,204.38
2/4/2022	Check #3501	150.00		382,054.38
2/8/2022	Check #3502	250.00		381,804.38
2/15/2022	Transfer from Savings	200,000.00		181,804.38
2/16/2022	Deposit		21,970.00	203,774.38
2/17/2022	Deposit		1,500.00	205,274.38
2/28/2022	Interest Earned		122.41	205,396.79
2/28/2022	Service Charge	25.00		205,371.79
2/28/2022	Ending Balance			205,371.79

4. Click **Reconcile Now** and then close the Select Reconciliation Report window.

REINFORCE YOUR SKILLS 5-3

Manage Credit Card Transactions

In this exercise, you will set up a new Visa company credit card for Colleen's use.

1. Choose **Lists→Chart of Accounts** and then choose **Account→New**.
2. Choose **Credit Card**, click **Continue**, and create the new credit card account:
   - Account Name: **Visa-7220**
   - Description: **Company Credit Card**
   - Credit Card Acct. No.: **4444 9999 2222 7220**
3. Click **Save & Close** to enter the new account and close the window, choosing **No** when asked about setting up bank feed services.
4. Close the Chart of Accounts window.

Enter a Credit Card Charge

Colleen has purchased protective cases for the company cell phones using the company Visa.

5. Choose **Banking→Enter Credit Card Charges** and ensure the **Visa-7220** is selected.

6. Complete the charge:

Vendor	**Oak Park Cellular** (Quick Add the new vendor)
Date	**022022**
Ref No.	**Ph-09**
Amount	**328.57**
Memo	**Cell phone protective cases**
Account	**Telephone Expense**

7. Copy and paste the memo text into the Expenses tab Memo field and then click **Save & New** to record the transaction.

Enter a Credit Card Refund/Credit

Colleen didn't realize that one of her employees already had a protective phone case, so she will return one of them to Oak Park Cellular. The Enter Credit Card Charges window should still be open; if it isn't, open it.

8. Choose **Refund/Credit** at the top of the window.

9. Complete the refund:

Purchased From	**Oak Park Cellular**
Date	**022522**
Ref No.	**Ph-09r**
Amount	**109.52**
Memo	**Returned cell phone case** (Also enter this text in the Memo field on the Expenses tab.)
Account	**Telephone Expense**

10. Click **Save & Close**.

Produce Banking and Balance Sheet Reports

In this exercise, you will run some banking reports to see the current status of the company's finances. You'll start out with banking reports and then produce a Balance Sheet report.

1. Choose **Reports→Banking→Previous Reconciliation**.
2. Choose the **Checking** account and then click the **2/28/2022** reconciliation.
3. Choose **Summary** and to view the transactions cleared at the time of reconciliation; click **Display**.

   You can save this report as a PDF file to keep for the company's records.

4. Close the Reconciliation Summary window.

Run a Deposit Detail Report

Now you will run a report to display all the bank deposits for April.

5. Choose **Reports→Banking→Deposit Detail**.
6. Change the From Date to **010122** and the To Date to **022822** and then click **Refresh**. Resize the window to view the data.

   If you need to edit a transaction, you can leave a report open and choose Refresh to bring in the new data.

Tip! Tap Tab after changing the date to have QuickBooks automatically refresh the report.

7. Close the Deposit Details report window, choosing **No** when asked to memorize the report.

Display a Balance Sheet Report

8. Choose **Reports→Company & Financial→Balance Sheet Standard**.
9. Type **a** to change the date range to **All**.

   Take a moment to review the report and notice how things are grouped: Assets and Liabilities & Equity. You can clearly see how Checking and Accounts Receivable fall under Assets. Also notice how Assets and Liabilities & Equity are in balance with each other.

10. Choose **Window→Close All** and don't save any memorized reports.
11. Close the company file.

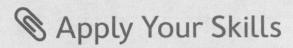# Apply Your Skills

Wet Noses Veterinary Clinic continues to do a thriving business. You will be staying on top of the necessary tasks on a day-to-day basis by entering credit card charges, reconciling and creating accounts, paying bills, and running reports. The password for all files unless otherwise stated is Password1.

APPLY YOUR SKILLS 5-1 QG

Perform Banking Tasks

In this exercise, you will create new accounts for Wet Noses Veterinary Clinic, choosing to not set up online services for either account. Leave the company file open unless otherwise stated.

1. Choose **File→Open or Restore Company**.
2. Open **AYS_Chapter05 (Company)** *or* restore **AYS_Chapter05 (Portable)** and save it as:
    `AYS_Chapter05 Wet Noses Clinic`
3. Create two new accounts for Wet Noses Veterinary Clinic:

Account Type	Bank	Credit Card
Account Name	Money Market	AmEx-9944
Description	Company Money Market Account	Company Credit Card
Account Number	3336665454	7777 888899 99944
Routing Number	010000001	

4. Make a deposit for all payments in the Undeposited Funds account into your Checking account on 06/09/2023.
5. Transfer 30000 on 06/10/2023 from Checking to Money Market.
6. Create an Account Listing report that displays a list of all accounts in the Chart of Accounts.
7. Click the **Excel** Excel ▾ button and export this list to a new workbook saved as:
    `CH5_A1 Account Listing`
8. Close Excel and then close the report, choosing not to memorize it.

Enter Credit Card Transactions

In this exercise, you will enter several credit card charges for purchases made and apply them to the appropriate expense account.

1. Enter these American Express charges for the month of June, Quick Adding vendors as necessary (all of these are original purchases and not bill payments):

Date	Vendor	Ref. No.	Amount	Memo
06/01/2023	Bothell Pet Supply Co.	06-01	$115.43	Boarding supplies
06/04/2023	Glen's Handyman Service	06-02	$108.70	12 door hinges – for maintenance
06/10/2023	Thrifty Grocery	06-03	$26.73	Bottled water and soda for office
06/14/2023	Karel's Gardening Service	06-04	$60.00	Monthly garden maintenance
06/20/2023	Bothell Pet Supply Co.	06-01r	$38.29	Return – Boarding supplies
06/22/2023	Laura's Café	06-05	$50.21	Business lunch with potential customer

2. Open the Chart of Accounts, select **AmEx-9944**, and run a QuickReport that displays charges from: 060123 through 063023.

3. Click the **Excel** button and export this list to a new workbook saved as:
   CH5_A2 June AMEX Charges

4. Close Excel and then close the Account QuickReport and Chart of Accounts.

Record a Bounced Check

In this exercise, you will help Dr. James handle check #6666 from Mary Ann Gulch for $145.65 that was returned for nonsufficient funds.

1. Locate the customer payment, **check #6666** from Mary Ann Gulch for $145.65, to record the bounced check.

2. Use this information for the fee in the Manage Bounced Check window:
   - Bank Fee: $25 on 06/06/2023 (use **Bank Service Charges** as the account)
   - Customer Fee: $45

3. Close any open windows and then run the **Open Invoice** report for 06/30/2023 to display the past-due invoices. You should see two for Mary Ann Gulch.

4. Click the **Excel** button and export this list to a new workbook saved as:
   CH5_A3 June Open Invoices

5. Close Excel and then close the report, choosing not to memorize it.

Pay a Bill with a Credit Card

In this exercise, you will use the American Express card to pay a vendor bill. You will need to select the appropriate expense account.

1. Create a bill, selecting the appropriate account, for Billy's Van Service:

Vendor	**Billy's Van Service**
Date	06/12/2023
Ref. No.	Van 01
Amount	$256.49
Memo	Travel: presentation May 2023

2. Open the Pay Bills window and pay the bill for Billy's Van Service on 06/12/2023 using the **AmEx-9944** account.

3. Open the Chart of Accounts, select **AmEx-9944**, and run a QuickReport that displays charges from: 06/01/2023 through 06/30/2023

4. Click the **Excel** button and export this list to a new workbook saved as:
   CH5_A4 AMEX QuickReport

5. Close Excel.

Reconcile a Credit Card Account

In this exercise, you will reconcile the American Express account.

1. Use this statement to reconcile the June American Express account:

American Express

75 Big Apple Way
New York, NY 10012
(800) 555-2639

Statement of Account
6/1/2023 – 6/30/2023
American Express Account #7777 888899 99944

		Account Summary	
New Balance	$579.27	Previous Balance	$0.00
Minimum Payment Due	$35.00	Payments and Credits:	-$38.29
Payment Due Date	07/30/2023	New Charges	$617.56
		Fees	$0.00
		Interest Charged	$0.00

Transaction Date	Details	Charge	Credit	Balance
	Beginning Balance			*0.00*
6/1/2023	Bothell Pet Supply Company	115.43		115.43
6/4/2023	Glen's Handyman Service	108.70		224.13
6/10/2023	Thrifty Grocery	26.73		250.86
6/12/2023	Billy's Van Service	256.49		507.35
6/14/2023	Karel's Gardening Service	60.00		567.35
6/20/2023	Bothell Pet Supply Company		38.29	529.06
6/22/2023	Laura's Café	50.21		579.27
2/28/2022	Interest Paid	0.00		579.27
2/28/2022	Fees	0.00		579.27
2/28/2022	Ending Balance			$579.27

---

2. Run the Summary Reconciliation report, write a check to American Express for the entire amount on **07/03/2023**, using **AMEX June 2023** for both memo fields. Choose to **Print Later** and then run the **Summary Reconciliation** report.

3. Ensure the Summary Reconciliation report is showing and then click the **Excel** button and export this list to a new workbook saved as: **CH5_A5 Summary Reconciliation**

4. Run the **Balance Sheet Standard** report as of 06/30/2023 to display the balance for all balance sheet accounts.

   Total Assets should equal Total Liabilities & Equity!

5. Click the **Excel** button and export this list to a new workbook saved as:
   CH5_A5 Balance Sheet

6. Close Excel and close the company file, choosing not to memorize the report.

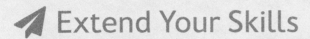 Extend Your Skills

Before You Begin: Open **EYS_Chapter05 (Company)** *or* restore **EYS_Chapter05 (Portable)**. The password is *Password1*.

You've been hired by Arlaine Cervantes to help her with her organization's books. She is the founder of Niños del Lago, a nonprofit organization that provides impoverished Guatemalan children with an engaging educational camp experience. You just sat down at your desk and opened a large envelope from Arlaine that contains a variety of documents; you also have several emails from her. It's your job to sort through the papers and emails and make sense of what you find, entering information into QuickBooks as appropriate and answering any questions in a word-processing document saved as: CH05_EYS_[LastnameFirstinitial]

Remember, you're dealing with random papers dumped out of an envelope and various emails, so part of your challenge is determining the order in which to complete the tasks.

- Scribbled note: I looked at QuickBooks and saw money in an account called Undeposited Funds. Why isn't it in the checking account? Can you move it for me? I deposited those funds into the Checking account on 7/11/2020!

- New credit card document: From Jasper State Bank, number 7777 2222 0000 2938, $7,500 credit limit.

- Note: Opened a new Money Market bank account at Jasper State Bank on 7/10/2020. Transferred $1,000 from savings to fund the new account. Need QuickBooks account set up.

- Bank deposit slip: Check #2323 dated 7/14/2020 for a $2,500 deposit to Checking. Handwritten message on slip reads, "From Hanson Family Trust."

- Credit card receipt: Dated 7/15/2020; for office supplies; $75.11; paid to Supplies Online.

- Note: Would you please create a report that shows all activity in the checking account for July 2020 and save it as a PDF file so I can email it to the accountant?

- Bank deposit slip: Dated 7/30/2020 for $750; handwritten on slip, check #1835 from Lakeside Christian School for remaining balance due.

- Credit card receipt: Dated 7/23/2020; payable to Casey's Service Station; for auto fuel; amount of $35.61. (Hint: This is for travel to a workshop site.)

- Scribbled note from Arlaine: Can you produce a report that shows the balances for all asset, liability, and equity accounts as of 7/31/2020?

6 Bringing It All Together: Service Project

Now that you've had the opportunity to learn the basics of using QuickBooks, you will create a company file from scratch with a greater understanding of *why* you're making certain choices. You'll then use that new company file to demonstrate your mastery of customer, vendor, and banking transactions.

📂 Project: Skortis Landscaping

Justin Skortis owns a landscaping company, Skortis Landscaping, that offers planning, installation, and monthly landscape maintenance services. Justin has decided to start using QuickBooks and has hired you as his bookkeeper. Your first project is to create list entries before entering customer, vendor, and banking transactions. Once you've set up the lists, you'll enter a variety of transactions for January 2022.

Note! This project is broken down into sessions. At the end of each session, you'll produce deliverables for evaluation. You will not be given specifics in many cases, just as you will not be given specifics when working with your own company. You may need to add new customers, vendors, or other information "on the fly" and use your own problem-solving and reasoning skills. Use QuickBooks' help and search features as needed. Now, let's get started!

Session 1: The Company File and Lists

In this session, you will create the new company file for Skortis Landscaping and set up the needed lists—Customers & Jobs, Vendors, Items, Chart of Accounts, and various profile lists.

Company Data

Create a new company file using the Detailed Start option, saving it as:

CH06_Skortis Landscaping

SKORTIS LANDSCAPING, LLC

876 MAIN STREET

POWAY, CA 92064

(858) 555-4589

SKORTISLAND@EMAIL.COM

COMPANY INFORMATION

Tax ID	98-7654321	Invoices	Yes
Industry	Lawn Care or Landscaping	Progress invoicing	No
Company Organization	Single-member LLC	Manage bills you owe	Yes
First Month of Fiscal and Tax Year	January	Do you want to track time in QuickBooks?	Yes
Administrator Password	Password1	Do you have employees?	Yes, W-2 employees

(cont.)

COMPANY INFORMATION (cont.)

What do you sell?	Services only	QuickBooks Start Date	12/31/2021
Sales tax	No	Use the Chart of Accounts information that follows to choose accounts to include/exclude.	
Estimates	Yes	Basis	Cash
Statements	Yes		

Turn off past and future date warnings in the Accounting category of the Preferences window before creating these accounts:

BANK AND CREDIT CARD ACCOUNTS

Account Name	Account Number	Opening Balance	Opening Balance Date
Checking	2009630-11	43,208.45	12/31/2021
Savings	2009630-99	127,402.78	12/31/2021
PayPal	skortisland@email.com	265.98	12/31/2021
Visa-0319	4444 2000 3000 0319	217.65	12/31/2021

Make sure your Chart of Accounts is set up with these income, cost of goods sold, and expense accounts. You can add many of these accounts during the setup process:

CHART OF ACCOUNTS

Income	Cost of Goods Sold	Expenses	
• Design Services • Installation Services • Maintenance Services	• Equipment Rental for Jobs • Material Costs • Merchant Account Fees • Tools and Small Equipment • Worker's Compensation Insurance	• Advertising and Promotion • Auto and Truck Expenses • Bank Service Charges • Business Licenses and Permits • Computer and Internet Expenses • Depreciation Expense • Insurance Expense • Interest Expense • Meals and Entertainment	• Office Supplies • Payroll Expenses • Postage and Delivery • Professional Fees • Rent Expense • Repairs and Maintenance • Telephone Expense • Uniforms • Utilities

CUSTOMER & VENDOR PROFILE LISTS

Customer Types	Vendor Types	Payment Methods	Terms List Entries
• Residential • Commercial	• Service Providers • Subcontractors • Suppliers • Tax Agency	• Cash • Check • MasterCard • Visa • Debit Card • PayPal (create an "Other" type)	• 1% 10 Net 30 • 2% 10 Net 25 • Due on receipt • Net 10 • Net 30

When entering the customers, be sure to copy the addresses to the Ship To fields.

CUSTOMERS

Customer / Name	Address	Phone	Terms	Customer Type
Mariner's Park, Inc. / Phoebe Martinez	1250 1st Ave. S. San Diego, CA 92128	(858) 555-3300	Net 10	Commercial
Maddy Gessford	2016 Ricardo Place Poway, CA 92064	(858) 555-1859	Net 10	Residential
Nathanial Jones	590 Piano Drive Poway, CA 92064	(858) 555-2201	Due upon receipt	Residential
Jurassic Ventures / Daniel Bennett	789 Epicodus Way San Diego, CA 92128	(858) 555-0857	Net 10	Commercial
Exploration Travel / Joseph Schmidt	18 Costa Rica Drive Poway, CA 92064	(858) 555-4788	Net 10	Commercial
Victoria Martusheff	4517 Hubbard Place San Diego, CA 92131	(858) 555-6429	Due upon receipt	Residential
Irie Spaeth	805 Fox Place San Diego, CA 92127	(858) 555-3319	Due upon receipt	Residential
Twin Peaks Realty / Lily Eberle	1456 Pine Street Poway, CA 92064	(858) 555-2018	Net 30	Commercial

VENDORS

Company / Name	Address	Phone	Account No. / Payment Terms	Type
Bark Girls / Jillian Murphy	18309 Industrial Way Poway, CA 92064	(858) 555-1059	PE-734 / Due upon receipt	Suppliers
Green Touch Nursery / Hwan Park	75 Greens Circle San Diego, CA 92127	(858) 555-0226	12-689-UV / Net 10	Suppliers
Rancho Properties / Ayana Chahine	16793 Club Pkwy San Diego, CA 92128	(858) 555-7822	78-453 / Due upon receipt	Service Providers
Hunter Cellular / Rick Hunter	7832 Pennoyer Place Portland, OR 97210	(503) 555-2098	430-320192-67 / Net 10	Service Providers
CA Tax Authority	309 Terwilliger Drive Sacramento, CA 95815	(916) 555-6736	987-6543-2 / Net 30	Tax Agency
McCall Equipment & Tools / Dee Dee McCall	10923 Devane Lane Poway, CA 92064	(858) 555-1984	LS-1991 / Due upon receipt	Suppliers

SERVICE ITEMS (NON-TAXABLE)

Item Name	Description	Rate	Account
Design	Landscape design services	$45.00	Design Services
Installation	Landscape installation	$65.00	Installation Service
Yard care	Residential yard maintenance	$50.00	Maintenance Services
Maintenance	Commercial landscape maintenance	$65.00	Maintenance Services

NON-INVENTORY ITEMS (NON-TAXABLE)

Item Name	Description	Preferred Vendor	Rate	Account
Mole repellant	Yard Safe natural, organic mole repellant, 10 lbs.	Green Touch Nursery	$56.15	Materials Costs
Lawn fertilizer	Green Touch Specialty Lawn Food, 33 lbs.	Green Touch Nursery	$45.13	Materials Costs
Monofilament line	String trimmer line, 3 lb. spool	McCall Equipment & Tools	$34.00	Tools and Small Equipment

Note! You will use the Preferred Vendor information when creating the purchase orders. It does not need to be entered in the New Item window.

Deliverables

Justin has asked you the following questions. For your response, you'll provide him with certain reports. (Hint: Display the Report Center in list view.)

> **Note!** If your class is using Quick Grader, be sure to export the reports to Excel, including the identifiers (e.g., "CH6-1") in the filenames.

QG **CH6-1**: What are the names of each of my company's accounts?

QG **CH6-2**: What is the contact information and current balance of each customer?

QG **CH6-3**: What is the phone number for each vendor?

QG **CH6-4**: What are the due dates and discounts available for customer payments and payments to vendors?

QG **CH6-5**: What is the price of each item or service my company sells?

Session 2: Transactions

Enter these transactions for Skortis Landscaping for January 2022. Create relevant memos for each transaction and Quick Add any new list entries.

WEEK 1	
1/3/2022	Create an invoice for Mariner's Park, Inc. for 8 hours of maintenance work.
1/4/2022	Enter a bill from Hunter Cellular for $230.45.
1/5/2022	Enter a cash sale for Nathanial Jones for 2 hours of installation work and 3 hours of yard care.
1/6/2022	Enter a bill from Bark Girls for a load of bark for $202.25. (Use Materials Cost as the account.)
1/7/2022	Create an invoice for Jurassic Ventures for 7 hours of design and 18 hours of installation.
1/8/2022	Pay all bills due by 1/8/2022 (checks to be printed), print all checks in the queue (first check number is 1892), and deposit all funds being held in Undeposited Funds to Checking.

 CHECK FIGURE *Checking $43,286.20 • A/R $2,005.00 • A/P $230.45 • Visa-0319 $217.65*

> **Note!** Check figure values come from the Chart of Accounts (which is accrual basis), not a balance sheet report (which for this company is cash basis).

WEEK 2	
1/10/2022	Enter a credit card charge for $175 for a 1-day tractor rental, payable to McCall Equipment & Tools. (Use Equipment Rental for Jobs as the account.)
1/11/2022	Enter a bill for 3 bags of mole repellant and 4 bags of lawn fertilizer from Green Touch Nursery.
1/12/2022	Create an invoice for Irie Spaeth for 2 hours of installation and 4 hours of yard care.
1/13/2022	Receive payments for the full amount due from Mariner's Park, Inc. (check #3280) and Jurassic Ventures (check #1090).
1/14/2022	Make a cash sale to Maddy Gessford for 5 hours of yard care.
1/15/2022	Pay all bills due by 1/15/2022 (checks to be printed), print all checks in the queue (first check number is 1893), and deposit all funds being held in Undeposited Funds to Checking.

 CHECK FIGURE *Checking $45,310.75 • A/R $330.00 • A/P $348.97 • Visa-0319 $392.65*

WEEK 3	
1/17/2022	Write a check to Office Superstore for $64.39 in office supplies and enter the number as 1895.
1/18/2022	Create an invoice for Exploration Travel for 4 hours of design and 12 hours of installation.
1/19/2022	Enter a sale for Victoria Martusheff, paid for by check #2017, for 4 hours of yard care.
1/20/2022	Purchase a set of hand tools from eBay for $90.43 using PayPal to pay for it.
1/21/2022	Create an invoice for Twin Peaks Realty for 9 hours of design work and 25 hours of installation.
1/22/2022	Pay all bills due by 1/22/2022 (use Credit Card as the Payment Method) and deposit all funds being held in Undeposited Funds to Checking.

 CHECK FIGURE *Checking $45,446.36 • A/R $3,320.00 • A/P $0.00 • Visa-0319 $741.62*

WEEK 4	
1/24/2022	Enter a bill for 5 spools of monofilament line from McCall Equipment & Tools.
1/25/2022	Enter an invoice for Mariner's Park, Inc. for 5 hours of installation and 7 hours of maintenance.
1/26/2022	Enter a bill for $1,875 to Rancho Properties for February 2022 rent.
1/27/2022	Enter a sale for Maddy Gessford, paid for by check #834, for 3 hours of installation and 6 hours of yard care.
1/28/2022	Receive payments for the full amount due from Irie Spaeth (check #763), Exploration Travel (check #1643), and Mariner's Park, Inc. (check #3291).
1/29/2022	Pay all bills due by 1/31/2022 (checks to be printed), print all checks in the queue (first check number is 1896), and deposit all funds being held in Undeposited Funds to Checking.

 CHECK FIGURE *Checking $45,966.36 • A/R $2,030.00 • A/P $0.00 • Visa-0319 $741.62*

Deliverables

Justin has asked you the following questions. For your response, you'll provide him with certain reports. (Hint: Display the Report Center in list view.)

> **Note!** If your class is using Quick Grader, be sure to export the reports to Excel.

QG **CH6-6**: What payments and invoices make up each customer's current balance?

QG **CH6-7**: What transactions has my company had with each vendor in January 2022?

QG **CH6-8**: Would you print me a list of all deposited and undeposited payments for January 2022?

QG **CH6-9**: What checks have been written, including the details of each one for January 2022?

Session 3: Wrap It Up

Complete the tasks required to address these items:

- The invoice for Twin Peaks Realty dated 1/21/2022 should have been for 8 hours of design work and 23 hours of installation. Correct the invoice to reflect this change.

- While reviewing your source documents, you realize that the bill from Bark Girls on 1/6/2022 for $220.25 was incorrectly entered into QuickBooks for $202.25.

- You received a damaged bag of mole repellant from Green Touch Nursery. The vendor issued you a credit on 1/31/2022 for $56.15 to account for the damaged goods. You will use this credit when paying a future bill to the vendor.

- On January 17, 2022, the bank advised you that check #3280 for $520.00 from Mariner's Park, Inc. was returned for nonsufficient funds. A $35 fee has been charged to your account. Pass this charge on to the customer.

- On 1/31/2022, pay all bills in Accounts Payable (checks to be printed) and print all checks in the queue (first check number: 1898).

- Reconcile the checking account using this bank statement:

Bates Bank

21 Poway Ranch Road
Poway, CA 92064
(858) 555-2999

Statement of Accounts
1/1/2022 – 1/31/2022
Checking Account #2009630-11

Total Deposits:	5,300.00		Total Payments:	3,097.09
Beginning Balance:	43,208.45		Ending Balance:	45,442.13

Date	Transaction Type	Payment	Deposit	Balance
1/1/2022	Beginning Balance			43,208.45
1/8/2022	Check 1892	202.25		43,006.20
1/8/2022	Deposit		280.00	43,286.20
1/15/2022	Check 1893	230.45		43,055.75
1/15/2022	Deposit		2,255.00	45,310.75
1/17/2022	NSF Check	520.00		44,790.75
1/17/2022	NSF Fee	35.00		44,755.75
1/17/2022	Check 1894	64.39		44,691.36
1/22/2022	Deposit		200.00	44,891.36
1/29/2022	Check 1895	170.00		44,721.36
1/29/2022	Check 1896	1,875.00		42,846.36
1/29/2022	Deposit		2,565.00	45,411.36
1/31/2022	Interest Earned		45.72	45,457.08
1/31/2022	Service Charge	14.95		45,442.13
1/31/2022	**Ending Balance**			**45,442.13**

 CHECK FIGURE *Checking $45,424.13 • A/R $2,410.00 • A/P –$56.15 • Visa $741.62*

Deliverables

Justin has asked you the following questions. For your response, you'll provide him with certain reports. (Hint: Display the Report Center in list view.)

> **Note!** If your class is using Quick Grader, be sure to export the reports to Excel.

QG **CH6-10**. What transactions were cleared or outstanding from the January 2022 checking account reconciliation? I need to see the details of each transaction.

QG **CH6-11**: What are the sales to each customer and job, broken down by transaction, for January 2022?

QG **CH6-12**: How much money did my company make or lose in January 2022?

QG **CH6-13**: What is the value of my company, showing me the individual balances for each account, as of January 31, 2022?

7 | Managing Physical Inventory

In this chapter, you will examine the QuickBooks inventory features that help you track the items (goods) you offer for sale. An example of a company needing to track inventory is a retail store that sells electronics or a salon that sells styling products. When the inventory function is turned on, QuickBooks provides additional features to create inventory items and purchase orders, receive items into inventory, sell inventory items, and run inventory-related reports. Additional accounts are created to track inventory—Inventory Assets and Cost of Goods Sold. You will also set up and track sales tax, deal with customer refunds, and explore common inventory and sales reports.

LEARNING OBJECTIVES

▸ Create and use items to track inventory

▸ Create purchase orders and receive items

▸ Adjust quantity/value on hand

▸ Sell items and process sales discounts and refunds

▸ Collect, track, and pay sales tax

▸ Use reports to manage inventory and sales

🗁 Project: Parrot's Paradise Resort

Jimmy Parrot is the owner of Parrot's Paradise Resort in Key West, Florida. He's been using QuickBooks to account for his service-based business for two months and is now opening a gift shop on the property, so he will need to begin using it to track inventory as well. In this chapter, as the bookkeeper for Parrot's Paradise Resort, you will help Jimmy set up inventory items in QuickBooks, order inventory, enter sales transactions, and track sales tax. You will also learn how to set up and receive payments when sales discounts are involved. Finally, you will explore sales reports and inventory reports to help manage inventory.

Tracking Inventory in QuickBooks

A useful feature in QuickBooks is inventory tracking. It must be turned on in the Preferences window. When activated, it will add links to the Home Page and options to the menu bar.

Should I Use QuickBooks to Track My Company's Inventory?

Not all companies are perfectly aligned to use QuickBooks to track their inventory. There are several factors you should consider before deciding to use QuickBooks to track your company's inventory items:

- **How many types of products do I sell?** QuickBooks Pro and Premier work well for companies that have up to a few hundred items. If you have more items, you may want to consider using QuickBooks' Point-of-Sale edition.

- **Does my inventory include perishable items?** The bookkeeping for perishable items can be a bit tedious due to differences between your on-hand quantities and what you have recorded in QuickBooks.

- **Do I sell unique, one-of-a-kind products?** If you sell items such as antiques, you will have to create a new QuickBooks item for each product you sell.

- **Do I manufacture the products that I sell?** If you purchase raw materials and assemble them into products, you may want to look at purchasing QuickBooks: Premier Manufacturing & Wholesale Edition or QuickBooks Enterprise Solutions: Manufacturing & Wholesale Edition, which address the unique needs of manufacturing businesses.

- **How fast do my inventory items become obsolete?** If this time frame is quite short, you may find that updating your inventory in QuickBooks is tedious.

- **How do I value my inventory?** QuickBooks Desktop uses the average cost method of inventory valuation. If you are using another one of the methods allowed by GAAP, such as LIFO or FIFO, or another method, you may want to look at using a different tool to track your inventory.

FLASHBACK TO GAAP: CONSISTENCY

Remember that the company should use the same accounting principles and methods from year to year.

Tracking Inventory Sales

You will likely need to create a new account and possibly subaccounts to track the sales of your inventory. In the following exercise, you will create three subaccounts to make sure you track your sales effectively. Once inventory preferences are turned on, the QuickBooks Inventory Center will become available. This center looks like the Customer and Vendor centers, providing a convenient place for you to manage your inventory items.

> **Note!** QuickBooks Premier and higher versions include a feature that allows you to convert units of measure, where you can work with either single units of measure (e.g., buy or sell a pound) or multiple units of measure (e.g., buy a yard, sell a foot).

Using Account Numbers in QuickBooks

Many businesses use account numbers for the accounts in their Chart of Accounts. You will be using account numbers as you work with the company file for Parrot's Paradise Resort. Account numbers are somewhat standard within the accounting world. "Somewhat" means that each account type begins with the same number, but the accounts listed within the account type are not universally numbered. Examine the following table to understand how account numbers work. Note that account numbers have a minimum of four characters, and you can use up to six. For instance, a checking account (which is an asset) could be numbered 1000, 10000, or 100000.

ACCOUNT TYPES AND NUMBERING CONVENTIONS		
Starts With	**Type of Account**	**Example**
1	Asset	Checking Account
2	Liability	Accounts Payable
3	Equity	Owner's Equity
4	Income	Service Income
5	Cost of Goods Sold	Purchases – Resale Items
6	Expenses	Utilities Expense
7	Other Income	Interest Income
8	Other Expense	Sales Tax Penalty

Show Lowest Subaccount Preference

When you use subaccounts to better categorize your QuickBooks data, it's often difficult to see the name and number of the subaccount that you used because of the narrow account fields in the windows. You can overcome this problem by choosing to see only the lowest subaccount in these fields. For example, if you need to choose the Clothing subaccount, it would normally be displayed as:

41000•Gift Shop and Vending Sales:41100•Clothing Sales

By choosing the Show Lowest Subaccount preference, it will simply be displayed as:

41100•Clothing Sales

> ↗ Edit→Preferences

In this exercise, you will turn on account numbers and the inventory features of QuickBooks.

Before You Begin: *Visit the Learning Resource Center at labyrinthelab.com/lrc to retrieve the exercise files for this course before beginning this exercise. Two versions of the files are available—portable company files and company files. The password for all files unless otherwise stated is Password1.*

1. Start QuickBooks 2020 and choose **File→Open or Restore Company**.

2. Open **DYS_Chapter07 (Company)** *or* restore **DYS_Chapter07 (Portable)** and save it as:
   DYS_Chapter07 Parrot's Paradise Resort

   You need to save the file with a different name only if you're using a portable company file. If you're using a company file, just open it and begin working.

   Now you'll set preferences to track inventory. Remember, preferences allow you to customize how you interact with QuickBooks. There are two that can be made: My Preferences and Company Preferences.

3. Choose **Edit→Preferences**.

4. Follow these steps to turn on the inventory feature:

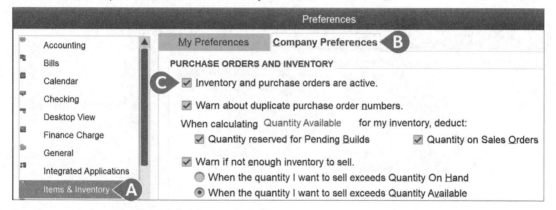

- Ⓐ Click **Items & Inventory**.
- Ⓑ Click the **Company Preferences** tab.
- Ⓒ Click the checkbox for **Inventory and purchase orders are active.**

You will be warned if you use a duplicate purchase order number and if your inventory quantity on hand is not enough.

Turn on Account Numbers and Set the Show Lowest Subaccount Preference

5. Click the **Accounting** category, click **Yes** in the Save Changes window, and then click **OK** to close all windows and make the preference change.

6. Click the checkboxes to the left of **Use account numbers** and **Show lowest subaccount only**.

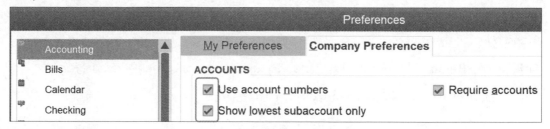

7. Click **OK** and then choose **Company→Home Page**.

Notice the new task icons in the Vendors area of the Home Page that are present now that inventory features are turned on.

Note! Unless otherwise instructed, always leave the company file open at the end of an exercise.

Tracking Inventory Sales

To most accurately track your inventory sales, you will create subaccounts for 41000•Gift Shop and Vending Sales. When using subaccounts, it's important to always direct funds toward them rather than the parent account.

NAME	TYPE
41000 · Gift Shop and Vending Sales	Income
41100 · Clothing Sales	Income
41200 · Food Sales	Income
41300 · Accessory Sales	Income
41400 · Souvenir Sales	Income
41500 · Sundry Sales	Income

The subaccounts that will be used to track retail sales are indented under the parent account, Gift Shop and Vending Sales, in the Chart of Accounts.

Cost of Goods Sold

The cost of goods sold (COGS) are the expenses directly related to the manufacture or acquisition of products or services that the company sells. In manufacturing, some expenses that might be considered COGS are labor, raw materials, depreciation, and overhead. In the case of a retail operation, the COGS is the wholesale cost of inventory. You do not pass on the COGS to a customer (it is instead incorporated into the final price of the product).

NAME	TYPE
50000 · Cost of Goods Sold	Cost of Goods Sold
51500 · Linens and Lodging Supplies	Cost of Goods Sold
51800 · Merchant Account Fees	Cost of Goods Sold
52900 · Purchases - Resale Items	Cost of Goods Sold

Four COGS accounts were created when the company file was set up using the Lodging (Hotel, Motel) industry as a starting point for the new company file.

In this exercise, you will first check that your accounts have numbers. Then you will create subaccounts to track inventory sales, which will help you to track inventory income.

Before You Begin: *If the Home Page is not displayed, choose Company→Home Page.*

1. Click the **Chart of Accounts** task icon in the Company area of the Home Page.

2. Scroll through the Chart of Accounts to see whether any do not have an account number.

    You will see that all accounts have a number assigned, which is necessary to show the lowest subaccounts only.

Create a New Subaccount to Track Inventory Sales

3. Click the **Account** drop-down arrow ▼ at the bottom of the window and choose **New** from the menu.

4. Choose **Income** as the Account Type and click **Continue**.

5. Follow these steps to create the new subaccount:

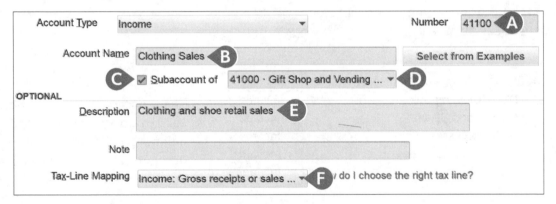

Ⓐ Type **41100** in the Number field.

Ⓑ Tap [Tab] and type: **Clothing Sales**

Ⓒ Click in the **Subaccount of** checkbox.

Ⓓ Click the drop-down arrow ▼ and choose **41000•Gift Shop and Vending Sales**.

Ⓔ Tap [Tab] and type: **Clothing and shoe retail sales**

Ⓕ Click the drop-down arrow ▼ and choose **Income: Gross receipts or sales…**.

6. Click **Save & New**.

Create Additional Subaccounts

You will now create four more subaccounts to further classify your retail sales income account.

7. Create the additional subaccounts for **41100•Gift Shop and Vending Sales**. All accounts map to **Income: Gross receipts or sales**. Click **Save & New** after each of the first three entries.

Number	Account Name	Description
41200	Food Sales	Food and beverage sales
41300	Accessory Sales	Accessory and jewelry sales
41400	Souvenir Sales	Souvenir and novelty sales
41500	Sundry Sales	Sundries and personal item sales

8. Click **Save & Close** after the last entry.

Notice that the five new subaccounts are indented under the parent account, 41100•Gift Shop and Vending Sales.

9. Close the Chart of Accounts window.

Dealing with Sales Tax in QuickBooks

If you live in a state that collects sales tax, or your business requires that you collect and remit it for other states, you will need to set it up in your company file. Thankfully, QuickBooks makes it easy to charge and collect sales tax for items. You can also choose whether to charge tax for customers who resell merchandise to *their* customers. How you set up sales tax in QuickBooks depends entirely on which state(s) you conduct business in. You must know the sales tax laws in your state/jurisdiction before you set up sales tax for your company and what type of items are taxable so you can properly designate them in QuickBooks.

Warning! When dealing with sales tax, learn about the sales tax laws in your jurisdiction. How you display items on invoices, whether items are stated separately or grouped together, can affect the amount of tax due on a transaction. Talk to an accountant, if necessary.

Behind the scenes, the sales tax collected will be directed to a Sales Tax Liability account that QuickBooks automatically creates for you. The funds will be held there until you pay them to the appropriate governing authority.

Sales Tax Items and Groups

To include sales tax on a sales form, you must set up the tax as an item. Often, you must pay the tax collected to multiple tax agencies. QuickBooks allows you to combine multiple sales tax items into a sales tax group. This is necessary, as you can apply only one sales tax item or group to a sales form. Before you can collect sales tax, you must turn on the preference and create the appropriate sales tax item(s) or group. In fact, you can create your sales tax items right from the Preferences window!

Default Tax Rate

Once you've created your sales tax item(s) and group(s), you should set the default to the most commonly used tax rate in Preferences. This rate will appear when you create a sales form for a customer for whom a tax rate is not specified; you can change it on a sale-by-sale basis.

Some companies conduct business in multiple jurisdictions. As such, the company must set up different sales tax items and/or groups with the different rates and taxing agencies. You can set one default tax rate for the company or default tax rates for each customer.

Sales Tax Codes

QuickBooks automatically sets up two sales tax codes when you turn on the preference, Taxable and Non-Taxable. These codes are assigned to customers and items. QuickBooks will apply sales tax to any customer or item where the code is set to Taxable, although this can be changed on an individual basis on the sales forms. You can even create additional sales tax codes, as needed, through the Sales Tax Code List.

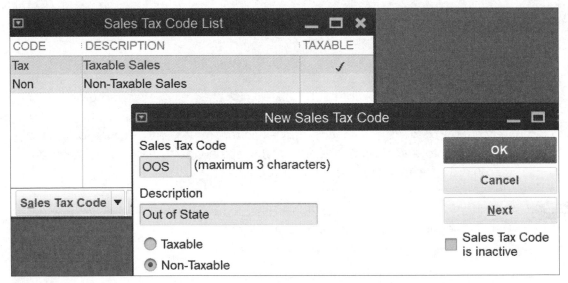

The Sales Tax Code List allows you to create additional codes such as Out of State, allowing you to track sales to customers who do not live in your state and are not required to pay your sales tax.

Edit→Preferences : Sales Tax→Company Preferences tab→[your most common sales tax item]

Customers→Customer Center : New Customer & Job→New Customer

In this exercise, you will turn on the sales tax preference and create a sales tax item. Then you will create a second sales tax item, a sales tax group, and an additional sales tax code.

1. Choose **Edit→Preferences**.

2. Click the **Sales Tax** category and the **Company Preferences** tab.

3. Follow these steps to set the sales tax preference and to set up your default sales tax item:

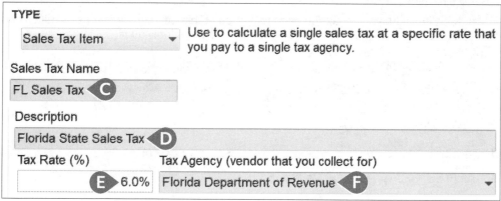

Ⓐ   Click in the circle next to **Yes**.

Ⓑ   Click **Add sales tax item...** and then tap Tab .

Ⓒ   Type: **FL Sales Tax**

Ⓓ   Tap Tab and type: **Florida State Sales Tax**

Ⓔ   Tap Tab and type: **6**

Ⓕ   Tap Tab and type: **Florida Department of Revenue**

4. Click **OK**, choose to **Quick Add**, and click **OK** again.

5. Click the **Your most common sales tax item** drop-down arrow ▼ and choose **FL Sales Tax**.

6. Click **OK** and then click **OK** in the Updating Sales Tax window, and, finally, click **OK** in the Warning window.

Create a Sales Tax Item and Group

In our example, there is a state tax rate and then each local area has an additional amount that is charged. You will now create another sales tax item and then create a sales tax group. Finally, you will update the most common sales tax item to this new group.

7. Choose **Company→Home Page** and then click the **Items & Services** task icon in the Company area of the Home Page.

Items & Services

8. Press ⌈Ctrl⌉+⌈n⌉ and click to choose **Sales Tax Item** as the new item type.

9. Complete the new sales tax item:
   - Sales Tax Name: `KW Local Tax`
   - Description: `Key West Local Sales Tax`
   - Tax Rate: `1.5`
   - Tax Agency: **Florida Department of Revenue**

10. Click **Next** and then follow these steps to create the sales tax group:

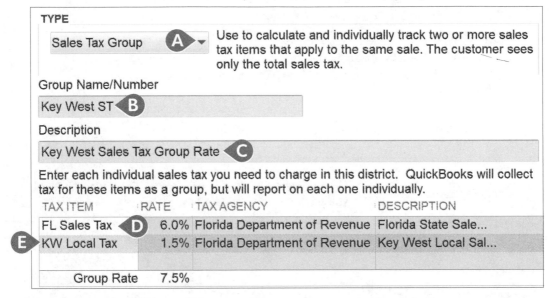

Ⓐ Click the drop-down arrow ▼ and choose **Sales Tax Group**.

Ⓑ Tap ⌈Tab⌉ and type: `Key West ST`

Ⓒ Tap ⌈Tab⌉ and type: `Key West Sales Tax Group Rate`

Ⓓ Click under **Tax Item** and then click the drop-down arrow ▼ and choose **FL Sales Tax**.

Ⓔ Tap ⌈Tab⌉, click the drop-down arrow ▼, and choose **KW Local Tax**.

Notice that after choosing the sales tax items, the group rate automatically calculates for you.

11. Click **OK** and then close the Item List and the Check Spelling on Form window, if necessary.

12. Choose **Edit→Preferences**.

13. Click the **Sales Tax** category and the **Company Preferences** tab.

14. Choose **Key West ST** as the most common sales tax item.

15. Click **OK**.

Work with the Sales Tax Code List

Now that you have set up your sales tax items, you will add an entry to the Sales Tax Code List.

16. Choose **Lists→Sales Tax Code List**.

Two sales tax codes were created automatically: Taxable and Non-Taxable. These codes are assigned to customers and items. QuickBooks will apply sales tax to any customer or item where the code is set to Taxable, although this can be changed on a case-by-case basis.

17. Click **Sales Tax Code** then choose **New**.

18. Create the new, non-taxable sales tax code:
    - Sales Tax Code: **OOS**
    - Description: **Out of State**

19. Click **OK** and then close the Sales Tax Code List window.

Setting Up Inventory Items

In order to select items you will be selling from a sales form or purchase order (PO), each one must first be set up as an item in the Item List. Setting up your inventory requires an understanding of when to classify items as inventory parts or non-inventory parts:

- Inventory parts are tracked and sold by quantity. Examples of inventory parts might be vitamins that a doctor purchases and sells to patients, lamps that an interior decorating company buys and resells, or branded ceramic coffee cups that a bakery might sell.

- Non-inventory parts include items you don't track as inventory, such as nails used by a contractor or thread used by a seamstress, or items you purchase for a particular customer or items you sell but don't first purchase, such as livestock that you breed and sell. These products are necessary for the business, but they are not being stocked for resale to customers.

The Item List for Parrot's Paradise Resort has been set up to group items that are sold by category, which are represented by numbers. Most of the categories represent service items; now you will be creating inventory items for the retail sales category. Sales from each category are directed into a separate income account.

Category Number	Category Description	Income Account
0	Lodging Services	Lodging Sales
1	Retail Sales	Gift Shop and Vending Sales
2	Event Services	Banquet and Events Income
3	Excursion Services	Excursion Income
4	Rental Services	Rental Income
5	Camp Services	Camp Income
6	Restaurant Sales	Food and Beverage Sales
7	Spa Services	Spa Income

Two-Sided Items

Inventory items have two sides: one for the purchase information and the other for the sales information. When you purchase items at wholesale to resell to your customers, the purchase price you pay is the COGS. Your profit is the difference between your sales price and COGS. All the information needed to track both sides of the item is detailed in the New Item window.

Units of measure allows you to purchase using one unit, such as yards, and sell at another, such as inches.

The sales side fields track price, tax code, and income account.

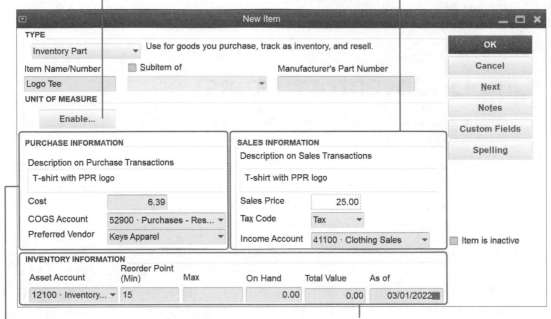

The purchase side fields track cost, COGS, and preferred vendor.

Set the information about the asset here: account, point to reorder, quantity, and value.

Add/Edit Multiple List Entries

If you're adding more than a few items at once, QuickBooks has a feature to easily record multiple entries in your lists. This feature is also available for customers and vendors to make your data entry faster. And you can quickly update several entries in your lists by right-clicking and choosing either the Clear Column or Copy Down command.

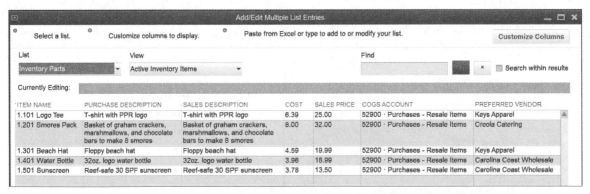

The Add/Edit Multiple List Entries window resembles an Excel spreadsheet and makes it easy to enter list entries efficiently.

Lists→Item List : Item→New

In this exercise, you will help Jimmy create inventory items for Parrot's Paradise Resort by entering a single item and then creating additional items using the Add/Edit Multiple List Entries feature.

1. Click the **Items & Services** task icon in the Company area of the Home Page.

Items & Services

2. Click the **Item** drop-down arrow ▼ from the bottom of the window and choose **New**.

3. Follow these steps to create an inventory item:

Ⓐ Click to choose **Inventory Part**.

Ⓑ Tap Tab and type: **1.101 Logo Tee**

Ⓒ Tap Tab four times and type: **T-shirt with PPR logo**

Ⓓ Tap Tab and type: **6.39**

Ⓔ Click the drop-down arrow ▼ and choose **52900•Purchases - Resale Items**.

Ⓕ Tap Tab and type: **Keys Apparel**

4. Tap Tab , click **Set Up**, and then set up the vendor, clicking **OK** when finished:

Company Name	Keys Apparel
Full Name	Ms. Angela Pepka
Job Title	Sales Manager
Main Phone	(305) 555-9442
Billed From/Shipped From Address	2016 Kirkland Drive, Marathon, FL 33050
Vendor Type	Suppliers

5. Follow these steps to finish setting up the new item:

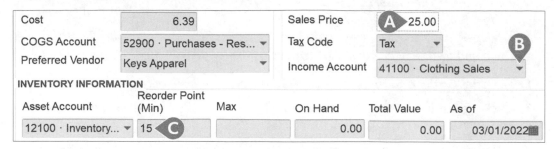

ⓐ Tap ⌑Tab⌑ twice and type **25** in the Sales Price field.

ⓑ Click the drop-down arrow ▼ and choose **41100•Clothing Sales**.

ⓒ Tap ⌑Tab⌑ twice and type: **15**

The description you enter for purchase transactions (which will appear on purchase orders) will automatically copy to the sales transactions side (which will appear on sales forms, such as invoices). You can leave it or edit it to meet your needs. The quantity on hand and total value are both zero because no items have been purchased yet.

6. Click **OK**.

Create Multiple Inventory Items

Next, you will create multiple inventory items using the Add/Edit Multiple List Entries window, but first you will customize the columns to include fields currently not displayed.

7. Click the **Item** drop-down arrow ▼ at the bottom of the window and choose **Add/Edit Multiple Items**. If the Time Saving Tip window appears at any time during this exercise, click **OK**.

Note that Inventory Parts is already selected as the list type ; however, if it isn't, choose to display Inventory Parts as the list before continuing.

8. Click **Customize Columns**.

9. Follow these steps to customize the columns for data entry of the inventory part items:

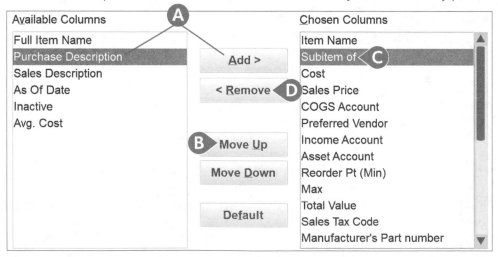

ⓐ Click **Purchase Description** and then click **Add**.

ⓑ Click **Move Up** until Purchase Description is displayed below *Item Name*.

ⓒ Click **Subitem of**.

ⓓ Click **Remove**.

10. Continue to add and remove columns, as well as move them up and down, until the Chosen Columns list matches the illustration.

11. Click **OK** to finish customizing the columns.

12. Click in the row below *Logo Tee* and enter the next four items.

   All items are taxable and share the same COGS account (52900•Purchases - Resale Items) and asset account (12100•Inventory Asset), so you can use the Copy Down command for each. Quick Add any vendors not on the Vendor List.

Chosen Columns
Item Name
Purchase Description
Sales Description
Cost
Sales Price
COGS Account
Preferred Vendor
Income Account
Asset Account
Reorder Pt (Min)
Sales Tax Code

Tip! Tapping Tab after each entry will move the cursor one field to the right, speeding up data entry. You can also right-click and select from a list to copy down, clear a column, and insert or delete lines.

Item Name	1.201 Smores Pack	1.301 Beach Hat	1.401 Water Bottle	1.501 Sunscreen
Purchase & Sales Description	Basket of graham crackers, marshmallows, and chocolate bars to make 8 smores	Floppy beach hat	32oz. logo water bottle	Reef-safe 30 SPF sunscreen
Cost	8.00	4.59	3.96	3.78
Sales Price	32.00	19.99	18.99	13.50
Preferred Vendor	Creola Catering	Keys Apparel	Carolina Coast Wholesale	Carolina Coast Wholesale
Income Account	41200•Food Sales	41300•Accessory Sales	41400•Souvenir Sales	41500•Sundry Sales
Reorder Point	20	25	20	35

13. Click **Save Changes** at the bottom of the window and then click **OK** in the Record(s) Saved window.

14. Close the Add/Edit Multiple List Entries.

   View the Item List to confirm that the entries were added.

15. Close the Item List window.

Purchase Orders

Many businesses use purchase orders for ordering items into inventory. When a PO is created, nothing occurs behind the scenes, as you have done nothing yet to debit or credit an account.

If you purchase items for sale to a specific customer, you can indicate that in the Customer column and select it in the Drop Ship To field.

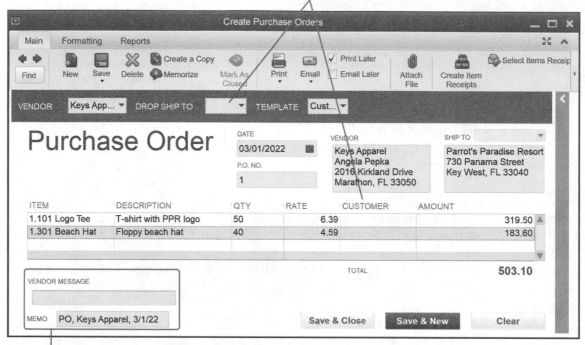

The Vendor Message field displays when the PO is produced for the vendor, whereas the Memo field is for your internal records.

FLASHBACK TO GAAP: COST

Remember that when a company purchases assets, it should record them at cost, not fair market value. For example, if you bought an item worth $750 for $100, it should be recorded at $100.

Non-Posting Accounts

When you create your first PO, QuickBooks creates a non-posting account (an account that *does not* affect your profit & loss or balance sheet reports) called Purchase Orders. Non-posting accounts appear at the end of your Chart of Accounts. By creating these accounts for you, QuickBooks allows you to create reports based on them.

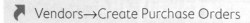

Vendors→Create Purchase Orders

DEVELOP YOUR SKILLS 7-5

In this exercise, you will create purchase orders for the inventory Jimmy will be selling. You will create a PO for an order of logo shirts and floppy hats from Keys Apparel, a second PO for smore packs from Creola Catering, and a third for sunscreen and water bottles from Carolina Coast Wholesale. Finally, you will review the Open Purchase Orders report.

1. Click the **Purchase Orders** task icon in the Vendors area of the Home Page.

2. Choose **Keys Apparel** as the Vendor and then follow these steps to complete the PO:

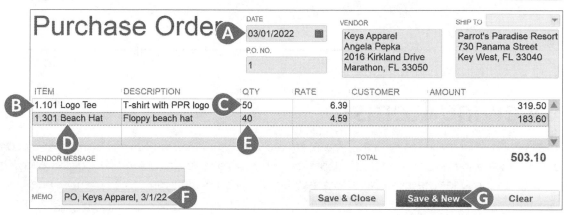

Ⓐ Tap ⌷Tab⌷ three times and enter the date: **030122**

Ⓓ Click the drop-down arrow ▾ and choose **1.101 Logo Tee**.

When you click in the Item column, the drop-down arrow will appear.

Ⓒ Tap ⌷Tab⌷ twice and type: **50**

Ⓓ Click the drop-down arrow ▾ and choose **1.301 Beach Hat**.

Ⓔ Tap ⌷Tab⌷ twice and type: **40**

Ⓕ In the Memo field, type: **PO, Keys Apparel, 3/1/22**

Ⓖ Click **Save & New**.

3. Create the next two POs on 3/1/2022, adding new words to the dictionary as needed:

Vendor	Creola Catering	Carolina Coast Wholesale
P.O. No.	2	3
Item/Quantity	1.201 Smores Pack/40 units	1.401 Water Bottle/50 units 1.501 Sunscreen/65 units
Memo	PO, Creola Catering, 3/1/22	PO, Carolina Coast, 3/1/22

4. Click **Save & Close** after the final PO.

View the Open Purchase Orders Report

Next, you will view the Purchase Orders non-posting account QuickBooks created when the first PO was entered and produce a QuickReport showing all open POs.

5. Click the **Chart of Accounts** task icon in the Company area of the Home Page.

6. Scroll to the bottom of the list and notice the non-posting 90100·Purchase Orders account.

7. Double-click the **Purchase Orders** account and tap a to set the date range to All.

   QuickBooks creates a QuickReport showing open POs.

8. Close the Account QuickReport and Chart of Accounts windows.

Receiving Items

When you receive the items on a PO, you need to enter them into inventory. This transaction can be handled in either one or two steps, depending on how your vendor delivers the accompanying bill. If a vendor sends the inventory items and the bill together, you can record them as one transaction. If you receive the items first and the bill later, you will enter them in two separate steps.

There is a drop-down arrow ▼ on the Receive Inventory task icon that allows you to choose whether to enter the bill for the items with the inventory receipt or later.

Including Expenses on a Bill for Items

You may incur additional shipping and handling charges when you order inventory items. These charges should not be entered on the Items tab, where the inventory is entered, but rather as an expense on the Expenses tab.

Expenses	$30.00	Items	$503.10		
ACCOUNT		AMOUNT	MEMO	CUSTOMER:JOB	BILLABLE?
67600 · Shipping Expense		30.00	Shipping, PO 1, 3/2022		▲

Expenditures listed on the Expenses tab will show up on a Profit & Loss report as an expense, whereas those on the Items tab will show up on the Balance Sheet as an asset.

Discount Payment Terms

Your vendors may offer you discount payment terms as incentive to pay your bills earlier (just as you may offer them to your customers). You can set default payment terms for a vendor; however, you may change the terms on an individual invoice as needed.

> **Note!** You will use the payment terms of 1% 10 Net 30 when entering a bill in this section. This means if you pay the bill within 10 days of receipt, you will receive a 1 percent discount. But if you don't pay within the first 10 days, the full bill is due in 30 days.

BEHIND THE SCENES: *Receive Items with the Bill*

12100•Inventory Asset	20000•Accounts Payable
INCREASE to Assets	*INCREASE to Liabilities*

→ **Equity**

Assets = **Liabilities** + (**Capital** + **Revenue** − **Expenses**)

$320.00 = $320.00 + $0.00 + $0.00 − $0.00

12100•Inventory Asset		20000•Accounts Payable	
Debit	*Credit*	*Debit*	*Credit*
$320.00			$320.00

↗ Vendors→Receive Items and Enter Bill

↗ Vendors→Receive Items

↗ Vendors→Enter Bill for Received Items

↗ Lists→Customer & Vendor Profile Lists→Terms List

DEVELOP YOUR SKILLS 7-6

In this exercise, you will receive inventory items for Parrot's Paradise Resort both with and without the bill.

1. Click the **Receive Inventory** task icon in the Vendors area of the Home Page and choose **Receive Inventory without Bill**.

2. Type **keys** and tap ⌷Tab⌷.

   QuickBooks fills in Keys Apparel, and the Open PO's Exist window appears.

3. Click **Yes** in the Open POs Exist window to receive inventory against your purchase order.

4. Click to place a checkmark in the first column for **PO NO. 1** (dated 3/1/2022) and then click **OK**.

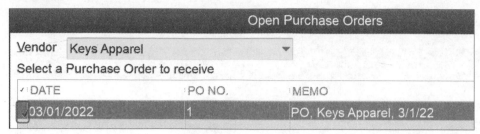

QuickBooks displays the Create Item Receipts window with the information from the PO filled in. Notice that the items appear on the Items tab at the bottom of the window, not on the Expenses tab!

5. Tap ⊞ on the keyboard to change the date to **03/06/2022**.

6. Click **Save & Close** to record the item receipt.

Receive the Bill and Add an Expense

The shirts and hats were entered into inventory when you received them. Now the bill for the items has arrived, and you need to enter it.

7. Click the **Enter Bills Against Inventory** task icon in the Vendors area of the Home Page.

8. Choose the correct item receipt:

- Vendor: **Keys Apparel**

- Click anywhere in the line to select the 03/06/2022 item receipt and click **OK**.

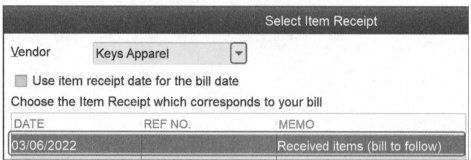

The Enter Bills window appears with the order information filled in and the invoice items on the Items tab.

9. Follow these steps to complete the bill:

Ⓐ Tap ⌈Tab⌉ and type the date: **031022**

Ⓑ Tap ⌈Tab⌉ and type: **PO1, Inv 2335**

Ⓒ Tap ⌈Tab⌉ and type: **533.1**

Ⓓ Tap ⌈Tab⌉ three times and type: **PO, Keys Apparel, 3/2022**

Ⓔ Click the **Expenses** tab.

Ⓕ Click the drop-down arrow ▾ and choose **67600•Shipping Expense**.

Ⓖ Tap ⌈Tab⌉ twice and type: **Shipping, PO 1, 3/2022**

10. Click **Save & Close** to record the new bill, choosing **Yes** to record your changes.

Receive Inventory Items with Bills

The smores packs and the bill for them were delivered to the resort at the same time.

11. Click the **Receive Inventory** task icon in the Vendor area of the Home Page and choose **Receive Inventory with Bill**.

12. Choose **Creola Catering** as the Vendor.

    QuickBooks fills in Creola Catering as the vendor, and the Open PO's Exist window appears.

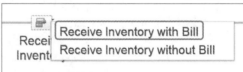

13. Click **Yes** in the Open PO's Exist window to receive inventory against the open PO.

14. Click to place a checkmark in the first column for **PO NO. 2**.

15. Click **OK** to move to the Enter Bills window; click **OK** in the Warning window, if necessary.

16. Complete the bill:

    • Date: **030722**

    • Ref. No.: **PO2, Inv. 145**

    • Amount Due: **320**

    • Memo: **PO, Creola, 3/2022**

17. Click **Save & New**.

18. Choose **Carolina Coast Wholesale** as the Vendor.

   QuickBooks will indicate that a PO exists for the vendor even if you don't initiate the bill through the Receive Inventory command.

19. Click **Yes** in the Open PO's Exist window to receive inventory against the open PO.

20. Click to place a checkmark in the first column for **PO NO. 3**.

21. Click **OK** to move to the Enter Bills window; click **OK** in the Warning window, if necessary.

22. Complete the bill:
    - Date: **030922**
    - Ref. No.: **PO3, Inv. 22-47**
    - Amount Due: **468.70**
    - Terms: **1% 10 Net 30**

      You will receive a 1 percent discount if you pay the bill by the Discount Date.
    - Memo: **PO, Carolina, 3/2022**

Enter an Expense on the Bill for Inventory Items

You will now enter the $25 shipping charge as an expense on the bill for Carolina Coast Wholesale.

23. Click the Expenses tab and complete the bill:
    - Account: **67600•Shipping Expense**
    - Amount: **25**
    - Memo: **Shipping, PO 3, 3/2022**

BEHIND THE SCENES BRIEF
12100•Inventory Asset DR 1,266.80 | 67600•Shipping Expense DR 55.00; **20000•Accounts Payable CR 1,321.80**
12100•Inventory Asset has **increased** | 67600•Shipping Expense has **increased**; Accounts Payable has **increased**
Check Figure: Accounts Payable $1,924.19

    Tip! You can easily compare these figures to those in your Chart of Accounts.

24. Click **Save & Close**.

   The Behind the Scenes Brief shows a summary of all three inventory receipt transactions.

25. Click **No** to reject changing the current terms for Carolina Coast Wholesale.

Selling Inventory Items

After you've ordered and received your items, it's time to start selling them! In this section, you will use the Create Invoices window, batch process invoices, and apply discount payment terms to a sales transaction.

There are two forms on which you process inventory sales in QuickBooks:

- The Create Invoices window (on account—it affects Accounts Receivable behind the scenes)
- The Enter Sales Receipts window (for immediate payment—it does *not* affect Accounts Receivable)

Switch between different templates.

Additional fields will aid in the shipment of inventory items.

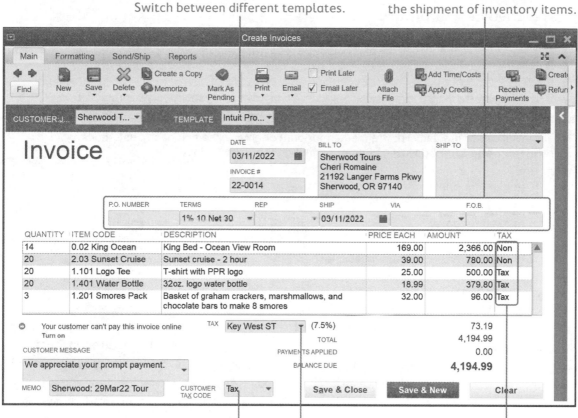

All customers have their own tax code, but if a customer is taxable and an item is not, it will be overridden by the individual item tax code.

You can change the sales tax item if it's not correct.

The tax code fills in from the item list entry, but if a customer is not taxable, the sale will not be taxed.

Batch Invoicing

The batch invoicing feature allows you to fill out an invoice just once for the customers in the batch and then create invoices for all of them. This is extremely efficient if your company charges a standard monthly fee for many customers. To complete this task, first create a billing group of the customers for whom you wish to batch invoice (although you can add customers one at a time as well).

> **Note!** Make sure the terms, sales tax code, and preferred delivery method are set up in the customer's record for any customer you wish to include in the batch. You also must have an email address entered for the customers you plan to batch invoice.

Batch Invoices Summary

After you've created a batch of invoices for customers, you will see the Batch Invoice Summary window. Here you can choose to either print or email the invoices (based on the preferred send method for each customer).

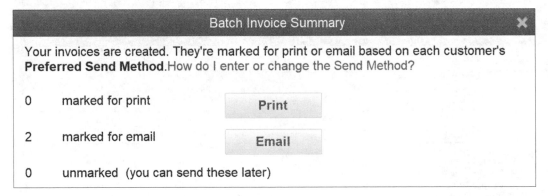

The Shipping Manager

You can ship a package right from QuickBooks from both the Create Invoices and Enter Sales Receipt windows using FedEx, UPS, and now the United States Postal Service (through Stamps. com). You can use either your existing account(s) for any of these services, or you can sign up right from the app. QuickBooks will process the shipment and create a shipping label for you with the customer information you've stored. In addition, you can track your shipments from within QuickBooks.

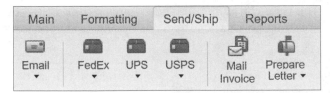

The Send/Ship tab of the Create Invoices window ribbon makes it easy to ship a package using the carrier of your choice.

11000•Accounts Receivable	41100•Clothing Sales 25500•Sales Tax Payable
INCREASE to Assets	*INCREASE to Revenue* *INCREASE to Liabilities*

→ **Equity**

Assets	=	**Liabilities**	+	(**Capital**	+	**Revenue**	−	**Expenses**)
$26.88	=	$1.88	+	$0.00	+	$25.00	−	$0.00

11000•Accounts Receivable		41100•Clothing Sales	
Debit	*Credit*	*Debit*	*Credit*
$26.88			$25.00

25500•Sales Tax Payable	
Debit	*Credit*
	$1.88

This example shows the behind-the-scenes activity for the sale of a logo tee.

↱ Customers→Create Invoices

↱ Customers→Create Batch Invoices

↱ Customers→Create Invoices : Send/Ship tab of ribbon

DEVELOP YOUR SKILLS 7-7

In this exercise, you will first help Parrot's Paradise Resort create an invoice for Sherwood Tours with discount payment terms. Since Sherwood Tours will be bringing multiple tour groups to the resort, you will be creating a job for each. Finally, you will create a batch of invoices for families that are participating in summer camps.

1. Click the **Customers** [CUSTOMERS] button in the Customers area of the Home Page.
2. Single-click **Sherwood Tours** on the Customers & Jobs List.

3. Click the **New Customer & Job** button on the toolbar above and choose **Add Job**.

4. Type **29Mar22** in the Job Name field and click **OK**.

Create an Invoice with Discount Payment Terms

Now that the job has been created, you will create an invoice with discount payment terms that will be emailed. The job you just created should still be selected in the Customers & Jobs List.

5. Click the **New Transactions** button on the toolbar and choose **Invoices**.

   The Create Invoices window will appear with the Customer:Job entered.

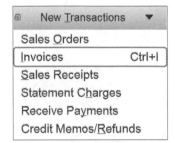

6. Follow these steps to complete the invoice:

Ⓐ Click the drop-down arrow ▼ and choose **Intuit Product Invoice**.

Ⓑ Tap ⌜Tab⌝ and type: **031122**

Ⓒ Click the drop-down arrow ▼ and choose **1% 10 Net 30** as the terms.

Nothing will be shipped to the customer, so you will leave the Ship To, Via, and FOB fields blank. If the customer had provided you with a PO number, you would enter it in the appropriate field.

7. Enter the items sold:

QUANTITY	ITEM CODE	DESCRIPTION	PRICE EACH	AMOUNT	TAX
14	0.02 King Ocean	King Bed - Ocean View Room	169.00	2,366.00	Non
20	2.03 Sunset Cruise	Sunset cruise - 2 hour	39.00	780.00	Non
20	1.101 Logo Tee	T-shirt with PPR logo	25.00	500.00	Tax
20	1.401 Water Bottle	32oz. logo water bottle	18.99	379.80	Tax
3	1.201 Smores Pack	Basket of graham crackers, marshmallows, and chocolate bars to make 8 smores	32.00	96.00	Tax

The Description, Price Each, Amount, and Tax columns for each item will fill in once the Item Code is selected.

8. Choose **We appreciate your prompt payment.** for the Customer Message.

9. Type this text for the memo: **Sherwood: 29Mar22 Tour**

10. On the ribbon, click the checkbox for **Email Later** and ensure Print Later is *not* selected.

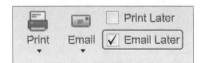

Tip! If the size of a field is not large enough to display the entire entry, you can hover your mouse pointer over the field and a pop-up will appear with the full list entry displayed.

11. Click **Save & Close**.

 An Information Missing or Invalid window will launch.

12. Type **SherwoodTours@email.com** and click **OK**.

13. Click **Yes** in the Information Changed window.

BEHIND THE SCENES BRIEF

11000•Accounts Receivable DR 4,194.99; **40000•Lodging Sales CR 2366.00 | 42000•Banquets and Events Income CR 780.00 | 41000•Gift Shop and Vending Sales CR 975.80 | 25500•Sales Tax Payable CR 73.19**

11000•Accounts Receivable has **increased**; 40000•Lodging Sales has **increased** | 42000•Banquets and Events Income has **increased** | 41000•Gift Shop and Vending Sales has **increased** | 25500•Sales Tax Payable has **increased**

Check Figure: Accounts Receivable $26,969.74

---

14. Leave the Customer Center open.

Set Up Customers for Batch Invoicing

With spring break fast approaching, Parrot's Paradise Resort is gearing up for the weeklong kids' camp. Many of the kids who attend camp over spring break also attend a summer session, so you will create a batch of invoices for two of these customers. First, you will need to ensure that the two customers are set up correctly.

15. Set up two customers for batch invoicing, double-clicking each customer to open it for editing and clicking **OK** to save the edits for each customer.

Customer	Angeles, Kyra	Laughlin, Tim
Main Email	KAngeles@email.com	TimL@email.com
Payment Terms	Net 15	Due on Receipt
Preferred Delivery Method	Email	Email
Tax Code	Tax	Tax
Tax Item	Key West ST	Key West ST

16. Close the Customer Center.

Create a New Billing Group

17. Choose **Customers→Create Batch Invoices** and then click **OK** in the "Is your customer info set up correctly?" window.

 The Batch Invoice window will appear.

18. Click the **Billing Group** drop-down arrow ▼ on the right side of the window and choose **Add New**.

19. Enter **Kids Camp-Week** as the Group Name and click **Save**.

20. Select two customers to be in the Billing Group as follows, resizing the Name field and scrolling, if necessary:

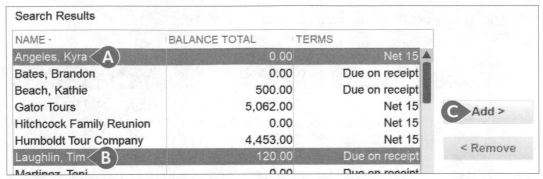

- Ⓐ Click to select **Angeles, Kyra**.
- Ⓑ Press Ctrl and click **Laughlin, Tim**.

    After clicking Laughlin, Tim, both customers should be highlighted in green so you can add them to the group at the same time.

- Ⓒ Click **Add**.

21. Click the **Save Group** button below the Customers in This Group list and click **Next** on the bottom-left portion of the window.

Create a Batch of Invoices

Now you will set up the invoice that will be sent to the batch of customers. In this case, the kids get a $5 logo tee when they attend camp, so you will include it on the invoice and change the price.

22. Follow these steps to create the batch invoice:

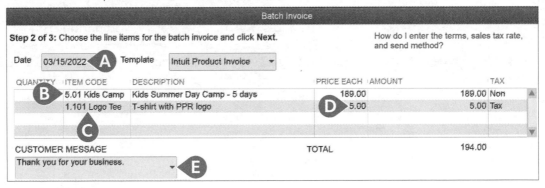

- Ⓐ Type: **031522**
- Ⓑ Click below *ITEM CODE* and then click the drop-down arrow ▾ and choose **5.01 Kids Camp**.
- Ⓒ Click in the next line down and then click the drop-down arrow ▾ and choose **1.101 Logo Tee**.
- Ⓓ Tap Tab twice and type: **5**
- Ⓔ Click the drop-down arrow ▾ and choose **Thank you for your business.**

    If the Price Levels window appears, click OK.

23. Click **Next** and then review the list of invoices you are preparing to create.

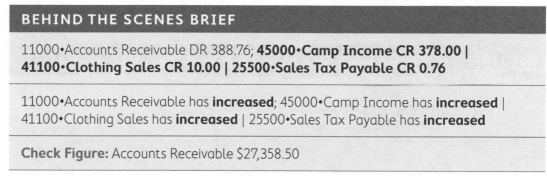

Invoice Date: 03/15/2022

SELECT	CUSTOMER	TERMS	SEND METHOD	AMOUNT	TAX CODE	TAX RATE	TAX	TOTAL	STATUS
✓	Angeles, Kyra	Net 15	Email	194.00	Tax	7.5%	0.38	194.38	OK
✓	Laughlin, Tim	Due on receipt	Email	194.00	Tax	7.5%	0.38	194.38	OK

The screen will show all invoices to be created. You could choose not to create an invoice for a member of the group by deselecting it.

24. Click **Create Invoices**.

The Batch Invoice Summary window displays.

> ## BEHIND THE SCENES BRIEF
>
> 11000•Accounts Receivable DR 388.76; **45000•Camp Income CR 378.00 | 41100•Clothing Sales CR 10.00 | 25500•Sales Tax Payable CR 0.76**
>
> 11000•Accounts Receivable has **increased**; 45000•Camp Income has **increased** | 41100•Clothing Sales has **increased** | 25500•Sales Tax Payable has **increased**
>
> **Check Figure:** Accounts Receivable $27,358.50

25. Click **Close** in the Batch Invoice Summary window.

Receiving Discounted and Electronic Payments

The procedure for receiving a discounted customer payment is similar to receiving a regular payment, except that you must identify the account to be debited for the discount amount.

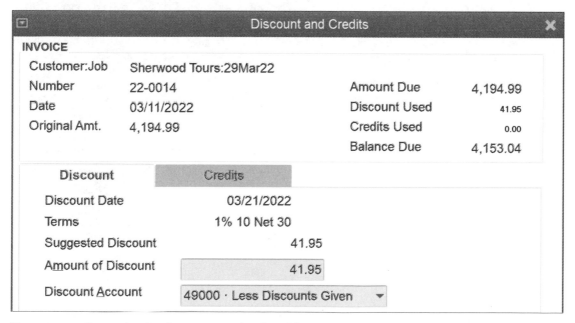

You can easily apply the discount in the QuickBooks Discount and Credits window. QuickBooks calculates the discount for you based on the payment terms.

Electronic Customer Payments

In some instances, you may receive payments from your customers electronically. When the bank notifies you that you have received an electronic payment, you enter the receipt in the Receive Payments window, noting e-Check as the payment type. You will then be able to run reports, filtering by payment type, if you need to track electronic customer payments.

Note! For a fee, you can subscribe to QuickBooks Payments. This service has a Pay Now button you can include on emailed invoices so customers can instantly make payments. The service also allows you to accept credit card payments and bank transfers. In addition, your books will be automatically updated when the money is deposited into your bank account. There are monthly plan and transaction fees for this service.

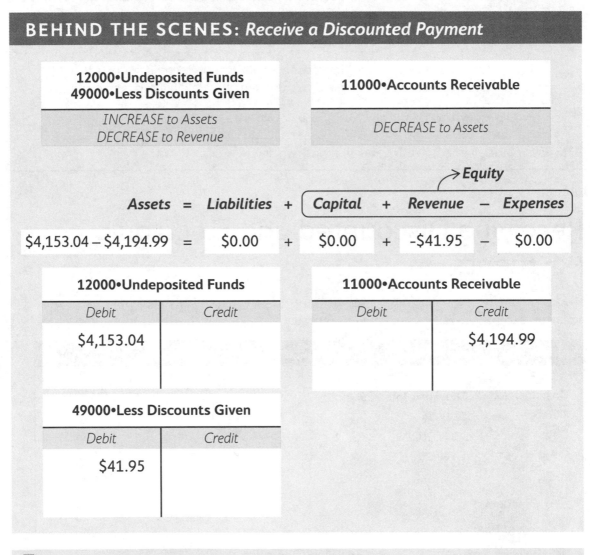

BEHIND THE SCENES: *Receive a Discounted Payment*

12000•Undeposited Funds 49000•Less Discounts Given	11000•Accounts Receivable
INCREASE to Assets *DECREASE to Revenue*	*DECREASE to Assets*

→ **Equity**

Assets	=	Liabilities	+	Capital	+	Revenue	−	Expenses
$4,153.04 − $4,194.99	=	$0.00	+	$0.00	+	-$41.95	−	$0.00

12000•Undeposited Funds

Debit	Credit
$4,153.04	

11000•Accounts Receivable

Debit	Credit
	$4,194.99

49000•Less Discounts Given

Debit	Credit
$41.95	

Customers→Receive Payments

In this exercise, you will record a discounted payment and process an electronic payment for Parrot's Paradise Resort. Sherwood Tours has made its payment within 10 days of the invoice, therefore qualifying for a discounted payment.

1. Click the **Receive Payments** task icon in the Customers area of the Home Page.

2. Follow these steps to receive the payment:

Ⓐ Click the drop-down arrow ▾ and choose **Sherwood Tours:29Mar22**.

Ⓑ Tap ⎡Tab⎤ and type: **4153.04**

Ⓒ Tap ⎡Tab⎤ and type: **031922**

Ⓓ Click **e-Check**.

Ⓔ Tap ⎡Tab⎤ and type: **2894**

Ⓕ Click **Discounts And Credits**.

Notice the Underpayment section on the bottom-left portion of the Receive Payments window. Whenever you enter a payment amount that is less than the total amount due, you will see this section. You can then choose how to handle the underpayment. You will leave this as an underpayment and apply the discount for early payment to the invoice to take care of the underpayment in this case.

3. In the Discount Account field, type: **Less Discounts Given**

4. Tap ⎡Tab⎤ and click **Set Up**.

5. Create the new income account:
   - Number: **49000**
   - Description: **Account to track discounts**

6. Click **Save & Close** and then click **Done** to return to the Receive Payments window.

   The discount has been applied so the underpayment information at the bottom left of the window is no longer displayed; the discount applied will be shown in the bottom right of the window.

7. Enter this in the Memo field: **Sherwood: Disc Pmt, 29Mar22 Tour**

BEHIND THE SCENES BRIEF

12000•Undeposited Funds DR 4,153.04 | 49000•Less Discounts Given DR 41.95; **11000•Accounts Receivable CR 4,194.99**

12000•Undeposited Funds has **increased** | 49000•Less Discounts Given has **decreased**; Accounts Receivable has **decreased**

Check Figure: 11000•Accounts Receivable $23,163.51

---

8. Click **Save & Close** to complete the payment receipt.

Deposit an Electronic Payment

Now you will record the deposit of the electronic payment into your bank account.

9. Click the **Record Deposits** task icon in the Banking area of the Home Page.

   The Payments to Deposit window appears. Note the 1 on the task icon, indicating one deposit is ready to be recorded.

Record Deposits

10. Click the **e-Check** you just entered and click **OK**.

11. Ensure the deposit will go to the **10300•Sailors Bank Checking** account and then click **OK** in the Setting Default Accounts window, if necessary.

12. Enter **031922** as the Date.

BEHIND THE SCENES BRIEF

10300•Sailors Bank Checking DR 4,153.04; **12000•Undeposited Funds CR 4,153.04**

10300•Sailors Bank Checking has **increased**; 12000•Undeposited Funds has **decreased**

Check Figure: Sailors Bank Checking $83,695.74

---

13. Click **Save & Close** to record the deposit to Sailors Bank Checking from Undeposited Funds where it was held prior to being deposited.

Refunds

There are many times when you may need to issue a refund to a customer and a variety of reasons for doing so, such as:

- For merchandise that has been returned

- For an order that was canceled

- To reimburse for an overpayment

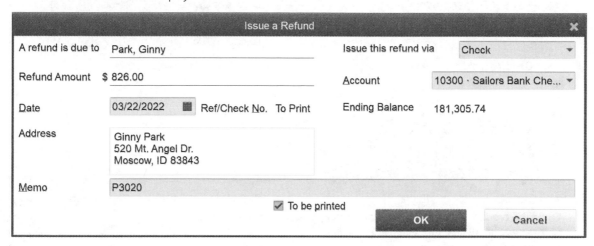

When you choose to issue a refund, the Issue a Refund window appears. Here you can enter the information for the refund check based on the amount from the invoice.

Credit Memos

To account for returned merchandise, you will create a credit memo. After a credit memo has been created, you can choose to apply the credit to an invoice (so the customer can apply it toward a future purchase) or issue a refund check or a return of funds to a credit card.

One-Click Credit Memo

If you need to refund a customer for a purchase that was made on an invoice, you can use a feature in QuickBooks that allows you to convert an invoice to a credit memo with one click. This can save you time as you will not have to retype the information for the new transaction.

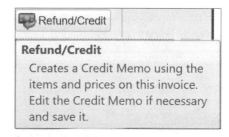

Convert an invoice to a credit memo by clicking the Refund/Credit button on the Create Invoices window ribbon.

Applying a Credit as a Part of a Payment

After a credit has been issued to a customer, you can apply it against invoices for future purchases. This is done through the Create Invoices or Receive Payments windows.

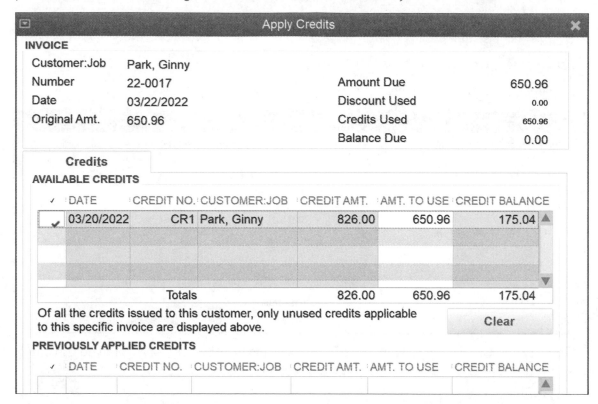

The Apply Credits window allows you to apply existing customer credits against an invoice.

Entering a Credit from a Vendor

If you're on the receiving end of a credit memo, you will need to enter it in your QuickBooks file as well. This is easily done through the Enter Bills window. After you have recorded the credit, use it when you pay bills to this vendor in the future.

DEVELOP YOUR SKILLS 7-9

In this exercise, you will create a credit memo and then apply the credit toward a future invoice. Ginny Park prepaid for a vacation and, because of a family matter, she has to cancel. You will create the credit for her to be applied to a future invoice.

1. Click the **Create Invoices** task icon in the Customers area of the Home Page.

2. Click the **Find** [Find] button on the ribbon.

3. Choose **Park, Ginny** as the Customer:Job and click **Find**.

   Invoice 22-0004 will display, as it's the only one created for Ginny Park.

4. Click the **Refund/Credit** button on the ribbon to convert the invoice to a credit memo.

   QuickBooks opens the Create Credit Memos/Refunds window with the information from the invoice displayed. This window looks like the Create Invoices window but does the opposite behind the scenes: It decreases Accounts Receivable and decreases the income account(s).

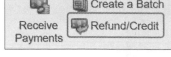

5. Create the credit memo:

- Date: **032122**
- Credit No.: **CR1**
- Tax: **Key West ST**
- Memo: `Park: refund Inv 22-0004`

Leave the Create Credit Memos/Refunds window open; you'll issue the refund from it in the next step. It may seem strange to enter a sales tax item when no tax is involved, but it's required to ensure non-taxable sales are reported correctly for each jurisdiction once the preference is turned on.

Apply a Credit and Create a New Invoice

Ginny will be rebooking a vacation on a different date, so you will now apply the credit to a new invoice, rather than issue a refund, and then create the new invoice.

6. Click the **Use credit to apply to invoice** button on the ribbon.

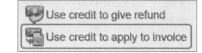

7. Click **OK** in the Warning window; click **Save & Close** to record the credit memo.

BEHIND THE SCENES BRIEF

40000•Lodging Sales DR 596.00 | 43000•Excursion Income DR 230.00; **11000•Accounts Receivable CR 826.00**

40000•Lodging Sales has **decreased** | 43000•Excursion Income has **decreased**; 11000•Accounts Receivable has **decreased**

Check Figure: Accounts Receivable $22,337.51

---

8. Click **Save & New** in the Create Invoices window and then create an invoice for the new vacation package:

Customer:Job	**Park, Ginny**
Date	**032222**
Invoice #	**22-0017**
Items/Quantity	**0.04 Fam Suite — Ocean/1** **3.03 Reef Excur/4** **2.01 Concert — Lawn/4**
Customer Message	**Thank you for your business.**
Memo	`Park: 5/2022 booking`

The product invoice template will be displayed since you used it last. You can use it for this invoice even though there are no inventory items being sold, as it affects the accounts the same behind the scenes. The product invoice template is just better designed to to deal with the sale of inventory items, especially if they are being shipped.

9. Click the **Apply Credits** button on the ribbon and then click **Yes** in the Recording Transaction window.

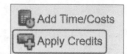

The Apply Credits window will launch. Look at how the credit has been applied to the invoice, and there is a remaining credit of $175.04.

BEHIND THE SCENES BRIEF
11000•Accounts Receivable DR 650.96; **40000•Lodging Sales CR 299.00 | 42000•Banquets and Events Income CR 71.96 | 43000•Excursion Income CR 280.00**
11000•Accounts Receivable has **increased**; 40000•Lodging Sales has **increased** | 42000•Banquets and Events Income has **increased** | 43000•Excursion Income has **increased**
Check Figure: Accounts Receivable $22,988.47

10. Click **Done** in the Apply Credits window and **Save & Close** in the Create Invoices window.

Inventory Reports

QuickBooks features many preset reports to help you efficiently manage inventory and sales as well as many other financial aspects of your company. These reports can be accessed via the Report Center or the menu bar. The reports in the Inventory category of the Report Center provide a great start for obtaining information about your inventory. If you don't find the exact report you need, you can create a custom one or search the reports for your industry submitted by other QuickBooks users, found on the Contributed tab. All of the reports in the Report Center can also be produced from the Reports option on the menu bar.

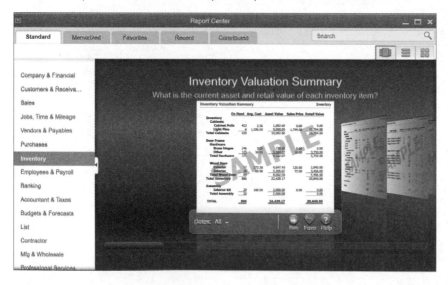

The Carousel View of the Report Center helps you find just the right report. Use the left ← and right → arrow keys to flip through the slides of the different reports in a category. Below the report slide are commands to set the report date range, run the report, mark it as a favorite, or search for help on it.

The report categories are the same in the Report Center and the Reports menu, though additional options are available via the menu.

Physical Inventory Worksheet

Periodically, it's important to physically count your inventory items to make sure what is "on the books" is actually what you have in stock. Many businesses do this type of procedure annually and adjust their books accordingly. QuickBooks provides a great report to aid in this process—the Physical Inventory Worksheet. It shows the name, description, preferred vendor, and on-hand quantity of each item you have in inventory. It also provides a column with blank lines, where you can record your actual count during a physical inventory count.

Parrot's Paradise Resort - Chapter 7
Physical Inventory Worksheet

Item	Description	Preferred Vendor	Quantity On Hand	Physical Count
1.101 Logo Tee	T-shirt with PPR logo	Keys Apparel	28	
1.201 Smores Pack	Basket of graham crackers, m...	Creola Catering	37	
1.301 Beach Hat	Floppy beach hat	Keys Apparel	40	
1.401 Water Bottle	32oz. logo water bottle	Carolina Coast Wholesale	30	
1.501 Sunscreen	Reef-safe 30 SPF sunscreen	Carolina Coast Wholesale	65	

The Physical Inventory Worksheet aids you in conducting a count of your inventory items to ensure the quantity on hand in QuickBooks matches the actual amount you physically have.

INVENTORY REPORTS AND THEIR PURPOSES

Inventory Report Name	What It Shows
Inventory Valuation Summary	The value of your inventory by item
Inventory Valuation Detail	The details of the transactions that affect the value of inventory
Inventory Stock Status by Item	The inventory items you need to reorder and the current number in stock of each item
Inventory Stock Status by Vendor	Similar to the Inventory Stock Status by Item report but arranged by vendor
Physical Inventory Worksheet	A printable worksheet used to count physical inventory or compare physical quantity to the number QuickBooks has recorded

Tracking Sales

The Sales category of the Report Center features reports and graphs that help you to analyze your company's sales. You can choose reports that show Sales by Customer, Sales by Item, and Sales by Rep. You can also view sales information by job if you have jobs set up for your company. The Sales Graph visually displays your sales by item, customer, and rep.

Note! Graphs are a great tool for data visualization. If QuickBooks doesn't provide a preset graph that works for you, you can export your data to Excel and create your graphs there.

QuickZoom Revisited

Recall that QuickBooks provides the QuickZoom tool that allows you to drill down to the source data found on a report. When you see the magnifying glass icon, just double-click to move to the next level down of data.

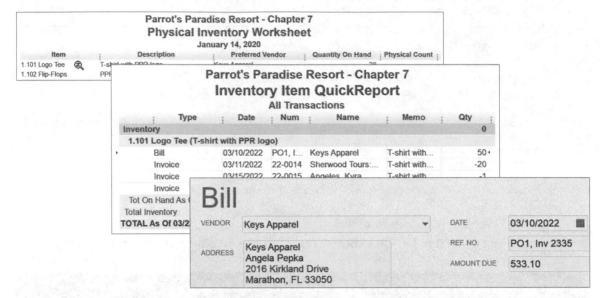

Double-clicking with the QuickZoom pointer on an item on the Physical Inventory Worksheet brings you to an Inventory Item QuickReport for the item. Double-clicking a transaction on the Inventory Item QuickReport opens the window where the transaction was entered.

Reports→Report Center: Inventory | Reports→Inventory

Reports→Report Center: Sales | Reports→Sales

DEVELOP YOUR SKILLS 7-10

In this exercise, you will run a report that will show the dollar value (based on purchase price) of the company's inventory.

1. Choose **Reports→Inventory→Inventory Valuation Summary**.

2. Tap a to set **All** as the date range for the report.

   The report will show the number of items you have in inventory as well as their asset value (cost) and retail value.

3. Close the Inventory Valuation Summary window, choosing not to memorize it.

Determine Which Items to Reorder

This report will help Jimmy to determine when he needs to order additional items.

4. Choose **Reports→Inventory→Inventory Stock Status by Item** and then tap a to set the date range to All.

When a checkmark is displayed in the Order column, you know it's time to place an order. In this case, the number of items on hand is greater than the Reorder Pt (Min) for each item, so no items need reordering.

	Pref Vendor	Reorder Pt (Min)	Max	On Hand	On Sales Order	For Assemblies	Available	Order	On PO	Reorder Qty	Next Deliv	Sales/Week
Parrot's Paradise Resort - Chapter 7 **Inventory Stock Status by Item** **All Transactions**												
Inventory												
1.101 Logo Tee (T-shirt with PPR logo)	›Keys App	15		28	0	0	28		0	0		10.3‹
1.201 Smores Pack (Basket of graham cracke...	Creola Ca...	20		37	0	0	37		0	0		1.9
1.301 Beach Hat (Floppy beach hat)	Keys App...	25		40	0	0	40		0	0		0
1.401 Water Bottle (32oz. logo water bottle)	Carolina C...	20		30	0	0	30		0	0		12.7
1.501 Sunscreen (Reef-safe 30 SPF sunscreen)	Carolina C...	35		65	0	0	65		0	0		0

5. Close the Inventory Stock Status by Item window, choosing not to memorize it.

Create a Sales Graph

Finally, you will create a graph that shows all sales by month and sales by customer.

6. Choose **Reports→Sales→Sales Graph**.

7. Click the **Dates** button on the toolbar and then type **a** and click **OK**.

8. Click the **By Item** button on the toolbar.

Note how the pie chart at the bottom changes.

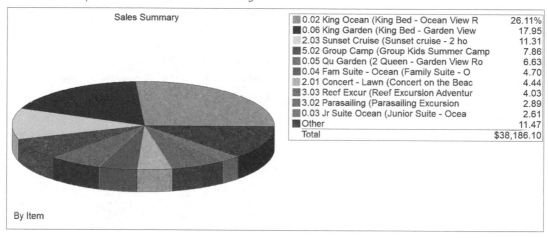

Notice the sales graph in the lower area of the window by item. There are so many items for the company that you will have to use QuickZoom to drill down to those classified as Other.

Note the Next Group button at the top right of the window that will allow you to see the remainder of the Other group.

9. Point to *Other* in the legend of the graph or on the dark purple pie slice and double-click to QuickZoom, displaying the detail of the Other grouping in a second graph.

10. Close the sales graph windows.

Tackle the Tasks

Now is your chance to work a little more with Parrot's Paradise Resort and apply the skills you've just learned to accomplish additional tasks. Continue with the same company file you've been using in this chapter so far. If you need to reopen the company file, the password is *Password1*.

Create an Inventory Item	Item Name: 1.102 Flip-Flops; Purchase Description: PPR logo flip-flops, various sizes; Sales Description: PPR logo flip-flops; Cost: 4.39; Sales Price: 25.00; COGS: 52900•Purchases - Resale Items; Pref. Vendor: Keys Apparel; Income Acct.: 41100•Clothing Sales; Asset Acct.: 12100•Inventory Asset; Reorder: 35; Qty on Hand: 0
Create a PO	On 03/16/2022 to purchase 50 of the flip-flops just entered as an inventory item
Receive Items	Receive the flip-flops with the bill on 3/20/2022, add a $15 shipping charge to the bill
Sell Items	Sell 20 pairs of flip-flops to Gator Tours on 3/22/2022, terms 2% 10 Net 30; terms are only for this invoice
Receive Payment	Receive an e-Check, 758946, from Gator Tours for both invoice 22-0009 and 22-0018 on 3/27/2022 for $5,588.75

Mary took advantage of the early payment discount (click the invoice to which you are applying the discount before clicking Discounts/Credits); deposit the payment to Sailors Bank Checking on the same day |
| **Run Reports** | Create a report that shows the inventory on hand and its value as of 3/31/2022

Create a report that shows the total sales for March 2022 |

Self-Assessment

Check your knowledge of this chapter's key concepts and skills using the Self-Assessment quiz here, in your ebook, or in your eLab course.

1. Non-posting accounts appear at the bottom of your Chart of Accounts.   *True   False*

2. QuickBooks Desktop uses the Last-In, First-Out (LIFO) method of inventory valuation.   *True   False*

3. The Show Lowest Subaccount preference helps you overcome the problem of narrow account fields in QuickBooks.   *True   False*

4. The Inventory Valuation Detail report tells you which items you need to reorder.   *True   False*

5. You must set up sales tax as an item to be able to include it on a sales form.   *True   False*

6. QuickBooks allows you to ship a package within the Create Invoices and Enter Sales Receipt windows using various services.   *True   False*

7. You can receive payments from your customers electronically.   *True   False*

8. The Sales Graph can display the total sales by item or by vendor.   *True   False*

9. When might QuickBooks NOT be a good tool for tracking inventory for a company?
    A. The company sells one-of-a-kind antiques.
    B. The company sells approximately 75 items.
    C. The company uses the average cost method for inventory valuation.
    D. The company's items are purchased at wholesale and sold at retail cost.

10. Which report do you run to determine the value of your inventory by item?
    A. Inventory Stock Status by Item
    B. Sales by Item Summary
    C. Inventory Valuation Detail
    D. Inventory Valuation Summary

11. What is the discount for early payment on an invoice for $100 with terms of 2% 10 Net 30?
    A. $10
    B. $2
    C. $4
    D. $20

12. What type of account is Purchase Orders?
    A. Inventory Asset
    B. COGS
    C. Inventory Expense
    D. Non-posting

13. Accounts Payable is _____ when you receive inventory with a bill.
    A. debited
    B. credited
    C. cleared out
    D. reconciled

Reinforce Your Skills

In the Reinforce Your Skills exercises, you will work with the company Donnell Construction, for which Colleen Donnell is the president. This limited liability company (LLC) provides general contracting services to residential and commercial customers, and you will assist Colleen in a variety of QuickBooks tasks. The company has decided to begin selling finished wood products, so you will help Colleen purchase, track, sell, and report on the inventory items. The password for all files unless otherwise stated is Password1.

REINFORCE YOUR SKILLS 7-1

Set Account Number and Sales Tax Preferences

In this exercise, you will set up a new Sales Tax Item for Cook County and set up inventory preferences, accounts, and items. The first steps are to turn on the sales tax preference and set up a sales tax item.

1. Choose **File→Open or Restore Company**.
2. Open **RYS_Chapter07 (Company)** or restore **RYS_Chapter07 (Portable)** and save it as: **RYS_Chapter07 Donnell Construction**
3. Choose **Edit→Preferences**.
4. Display the **Company Preferences** tab of the **Accounting** category.
5. Choose to **Use account numbers** and **Show lowest subaccount only**.
6. Click the **Sales Tax** category; click **Yes** to save changes.
7. Click in the circle to the left of **Yes** to indicate you charge sales tax.
8. Add a new sales tax item:
   - Sales Tax Name: **IL State**
   - Description: **IL State Sales Tax**
   - Tax Rate: **6.25%**
   - Tax Agency: **Illinois Treasury Department** (Quick Add the new vendor)
9. Click **OK** to add the new sales tax item.
10. Set **IL State** as the most common sales tax item and then click **OK** three times, closing the Preferences, Updating Sales Tax, and Warning windows.
11. Create an additional sales tax item:
    - Sales Tax Name: **Cook County**
    - Description: **Cook County Sales Tax**
    - Tax Rate: **2.75%**
    - Tax Agency: **Illinois Treasury Department**

12. Create a sales tax group called **Oak Park ST** using the **IL State** and **Cook County** sales tax items.

13. Choose **Edit→Preferences**, set **Oak Park ST** as the most common sales tax item in the preferences, and click **OK**.

Turn On Inventory Preferences and Set Up Inventory Items

Colleen Donnell wants to start offering custom wood products for sale to her customers. You will now set up QuickBooks to deal with inventory along with the new necessary accounts.

14. Choose **Edit→Preferences**.

15. Click the **Items & Inventory** category and then click the **Company Preferences** tab.

16. Click the checkbox to turn on **Inventory and Purchase Orders Are Active**.

17. Click **OK** to close the Preferences window and then click **OK** to close the Warning window, if necessary.

Create New Accounts

The next step is to set up separate income and cost of goods sold accounts for the product sales.

18. Choose **Lists→Chart of Accounts**.

19. Click the **Account** drop-down arrow ▼ and choose **New**.

20. Create two new accounts:

Account Type	Income	Cost of Goods Sold
Number	45000	55000
Account Name	Product Sales	Purchases - Retail Sales
Description	Gross revenue for product sales	Wholesale cost for product sales
Tax-Line Mapping	Schedule C: Gross receipts or s...	Schedule C: Purchases, cost of...

21. Click **Save & Close** and then close the Chart of Accounts window.

Create a New Inventory Item

Now you will set up a taxable inventory item that Donnell Construction will sell on sales forms.

22. Choose **Lists→Item List**, click the **Item** drop-down arrow ▼, and choose **New**.

23. Choose **Inventory Part** as the item type.

24. Create three new inventory items:

All items are taxable and will use 45000•Product Sales as the Income Account and 55000•Purchases – Retail Sales as the Cost of Goods Sold account:

Item Name	Wine Cart	Roll Top Desk	Hall Mirror
Purchase/Sales Description	`Solid oak 36 bottle wine cart`	`Solid oak roll top desk`	`Solid oak ornate large framed mirror`
Cost	225	489	94
Preferred Vendor	`Oak Park Oak Factory`	`Oak Park Oak Factory`	`Oak Park Oak Factory`
Sales Price	475	1,200	350
Reorder Point (Min)	10	4	12

Click Next after each of the first two items; Quick Add the vendor the first time you enter it.

25. Click **OK** and then close the Item List.

REINFORCE YOUR SKILLS 7-2

Create POs and Receive Items

In this exercise, you will help Donnell Construction order and receive inventory items. You will begin by creating a PO for Oak Park Oak Factory.

1. Choose **Vendors→Create Purchase Orders** and create the PO:

Vendor	`Oak Park Oak Factory`
Date	`030122`
PO No.	`22-01`
Vendor Address	`302 Hidden Lake Drive` `Oak Park, IL 60302`

Items/Quantities	`Wine Cart/15`
	`Roll Top Desk/7`
	`Hall Mirror/20`

Memo	`Oak Factory: PO 3/2022`

Type in the vendor address under the name in the Vendor field.

2. Click **Save & Close** and click **Yes** to make the address for the vendor permanent.

The inventory from Oak Park Oak Factory has arrived without the bill, so you will receive them into QuickBooks for Colleen.

3. Choose **Vendors→Receive Items**.

4. Choose **Oak Park Oak Factory** as the vendor and then click **Yes** to receive against an open PO.

5. Click the checkmark column to select the PO dated **03/01/2022** and click **OK**.

6. Change the date of the Item Receipt to **031022** and then click **Save & Close**.

Receive the Bill

The bill for the inventory has just arrived, so it's time to enter it into QuickBooks.

7. Choose **Vendors→Enter Bill for Received Items** and then choose **Oak Park Oak Factory** as the vendor.

8. Click the item receipt dated **03/10/2022** and then click **OK**.

9. Complete the bill:

Date	031522
Ref. No.	Inv 22031
Terms	Net 15
Memo	Oak Park: Inventory 3/2022
Shipping Expense (Expense tab)	85

10. Click **Save & Close**, click **Yes** to agree to change the transaction, and click **Yes** to permanently change the information for Oak Park Oak Factory.

REINFORCE YOUR SKILLS 7-3

Sell Inventory Items and Process Payments

Once the products have been entered into inventory, it's time to start selling! In this exercise, you will record an inventory sale for Hayden Popelka and a friend of Hayden's who liked her desk so much that she wants one as well. You will record the second sale without listing the customer, as you don't foresee completing any construction projects for her. Next, you will deposit the payments received into the company Checking account.

All sales will use the default tax rate for Oak Park.

1. Choose **Customers→Enter Sales Receipts**.

2. Choose **Popelka, Hayden** as the Customer:Job and then use this information to complete the sales receipts, taking care to click **Save & New** after the first sale and **Save & Close** after the second:

Customer:Job	Popelka, Hayden	[Select no customer]
Payment Method	**Check**	**Cash**
Date	**032322**	**033022**
Check No.	**3320**	[none]
Item	**Roll Top Desk**	**Roll Top Desk**
Customer Message	**Thank you for your business.**	**Thank you for your business.**
Memo	`Popelka: Desk 3/2022`	`Cash sale: Desk 3/2022`

3. Choose **Banking→Make Deposits**.
4. Click the **Select All** button and then click **OK**.
5. Ensure the date of the deposit is **03/30/2022** and *10100•Checking* is the account displayed.
6. Click **Save & Close**.

All payments that were waiting in the Undeposited Funds account have been deposited into the Checking account.

REINFORCE YOUR SKILLS 7-4

Produce a Report

In this exercise, you will create an inventory report that details the quantity and value of inventory on hand and use QuickZoom to make a change to an underlying form.

1. Choose **Reports→Inventory→Inventory Valuation Detail** and then type **a** to set the date range to All.
2. Using **QuickZoom**, go to the bill for the Oak Park Oak Factory.
3. Change the terms of the bill to **Net 30**.
4. Save the bill with the changes, choosing to have the new terms appear next time and become a permanent change to the vendor record.
5. Click **Yes** to refresh the report.
6. Close the report, choosing not to memorize it, and then close the company file.

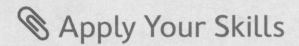 Apply Your Skills

In the Apply Your Skills exercises, you will work with a company called Wet Noses Veterinary Clinic. It's run by Dr. Sadie James, DMV, a small-animal veterinarian specializing in dogs and cats. Wet Noses has started buying and selling inventory, and you will manage the sales tax, purchase and receive inventory items, and sell products to customers. As needed, you will issue credit memos and discount purchases based on payment terms. The password for all files unless otherwise stated is Password1.

APPLY YOUR SKILLS 7-1 [QG]

Set Up Sales Tax and Inventory Items

In this exercise, you will set up sales tax and items to begin selling to customers.

1. Choose **File→Open or Restore Company**.
2. Open **AYS_Chapter07 (Company)** *or* restore **AYS_Chapter07 (Portable)** and save it as: **AYS_Chapter07 Wet Noses Clinic**
3. Open the **Preferences** window and set the preference to collect sales tax.
4. Set up a new sales tax item, setting it as the most common sales tax item:
   - Name: King County Sales Tax
   - Rate: 10%
   - Payable to: King County Treasurer
5. Choose to make all existing customers taxable but NOT all existing non-inventory and inventory parts.
6. Open the **Preferences** window and turn on the **Inventory and Purchase Order** feature and set the company to **Use account numbers**.
7. Open the **Chart of Accounts** and create a new income account named Inventory Sales and numbered 45000.
8. Add account numbers to these accounts:
   - **Money Market** – 10800
   - **AmEx-9944** – 21000

9. Create these inventory part items using **50000•Cost of Goods Sold** as the COGS account.

Item Name	Toothbrush	Chew Toy	Cat Collar
Purchase/Sales Description	Dog toothbrush and paste kit	The great indestructible ball!	Designer cat collar
Cost	2.49	1.71	5.00
Preferred Vendor	**Seattle Vet Supply**	**Bothell Pet Supply Co.**	**Take a Walk**
Sales Price	14.99	8.99	19.99
Income Account	**45000•Inventory Sales**	**45000•Inventory Sales**	**45000•Inventory Sales**
Reorder Point	15	20	10

10. Run the **Item Listing** report for detailed information about each item.

11. Click the **Excel** ⌐Excel ▾⌐ button and export this list to a new workbook saved to your file storage location as: **CH7_A1 New Item Listing**

12. Close Excel.

APPLY YOUR SKILLS 7-2 QG

Purchase and Receive Inventory Items

In this exercise, you will purchase and receive new inventory items in order to have them in stock.

1. Create POs for these three items:
   - 25 toothbrushes from Seattle Vet Supply on 07/01/2023
   - 40 chew toys from Bothell Pet Supply Co. on 07/02/2023
   - 15 cat collars from Take a Walk on 07/02/2023

2. You received all 25 toothbrushes from Seattle Vet Supply on 07/07/2023, along with the bill. Receive the items and enter the bill, making sure to receive against the PO you created.

3. You received 33 of the chew toys from Bothell Pet Supply Co. The rest are on back order, so you did not receive the bill yet. Receive these 33 items into inventory on 07/08/2023.

4. You received all 15 of the cat collars from Take a Walk on 07/12/2023, along with the bill. Included on the bill was a shipping charge of $12.95. Receive the items into inventory and enter the bill and create a 66500•Postage and Delivery account for the shipping charge.

5. On 07/14/2023 you received a bill for the chew toys you received on 07/08/2023, along with a shipping charge of $13.50. You then receive the seven chew toys that were on back order, along with a bill for the items with no shipping charge, on 07/25/2023.

6. Run the **Inventory Stock Status by Item** report for all dates to determine how many inventory items are currently in stock.

7. Click the **Excel** button and export this report to a new workbook saved to your file storage location as: **CH7_A2 Current Inventory Status**

8. Close Excel.

Sell Inventory

In this exercise, you will process sales of inventory items.

1. Sell two of the new designer cat collars to Jill Ann Tank on 07/14/2023. She pays with cash.

2. Sell seven toothbrushes and seven chew toys to King County Sheriff K-9 Unit on 07/15/2023. The Terms should be 2% 10 Net 30 and should not be made permanent.

3. Create an invoice for Stacy LiMarzi's cat, Reagan, dated 07/19/2023. The invoice should include a New Patient Exam, a FIV/FeLV test, a dose of Revolution-Cat/Small Dog for a cat, and a cat collar. Only the collar is taxable.

4. Run the **Sales by Customer Summary** report to show the sales amount for each customer for the month from 07/01/2023 to 07/31/2023.

5. Click the **Excel** button and export this report to a new workbook saved to your file storage location as: `CH7_A3 Sales by Customer Summary`

6. On 07/21/2023, King County Sheriff K-9 Unit has paid the invoice from 07/15/2023 in the amount of $180.96 with check 7796. Because the payment was received within 10 days, a 2 percent discount of $3.69 will be applied and should be reflected in the 47320•Less Discounts Given income account. (Make sure to click the invoice to which you want to apply the discount before clicking the Discounts/Credits button.)

7. Stacy LiMarzi has paid the entire amount of the invoice for her cat, Reagan, with check 448 on 07/22/2023.

8. Run the **Sales by Item Summary** report that shows which items sold the most during the month of July 2023.

9. Click the **Excel** button and export this report to a new workbook saved to your file storage location as: `CH7_A3 Sales by Item Summary`

10. Close Excel.

Issue Credits and Refunds and Manage Returned Inventory

In this exercise, you will issue a credit memo, process a refund check, and review inventory on hand.

1. Sampson, a King County Sheriff K-9 Unit dog, did not receive the nail trim he was charged for. Create a Credit Memo numbered RF1 on 07/14/2023 and use the credit to apply to an invoice. Nail trims are a service and therefore not a taxable item.

2. Run the **Item Listing** report to view Quantity on Hand for each item on the Item List.

3. On 7/19/2023 Jill Ann Tank returned one of the cat collars she purchased. Process a refund check that will be printed later.

4. Run the **Inventory Stock Status by Item** report for All dates to display total inventory on hand by item.

5. Click the **Excel** button and export this list to a new workbook saved to your file storage location as: `CH7_A4 Stock Status by Item`

   Notice the returned cat collar has changed the On Hand amount from 12 to 13; the item was added back into inventory.

6. Close Excel and the company file.

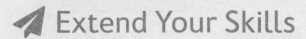

Extend Your Skills

Before You Begin: Open **EYS_Chapter07 (Company)** *or* restore **EYS_Chapter07 (Portable)**. The password is *Password1*.

You've been hired by Arlaine Cervantes to help her with her organization's books. She is the founder of Niños del Lago, a nonprofit organization that provides impoverished Guatemalan children with an engaging educational camp experience. You just sat down at your desk and opened a large envelope from Arlaine that contains a variety of documents; you also have several emails from her. It's your job to sort through the papers and emails and make sense of what you find, entering information into QuickBooks as appropriate and answering any questions in a word-processing document saved as: CH07_EYS_[LastnameFirstinitial]

Remember, you're dealing with random papers dumped out of an envelope and various emails, so part of your challenge is determining the order in which to complete the tasks.

- Sticky note from Arlaine: We're going to start selling items made by Guatemalan women. I want to see if we can set them up in QuickBooks. Our accountant said we should use "average cost" to track our inventory. Will we be able to track this in QuickBooks? (Explain your answer.)

- Packing slip and bill from Guatemalan Women's Art Alliance (GWAA) dated 8/14/2020. You've received the rest of the scarves and cosmetic bags, and a $45 shipping charge was included on the bill.

- Scrap of paper: If we can track inventory in QuickBooks, please set up "Traditional Guatemalan Scarf" as an inventory item; the cost from GWAA is $7.00 and the resale price is $20.00. Also, please set up two more inventory items to track "Cosmetic Bag" and "Handbag." The cost from GWAA for the cosmetic bag is $8.00 with a resale price of $18.00, and the cost for the handbag is $15.00 with a resale price of $35.00. As of 8/1/2020, order the following inventory: 50 scarves, 40 cosmetic bags, and 25 handbags.

- Handwritten invoice: 10 scarves and 5 handbags sold to Parrot's Paradise Resort, dated 8/16/2020, due 2% 10 Net 30.

- Packing slip from GWAA: Dated 8/5/2020 for receipt of 45 scarves, 30 cosmetic bags, and 25 handbags; the rest are on backorder.

- Photocopy of a check: Check 2007 from Parrot's Paradise Resort dated 8/23/2020 written for the total amount due and with a memo stating the company took advantage of the 2 percent discount.

- Scribbled note from Arlaine: Can you produce a report for me that shows the value of the inventory we currently have in stock? How about the number of each item?

8 Working with Balance Sheet Accounts and Budgets

In this chapter, you will work with additional accounts that are reported on a company's balance sheet: Other Current Assets, Fixed Assets, Current Liabilities, Long Term Liabilities, and Equity. These other balance sheet accounts allow you to track the various assets owned by your business, liabilities owed by your business, loans that span more than one year, prepaid expenses, and owner/shareholder investments in a company. You will also work with the QuickBooks budgeting feature.

LEARNING OBJECTIVES

▸ Create and use current asset accounts and transfer funds between accounts

▸ Track petty cash

▸ Create and use fixed asset accounts and items

▸ Record depreciation of assets

▸ Pay current liabilities and set up a long term liability

▸ Create and manage equity accounts

▸ Set up and use QuickBooks budgets

📁 Project: Parrot's Paradise Resort

Parrot's Paradise Resort has received an offer to prepay their business insurance for six months for a discounted amount. Jimmy has decided to take advantage of this offer and will use QuickBooks to track this insurance prepayment. Jimmy has also just purchased a new boat for the resort. You will set up the boat as a fixed asset and set up a long term liability account to track the loan.

One company task that comes due periodically is paying the sales tax collected from sales of inventory. This tax will be paid from the current liability account, Sales Tax Payable. You will also explore how to work with budgets in QuickBooks for Jimmy.

Working with Other Current Assets

Companies use other current assets to help them match their expenses to income within the same reporting period. This is a particularly important aspect when you use the accrual basis of accounting, which means that expenses are recorded when accrued, not when cash is paid. This means that even if you pay a six-month insurance policy or six months of rent up front, you must expense it during the month that it covers.

April 1st
Check written for six months of insurance $1,770

April 1st
$295 Insurance Expense
$1,475 Prepaid Insurance

May 1st
$295 Insurance Expense
$1,180 Prepaid Insurance

June 1st
$295 Insurance Expense
$885 Prepaid Insurance

FLASHBACK TO GAAP

Expenses are matched with revenues during the same accounting period. This allows for better evaluation of profitability and performance (how much did you spend to earn the revenue?).

Balance Sheet Accounts

Remember, the balance sheet accounts are the asset, liability, and equity accounts. You already know about many balance sheet accounts: bank, credit card, current liabilities (sales tax payable), Accounts Receivable, and Accounts Payable. Now you will focus on the remaining ones.

ADDITIONAL TYPES OF BALANCE SHEET ACCOUNTS

Account Type	Description	Examples
Other Current Asset	Assets you plan to either use or convert to cash within one year	• Prepaid Insurance • Security Deposit
Fixed Asset	Assets you do not plan to convert to cash within one year; they are usually depreciable	• Vehicle • Equipment
Other Current Liability	Funds your business owes and plans to pay within a year	• Sales Tax Payable • Payroll Liabilities
Long Term Liability	Liabilities (loans) you do not plan to pay off within the next year	• Mortgage • Auto Loan
Equity	The owner's equity in the company, whether it is a sole proprietor, a partner, or shareholders	• Owner's Equity • Retained Earnings

Tracking Supplies as an Other Current Asset

Some companies that operate using the accrual basis will track supplies in an other current asset account. However, because of the low cost of supplies, many companies simply expense them when they're purchased. When tracking office supplies using an asset account, the transactions will look similar to the ones used to track prepaid expenses. A Supplies on Hand account will hold the purchased supplies until they are used. Once the supplies are consumed, you'll transfer the amount used to the expense account that tracks supplies.

Here you see a purchase of supplies recorded in 12200•Supplies on Hand, an other current asset account. At the end of the accounting period, a transfer is made for the supplies that have been consumed to 64900•Office Supplies, the supply expense account.

Notes Receivable

Another asset you may see on the balance sheet is Notes Receivable. This account tracks promissory notes, or loans, you've issued to another individual or organization. They're classified as other current assets if they are to be repaid within a year or other asset if it will take more than a year for the loan to be repaid to you.

Notes receivable and accounts receivable are both assets for the company, with the difference being that accounts receivable are the funds owed by customers and notes receivable are based on a written promise to repay funds at some future date. The interest earned from a notes receivable should be recorded in 70000•Interest Income, an other interest account, if they're not earned through a company's normal business operation. So, unless you are running a company such as a bank or a consumer loan company, the interest is not earned as a normal business activity and therefore should not be tracked in a regular income account.

BEHIND THE SCENES: *Prepaid Funds*

13100•Prepaid Insurance 63300•Insurance Expense	10300•Sailors Bank Checking
INCREASE to Assets INCREASE to Expenses	DECREASE to Assets

→ **Equity**

Assets	=	Liabilities	+	Capital	+	Revenue	−	Expenses
$1,475.00 − $1,770.00	=	$0.00	+	$0.00	+	$0.00	−	$295.00

13100•Prepaid Insurance

Debit	Credit
$1,475.00	

10300•Sailors Bank Checking

Debit	Credit
	$1,770.00

63300•Insurance Expense

Debit	Credit
$295.00	

↗ Company→Chart of Accounts : Account→New : Other Account Types→Other Current Asset

↗ Banking→Transfer Funds

DEVELOP YOUR SKILLS 8-1

In this exercise, you will help set up QuickBooks to track the prepayment of insurance for the company, and then you will write a check to pay the rent for six months, April through September. The password for all files unless otherwise stated is Password1. *Leave the company file open unless otherwise instructed.*

1. Start QuickBooks 2020 and choose **File→Open or Restore Company**.

2. Open **DYS_Chapter08 (Company)** *or* restore **DYS_Chapter08 (Portable)** and save it as:

   DYS_Chapter08 Parrot's Paradise Resort

   First you will create a prepaid insurance account.

3. Click the **Chart of Accounts** task icon in the Company area of the Home Page.

4. Click the **Account** drop-down arrow ▼ at the bottom of the window and choose **New**.

Chart of Accounts

5. Choose **Other Current Asset** from the Other Account Types menu and click **Continue**.

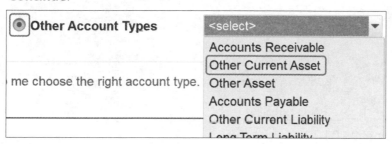

6. Create the new account:

Account Number	13100
Account Name	Prepaid Insurance
Description	Prepaid insurance holding account
Tax-Line Mapping	B/S-Assets: Other current assets

7. Click **Save & Close** and then close the Chart of Accounts window.

Write a Check to Prepay the Insurance

You will now write the check for the insurance payment, expensing the current month and placing the rest in the prepaid rent account.

8. Click the **Write Checks** task icon in the Banking area of the Home Page.

9. Follow these steps to write the rent check:

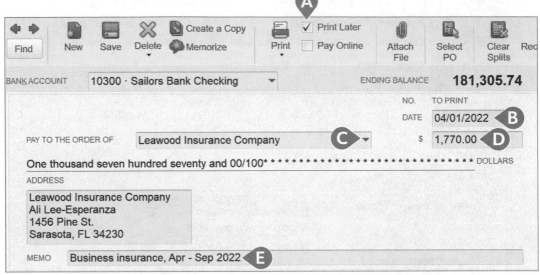

Ⓐ Click checkbox to choose **Print Later**.

Ⓑ Tap Tab and type: **040122**

Ⓒ Click the drop-down arrow ▾ and choose **Leawood Insurance Company**.

Ⓓ Tap Tab and type: **1770**

Ⓔ Tap Tab twice and type: **Business insurance, Apr – Sep 2022**

There are two separate line items that must be entered under Expenses to split the total amount of the check. The first line is the April rent that you will expense for the month, and the second line is the prepaid insurance account that will hold the remainder.

10. Follow these steps to enter the line items and complete the check:

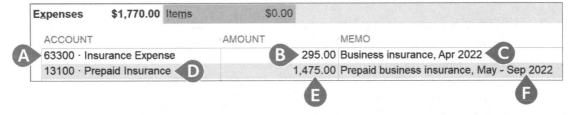

Ⓐ Click the drop-down arrow ▾ and choose **63300•Insurance Expense**.

Ⓑ Tap Tab and type: **295**

Ⓒ Tap Tab and type: **Business insurance, Apr 2022**

Ⓓ Click the drop-down arrow ▾ and choose **13100•Prepaid Insurance**.

Ⓔ Tap Tab and type: **1475**

Ⓕ Tap Tab and type: **Prepaid business insurance, May - Sep 2022**

BEHIND THE SCENES BRIEF

13100•Prepaid Insurance DR 1,475.00 | 63300•Insurance Expense DR 295.00;
10300•Sailors Bank Checking CR 1,770.00

13100•Prepaid Insurance has **increased** | 63300•Insurance Expense has **increased**;
10300•Sailors Bank Checking has **decreased**

Check Figure: Prepaid Insurance $1,475.00

11. Click **Save & Close**.

Paying Down Other Current Assets

After you place funds in an other current asset account, you will expense them when they are used. It's important to match expenses to income during the period in which they're used. Another term for this movement of funds from the asset to the expense account for an intangible asset is amortization. Amortization is simply the process of a balance decreasing over time. For instance, if you have a mortgage on a company property, prorating the cost over 30 years is amortization. You can accomplish this transfer in the register window of the asset.

Memorizing Transactions

There are many transactions (such as the expensing of other current assets) that you will repeat over and over. You can have QuickBooks memorize these transactions to increase your efficiency. When QuickBooks memorizes a transaction, you can choose:

• To be reminded about the transaction

• Not to be reminded and simply have it listed on the Memorized Transaction List

• To have QuickBooks automatically enter it based on a set schedule

By default, QuickBooks will choose for you to be reminded of the memorized transaction. You must make sure to choose one of the other options if you want the transaction to be listed or to occur automatically.

Recurring Transactions

When you are creating a new memorized transaction that you want QuickBooks to enter automatically for you, you can group it with other transactions you have memorized. Whenever you open QuickBooks, if you have memorized transactions, the Enter Memorized Transactions window appears with a list of those scheduled to be entered. This detailed list includes automatic transactions and helps you to stay on top of which transactions are slated to be recorded.

Memorized Transaction List								
TRANSACTION NAME	TYPE	SOURCE ACCOUNT	AMOUNT	FREQUENCY	AUTO	NEXT DATE		
Monthly	Group			Monthly	✓	06/01/2022		
⌐PP Insurance Txfr	General Journal	13100 · Prepaid Insurance	295.00					

Memorized Transaction ▼   Enter Transaction

The Memorized Transaction List keeps track of all your memorized transactions. Access it via the Lists option on the menu bar.

Using Memorized Transactions for Common Transactions

You can use the Memorized Transaction List for those transactions you complete on a regular basis. For instance, if you send an invoice to the same customer monthly, you can set up the invoice and memorize it. Then when you need to enter it, just double-click it in the Memorized Transaction List.

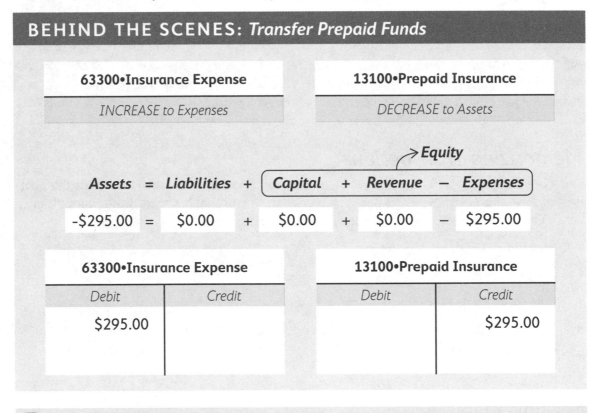

BEHIND THE SCENES: *Transfer Prepaid Funds*

63300•Insurance Expense	
INCREASE to Expenses	

13100•Prepaid Insurance	
DECREASE to Assets	

→ **Equity**

$$\text{Assets} = \text{Liabilities} + (\text{Capital} + \text{Revenue} - \text{Expenses})$$

$$-\$295.00 = \$0.00 + \$0.00 + \$0.00 - \$295.00$$

63300•Insurance Expense		13100•Prepaid Insurance	
Debit	Credit	Debit	Credit
$295.00			$295.00

Lists→Memorized Transaction List

DEVELOP YOUR SKILLS 8-2

In this exercise, you will record the first transfer of funds from Prepaid Insurance to Insurance Expense. After the transfer is set up, you will memorize it to occur automatically. Before you set up your first recurring monthly transaction in your Memorized Transaction List, you will create a group called "Monthly" for this list entry. You can then add new monthly transactions as they are created.

1. Choose **Lists→Memorized Transaction List**, resizing the window if necessary.
2. Click the **Memorized Transaction** drop-down arrow ▼ at the bottom of the window and choose **New Group**.

3. Follow these steps to create the new group:

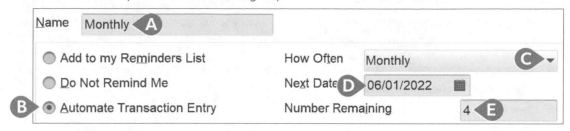

- Ⓐ Type **Monthly** in the Name field.
- Ⓑ Click to select **Automate Transaction Entry**.
- Ⓒ Click the drop-down arrow ▾ and choose **Monthly**.

  You will create the transaction to move $295 from Prepaid Insurance to Insurance Expense for May, which you will then memorize. So, the first automatic transaction will begin in June.

- Ⓓ Tap Tab and type: **060122**
- Ⓔ Tap Tab and type: **4**

4. Click **OK** to record the new memorized group and then close the Memorized Transaction List.

Record Next Month's Insurance Expense

5. Click the **Chart of Accounts** task icon in the Company area of the Home Page.

Chart of Accounts

6. Double-click the **13100•Prepaid Insurance** account and resize the window.

The register for the asset account opens. Notice that QuickBooks has registered an increase in the Prepaid Insurance account for $1,475.

7. On the next blank line, follow these steps to record a transfer of $295 from Prepaid Insurance to the Insurance Expense account for May:

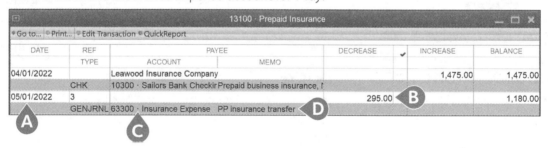

- Ⓐ Type: **050122**
- Ⓑ Tap Tab three times and type: **295**
- Ⓒ Click the drop-down arrow ▾ and choose **63300•Insurance Expense**.
- Ⓓ Tap Tab and type: **PP insurance transfer**

BEHIND THE SCENES BRIEF
63300•Insurance Expense DR 295.00; **13100•Prepaid Insurance CR 295.00**
63300•Insurance Expense has **increased**; 13100•Prepaid Insurance has **decreased**
Check Figure: Prepaid Insurance $1,180.00

8. Click **Record** at the bottom-right portion of the register window.

Memorize the Transaction

To avoid having to sit down at the computer at the first of each month to record this transfer, you will memorize it and choose for QuickBooks to include it in the Enter Memorized Transactions list.

9. Click anywhere within the two lines of the transaction you just recorded and choose **Edit→ Memorize General Journal**.

   This transaction is considered a General Journal Entry because it's a basic transfer between accounts.

10. Memorize the transaction in the Monthly group:
    - Name: `PP Insurance Txfr`
    - Choose **Add to Group**
    - Group Name: **Monthly**

11. Click **OK** to memorize the transaction.

12. Close the Prepaid Insurance and the Chart of Accounts windows.

13. Choose **Lists→Memorized Transaction List**.

    Look at the Memorized Transaction List and notice the new group and insurance transfer entries. If you do not continue to take advantage of prepaid insurance, you will need to delete this memorized transaction when the last transfer has been completed.

14. Close the Memorized Transaction List window.

Tracking Petty Cash

Most businesses keep cash around for small expenditures. This is known as petty cash. In QuickBooks, you set up Petty Cash as a bank account in your Chart of Accounts. You fund it by transferring money from another account or keeping cash back when you make a deposit.

End-of-Month Entry Option

Many businesses track petty cash expenditures at the end of the month with one journal entry. This text will show you how to track expenditures individually; however, you should be aware that they can also be handled in a different manner.

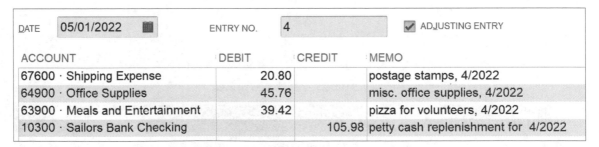

DATE 05/01/2022		ENTRY NO. 4		✔ ADJUSTING ENTRY
ACCOUNT	DEBIT	CREDIT	MEMO	
67600 · Shipping Expense	20.80		postage stamps, 4/2022	
64900 · Office Supplies	45.76		misc. office supplies, 4/2022	
63900 · Meals and Entertainment	39.42		pizza for volunteers, 4/2022	
10300 · Sailors Bank Checking		105.98	petty cash replenishment for 4/2022	

Here is a monthly journal entry to replenish Petty Cash. In this method, you don't credit Petty Cash but rather Checking. Petty Cash is affected only if the amount contained in the fund is changed or if you close the petty cash account.

Recording Methods

QuickBooks offers two methods to record individual petty cash expenditures:

- **Write Checks Method:** Choose Petty Cash as the account and use the Write Checks window to record your petty cash expenses.

- **The Register Method:** Enter petty cash expenditures directly into the Petty Cash register.

Tip! The register method allows you to enter your petty cash expenditures more quickly, as you can tab through it faster.

BEHIND THE SCENES: *Fund Petty Cash*

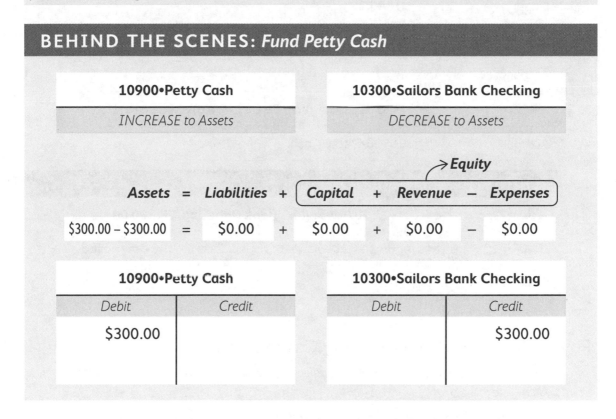

10900•Petty Cash
INCREASE to Assets

10300•Sailors Bank Checking
DECREASE to Assets

Equity

$$Assets = Liabilities + (\;Capital\; + \;Revenue\; - \;Expenses\;)$$

Assets	=	Liabilities	+	Capital	+	Revenue	−	Expenses
$300.00 – $300.00	=	$0.00	+	$0.00	+	$0.00	−	$0.00

10900•Petty Cash	
Debit	Credit
$300.00	

10300•Sailors Bank Checking	
Debit	Credit
	$300.00

DEVELOP YOUR SKILLS 8-3

In this exercise, you will create, fund, and use a petty cash account. You'll also memorize a transaction.

1. Click the **Chart of Accounts** task icon in the Company area of the Home Page.

   Note that, currently, there is no account set up to track petty cash.

Chart of Accounts

2. Click the **Account** drop-down arrow ▾ and choose **New**.

3. Choose **Bank** as the account type and then click **Continue**.

4. Create the new account:

   - Number: **10900**

   - Account Name: **Petty Cash**

5. Click **Save & Close**, choosing **No** in the Set Up Bank Feed window.

6. Close the Chart of Accounts window.

Fund the Petty Cash Account and Memorize the Transaction

Next you will transfer $300 from the Sailors Bank Checking account to the Petty Cash account.

7. Click the **Write Checks** task icon in the Banking area of the Home Page.

8. With Sailors Bank Checking as the account, complete the check and fund petty cash:

Write Checks

Number	**3805**
Date	**040122**
Pay to the Order of	**Cashier** (**Quick Add** it as a **Vendor**)
Amount	**300**
Memo	**Add funds to Petty Cash account**
Account	**10900•Petty Cash**

BEHIND THE SCENES BRIEF
10900•Petty Cash DR 300.00; **10300•Sailors Bank Checking CR 300.00**
10900•Petty Cash has **increased**; 10300•Sailors Bank Checking has **decreased**
Check Figure: Petty Cash $300.00

9. Click **Save & Close**.

Pay for Supplies Using the Petty Cash Register

You will now use petty cash to pay for miscellaneous office supplies and record the transaction in the Petty Cash register.

10. Click the **Chart of Accounts** task icon in the Company area of the Home Page.

11. Double-click the **Petty Cash** account in the Chart of Accounts window, resize the window, and record the charge to petty cash:

Chart of Accounts

Date	**041022**
Number	Delete the check number in this field.
Payee	**Nautical Wheelers Stationary** (**Quick Add** it as a **Vendor**)
Amount	**38.49**
Account	**64900•Office Supplies**
Memo	**misc. office supplies, 4/2022**

BEHIND THE SCENES BRIEF

64900•Office Supplies DR 38.49; **10900•Petty Cash CR 38.49**

64900•Office Supplies has **increased**; 10900•Petty Cash has **decreased**

Check Figure: Petty Cash $261.51

12. Click **Record** and then close the Petty Cash register window.

13. Close the Chart of Accounts window.

Writing Off Uncollectable Receivables

Almost every business writes off money owed as bad debt at some point or another and removes it from Accounts Receivable. QuickBooks allows you to do this via one of two methods: treating it as a discount or using a credit memo. Regardless of the method selected, you will need to create an expense account to which you will direct the bad debt. An example of when you may choose to write off receivables is when you learn that a customer's company has gone out of business. If you believe it's unlikely that you'll be able to collect for the amount due, you can decide to write off the amount owed by this customer as a bad debt.

 **Best Practice**

Your sales tax liability will not be affected if you treat bad debt as a discount, whereas it will be reduced if you use the credit memo method. This is why the credit memo is recommended when sales tax is involved.

FLASHBACK TO GAAP: MATERIALITY

Remember that when an item is reported, its significance should be considered.

Treating Bad Debt as a Discount

To treat bad debt as a discount (not recommended for a receivable associated with sales tax), you enter it as a discount in the Discount and Credits window launched from the Receive Payments window. Make sure, though, that you use the proper expense account for the bad debt (e.g., Bad Debt Expense).

Note! If you receive a partial payment from a customer, you can also choose to write off the extra amount in the Receive Payments window if you don't expect to ever receive the remaining balance.

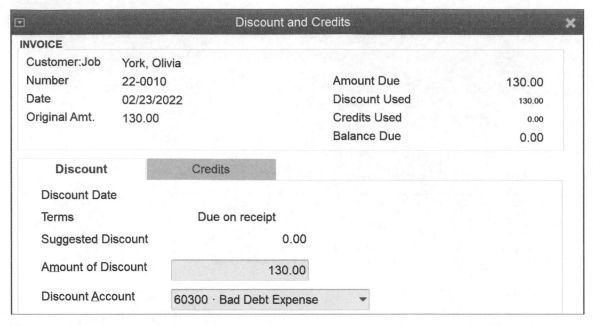

If you were to choose to use the discount method to write off the amount of Olivia York's invoice, you would launch the Discount and Credits window from the Receive Payments window and choose 60300•Bad Debt Expense as the account.

Using a Credit Memo to Write Off a Bad Debt

If you create a credit memo to write off a bad debt, you will use an Other Charge item to route the bad debt to the appropriate expense account (which will be debited). Accounts Receivable will be credited. You can include both taxable and nontaxable bad debts on a single credit memo. Using this method, the credit memo is applied to the original invoice.

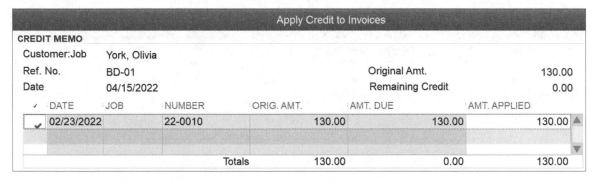

The Apply Credit to Invoices window appears after you create a credit memo. Here, Credit Memo BD-01 is applied to Invoice #22-0010 by checking the checkbox, writing off the bad debt.

Treating Bad Debt as an Allowance

Another way companies deal with bad debt is by treating it as an allowance. In this method, which follows the GAAP matching principle, a business can estimate what the bad debts will be as either a percentage of sales or percentage of receivables. This amount is written off by debiting Bad Debt Expense and crediting an Allowance for Doubtful Accounts account, which is a *contra account* because it's an asset with a credit normal balance. When an account is then determined to be uncollectable, the funds are removed from Accounts Receivable (it's credited) and the Allowance for Doubtful Accounts account is debited. There are potentially three sets of accounting entries you would encounter when using this method.

An Example

Let's look at how to handle bad debts using the allowance method. First, an adjusting entry is made to record the bad debt expense. In this example, $1,000 of bad debt was estimated for the fiscal period.

Bad Debt Expense		Allowance for Doubtful Accounts	
1,000.00			1,000.00

When a debt is determined to be uncollectable, it's removed from Accounts Receivable by debiting the allowance contra account. Here, the uncollectable debt is for $200.

Allowance for Doubtful Accounts		Bad Debt Expense	
200.00			200.00

The final accounting takes place only if the debt was collected after being written off. It's a two-step process where you first reverse the previous entry and then record receipt of the payment.

Accounts Receivable		Allowance for Doubtful Accounts	
200.00			200.00

Cash		Accounts Receivable	
200.00			200.00

In the next exercise, you'll account for bad debit using the credit memo method. The accounting that QuickBooks takes care of for you is shown here:

BEHIND THE SCENES: *Accounting for Bad Debt*

60300•Bad Debt Expense	**11000•Accounts Receivable**
INCREASE to Expenses	*DECREASE to Assets*

→ *Equity*

Assets	**=**	**Liabilities**	**+**	**Capital**	**+**	**Revenue**	**−**	**Expenses**
-$130.00	=	$0.00	+	$0.00	+	$0.00	−	$130.00

60300•Bad Debt Expense		**11000•Accounts Receivable**	
Debit	*Credit*	*Debit*	*Credit*
$130.00			$130.00

↗ Customers→Receive Payments

↗ Customers→Create Credit Memos/Refunds

In this exercise, you will use the credit memo method to write off the amount owed by Olivia York. The first step is to create an expense account for the payment.

1. Click the **Chart of Accounts** task icon in the Company area of the Home Page.

2. Click the **Account** drop-down arrow ▼ and choose **New**.

3. Choose **Expense** as the account type and click **Continue**.

Chart of Accounts

4. Create the new account:

   • Number: **60300**

   • Account Name: **Bad Debt Expense**

   • Description: **Expense account to write off uncollectible receivables**

5. Click **Save & Close** and then close the Chart of Accounts window.

Set Up the Bad Debt Item

The next step in writing off a bad debt using a credit memo is to create the item.

6. Click the **Items & Services** task icon in the Company area of the Home Page.

7. Click the **Item** drop-down arrow ▼ and choose **New**.

8. Create the new item:

Items & Services

Type	**Other Charge**
Item Name/Number	**Bad Debt**
Description	**Bad Debt Write-off** The amount is left blank here so you can fill in the correct amount for each transaction on the credit memo.
Tax Code	**Non** The Tax Code is set to Non, but you can change this on the credit memo for each receivable written off when necessary.
Account	**60300•Bad Debt Expense**

9. Click **OK** and then close the Item List window.

Create the Credit Memo and Apply It to an Invoice

Finally, you will create the credit memo to write off the bad debt and choose to which invoice(s) it should be applied.

10. Click the **Refunds & Credits** task icon in the Customers area of the Home Page.

Refunds & Credits

11. Click to remove the checkmark from **Print Later** on the ribbon and then complete the credit memo:

Customer:Job	**York, Olivia**
Date	**041522**
Credit No.	**BD-01**
Item	**Bad Debt** (click **OK** in the Warning window)
Rate	**130**
Tax	**Non**
Memo	**York: bad debt write-off, 4/15/22**

You will leave the transaction as nontaxable, as the original invoice did not include tax.

12. Click **Save & Close**.

An Available Credit window appears from which you can decide what to do with the resulting credit.

13. Choose **Apply to an Invoice** and click **OK**.

The Apply Credits to Invoice window appears, listing all open invoices for the customer. Be sure QuickBooks has checked the correct invoice to apply the credit to, in this case number 22-0010.

BEHIND THE SCENES BRIEF
60300•Bad Debt Expense DR 130.00; **11000•Accounts Receivable CR 130.00**
60300•Bad Debt Expense has **increased**; 11000•Accounts Receivable has **decreased**
Check Figure: Accounts Receivable –$175.04

14. Click **Done** in the Apply Credits to Invoice window.

The total amount owed by Olivia York has now been transferred to the Bad Debt Expense account.

Current Liabilities

Current liabilities are funds your company owes and expects to pay within a year. You've been collecting sales tax for your inventory sales, and now it's time to learn how to pay the collected tax (a current liability) to the appropriate tax agencies.

Notes Payable

Just as notes receivable track loans based on written promissory notes owed to you, notes payable are promissory note loans you owe to other entities. In this situation, you have promised to pay back the loan with interest by a future date. If the amount is to be paid back within a year, it's classified as a current liability; if it's due more than a year in the future, it's considered a long term liability.

There's a difference between notes payable and accounts payable. Accounts payable are amounts a business owes to an entity for products or services purchased from it and are usually due within a short time frame, whereas notes payable are based on promissory notes and typically due on a later date.

A Notes Payable Example: Construction Style

An example of a way that a construction company may use notes payable accounts is to track loans for specific homes being built. They will draw on the loans as the homes are built and repay them once the houses are sold.

Sales Tax Payable

When you bill a customer and collect sales tax, QuickBooks holds the funds in a current liability account. These taxes are never actually the property of your business, so you've been using a liabilities payable account as a place to store the taxes until it's time to pay them.

When you're ready to pay your sales tax, it's *imperative* that you do so through the Pay Sales Tax window. This ensures the proper liability account is affected behind the scenes when the payment is processed.

Warning! When you pay sales tax, you *must* use the proper procedure or you won't empty the Sales Tax Payable account behind the scenes.

The Sales Tax Liability Report

You can choose to run a Sales Tax Liability report to see what funds you're holding in your Sales Tax Payable account. This report will give you the values you need to file your sales tax return: total sales, taxable sales, nontaxable sales, and the amount of tax collected.

The Manage Sales Tax Window

The Manage Sales Tax window helps you manage all your sales tax activities and reports by providing links to all the tasks you'll be performing when working with sales tax, from setting it up to paying it.

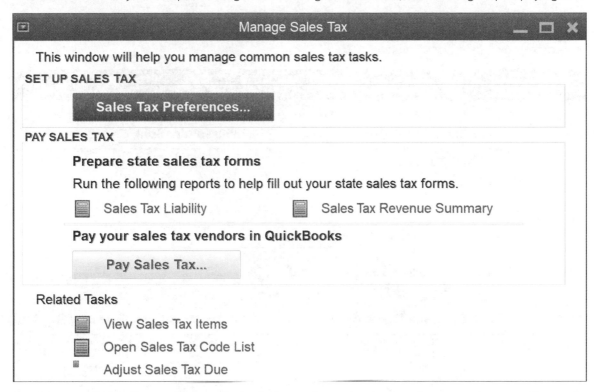

The Manage Sales Tax window includes links to the tasks you need to complete to effectively manage the sales tax you collect.

Sales Tax Adjustments

There are many situations that could result in an incorrect amount in the Pay Sales Tax window or on the Sales Tax Liability report. You may have charged a customer a tax rate for the wrong jurisdiction, or tax may have been charged for a nontaxable item. There could also be rounding errors, penalties, or credits/discounts that you need to consider. You can make an adjustment to the tax owed through the Pay Sales Tax window or by choosing Adjust Sales Tax Due from the Vendors menu. Don't use Sales Tax Payable as the "pay from" account. Instead, you should use these types of accounts:

- **For a rounding error:** You can set up a special account or use Miscellaneous Expense. Some businesses opt to create a special income account for a negative error or a special expense account for a positive error.

- **For a credit or to apply a discount:** Use an income account such as Other Income.

- **For interest due, fines, or penalties:** Use an expense account such as Interest Expense or Non-deductible Penalties.

If you make an adjustment to the Sales Tax Liability account, you will need to choose the adjustment the next time you pay sales tax in order to get the correct amount to pay.

Changing a Tax Jurisdiction

If a customer is charged sales tax for the wrong jurisdiction, you need to go back to the original transaction and choose the correct sales tax item or group. If you charged tax on a nontaxable item (or vice versa), you need to adjust the invoice or sales receipt where the sale was made. This may require you to issue a credit to the customer who overpaid or reissue the invoice/receipt (or a statement) to a customer who underpaid.

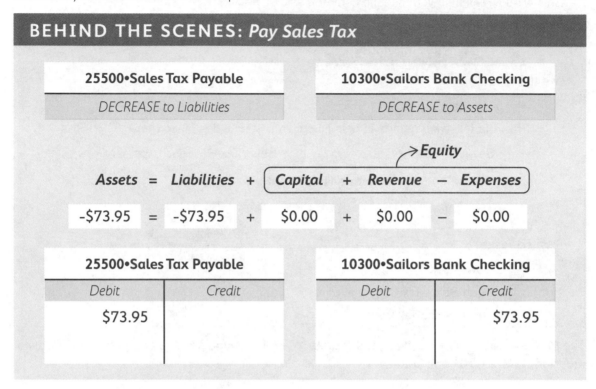

BEHIND THE SCENES: *Pay Sales Tax*

25500•Sales Tax Payable	
DECREASE to Liabilities	

10300•Sailors Bank Checking	
DECREASE to Assets	

→Equity

Assets = **Liabilities** + (**Capital** + **Revenue** − **Expenses**)

-$73.95 = -$73.95 + $0.00 + $0.00 − $0.00

25500•Sales Tax Payable	
Debit	*Credit*
$73.95	

10300•Sailors Bank Checking	
Debit	*Credit*
	$73.95

↗ Vendors→Sales Tax→Manage Sales Tax *or* Pay Sales Tax *or* Sales Tax Liability

↗ Reports→Vendors & Payables→Sales Tax Liability

DEVELOP YOUR SKILLS 8-5

In this exercise, you will pay the sales tax collected for March 2022. The first step is to run a report to determine how much sales tax is owed and to whom.

1. Click the **Manage Sales Tax** task icon in the Vendors area of the Home Page.
2. Click the **Sales Tax Liability** link in the middle of the Manage Sales Tax window.

Manage Sales Tax

3. Set the date range for the report:
   - From: **030122**
   - To: **033122**
   - Click **Refresh** on the report toolbar (resize the window to view the data)

	Total Sales	Non-Taxable...	Taxable Sales	Tax Rate	Tax Collected	Sales Tax Payable As of Mar 31, 22
Florida Department of Revenue						
FL Sales Tax	4,834.76	3,348.96	1,485.80	6.0%	89.15	89.15
KW Local Tax	4,834.76	3,348.96	1,485.80	1.5%	22.30	22.30
Multiple taxes for Florida Department of Revenue	-4,834.76	-3,348.96	-1,485.80		0.00	0.00
Total Florida Department of Revenue	4,834.76	3,348.96	1,485.80		111.45	111.45
TOTAL	4,834.76	3,348.96	1,485.80		111.45	111.45

Parrot's Paradise Resort - Chapter 8
Sales Tax Liability
March 2022

The information you need to pay and file your taxes is in the last column, which is $111.45. Notice that all the nontaxable sales are also included on the report.

4. Close the Sales Tax Liability report, choosing not to memorize it.

Pay the Sales Tax

From the report you just ran, you know that Parrot's Paradise Resort owes $111.45 as of 3/31/2022 to the Florida Department of Revenue.

5. Click the **Pay Sales Tax...** button in the Manage Sales Tax window.

6. Follow these steps to pay the taxes due:

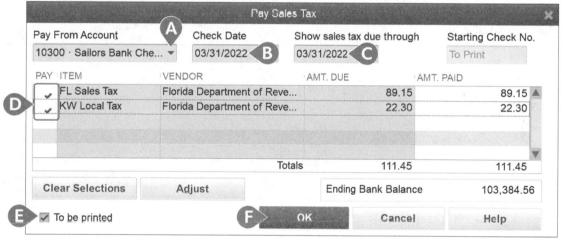

Ⓐ Click the drop-down arrow ▼ and choose **10300•Sailors Bank Checking**. Click **OK** in the Setting Default Accounts window, if necessary.

Ⓑ Tap ⌈Tab⌉ and type: **033122**

Ⓒ Tap ⌈Tab⌉ and type: **033122**

Ⓓ Tap ⌈Tab⌉ and then click to the left of each of the taxes to be paid.

Ⓔ Click to choose to print the check.

Ⓕ Click **OK**.

The Clear Selections button was the Pay All Tax button before you selected a tax bill. You could have clicked that button to select the two tax bills. In this situation, there are only two bills, which are payable to the same vendor. When you collect tax for multiple jurisdictions, make sure to choose the specific taxes you intend to pay. The liability check has now been entered into the queue of checks to be printed.

BEHIND THE SCENES BRIEF

25500•Sales Tax Payable DR 111.45; **10300•Sailors Bank Checking CR 111.45**

25500•Sales Tax Payable has **decreased**; 10300•Sailors Bank Checking has **decreased**

Check Figure: Sales Tax Payable $0.00

7. Close the Manage Sales Tax window.

8. Click the **Print Checks** task icon in the Banking area of the Home Page.

Print
Checks

> **Note!** If you don't see the Print Checks task icon, use the sizing arrow to enlarge the Home Page or choose File→Print Forms→Checks.

9. Use **10300•Sailors Bank Checking** as the account and **3806** as the first check number and then click **OK**.

10. Click the **Printer Name** drop-down arrow ▼ and choose a PDF driver (or a printer for physical checks), ensuring that **Voucher** is chosen as the check style.

11. Click **Print** and then click **Save** to save the PDF file in your default file location.

    When complete, QuickBooks will display a Print Checks – Confirmation window. Here you can choose to reprint any checks that did not print correctly or to troubleshoot the order in which your checks printed.

12. Click **OK** in the Print Checks - Confirmation window.

Fixed Assets

A fixed asset is one you don't plan to use up or turn into cash within the next year. A business uses fixed assets in a productive capacity to promote the main operations of the company. Fixed assets are depreciable, which means you don't expense the assets when you purchase them but rather over the useful life of the asset. The main types of fixed assets in QuickBooks are Land, Buildings, Leasehold Improvements, Furniture & Equipment, and Vehicles.

> **Note!** While land is a fixed asset for a company, it is not depreciable.

Setting Up Fixed Assets in QuickBooks

There is more than one correct way to set up your fixed assets in QuickBooks, so ask your accountant which method is preferred for your company. One method involves creating a fixed asset account for each major type of fixed asset and then an account to track accumulated depreciation for all fixed assets. Another method, which we will use in this book, involves creating a cost and accumulated depreciation account for each fixed asset. This results in the current book value of each asset being displayed in the Chart of Accounts and on the balance sheet.

When you enter fixed assets upon creation of a new company, you will debit the fixed asset account and credit the Opening Balance Equity account; this account is created by QuickBooks when the first balance sheet account is created so you have an accurate balance sheet from the beginning. If a loan is associated with the fixed asset, the loan amount will be entered in a Long Term Liability account and the difference in an equity or bank account.

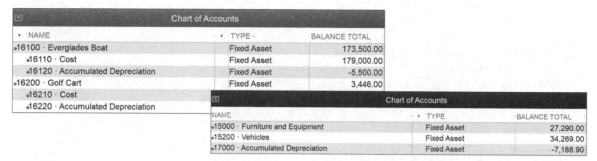

The top figure shows how to track fixed assets with individual cost and accumulated depreciation subaccounts, which results in the book value of the asset displayed in the parent account. The bottom figure shows a method of tracking fixed assets that uses one account to track accumulated depreciation.

Depreciation

Depreciation provides a business with a way to match income to expenses. A fixed asset is used to produce income over a period of time, and depreciation allows you to record the appropriate expense for each accounting period. Many small businesses record depreciation transactions just once a year, but they can be entered monthly or quarterly if the business produces financial statements for those periods.

> **FLASHBACK TO GAAP: MATCHING**
>
> Remember that expenses need to be matched with revenues.

Accumulated Depreciation

Each accounting period, a business records a depreciation expense for the fixed asset(s). These depreciation expenses accumulate in an account called Accumulated Depreciation, which is also a fixed asset account. Accumulated Depreciation is a contra account, which means it offsets the balance of the related fixed asset accounts by entering a negative amount so the book value is displayed rather than the original cost on the balance sheet report.

> **Note!** You need to consult with your accountant before entering depreciation, and often she will enter it for you at the end of the accounting period.

Fixed Asset Items

Fixed asset items provide a convenient way to track your fixed assets. After creating your fixed asset account and subaccounts, set up the fixed asset items through the Fixed Asset Item List. These items help you consolidate the important information about each fixed asset in a convenient place. In addition, your accountant can transfer information from your Fixed Asset Item List to the Fixed Asset Manager, if they use that feature of QuickBooks. Fixed asset items do *not* affect anything behind the scenes.

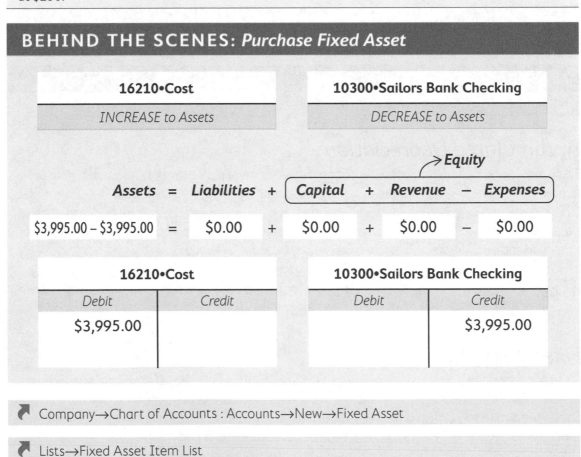

NAME	FAM NUMBER	PURCHASE ...	PURCHASE DESCRIPTION	ACCOUNT	COST	ATTACH
Everglades Boat		04/16/2022	2011 Everglades Boat	16110 · Cost	179,000.00	
Golf Cart		04/28/2022	2020 Club Car Golf Cart	16210 · Cost	3,995.00	

Item ▼ Activities ▼ Reports ▼ Attach ☐ Include inactive

Note! When you set up a fixed asset item, you indicate the account into which it's been entered. This doesn't enter it into the account or affect things behind the scenes. You must also complete the transactions to purchase the assets, pay for those assets, and set up the accumulated depreciation account to make sure it's tracked properly.

Accountant Tool: Fixed Asset Manager

If your accountant uses the Premier Accountant version of QuickBooks, fixed asset information can be pulled from your Fixed Asset Item list into the Fixed Asset Manager. This tool will help determine how to depreciate the fixed assets as well as the amount that needs to be posted back to the company file as an adjusting entry.

FLASHBACK TO GAAP: COST

Remember that when a company purchases assets, it should record them at cost, not fair market value. For example, if you bought an item worth $750 for $100, it should be recorded at $100.

BEHIND THE SCENES: *Purchase Fixed Asset*

16210•Cost	10300•Sailors Bank Checking
INCREASE to Assets	*DECREASE to Assets*

→**Equity**

Assets	=	Liabilities	+	Capital	+	Revenue	−	Expenses
$3,995.00 − $3,995.00	=	$0.00	+	$0.00	+	$0.00	−	$0.00

16210•Cost		10300•Sailors Bank Checking	
Debit	*Credit*	*Debit*	*Credit*
$3,995.00			$3,995.00

🏹 Company→Chart of Accounts : Accounts→New→Fixed Asset

🏹 Lists→Fixed Asset Item List

DEVELOP YOUR SKILLS 8-6

In this exercise, you will set up two new fixed asset items for Parrot's Paradise Resort—a used center console boat for diving and fishing excursions and a new golf cart. To begin, create fixed asset, cost, and accumulated depreciation accounts for the new assets.

1. Click the **Chart of Accounts** task icon in the Company area of the Home Page.
2. Click the **Account** drop-down arrow ▼ and choose **New**.
3. Choose **Fixed Asset** as the account type and click **Continue**.
4. Create the first three fixed asset accounts, clicking **Save & New** after each:

Account Number	Account Name	Description
16100	Everglades Boat	2011 Everglades 3500CC
The following are subaccounts of 16100•Everglades Boat:		
16110	Cost	Original cost of Everglades Boat
16120	Accumulated Depreciation	Accumulated depreciation for Everglades Boat

5. Create the remaining new accounts, clicking **Save & New** after the first two:

Account Number	Account Name	Description
16200	Golf Cart	Club Car electric golf cart
The following are subaccounts of 16200•Golf Cart:		
16210	Cost	Original cost of golf cart
16220	Accumulated Depreciation	Accumulated depreciation for golf cart

6. Click **Save & Close** and close the Chart of Accounts.

Set Up Purchase Vendors

Next, you will set up the two vendors from whom Jimmy purchased the fixed assets.

7. Click the **Vendors** [VENDORS] button in the Vendors area of the Home Page.
8. Click the **New Vendor** button and choose **New Vendor**.

9. Set up the two vendors, clicking **OK** after each entry:

Vendor/Company Name	`Pirate Boat Sales`	`Sunland Golf Equipment`
Full Name	`Mr. Tony Tarracino`	`Ms. Miriam Law`
Job Title	`Sales Captain`	`Sales Rep`
Main Phone	`(305) 555-1838`	`(561) 555-2222`
Address	`428 Black Street, Key West, FL 33040`	`1505 Clemson St., West Palm Beach, FL 33401`

10. Close the Vendor Center.

Create Fixed Asset Items

You've created the fixed asset accounts, so it's now time to set up the fixed asset items.

11. Choose **Lists→Fixed Asset Item List**.

12. Click the **Item** drop-down arrow ▼ and choose **New**.

13. Follow these steps to create the new fixed asset items:

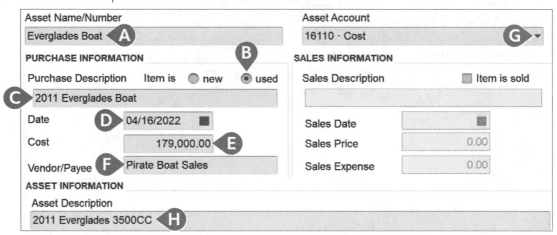

ⓐ Type **Everglades Boat** in the Asset Name/Number field.

ⓑ Click to choose **used**.

ⓒ Tap ⌷Tab⌷ and type: **2011 Everglades Boat**

ⓓ Tap ⌷Tab⌷ and type: **041622**

ⓔ Tap ⌷Tab⌷ and type: **179000**

ⓕ Tap ⌷Tab⌷ and type: **Pirate Boat Sales**

ⓖ Click the drop-down arrow ▼ and choose **16110•Cost**.

   Make sure you choose the Cost account for the boat!

ⓗ Tap ⌷Tab⌷ twice and type: **2011 Everglades 3500CC**

14. Click **Next**.

15. Create the second fixed asset item:

Asset Name/Number	**Golf Cart**
Item is	**New**
Purchase Description	**2020 Club Car Golf Cart**
Date	**042822**
Cost	**3995**
Vendor/Payee	**Sunland Golf Equipment**
Asset Account	**16210•Cost**
Asset Description	**2020 48V Club Car Precedent Golf Cart**

16. Click **OK** and then close the Fixed Asset Item List.

You did not affect anything behind the scenes in this exercise. You just set up the item that will be tracked and the account that will be used to track it.

Purchase Fixed Assets

The Everglades boat was purchased with a long term loan, whereas the golf cart was purchased with cash. You will account for the purchase of the golf cart in this exercise and the boat in Develop Your Skills 8-7.

17. Click the **Write Checks** task icon in the Banking area of the Home Page.

18. Enter the check:

Account	**10300•Sailors Bank Checking**
No.	**3808**
Date	**042822**
Pay to the Order of	**Sunland Golf Equipment**
Amount	**3995**
Memo	**Purchase of golf cart, 4/2022**
Account	**16200•Golf Cart:16210•Cost**

BEHIND THE SCENES BRIEF

16210•Cost DR 3,995.00; **10300•Sailors Bank Checking CR 3,995.00**

16210•Cost has **increased**; 10300•Sailors Bank Checking has **decreased**

Check Figure: 10300•Sailors Bank Checking $99,389.56

19. Click **Save & Close** and then close the Set Check Reminder window, if necessary.

Setting Up a Long Term Liability

Most companies have to take out a loan for a fixed asset; a Long Term Liability account is used to track a loan scheduled to take longer than a year to pay off. In this section, you will create a Long Term Liability account to track a boat loan.

The QuickBooks Loan Manager

QuickBooks provides a tool for you to track your loans, similar to the Fixed Asset Item List for tracking your fixed assets. The Loan Manager allows you to set up loans based on information you've entered in a Long Term Liability or Other Current Liability account. The Loan Manager tracks the principal and interest payments without having to set up separate amortization schedules. You can also use the Loan Manager to compare different loan scenarios.

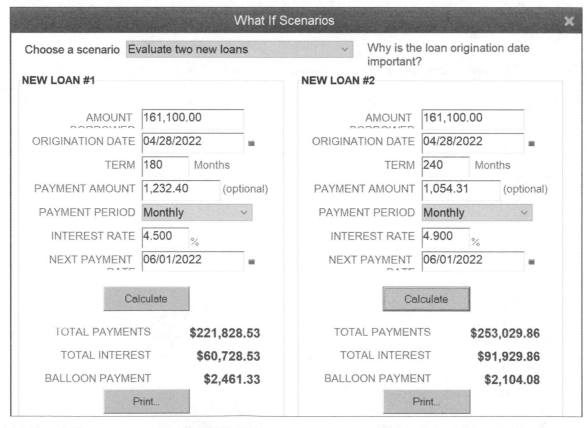

The Loan Manager includes a "what if" tool that allows you to see whether you can afford a loan and to compare multiple loan options. In this case, review the comparison between a 15-year vs. a 20-year loan for the Everglades boat.

There are a number of items you should prepare before you set up a loan in the Loan Manager:

- **Set up your accounts.** Set up any liability (e.g., 26000•Loan – Everglades Boat), expense (e.g., 63400•Interest Expense), and escrow (if required) accounts that will be affected by the loan.

- **Set up the vendor, if not already in your Vendor List.**

- **Check previous transactions.** If you're working with an existing loan, confirm that all the transactions related to it are entered into QuickBooks.

- **Gather your loan documents.** Have all your original loan documents handy so you properly enter the opening balance and other information.

Once all transactions are up to date and the loan is entered into the Loan Manager, you will be able to record future loan payments in the Set Up Payment window.

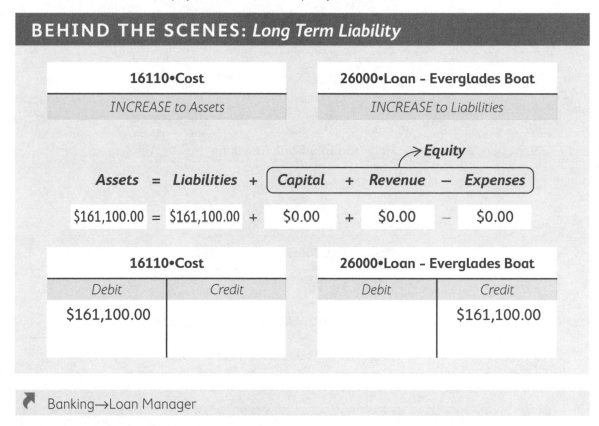

BEHIND THE SCENES: *Long Term Liability*

16110•Cost	26000•Loan – Everglades Boat
INCREASE to Assets	INCREASE to Liabilities

$$\text{Assets} = \text{Liabilities} + \overbrace{(\text{Capital} + \text{Revenue} - \text{Expenses})}^{\text{Equity}}$$

$$\$161,100.00 = \$161,100.00 + \$0.00 + \$0.00 - \$0.00$$

16110•Cost		26000•Loan – Everglades Boat	
Debit	Credit	Debit	Credit
$161,100.00			$161,100.00

Banking→Loan Manager

DEVELOP YOUR SKILLS 8-7

In this exercise, you will set up the long term loan account for the Everglades boat, issue a down payment, fund the loan, and set up the loan in the Loan Manager. First, you will create the new liability account.

1. Click the **Chart of Accounts** task icon in the Company area of the Home Page.
2. Click the **Account** drop-down arrow ▾ and choose **New**.
3. Choose **Long Term Liability** from the Other Account Types menu and click **Continue**.

Chart of Accounts

4. Create the long term liability account:

Number	26000
Account Name	Loan - Everglades Boat
Description	Sailors Bank loan for 2011 Everglades boat
Account Number	5493-7715

Note that the Tax-Line Mapping information was automatically filled in for you.

5. Click **Save & Close** to record the new account and then close the Chart of Accounts window.

Write a Check for the Down Payment

Jimmy made a 10 percent down payment on the boat, so you will write the check for that next.

6. Click the **Write Checks** task icon in the Banking area of the Home Page.

Write
Checks

7. Create the check for the down payment:

Bank Account	10300•Sailors Bank Checking
Number	3809
Date	041622
Pay to the Order of	Pirate Boat Sales
Amount	17900
Memo	Down payment, 2011 Everglades boat
Account	16100•Everglades Boat:16110•Cost

Make sure to choose the Cost subaccount for Everglades Boat!

BEHIND THE SCENES BRIEF

16110•Cost DR 17,900.00; **10300•Sailors Bank Checking CR 17,900.00**

16110•Cost has **increased**; 10300•Sailors Bank Checking has **decreased**

Check Figure: Sailors Bank Checking $81,489.56

---

8. Click **Save & Close** to record the transaction.

Fund the Long Term Liability Account

Sailors Bank Checking has issued the funds on your behalf to Pirate Boat Sales for the financed amount. You will fund the loan next.

9. Click the **Chart of Accounts** task icon in the Company area of the Home Page.

10. Double-click the **26000•Loan – Everglades Boat** account and then resize the window.

Chart of Accounts

The register window for the liability account will appear.

11. Record the funding of the loan:

Date	**041622**
Increase	**161100**
Account	**16100•Everglades Boat: 16110•Cost**
Memo	**Funding of Everglades boat loan**

BEHIND THE SCENES BRIEF
16110•Cost DR 161,100.00; **26000•Loan – Everglades Boat CR 161,100.00**
16110•Cost has **increased**; 26000•Loan – Everglades Boat has **increased**
Check Figure: 16100•Cost $179,000.00

12. Click **Record** and close the register window; close the Chart of Accounts window.

Enter a Loan in the Loan Manager

You will enter a 15-year loan from the bank. Some students have had issues with the Loan Manager. If this happens to you, you can skip the exercise and continue with the rest of the chapter.

13. Choose **Banking→Loan Manager**.

If the Feature Update window appears, you'll need to reboot your computer before you can use the Loan Manager. You can continue using other features of QuickBooks if you don't reboot.

14. Click the **Add a Loan...** button.

15. Enter the account information for the loan:

Account Name	**Loan – Everglades Boat**
Lender	**Sailors Bank**
Origination Date	**041622**
Original Amount	**161100**
Term	(Choose **Months**.) **180**

16. Click **Next** and enter the payment information:

- Due Date of Next Payment: **060122**
- Payment Amount: **1232.40**

See your accountant, use a loan calculator, or complete a what-if scenario prior to this step to determine affordability of monthly payments (principal + interest) based on criteria such as origination date, loan amount, interest rate, and term. It can also be used to evaluate two loans to determine the best option.

17. Click **Next** and enter the interest information:

Interest Rate	**4.5**
Payment Account	**Sailors Bank Checking**
Interest Expense Account	**Interest Expense**

The loan is now set up in the Loan Manager, ready for you to track. Due to the dates of this exercise being in the future, you will see the loan in the list with a zero balance for the amount, and the payment schedule won't display since it is based off of your computer clock.

18. Click **Finish** and then close the Loan Manager window.

Equity Accounts

Equity accounts reflect the net worth of a company. In Appendix A, "Need-To-Know Accounting," notice the accounting equation teaches that the sum of the equity accounts is equal to assets (what you own) less liabilities (what you owe):

$$Equity = Assets - Liabilities$$

An equity account has a credit normal balance. It represents how viable your company is, as it shows how much you would have left if you sold all your assets and then paid off the liabilities.

Owner's Equity / Capital Stock

In a sole proprietorship, the equity is what the owner has invested in the company. In a corporation, the equity is what the shareholders have invested in the company (capital stock). An owner's investment occurs when an owner deposits funds or other assets into the company or shareholders purchase stock. An owner's withdrawal of funds from the company is known as a draw; if it's a corporation, you will see shareholder distributions.

Retained Earnings

At the end of the fiscal year, a business will show either a net income or a net loss. When the books are closed, this amount is transferred into the Retained Earnings account to clear out all income and expense accounts for the next year. When the fiscal year ends, QuickBooks automatically makes this transfer.

Opening Balance Equity

QuickBooks creates the Opening Balance Equity account when you first create your company. As you enter opening balances into the accounts, QuickBooks uses Opening Balance Equity as the offset account so you can have a working balance sheet right from the beginning. You may need to enter a transfer between accounts if there's a balance in the Opening Balance Equity account after all your new accounts are entered into QuickBooks.

There are other times when QuickBooks may use the Opening Balance Equity account and an adjustment must be made. For instance, when you set QuickBooks up to track inventory and enter a beginning number of inventory items on hand, you debit 12100•Inventory Asset, and 30000•Opening Balance Equity is credited behind the scenes. Talk to your accountant about how to deal with equity transactions for your unique company.

FLASHBACK TO GAAP: BUSINESS ENTITY

Remember that the first assumption of GAAP is that the business is separate from the owners and from other businesses. Business revenues and expenses should be kept separate from the business owner's personal expenses.

BEHIND THE SCENES: *Equity Draw*

31400•Shareholder Distributions	10300•Sailors Bank Checking
DECREASE to Capital	DECREASE to Assets

→ **Equity**

$$Assets\ =\ Liabilities\ +\ (\ Capital\ +\ Revenue\ -\ Expenses\ )$$

$$-\$20,000.00\ =\ \$0.00\ +\ -\$20,000.00\ +\ \$0.00\ -\ \$0.00$$

31400•Shareholder Distributions		10300•Sailors Bank Checking	
Debit	Credit	Debit	Credit
$20,000.00			$20,000.00

 Banking→Make Deposits [use Owner's Equity in the From Account field]

 Banking→Write Checks

Jimmy and his sister, Laurie, are stockholders in Parrot's Paradise Resort. In this exercise, you will record distributions to them.

1. Click the **Write Checks** task icon in the Banking area of the Home Page.

2. Produce shareholder distribution checks on **5/31/2022** for Jimmy and Laurie (both checks are drawn from **10300·Sailors Bank Checking** and will be printed later), clicking **Save & New** after the first:

Write Checks

Pay to the Order of (add both to Other Names)	Jimmy Parrot	Laurie Parrot
Amount	10000	10000
Memo	Shareholder distribution, 5/31/2022	Shareholder distribution, 5/31/2022
Account	31400·Shareholder Distributions	31400·Shareholder Distributions

BEHIND THE SCENES BRIEF

31400·Shareholder Distributions DR 20,000.00; **10300·Sailors Bank Checking CR 20,000.00**

31400·Shareholder Distributions has **decreased**; 10300·Sailors Bank Checking has **decreased**

Check Figure: Sailors Bank Checking $61,489.56

3. Click **Save & Close**.

Budgeting and Predicting in QuickBooks

QuickBooks includes a budgeting feature that allows you to create account-based budgets for Balance Sheet and Profit & Loss accounts. Budgets can be created based on a previous year's budget or from scratch—or, if you've been using QuickBooks for a year, the actual figures from the previous year. After you've created a budget or a forecast, you will run a report to view the information. QuickBooks provides several reports that will allow you to view the information in your budgets and forecasts.

BUDGET & FORECAST REPORTS AND THEIR PURPOSES

Budget Report Name	What It Tells You
Budget Overview	Company's projected income and expenses for each month
Budget vs. Actual	Actual income and expenses compared to budgeted amounts for the company as a whole
Profit & Loss Budget Performance	Actual income and expenses compared to budgeted amounts for the current month and year

(cont.)

BUDGET & FORECAST REPORTS AND THEIR PURPOSES (cont.)	
Budget vs. Actual Graph	Income and expenses as over or under budget
Forecast Overview	Company's forecasted income and expenses for each month
Forecast vs. Actual	Actual income and expenses compared to what has been forecasted

Predicting the Future Cash Flow

In addition to budgets, QuickBooks supplies you with a Cash Flow Projector feature that assists with making future predictions. It allows you to conduct what-if analyses as well as look at future cash flow or revenue. Projections can be based on actual figures from the last year or from scratch.

The Balance Sheet in Review

In this chapter, you've worked with a variety of asset, liability, and equity accounts, collectively known as the balance sheet accounts. The balance sheet is a report that shows the balances of all these accounts as of a specific date. Now that you've set up the majority of the balance sheet accounts, you'll run a report to take a look at how Parrot's Paradise Resort's books are shaping up.

Parrot's Paradise Resort - Chapter 8
Balance Sheet
As of May 31, 2022

	May 31, 22
▾ASSETS	
▾Current Assets	
▾Checking/Savings	
10100 · Money Market	37,302.35
10200 · Payroll Checking	100,000.00
10300 · Sailors Bank Checking	61,489.56
10400 · Sailors Bank Savings	347,091.49
10900 · Petty Cash	261.51
Total Checking/Savings	546,224.91
▾Accounts Receivable	
11000 · Accounts Receivable	-175.04
Total Accounts Receivable	-175.04
▾Other Current Assets	
12100 · Inventory Asset	1,154.72
13100 · Prepaid Insurance	1,180.00
Total Other Current Assets	2,334.72
Total Current Assets	548,384.59
▾Fixed Assets	
▾16100 · Everglades Boat	
16110 · Cost	179,000.00
Total 16100 · Everglades Boat	179,000.00
▾16200 · Golf Cart	
16210 · Cost	3,995.00
Total 16200 · Golf Cart	3,995.00
Total Fixed Assets	182,995.00
TOTAL ASSETS	**731,379.59**

▾LIABILITIES & EQUITY	
▾Liabilities	
▾Current Liabilities	
▾Accounts Payable	
20000 · Accounts Payable	468.70
Total Accounts Payable	468.70
▾Credit Cards	
21400 · Visa-4545	227.20
Total Credit Cards	227.20
Total Current Liabilities	695.90
▾Long Term Liabilities	
26000 · Loan - Everglades Boat	161,100.00
Total Long Term Liabilities	161,100.00
Total Liabilities	161,795.90
▾Equity	
30000 · Opening Balance Equity	549,860.32
31400 · Shareholder Distributio...	-20,000.00
Net Income	39,723.37
Total Equity	569,583.69
TOTAL LIABILITIES & EQUITY	**731,379.59**

With the addition of the accounts from this chapter, the Balance Sheet report will now break assets and liabilities down by current and fixed/long term.

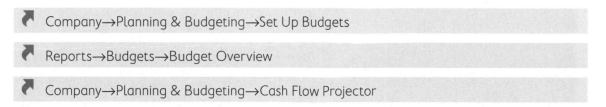

Company→Planning & Budgeting→Set Up Budgets

Reports→Budgets→Budget Overview

Company→Planning & Budgeting→Cash Flow Projector

In this exercise, you will create a budget for 2023.

1. Choose **Company→Planning & Budgeting→Set Up Budgets**.

2. Set **2023** as the year and **Profit and Loss** as the type and then click **Next**.

3. Ensure that **No Additional Criteria** is selected and then click **Next**.

   Your budget will be based on all Customers:Jobs, so you don't need to provide additional criteria at this time.

4. Ensure **Create Budget from Scratch** is selected and then click **Finish**.

   A blank budget displays with all your income and expense accounts included. To populate the budget, you will enter a monthly amount in the January column for each account and then copy the amount across. The amounts are averages in this example, but when creating your own company's budget, you can choose to enter a different amount for each month.

   Warning! If you press ⌷Enter⌷, you'll leave the Set Up Budgets screen. To bring it back, choose Company→Planning & Budgeting→Set Up Budgets.

5. Click in the **JAN23** column of the 40000•Lodging Sales row and then type **45000** and click **Copy Across**.

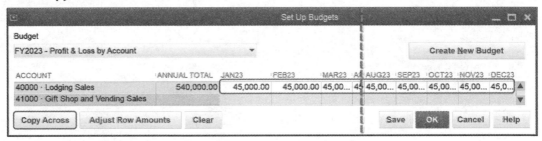

   When you click Copy Across, the amount fills in for all months of 2023.

6. Click **Save** to update the budget with what you've entered so far.

7. Enter the January 2023 income amounts, making sure to click **Copy Across** after each:

Gift Shop and Vending Sales (all subaccounts are grouped)	10000	Food and Beverage Sales	0
Banquets and Events Income	15000	Spa Income	6000
Excursion Income	10000	Returned Check Charges	120
Rental Income	5000	Less Discounts Given	100
Camp Income	5000		

8. Enter the January 2023 COGS and expense amounts, clicking **Copy Across** after each:

Cost of Goods Sold	0	Interest Expense	600
Linens and Lodging Supplies	4000	Landscaping and Groundskeeping	2000
Merchant Account Fees	2000	Meals and Entertainment	200
Purchases – Resale Items	2000	Office Supplies	300
Advertising/Promotion	500	Payroll Expense	35000
Automobile Expense	3500	Professional Fees	50
Bad Debt Expense	500	Repairs and Maintenance	1300
Bank Service Charges	20	Service Supplies	2000
Business Licenses and Permits	100	Shipping Expense	75
Computer and Internet (all subaccounts are grouped)	400	Small Tools and Equipment	500
Depreciation Expense	10000	Subcontractor Expense	3000
Dues and Subscriptions	100	Telephone Expense	950
Event Entertainment	2500	Uniforms	500
Event Rentals	1000	Utilities (all subaccounts are grouped)	2500
Insurance Expense	500		

9. Click **Save** and then click **OK**.

Produce a Budget Report

Now that the budget for 2023 has been produced, Jimmy would like to see a report showing an overview of it.

10. Choose **Reports→Budgets & Forecasts→Budget Overview**.

A Budget Report wizard will help you create the report you desire.

11. Click **Next** two times and then click **Finish**.

The budget for 2023 will be displayed by month.

12. Scroll down and note whether there is a net income or loss projected for each month.

You will see that there is a $20,125 net income budgeted per month.

13. Close the budget report window.

Produce a Balance Sheet Report

Jimmy has asked for a balance sheet report that displays all the balance sheet accounts you've entered.

14. Choose **Reports→Company & Financial→Balance Sheet Standard**.

15. Tap ⌈Tab⌉ and type: **053122**

16. Click **Refresh**.

You will see a balance sheet report breaking down assets by current and fixed and liabilities by current and long term.

17. Close the report, choosing not to memorize it.

Tackle the Tasks

Now is your chance to work a little more with Parrot's Paradise Resort and apply the skills you've just learned to accomplish additional tasks. Continue with the same company file you've been using in this chapter so far. If you need to reopen the company file, the password is *Password1*.

Create and Fund a Prepaid Insurance Account	Jimmy has been paying a monthly fee of $200 for professional pool service and was offered a deal of $175/month if he prepays for a year; he's decided to go with that option Create 13200•Prepaid Pool Service as an Other Current Asset account; write a check to be printed to Barefoot Children Pools on 05/01/2022 for $2,100, expensing $175 in May to 63700•Landscaping and Groundskeeping; place the rest in the Prepaid Pool Service account
Record and Memorize a Transfer of Funds	Record a transfer of $175 from 13200•Prepaid Pool Service to 63700•Landscaping and Groundskeeping on 06/01/2022; memorize the transaction in the Monthly group to occur through April 2023
Make a Petty Cash Expenditure	Use 10900•Petty Cash to purchase a birthday cake on 05/31/2022 for all employees with May birthdays; the total is $43.75, payable to Jordan Bakery, expensed to 64300•Meals and Entertainment
Create a New Fixed Asset Item	Jimmy purchased new furniture for the office on 05/25/2022 for $22,639 from Pa's Custom Furniture; create a new Fixed Asset Item called Office Furniture and a new fixed asset account called 16300•Office Furniture with Cost and Accumulated Depreciation subaccounts; write check #3810 to pay for the down payment for the furniture, which is 5,000, expensing it to the Cost subaccount
Create a Long Term Liability	Create a Long Term Liability account for the new furniture called 27000•Loan - Furniture (Office); on 05/25/2022, enter the remaining amount of the furniture ($22,639 less the down payment) as an increase in the new liability account you just created, with the 16300•Office Furniture Cost subaccount increasing as well
Use the Loan Manager	Create a what-if scenario to calculate the monthly payment for the loan of $17,639 for the furniture, using the Loan Origination date of 05/25/2022; the interest rate is 5.25%, the loan is for 24 months, and the next payment date is 07/01/2022; click Calculate to see the monthly payment amount and write it down Enter the furniture loan in the Loan Manager; the loan is issued by Sailors Bank, the Payment Account is Sailors Bank Checking, and the Interest Expense account is Interest Expense
Create a Forecast and Reports	Create a new forecast for FY2024; increase each amount used for the FY2023 by 5% for the forecast *(Hint: Use the amounts in* Develop Your Skills *8-9, multiplying each by 1.05. You can even do the multiplication right in the field by typing the original value followed by *1.05)* Run a report showing an overview of this new forecast Create a Balance Sheet Detail report from 05/01/2022 to 5/31/2022

Self-Assessment

Check your knowledge of this chapter's key concepts and skills using the Self-Assessment in your ebook or eLab course.

1. When you memorize a transaction, QuickBooks always automatically enters the transaction for you. *True   False*

2. Petty Cash is set up as an expense account in your Chart of Accounts. *True   False*

3. You can fund your Petty Cash account by holding cash back from a deposit. *True   False*

4. Depreciation allows a business to match income to expenses. *True   False*

5. Accumulated Depreciation is an example of a contra account. *True   False*

6. A Long Term Liability is a loan that will be paid off in less than a year. *True   False*

7. A company's net income or loss is transferred into the Retained Earnings account at the end of the accounting period. *True   False*

8. A Prepaid Expense is depreciated. *True   False*

9. You can enter petty cash expenditures just as you enter checks. *True   False*

10. Budgets that you create in QuickBooks must be account based. *True   False*

11. Which is NOT a method used to account for petty cash?
    A. Register method
    B. End-of-month journal entry method
    C. Chart of Accounts method
    D. Write checks method

12. Which of these is an Other Current Asset account?
    A. Checking
    B. Land
    C. Money Market
    D. Prepaid Rent

13. What type of accounts do you depreciate?
    A. Long Term Liabilities
    B. Fixed Assets
    C. Equity Accounts
    D. Other Current Assets

14. Which account does QuickBooks create so you have a working balance sheet account from the start?
    A. Retained Earnings
    B. Opening Balance Equity
    C. Owner's Equity
    D. Accounts Receivable

⫶ Reinforce Your Skills

It's now time for you to help Colleen manage the other balance sheet accounts for Donnell Construction. You will help her set up a prepaid expense account, track petty cash, remit the collected sales tax, and track fixed assets and long term liabilities. The password for all files unless otherwise stated is Password1.

REINFORCE YOUR SKILLS 8-1

Use a Prepaid Rent Account and Write a Rent Check

In this exercise, you will set up and use a Prepaid Rent account. The first step is to set up an Other Current Asset account.

1. Choose **File→Open or Restore Company**.
2. Open **RYS_Chapter08 (Company)** *or* restore **RYS_Chapter08 (Portable)** and save it as: **RYS_Chapter08 Donnell Construction**
3. Choose **Lists→Chart of Accounts**, click the **Account** drop-down arrow ▼, and choose **New**.
4. Create a new **Other Current Asset** account called: **13000•Prepaid Rent**

   Leave the Chart of Accounts open.
5. Choose **Banking→Write Checks** and complete the check to be printed later:

Date	**040122**
Pay to the Order of	**Toros Property Management**
Amount	**10800**
Memo	**Toros: Rent Apr 2022 – Sep 2022**
First line account	**67000•Rent Expense**
First line amount	**1800**
Second line account	**13000•Prepaid Rent**
Second line amount	**9000**

6. Save the check and close the Write Checks window.

Memorize a Funds Transfer

Now you will make the first transfer from Prepaid Rent to Rent Expense. The Chart of Accounts should still be open. If it isn't, choose Lists→Chart of Accounts.

7. Double-click the **1300•Prepaid Rent** account to open the register and record the transfer:

Amount	**$1800**
Account	**67100•Rent Expense**
Date	**5/01/2022**

8. Click within the transaction and choose **Edit→Memorize General Journal**.

9. Create a **Rent Transfer** memorized transaction that is a monthly automated transaction entry:

   • Next transfer: **6/01/2022**

   • Remaining transfers: **4**

10. Close the Memorized Transaction window, click **Record**, and then close the Prepaid Rent register window.

REINFORCE YOUR SKILLS 8-2

Track Petty Cash

In this exercise, you will fund Petty Cash and then make a purchase using it.

1. Choose **Banking→Write Checks** and then choose **10100•Checking**.

2. Complete the check:

No.	**11358**
Date	**040522**
Pay to the Order of	**Cashier** (Quick Add the new vendor)
Amount	**300**
Memo	**Fund Petty Cash, 4/2022**

3. In the Account section, type **Petty Cash** and tap ⎘Tab and then choose **Set Up**.

4. Set up the Petty Cash account as a **Bank** account numbered **10300**, click **Save & Close**, and then **Save & Close** the check.

Make a Purchase with Petty Cash

Now that the Petty Cash account is set up, you will use it to purchase postage stamps. If the Chart of Accounts window is not still open, choose Lists→Chart of Accounts.

5. Double-click the **10300•Petty Cash** account from the Chart of Accounts window.

6. Complete the transaction:

Date	**041222**
Payee	**USPS** (Quick Add the new vendor)
Payment	**52.00**
Account	**66500•Postage and Delivery** (Set up and create a new expense account)
Memo	**postage stamps**

7. Record the transaction and then close the Petty Cash register and the Chart of Accounts window.

Record a Bad Debt and Pay Sales Tax

Unfortunately, a check from one of Colleen's customers was returned for nonsufficient funds. In addition, it's time for Colleen to pay the sales tax collected on the product sales. In this exercise, you will record a bounced check and pay the sales tax due.

1. Choose **Lists→Chart of Accounts**.

2. Create a **Bad Debt Expense** account numbered: **60300**

3. Close the Chart of Accounts and then choose **Lists→Item List**.

4. Create an **Other Charge** item called **Bad Debt**, routing it to **60300•Bad Debt Expense**.

5. Close the Item List and then choose **Customers→Create Credit Memos/Refunds**.

6. Remove the checkmark from **Print Later** on the ribbon and then complete the credit memo:

Customer:Job	**Estes, Kathy**
Date	**041122**
Credit No.	**BD1**
Item	**Bad Debt**
Rate	**1,500**
Tax	**Non**
Memo	**Estes: bad debt write-off 4/11/22**

7. Click **Save & Close**, choose to apply it to invoice **22-006**, and click **Done**.

8. Choose **Vendors→Sales Tax→Pay Sales Tax** and pay the sales tax:

- Pay From Account: **10000•Checking**
- Check Date: **043022**
- Show sales tax due through: **033122**

9. Click to add a checkmark for **To Be Printed**.

10. Click **Pay All Tax** and then click **OK** to send the liability checks to the queue to be printed.

REINFORCE YOUR SKILLS 8-4

Purchase and Fund a New Fixed Asset

Colleen purchased a new Ford F-150 truck for the business. In this exercise, you will set up the purchase as a fixed asset item in the QuickBooks company file.

1. Choose **List→Fixed Asset Item List** and create a new **Fixed Asset Item** for the vehicle:

Asset Name	**Ford F-150**
Item is	**Used**
Purchase Description	**2018 Ford F-150**
Date	**041322**
Cost	**34269**
Vendor	**Carmel Auto Sales**
Asset Account	**15200•Vehicles** (**Set Up** and create the account)
Asset Description	**2018 Ford F-150 Lariat**

2. Save the new fixed asset item and then close the Fixed Asset Item List.

Create the Long Term Liability Account

3. Choose **Lists→Chart of Accounts**.

4. Click the **Account** drop-down arrow ▼ in the Chart of Accounts window and choose **New**.

5. Choose to create a new **Long Term Liability** account (an Other Account Type) and click **Continue**.

6. Create the account:
   - Number: **28000**
   - Account Name: **Loan - Ford F-150**

7. Click **Save & Close**.

Enter the Down Payment Transaction

You will now enter the two transactions to account for the full purchase price of the truck. The first is the down payment.

8. Choose **Banking→Write Checks** and create the check, which is to be printed later:

Bank Account	**10100•Checking**
Date	**041322**
Payee	**Carmel Auto Sales** (**Quick Add** the new vendor)
Amount	**3427**
Memo	**Carmel: Ford truck down payment, 4/2022**
Account	**15200•Vehicles**

9. Click **Save & Close**.

Enter the Loan Transaction

The loan has been funded by the bank, so now you need to account for it in QuickBooks.

10. In the Chart of Accounts window, double-click the **28000•Loan - Ford F-150** long term liability account and enter the loan transaction:

- Date: **041322**
- Increase: **30842**
- Account: **15200•Vehicles**

11. Click **Record**, close the Loan - Vehicle and Chart of Accounts windows, and close the company file.

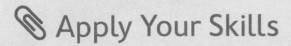

Apply Your Skills

Wet Noses Veterinary Clinic is ready to work with fixed asset, current liability, long term liability, and equity accounts. In addition to prepaying expenses, buying equipment, and drawing from the owner's equity, the clinic will also have to account for bad debt. The password for all files unless otherwise stated is Password1.

APPLY YOUR SKILLS 8-1 QG

Set Up Prepaid Expenses

Wet Noses Veterinary Clinic will pay a website hosting fee for one year in advance. In this exercise, you will set up an Other Current Asset account to track the prepaid web hosting expense, transfer funds to the expense account, and set up a monthly automatic transfer for the remainder of the year.

1. Choose **File→Open or Restore Company**.
2. Open **AYS_Chapter08 (Company)** *or* restore **AYS_Chapter08 (Portable)** and save it as:
    AYS_Chapter08 Wet Noses Clinic
3. Create a Prepaid Web Hosting **Other Current Asset** account using number 12200.
4. Write a check on 07/22/2023 for $1,068.00 to Zoom Web Services for a year's worth of monthly web hosting, to be printed later. Expense the month of July's to **Computer and Internet Expense** and send the remainder to the **Prepaid Web Hosting** account.
5. Record a transaction in the **Prepaid Web Hosting** register to decrease the prepaid account for Computer and Internet Expenses by $89 for the month of August on 08/22/2023.
6. Memorize the transaction as Web Host Transfer and set it to be automated monthly beginning 9/22/2023 for the remaining 10 months.
7. Run a **QuickReport** on the **Prepaid Web Hosting** account to show the transaction detail for this account.
8. Click the **Excel** button and export this report to a new workbook saved as:
    CH8_A1 Prepaid Web QuickReport

APPLY YOUR SKILLS 8-2 QG

Track and Use Petty Cash and Take an Owner's Draw

In this exercise, you will create a petty cash account and use it to pay for expenses. Then you will process an equity transaction for Dr. James.

1. Create a Petty Cash account numbered 10700 and write a check to **Cashier**, to be printed later, for $200 from the Checking account on 07/08/2023 to fund the account.
2. Choose **File→Print Forms→Checks**. Choose to print all checks in the queue, starting with number 1436. Print to PDF and save to your file storage location.
3. Purchase an appetizer platter for $44.95 (use funds from **Petty Cash** to pay for it) from Laura's Café for an office party on 07/12/2023.
4. Purchase postage stamps for $52.00 on 07/14/2023 from the USPS, again using **Petty Cash** to pay for it.
5. Purchase a ream of paper from Whoville Office Supplies for $10.98 of **Petty Cash** on 07/15/2023.

6. Create a transaction for **Sadie James, Partner**, as a Partner's Draw for Partner 1 of $2,000 on 07/15/2023 from her equity in the business, choosing to print the check later.

7. Run the **Balance Sheet Standard** report to show a snapshot of the business for all dates.

8. Click the **Excel** button and export this report to a new workbook saved as:
   `CH8_A2 Balance Sheet Standard`

9. Close Excel and the report.

APPLY YOUR SKILLS 8-3

Account for Bad Debt and Pay Sales Tax Due

You have learned that a customer has moved out of town. You don't expect to receive payment for her outstanding invoices. In this exercise, you will write off the amount as bad debt using a credit memo and then pay the sales tax due.

1. Create a Bad Debt Expense account using number 60300.

2. Create a new **Other Charge** item called Bad Debt that is nontaxable and routed to the Bad Debt Expense account you just created. Leave the amount as zero.

3. Generate a **Credit Memo/Refund** on 07/13/2023 for **Natalie Sheehan: Dog-Sandy**. Use BD1 as the credit number for the **Bad Debt** item in the amount of $148.10 (nontaxable).

   All the items on the invoice were nontaxable. The credit memo will not be printed.

4. Apply the amount of the credit to the outstanding invoice.

5. Run the **Sales Tax Liability** report for July 2023. Close the report after noting the total amount due.

6. Pay the sales tax on 07/31/2023 through 07/31/2023 and ensure **Checking** is the payment account. Choose for the check to be printed and to pay all tax due.

APPLY YOUR SKILLS 8-4 QG

Buy a New Fixed Asset and Work with Liabilities

In this exercise, you will enter a new ultrasound machine into the Fixed Asset Item List. Then you will use the Loan Manager to track the loan that you took out for the ultrasound machine.

1. Create a new fixed asset item:

Asset Name	Ultrasound Machine
Purchase Description	New Health Power Ultrasound Machine
Date	07/21/2023
Cost	$2,050
Vendor	Seattle Vet Supply
Asset Account	15000•Furniture and Equipment
Asset Description	High Performance +7.5 MHz Vet Ultrasound

2. Create a new Long Term Liability account numbered 26000 called Loan-Ultrasound and then fund the loan by entering an increase to the Ultrasound Loan account for $2,050 on 07/22/2023 and debiting the 15000•Furniture and Equipment fixed asset account.

3. Use a what-if scenario to calculate the monthly payment amount of a loan for $2,050 for 36 months at 7.8% interest.

4. Create a new loan in the Loan Manager:

Account Name	**Loan-Ultrasound**	Payment Amount	$64.05
Lender	**Bank of Bothell**	Payment Period	**Monthly**
Origination Date	07/21/2023	Interest Rate	7.8%
Original Amount	$2,050	Payment Account	**Checking**
Term	36 months	Interest Expense Account	**Interest Expense**
Due Date of Next Payment	08/21/2023	Fees/Charges Expense Account	**Bank Service Charge**

5. Run the **Account Listing** report.

6. Click the **Excel** button and export this report to a new workbook saved as:
   `CH8_A4 Account Listing`

7. Close Excel and then close your company file.

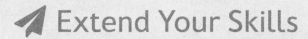

Extend Your Skills

Before You Begin: Open **EYS_Chapter08 (Company)** *or* restore **EYS_Chapter08 (Portable)**. The password is *Password1*.

You've been hired by Arlaine Cervantes to help her with her organization's books. She is the founder of Niños del Lago, a nonprofit organization that provides impoverished Guatemalan children with an engaging educational camp experience. You just sat down at your desk and opened a large envelope from Arlaine that contains a variety of documents; you also have several emails from her. It's your job to sort through the papers and emails and make sense of what you find, entering information into QuickBooks as appropriate and answering any questions in a word-processing document saved as: CH08_EYS_[LastnameFirstinitial]

Remember, you're dealing with random papers dumped out of an envelope and various emails, so part of your challenge is determining the order in which to complete the tasks.

- Receipt from USPS: Dated 8/15/2020, $46.00 for 100 first-class stamps, paid for with petty cash.

- Deposit slip: Check #578 for $5,000 from the House Foundation, deposited in the Checking account on 8/12/2020; $200 was kept back for petty cash.

- Bill from landlord of U.S. office for six months of rent at a discount: Arlaine wrote in a note on the bill that she wants to take advantage of the discounted rent by prepaying it for six months. The amount per month is $500, payable to Keely Amaral Properties, LLC. Pay the rent for August 2020 on 8/5/2020 and then set it up for the remaining months of rent to automatically transfer on the fifth of each month for the remainder of the six-month term.

- Note from the accountant: Need to set up account for loan for new computer equipment for U.S. office. Total financed is $3,029. Loan was funded on 8/10/2020. Set up the equipment as a fixed asset item as well, using Furniture & Equipment as the account. Description of equipment is two new Sony desktop computers, two 21-inch dual monitors, and a new laser printer. The vendor is Lancaster Computer Sales. It was financed by Cherry City Finance.

- Scribbled note from Arlaine: The accountant asked me for a balance sheet report dated August 31, 2020. Please run it and save it as a PDF so that I can email it to her.

9 Using QuickBooks for Payroll

Payroll is a sensitive subject because it affects people's livelihoods. As an employer, you should be well-informed of all payroll options and well-equipped to efficiently manage payroll for your business. In this chapter, you will first set up QuickBooks to run payroll and manage the Employees List. Then you will examine how QuickBooks deals with payroll by creating paychecks, tracking payroll liabilities, and processing payroll forms by using a sample company file that includes a free payroll subscription. Finally, you will account for payroll completed by an outside payroll service.

LEARNING OBJECTIVES

▸ Set up QuickBooks to run payroll

▸ Manage the Employees List

▸ Create paychecks

▸ Track and pay payroll liabilities

▸ Fix payroll errors

▸ Process payroll forms and reports

▸ Input information from an outside payroll service into QuickBooks

📁 Project: Rock Castle Construction

We're taking a break from Parrot's Paradise Resort in sunny Key West and traveling west to California, where we'll work with Rock Castle Construction as we learn about payroll. The Rock Castle QuickBooks file is a sample company file, which means it's set to open on a specific date and has a sample payroll subscription.

Warning! This book teaches how to use QuickBooks to run payroll for a company using fictitious information from an outside payroll service. Contact your local tax agency to determine which tax laws apply to you and to whom you should submit taxes. DON'T use the specific percentages, vendors, or amounts shown, even if from your local jurisdiction, because tax laws change all the time! It's your responsibility to stay informed on your own or through a paid service (such as those offered by Intuit).

Setting Up QuickBooks to Run Payroll

We begin our payroll journey by looking at the payroll options in QuickBooks and learning which payroll items to include and how to manage payroll preferences.

All payroll preferences are set by the administrator on the Company Preferences tab.

New windows will open to work with these preferences.

My Preferences	**Company Preferences**

QUICKBOOKS DESKTOP PAYROLL FEATURES   **SET PREFERENCES FOR**

- ⦿ <u>F</u>ull payroll
- ○ <u>N</u>o payroll

- ○ <u>O</u>nline payroll

        Pay Stub & Voucher Printing

        Workers Compensation

        Sick and Vacation

- ☐ Copy earnings details from pre<u>v</u>ious paycheck
- ☑ Recall <u>q</u>uantity field on paychecks   ☑ Recall <u>h</u>our field on paychecks
- ☑ Job Costing, Class and Item tracking for paycheck expenses
  - Assign one class per   ⦿ Entire paycheck   ○ Earnings item

Changing the employee name display preferences will cause all QuickBooks Desktop windows to close. Please finish paying your employees before you do this.

DISPLAY EMPLOYEE LIST BY:
- ⦿ First Name   ○ Last Name

        Employee Defaults...

- ☐ <u>M</u>ark new employees as sales reps
- ☐ <u>D</u>isplay employee social security numbers in headers on reports

Some preferences help you increase efficiency when processing payroll.

You can set defaults to apply to all new employees.

Payroll Recordkeeping in QuickBooks

To produce the required federal, state, and local payroll forms and reports, QuickBooks keeps a separate set of records for payroll. These records track payroll liabilities, paychecks (and the items listed on them), and taxes. Due to this method of payroll recordkeeping, only those transactions entered via QuickBooks' payroll features will affect payroll reporting.

Payroll Options

QuickBooks payroll offers multiple options: Manual, Basic, Enhanced, and Full Service. There are also separate services for accountants, online edition users, and those who need to process household and nanny payroll. And there are mobile payroll apps so you can keep up with your payroll tasks on the go. Each option has its pros and cons, and all but the Manual option are associated with a fee. Intuit does not recommend the Manual option, as it requires you to stay abreast of all tax law changes and there's a higher likelihood of error and resulting penalties when you enter everything yourself.

> **Note!** Intuit produces a separate line of products for the Canadian market that addresses multiple currencies and Canadian payroll regulations. Find more information at: quickbooks.ca

To learn more about the payroll options available through QuickBooks, visit the Intuit website at quickbooks.intuit.com. QuickBooks can change its payroll options at any time, so check out the website to ensure you're dealing with the most current information. QuickBooks is not ideal for all companies' payroll needs. If multiple states require you run payroll for an individual employee, or you withhold a certain percentage of wages on paychecks, using QuickBooks for payroll may not be the best solution for you.

Common Mistakes When Using QuickBooks for Payroll

There are two common mistakes people make when using QuickBooks for payroll:

- Making a payroll liabilities adjustment with a journal entry

- Paying the liabilities with a "regular check" rather than a liability check similar to what you used when paying sales tax

In both cases, the Chart of Accounts is affected, but the separate payroll records that QuickBooks keeps is not. If you've used a regular check for payroll liabilities, you'll need to make an adjustment in the Liability Adjustment window, from where you can choose for QuickBooks to not affect the Chart of Accounts. Another common error is for people to set up their payroll items incorrectly. If you use subaccounts and remap your payroll accounts manually, take care to map the payroll items correctly!

Historical Amounts

If you're beginning to use the QuickBooks payroll feature for existing employees who have received at least one paycheck from you (and it's not the first day of January), you must enter the payroll history amounts. This ensures that QuickBooks properly calculates taxes with thresholds. It also ensures you'll be able to produce accurate W-2s at the end of the year. QuickBooks can assist you in entering the required payroll history. Before you begin setting up historical amounts, make sure you have:

- Prior-period paychecks

- Prior liability payments

Step-by-step help for this task is accessible through the QuickBooks Payroll Setup Interview. After you've entered the information, you'll have the opportunity to reconcile and verify your data to ensure it's correct.

FLASHBACK TO GAAP: TIME PERIOD

Remember that the activities of the business can be divided into time periods.

➤ Edit→Preferences : Payroll & Employees→Company Preferences tab

DEVELOP YOUR SKILLS 9-1

In this exercise, you will view how to set the payroll preference for a company. The first step is to open a QuickBooks sample file for Rock Castle Construction that includes a payroll service. If you're setting up QuickBooks to run payroll for the first time in your company file, you must set the preference. In this case, you will verify that it's set correctly. Leave the company file open unless otherwise instructed.

Note! You will be using an Intuit sample data file with dates set in 2024. Net amounts and tax amounts may vary depending on your QuickBooks release. If prompted, you can choose Update Now—but if you do, you won't be able to open your company file in an older release of QuickBooks.

1. Start QuickBooks 2020.
2. Open **DYS_Chapter09 (Company)** *or* restore **DYS_Chapter09 (Portable)** and save it as: **DYS_Chapter09 Rock Castle Construction**
3. Click **OK** to acknowledge you're using a sample company file.
4. Choose **Edit→Preferences** and then click the **Payroll & Employees** category and the **Company Preferences** tab.
5. Confirm the Full Payroll option is turned on for this company file.
6. Click **Cancel** to close the Preferences window.

Payroll Items

Before you can run payroll for a company, you must set up the taxes and deductions to collect and indicate to whom they will be paid. You can use the Payroll Item List or the QuickBooks Payroll Setup Interview to set up and edit payroll items. In addition, you can view the Payroll Item Listing report to verify that the taxes and deductions are being routed to the right expense and liability accounts, as well as the actual Payroll Item List to make sure the vendors to whom you pay them are correct.

You must have your Federal Employer Identification Number (FEIN or EIN for Employer Identification Number) listed in your company file for payroll to be processed correctly. If you didn't enter this correctly when you created your company file, you can make that change at any time.

The Payroll Setup Interview

The Payroll Setup Interview walks you through the steps of setting up payroll in QuickBooks to make sure you set up taxes, compensation, and benefits correctly. This feature also helps you set up your employees and enter historical amounts so you can begin doing your company's payroll in QuickBooks.

 Employees→Payroll Setup

Payroll Item List

Anything you wish to include on a paycheck—such as wages, taxes, employee loans, and 401(k) withholdings—must first be set up as a payroll item. Most payroll mistakes are made because payroll items were not set up properly.

ITEM NAME	TYPE	AMOUNT	LIMIT	TAX TRACKING	PAYABLE TO	ACCOUNT ID
Salary	Yearly Salary			Compensation		
Sick Salary	Yearly Salary			Compensation		
Vacation Salary	Yearly Salary			Compensation		
Overtime Rate	Hourly Wage			Compensation		
Regular Pay	Hourly Wage			Compensation		
Sick Hourly	Hourly Wage			Compensation		
Vacation Hourly	Hourly Wage			Compensation		
Bonus	Bonus	0.00		Compensation		
Mileage Reimb.	Addition	0.45		Compensation		
401k Emp.	Deduction	0.00		401(k)	Great Statewide Bank	52209-CA9
Charity Donation	Deduction	0.00		Other	Ninos del Lago	CC-4479
Child Support	Deduction	0.00		Other	County Financial Services	00-7904153
Health Insurance	Deduction	-500.00	-1,200.00	Premium Only/125	Sergeant Insurance	382-1YRN2
401k Co. Match	Company Contribution	0.00		401(k) Co. Match	Great Statewide Bank	52209-CA9
Workers Compensation	Company Contribution			None	State Fund	
Advance Earned Income Credit	Federal Tax			Advance EIC Payment	Great Statewide Bank	00-7904153
Federal Unemployment	Federal Tax	0.6%	7,000.00	FUTA	Great Statewide Bank	00-7904153
Federal Withholding	Federal Tax			Federal	Great Statewide Bank	00-7904153
Medicare Company	Federal Tax	1.45%		Comp. Medicare	Great Statewide Bank	00-7904153
Medicare Employee	Federal Tax	1.45%		Medicare	Great Statewide Bank	00-7904153
Social Security Company	Federal Tax	6.2%	132,900.00	Comp. SS Tax	Great Statewide Bank	00-7904153
Social Security Employee	Federal Tax	6.2%	-132,900.00	SS Tax	Great Statewide Bank	00-7904153
CA - Withholding	State Withholding Tax			SWH	Employment Development Department	987-6543-2
CA - Disability Employee	State Disability Tax	1.0%	-118,371.00	SDI	Employment Development Department	987-6543-2
CA - Unemployment Company	State Unemployment Tax	5.25%	7,000.00	Comp. SUI	Employment Development Department	987-6543-2
CA - Employee Training Tax	Other Tax	0.1%	7,000.00	Co. Paid Other Tax	Employment Development Department	987-6543-2
Medicare Employee Addl Tax	Other Tax	0.9%		Medicare Addl Tax	Great Statewide Bank	00-7904153
Direct Deposit	Direct Deposit			None		

The Payroll Item List displays all payroll items, from compensation to taxes and other deductions. Remember, payroll item limits change often. Figures are for example only; do not use them for your own company.

> **Tip!** If you need to add payroll items later, you can always return to the QuickBooks Payroll Setup Interview or access the Payroll Item List from the menu bar.

Making Payroll Data More Meaningful

When you turn on the payroll preference in QuickBooks, the payroll expense and liability accounts are created for you. QuickBooks then routes payroll items set up through the QuickBooks Payroll Setup to these accounts. To provide more meaningful information in your reports and make troubleshooting more user-friendly, you may want to set up subaccounts for the payroll accounts QuickBooks creates for you. When you create subaccounts, you must remap each payroll item to the correct one through the Payroll Item List.

Verifying Correct Payroll Item Setup

To verify the payroll items are set up correctly and mapped to the correct accounts, run the Payroll Item Listing report. If you see either Payroll Liability-Other or Payroll Expense-Other on a balance sheet or P&L, you know a payroll item is mapped to a parent account rather than to a subaccount.

Rock Castle Construction - Chapter 9
Payroll Item Listing

Payroll Item	Type	Amount	Limit	Expense Account	Liability Account	Tax Tracking
Salary	Yearly Salary			62710 · Gross Wages		Compensation
Sick Salary	Yearly Salary			62710 · Gross Wages		Compensation
Vacation Salary	Yearly Salary			62710 · Gross Wages		Compensation
Overtime Rate	Hourly Wage			62710 · Gross Wages		Compensation
Regular Pay	Hourly Wage			62710 · Gross Wages		Compensation
Sick Hourly	Hourly Wage			62710 · Gross Wages		Compensation
Vacation Hourly	Hourly Wage			62710 · Gross Wages		Compensation
Bonus	Bonus	0.00		62710 · Gross Wages		Compensation
Mileage Reimb.	Addition	0.45		62710 · Gross Wages		Compensation
401k Emp.	Deduction	0.00			24400 · 401k Retirement Payable	401(k)
Charity Donation	Deduction	0.00			24200 · Charity Payable	Other
Child Support	Deduction	0.00			24300 · Child Support Payable	Other
Health Insurance	Deduction	500.00	1,200.00		24100 · Emp. Health Ins Payable	Premium Only/125
401k Co. Match	Company Contribution	0.00		62750 · Co. 401k Retirement Match	24400 · 401k Retirement Payable	401(k) Co. Match
Workers Compensation	Company Contribution			62130 · Work Comp	24080 · Worker's Compensation	None
Advance Earned Income Cre...	Federal Tax				24030 · AEIC Payable	Advance EIC Payment
Federal Unemployment	Federal Tax	0.6%	7,000.00	62730 · FUTA Expense	24040 · FUTA Payable	FUTA
Federal Withholding	Federal Tax				24010 · Federal Withholding	Federal
Medicare Company	Federal Tax	1.45%		62720 · Payroll Taxes	24020 · FICA Payable	Comp. Medicare
Medicare Employee	Federal Tax	1.45%			24020 · FICA Payable	Medicare
Social Security Company	Federal Tax	6.2%	132,900.00	62720 · Payroll Taxes	24020 · FICA Payable	Comp. SS Tax
Social Security Employee	Federal Tax	6.2%	132,900.00		24020 · FICA Payable	SS Tax
CA - Withholding	State Withholding Tax				24050 · State Withholding	SWH
CA - Disability Employee	State Disability Tax	1.0%	118,371.00		24070 · State Disability Payable	SDI
CA - Unemployment Company	State Unemployment Tax	5.25%	7,000.00	62740 · SUTA Expense	24060 · SUTA Payable	Comp. SUI
CA - Employee Training Tax	Other Tax	0.1%	7,000.00	62740 · SUTA Expense	24060 · SUTA Payable	Co. Paid Other Tax
Medicare Employee Addl Tax	Other Tax	0.9%			24000 · Payroll Liabilities	Medicare Addl Tax
Direct Deposit	Direct Deposit				24090 · Direct Deposit Liabilities	None

The Payroll Item Listing report shows what happens behind the scenes with expense and liability accounts when you use a payroll item.

 Reports→Employees & Payroll→Payroll Item Listing | Reports→Report Center : Employees & Payroll→Payroll Item Listing

 Lists→Payroll Items List

Sick and Vacation Time

QuickBooks allows you to easily track employee sick and vacation time. Sick and vacation time defaults apply to all new employees created. To update this information for existing employees, you will need to open each employee record and make the changes. You have three options for the accrual period: beginning of year, every paycheck, and every hour on paycheck.

Note! Your local jurisdiction may have regulations governing sick time, so make sure you understand them before setting it up for your company.

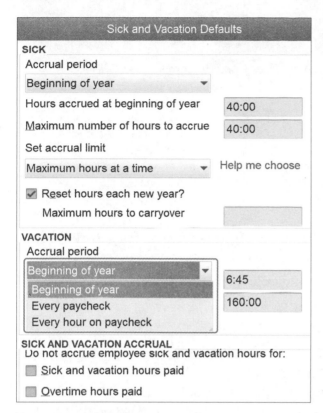

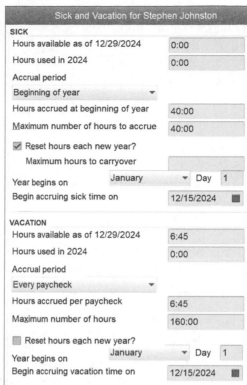

You can set default sick and vacation options that will apply to all new employees as well as edit options for each individual employee. Note the three accrual-period options for both vacation and sick time.

Edit→Preferences : Payroll & Employees→Company Preferences tab : Sick and Vacation

Employees→Employee Center : [double-click customer] : Payroll Info tab→Sick/Vacation...

Workers' Compensation Insurance

QuickBooks can process workers' compensation insurance in much the same way it processes payroll taxes. To track this payroll expense, your first step is to turn on the preference.

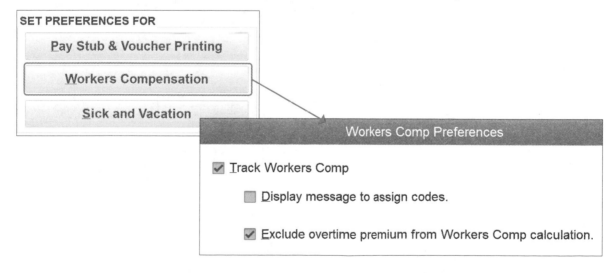

In this exercise, you will make sure the EIN is entered properly and the company is set up as necessary to account for payroll taxes and deductions.

1. Choose **Company→My Company**, resizing the window, if necessary.

2. Verify that **00-7904153** is the EIN entered for Rock Castle Construction and then close the My Company window.

Legal Name & Address	Rock Castle Construction, Inc. 1735 County Road Bayshore CA 94326 US
	EIN 00-7904153

Payroll items should link to the proper accounts in your Chart of Accounts. You will now review a report that shows how the items are linked so you can ensure you're doing payroll properly.

3. Choose **Reports→Employees & Payroll→Payroll Item Listing**.

The Payroll Item Listing report will be displayed.

4. Note the Expense Account and Liability Account columns.

The expense accounts indicate the payroll expenses for your company, from salaries and benefits to the employer taxes you're required to pay. The liability accounts are where you "hold" the funds until you pay them to the proper taxing authority. QuickBooks keeps a separate set of records for payroll behind the scenes, so when you pay your payroll liabilities with a special Liability Check window, it will "empty" these accounts properly.

5. Close the Payroll Item Listing window.

Verify Vendors and Edit a Payroll Item

Next, you will verify that your payroll taxes are set up properly to ensure you're paying taxes to the proper vendors.

6. Choose **Lists→Payroll Item List**.

Look in the Payable To column, which shows to whom you must pay each tax you're holding in your liability accounts. Notice there is no vendor listed for Health Insurance. You will add this information now.

7. Double-click **Health Insurance** to open it for editing.

An Edit Payroll Item window displays. You will be clicking Next to move through the screens to modify this item.

8. Click **Next** and then follow these steps to set up the vendor to whom you will pay insurance premiums:

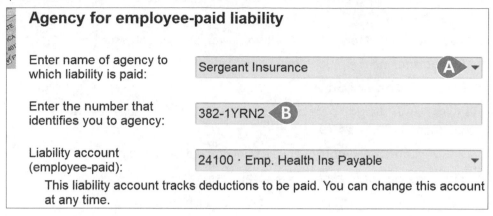

Agency for employee-paid liability

Enter name of agency to which liability is paid:	Sergeant Insurance Ⓐ ▾
Enter the number that identifies you to agency:	382-1YRN2 Ⓑ
Liability account (employee-paid):	24100 · Emp. Health Ins Payable ▾

This liability account tracks deductions to be paid. You can change this account at any time.

Ⓐ Click the drop-down arrow ▾, scroll down, and choose **Sergeant Insurance**.

Ⓑ Tap [Tab] and type: **382-1YRN2**

The liability account is correct, as it points to a subaccount of 24000•Payroll Liabilities, so you don't need to edit it.

9. Click **Next** and then click the drop-down arrow ▾, scroll down, and choose **Premium Only/125** in the Tax tracking type screen; click **Next**.

10. Click **Next** in the next two screens (Taxes and Calculate Based on Quantity).

11. Type **500** and then click **Finish** in the Default Rate and Limit window.

12. Click **Yes** in the *Apply new rate to employees?* window and then click **Finish** again.

You can change the deduction amount when you set up each new employee, if necessary.

Create Liability Accounts and Payroll Items

You will now create two new deduction payroll items: child support and charity donation.

13. Choose **Lists→Chart of Accounts** and then click the **Account** drop-down arrow ▾ and choose **New**.

14. Create two new Payroll Liabilities subaccounts, clicking **Save & New** after the first one:

Account Type	**Other Current Liability**	**Other Current Liability**
Number	**24200**	**24300**
Account Name	**Charity Payable**	**Child Support Payable**
Subaccount of	**24000•Payroll Liabilities**	**24000•Payroll Liabilities**

15. Click **Save & Close** and then close the Chart of Accounts window.

    Now you will create the new payroll items. If the Payroll Item List is not open, choose Lists→Payroll Item List.

16. Choose **Payroll Item→New**, select **Custom Setup**, and click **Next**.

17. Choose **Deduction** and then click **Next**.

18. Type **Charity Donation** as the name for the deduction and then click **Next**.

19. Type **Ninos del Lago** as the payee, QuickAdd it as a Vendor, tap ⌴Tab⌴, and enter this account number: **CC-4479**

20. Choose **24200·Charity Payable** as the liability account and then click **Next**.

21. Choose **Other** as the Tax Tracking type and click **Next** four times.

22. Click **Finish** and then click **OK** in the Schedule Payments window.

23. Set up the child support payroll item, accepting the default for any field not displayed below:

Name for Deduction	**Child Support**
Payee (Vendor)	**County Financial Services** (QuickAdd as a Vendor)
Account	**00-7904153**
Liability Account	**24300·Child Support Payable**
Tax Tracking Type	**Other**

    You will now see the Payroll Item List displayed with your two new payroll items added to it.

24. Close the Payroll Item List.

Working with Employees in QuickBooks

The QuickBooks definition of an employee is someone to whom you issue a W-2 at the end of the year. Subcontractors *are not* entered into the Employees List but *are* entered as vendors. You will use the Employee Center to track employees.

The Employees List

You will edit, delete, and create new employees the same way you did for customers and vendors. New employees can also be set up as part of the QuickBooks Payroll Setup Interview.

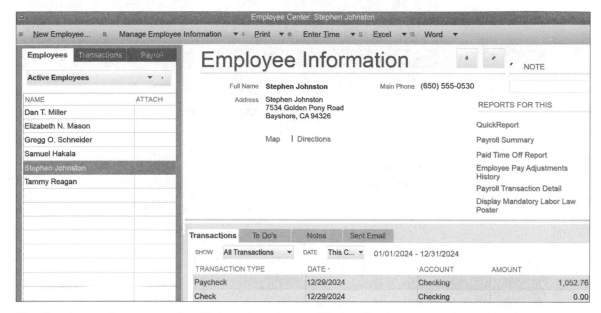

The Employee Center tracks all demographic and payroll information for employees.

The employee information required for payroll setup includes name, address, Social Security number, birth date, and federal and state exemption information. Also needed are the salaries, hourly wages, bonuses, and additional deductions to be withheld, such as investment plan contributions or child support payments for your employees.

To run payroll, you must enter tax information for each employee. If you don't have your employees' W-4 forms handy, you can add the information later—if it's entered before you first run payroll (*not* optional!). It's important to have all your employees' W-4 and I-9 forms neatly organized with all personnel records (or that your outside payroll service has them all completed). Workers' compensation companies thoroughly review company payroll records. Even though you don't treat independent contractors as employees in QuickBooks, keep an I-9 form on file for each subcontractor.

Employee Defaults

Before setting up your employees, set the employee defaults. When doing so, choose the options that apply to the majority of employees you will create, such as pay schedule, health insurance, and 401(k). These preferences are applied to each new employee you create, and you can change them as needed.

 Employees→Employee Center : New Employee

---

DEVELOP YOUR SKILLS 9-3

In this exercise, you will set employee defaults and then create two additional employees for Rock Castle Construction.

1. Choose **Edit→Preferences** and then click the **Payroll & Employees** category and the **Company Preferences** tab.

2. Click the **Employee Defaults** button and then follow these steps to set the employee defaults:

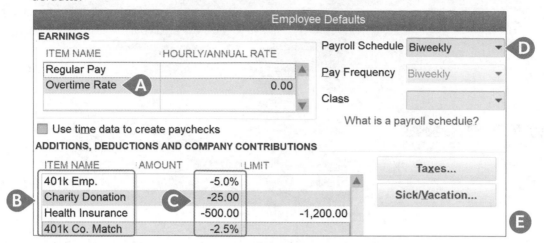

Ⓐ Click the drop-down arrow ▾ and choose **Overtime Rate**.

Ⓑ Click the drop-down arrow ▾ for each line and choose the items displayed.

Ⓒ Enter the amounts for each item (including the minus signs).

Ⓓ Click the drop-down arrow ▾ and choose **Biweekly**.

Ⓔ Click **OK**.

3. Click **OK** to close the Preferences window.

The defaults for Taxes and Sick/Vacation have already been set, but you could set them in your own company through this window.

Create Employees

4. Click the **Employees** [EMPLOYEES] button in the Employees area of the Home Page.

5. Click the **New Employee** button on the Employee Center toolbar.

6. Enter the personal information for the first employee:

7. Click the **Address & Contact** tab and enter Stephen's address and phone number:

8. Click the **Payroll Info** tab and enter **25** in the Regular Pay field.

The overtime rate will automatically calculate.

9. Click the **Taxes** button and follow these steps to set the federal tax withholding information:

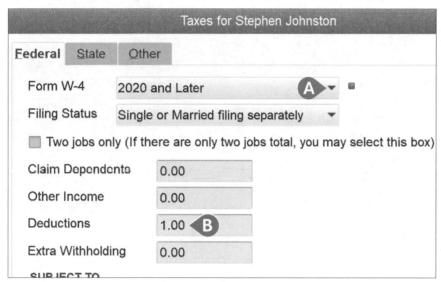

Ⓐ Click the **Form W-4** drop-down arrow and choose **2020 and Later**.

A Federal W-4 2020 Form window will appear. Read the information in the window to acquaint yourself with the changes.

Ⓑ Click **OK** and then enter **1** in the Deductions field.

10. Click the **State** tab and enter **1** for the number of allowances; click the **Other** tab.

The local tax is already set up, so you are done setting up the new employee.

11. Click **OK** twice and then click **Leave As Is** to save the new employee.

Add an Additional Employee

You will now add one more employee—Samuel Hakala.

12. Click the **New Employee** button on the Employee Center toolbar and create another employee:

Legal Name	**Mr. Samuel Hakala**	Address	**303 Pilot Place, Bayshore, CA 94326**
Social Security No.	**999-88-7777**	Main Phone	**(650) 555-4673**
Gender	**Male**	Regular Pay Amount	**25**
Date of Birth	**013078**	401k Emp.	**-4%**
Marital Status	**Married**	Charity Donation	**-50**
U.S. Citizen	**Yes**	Form W-4	**2020 and Later**
Ethnicity	**Hawaiian/Pacific Islander**	Federal Filing Status	**Married filed jointly**
Disabled	**No**	Deductions	**3**
I-9 on File	**Yes**	State Filing Status	**Married (two incomes)**
U.S. Veteran/ Status	**Yes / Reserve**	Allowances	**3**

13. Click **OK** twice, click **Leave As Is**, and then close the Employee Center.

Creating Paychecks

After you've chosen your payroll method, made sure your payroll items are set up properly, and set up your employees and payroll tax information, you can begin creating paychecks for your employees. When you first choose to pay employees, you will see an Enter Hours window displayed. After you've entered the paycheck information for each employee, you will see all the data in the Review and Create Paychecks window.

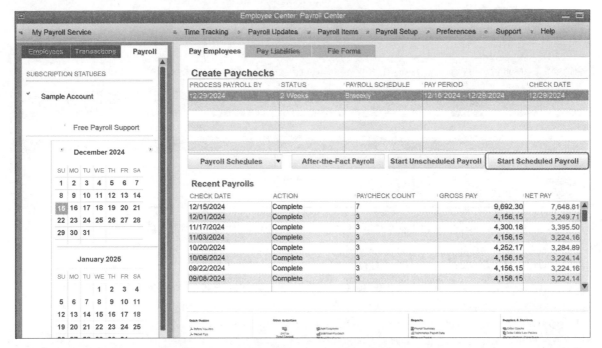

The Payroll Center, an element of the Employee Center, becomes active once you turn on the QuickBooks payroll feature. You can easily start a scheduled payroll with the click of a button.

After entering the hours worked in the Enter Payroll Information window, the Review and Create Paycheck window allows you to view a summary of all paychecks you are about to create.

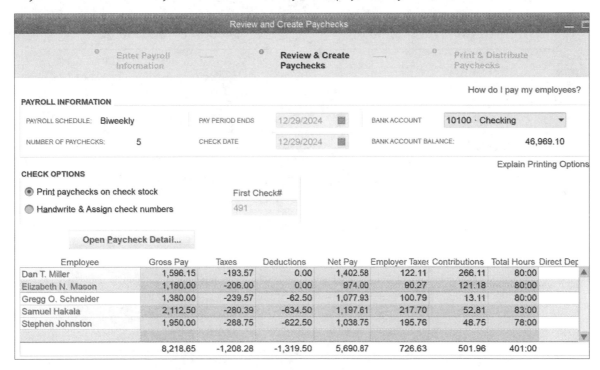

Payroll Schedules

When you use QuickBooks for payroll, you have the option to set up payroll schedules so payroll runs more efficiently. Payroll schedules allow you to set how often you pay employees, the date on which the paychecks are due, and the date on which you will run payroll, all the while considering holidays and weekends to ensure you pay employees on time. Another benefit of using scheduled payroll is that you can choose to pay employees by group or by batch. Payroll schedules are created from the Payroll Center or via the Payroll Schedule List. Using scheduled payroll does not limit you from creating a paycheck for an employee "off schedule."

NAME	PAY FREQUENCY	NEXT CHECK DATE	NEXT PAY PERIOD END DATE
Biweekly	Biweekly	12/29/2024	12/29/2024

Payroll Schedule ▼ ☐ Include inactive

The Payroll Schedule List displays all the payroll schedules in use for the company.

Passing On Billable Time to Customers

If an employee has time spent on a job, those billable payroll expenses can be passed on to customers. When you create a paycheck for an employee who has billable hours, make sure to choose the correct customer or job to which to pass on the expense.

In this Behind the Scenes, you're viewing the parent accounts for the payroll liabilities and expenses, not the subaccounts.

BEHIND THE SCENES: *Create Paychecks*

62700•Payroll Expenses 62130•Work Comp	10100•Checking 24000•Payroll Liabilities
INCREASE to Expenses	DECREASE to Assets INCREASE to Payroll Liabilities

$$\text{Assets} = \text{Liabilities} + (\text{Capital} + \text{Revenue} - \text{Expenses}) \rightarrow \text{Equity}$$

$$-\$5,759.88 = \$3,687.36 + \$0.00 + \$0.00 - \$9,447.24$$

62700•Payroll Expenses		10100•Checking	
Debit	Credit	Debit	Credit
$9,046.84			$5,759.88

62130•Work Comp		24000•Payroll Liabilities	
Debit	Credit	Debit	Credit
$400.40			$3,687.36

Note! All of the Behind the Scenes and BTS Brief features in this chapter may not match your file due to payroll table updates.

↗ Employees→Payroll Center *or* Pay Employees

↗ File→Print Forms→Paychecks *or* Pay Stubs

DEVELOP YOUR SKILLS 9-4

In this exercise, you will run payroll for your employees for the period ending 12/31/2024.

1. Click the **Pay Employees** task icon in the Employees area of the Home Page.

   The Employee Center: Payroll Center window opens.

2. Click the **Start Scheduled Payroll** button in the middle of the Pay Employees tab.

   The Enter Payroll Information window displays with the Check Date field selected. All five employees are selected because the Biweekly scheduled payroll is assigned to each.

3. Follow these steps to enter the payroll hours:

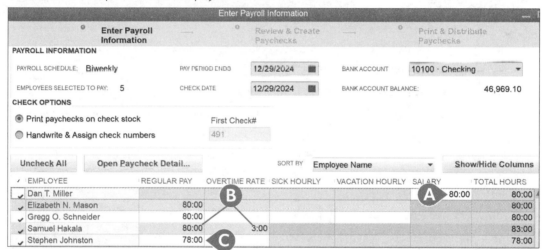

Ⓐ Click and enter **80** for Dan's salary

Ⓑ Click and enter **80** for Samuel's regular pay, tap [Tab], and type **3** as his overtime rate.

Ⓒ Click and enter **78** for Stephen's regular pay.

4. Click **Samuel Hakala**.

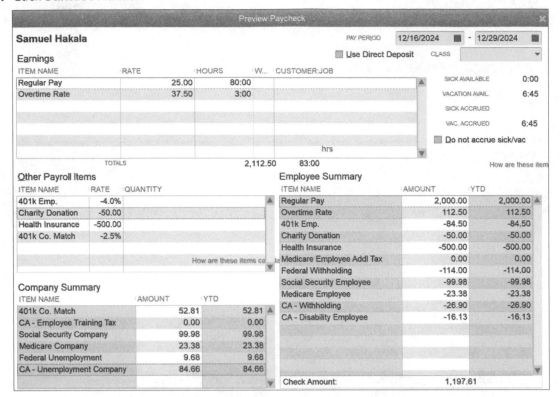

In the Preview Paycheck window, you can edit amounts for individual employees. The amounts displayed may be different due to updates to the tax tables.

5. Click **Save & Close** and then click **Continue**.

The Review and Create Paychecks window appears. When you enter the hours for each employee, QuickBooks calculates payroll taxes automatically. This will happen for your own company, as well, if you've subscribed to a QuickBooks payroll service. You can choose to do paychecks manually, but that will require you to enter each amount manually and to stay on top of all tax law changes. It results in a much greater chance for error.

6. Click **Create Paychecks**.

The Confirmation and Next Steps window appears. This window shows you the payroll flow and allows you to print paychecks and pay stubs.

BEHIND THE SCENES BRIEF

62700•Payroll Expenses DR 9,046.84 | 62130•Work Comp DR 400.40;
10100•Checking CR 5,690.87 | 24000•Payroll Liabilities CR 3,756.37

62700•Payroll Expenses has **increased** | 62130•Work Comp has **increased**;
10100•Checking has **decreased** | 24000•Payroll Liabilities has **increased**

Check Figure: Checking $41,278.23

These numbers reflect all paychecks. You're also viewing the parent accounts for the payroll liabilities and expenses in this case, not the various subaccounts.

Print Paychecks and Pay Stubs

After creating the paychecks, you print them. Here you'll print from the Confirmation and Next Steps window and then print the pay stubs using the menu bar command that's always available.

7. Click the **Print Paychecks** button in the Confirmation and Next Steps window.

The Select Paychecks to Print window displays. At this point, you would place preprinted checks into the printer. For this exercise, you will print to a PDF file.

	Select Paychecks to Print		
Bank Account 10100 · Checking	**First Check Number** 10080		

Select Paychecks to print, then click OK.
There are 5 Paychecks to print for $5,759.88.

✓	DATE	EMPLOYEE	AMOUNT
✓	12/29/2024	Dan T. Miller	1,402.58
✓	12/29/2024	Elizabeth N. Mason	974.00
✓	12/29/2024	Gregg O. Schneider	1,077.93
✓	12/29/2024	Samuel Hakala	1,252.61
✓	12/29/2024	Stephen Johnston	1,052.76

8. Click **OK** to choose to print all five paychecks.

9. Choose the option that allows you to print/save to a PDF file and click **Print**, navigate to your file storage location, and click **Save**.

10. Click **OK** to verify that all checks printed correctly and then **Close** the Confirmation and Next Steps window.

Yes, you can print pay stubs from that window, but it's important to know how to print paychecks and pay stubs from the menu bar as well.

11. Choose **File→Print Forms→Pay Stubs**.

12. Change the Checks Dated dates to: **122924** through **122924**

Now only the pay stubs for the paychecks you just created display.

13. Click **Preview** to see how the employee pay stubs will look, click **OK** in the Paystub Information window, and then close the Print Preview window.

14. Close the Select Pay Stubs and the Employee Center: Payroll Center windows.

Tracking and Paying Payroll Liabilities

When you run payroll, you must collect taxes and other deductions and hold them in a current liability account until you're required to pay them. QuickBooks has preset reports for the employee and payroll aspects of your business. One such report, Payroll Liability Balances, shows the amount you owe to various vendors that is being held in these liability accounts (you may have only one account, Payroll Liabilities, if you don't use subaccounts).

The Pay Payroll Liabilities Window

Just as you used the Pay Sales Tax window to pay your sales tax liabilities, you will use a special Pay Liabilities window to pay your payroll taxes and deductions. *Never* use Write Checks for your payroll taxes if you're using QuickBooks Payroll because QuickBooks will not properly debit the liability accounts. After you choose which liabilities to pay, the Liability Payment – Checking window launches, which will debit the payroll liability account in which the funds are held.

Rock Castle Construction - Chapter 9
Payroll Liability Balances
December 2024

	BALANCE
Payroll Liabilities	
Advance Earned Income Cre...	0.00
Federal Withholding	1,900.00
Medicare Employee	304.57
Social Security Employee	1,302.30
Federal Unemployment	118.38
Medicare Company	304.57
Social Security Company	1,302.30
CA - Withholding	405.38
CA - Disability Employee	95.96
CA - Unemployment Compa...	260.79
Medicare Employee Addl Tax	0.00
CA - Employee Training Tax	10.00
401k Emp.	182.00
Charity Donation	75.00
Health Insurance	1,212.50
401k Co. Match	101.56
Workers Compensation	1,614.71
Total Payroll Liabilities	**9,190.02**

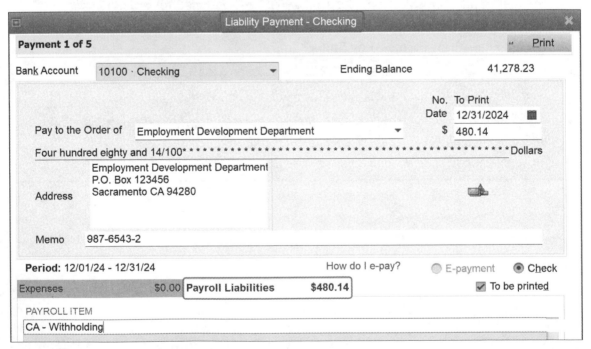

You pay payroll liabilities via a Liability Payment window. The payroll liabilities to be paid are listed on the Payroll Liabilities tab. One check is produced for each vendor. If multiple payroll items are to be paid, they will be listed on separate lines on the Payroll Liabilities tab.

Tip! If your bank sends your federal payroll taxes electronically, clear the Print Later checkbox and enter EFTPS (Electronic Federal Tax Payment Service) in the check number field.

BEHIND THE SCENES: *Pay Payroll Liabilities*

24000•Payroll Liabilities
DECREASE to Liabilities

10100•Checking
DECREASE to Assets

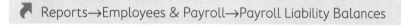

				→Equity		
Assets	=	*Liabilities*	+	*Capital*	+ *Revenue*	− *Expenses*
-$5,031.74	=	-$5,031.74	+	$0.00	+ $0.00	− $0.00

24000•Payroll Liabilities	
Debit	*Credit*
$5,031.74	

10100•Checking	
Debit	*Credit*
	$5,031.74

➦ Reports→Employees & Payroll→Payroll Liability Balances

➦ Employees→Payroll Tax and Liabilities→Pay Scheduled Liabilities

DEVELOP YOUR SKILLS 9-5

In this exercise, you will pay the payroll liabilities that have been collected for December 2024. To see exactly how much to pay to the various payroll vendors, you will run a report that shows all taxes and deductions being held in the payroll liability accounts.

1. Choose **Reports→Employees & Payroll→Payroll Liability Balances**.
2. Set the date range for the report:
    - From: **120124**
    - Io: **123124**
3. Click the **Refresh** button.

    Note the balance shown on the report.
4. Close the Payroll Liability Balances report, choosing not to memorize it.

Pay the Liabilities

You're now ready to pay the payroll liabilities due for December 2024. You will do so using a liability check. Remember, when paying liabilities for your own company, you need to pay them based on the schedule that applies to your business.

5. Click the **Pay Liabilities** task icon in the Employees area of the Home Page.

    The Employee Center: Payroll Center will launch with the Pay Liabilities tab displayed.

6. Follow these steps to pay the liabilities due in January:

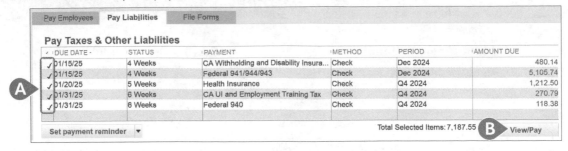

Ⓐ Click to the left of each of the five liabilities due through 01/31/25.

Ⓑ Click **View/Pay**.

The Liability Payment – Checking window (not the Write Checks window) appears with the check information for the first payroll vendor filled in.

7. Change the check date to **12/31/2024** and click **Save & Next**.

Because this is a sample company file, QuickBooks loads 12/15/2024 as the date each time you create a new transaction. In your own company file, the date will be the last date you used in another transaction.

The second liability payment information displays in the window.

8. Change the date on the rest of the liability checks to **12/31/2024**, clicking **Save & Next** after each until the last one, on which you should click **Save & Close**.

The Payment Summary window displays. You can print the checks from this window; if you don't, they'll be placed in the queue of checks waiting to be printed (accessed from the menu bar).

In this Behind the Scenes Brief, you're viewing the parent account for Payroll Liabilities, not the various subaccounts.

BEHIND THE SCENES BRIEF

24000•Payroll Liabilities DR 7,187.55; **10100•Checking CR 7,187.55**

24000•Payroll Liabilities has **decreased**; 10100•Checking has **decreased**

Check Figure: Checking $34,090.68

---

9. Close the Payment Summary and Employee Center: Payroll Center windows.

Correcting Payroll Errors

When correcting payroll errors, ensure you do so properly. Remember that QuickBooks keeps a separate "set of books" for payroll, so you must make changes via the payroll features. The Edit/Void Paychecks window allows you to choose which paycheck to edit/void and provides guidance.

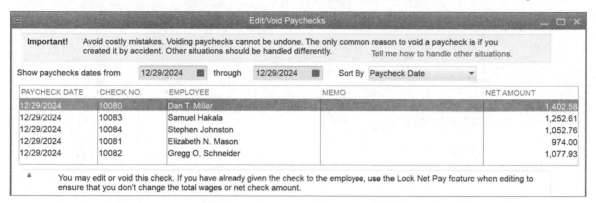

Note the important message at the top of the window regarding voiding paychecks as well as the message at the bottom that refers to the selected paycheck (Dan T. Miller's).

Fixing a Paycheck

It is only on rare occasions that you should void a paycheck. Two such times are when you accidentally created a paycheck or when you must correct a paycheck from a prior year.

Correcting a Paycheck Error from a Prior Year

If you need to change the date of a paycheck from one year to another, you must void the existing paycheck and issue a new one. Voiding a paycheck is done in basically the same way as voiding any transaction in QuickBooks. Just remember that when you re-create the paycheck, you must do so through the proper method. That is, you *cannot* just create a new check in the Write Checks window.

Lock Net Pay Feature

If you need to make changes to a paycheck and want to make sure you don't change the amount (which is dealt with differently), use the Lock Net Pay feature. It prevents you from changing the amount of the paycheck or the total wages, but you can make changes to things that don't affect the amount of the check, such as the class to which it is assigned, vacation or sick time accrual, or direct deposit signup.

Unscheduled Payroll Checks

There may be times you need to issue a paycheck to an employee when it's not at the end of a pay period. For instance, you may have underpaid an employee and don't want that employee to have to wait until the next payday to receive the compensation, or you may need to issue a final paycheck. These situations are easily dealt with in QuickBooks from the Payroll Center window by choosing either to conduct an unscheduled payroll or to create a termination check.

COMMON PAYROLL ERRORS AND THEIR FIXES

The Error	The Fix
An issued paycheck was lost or damaged.	Reprint and reissue the check with the next check number; document the lost check by creating and then voiding a check.
The pay period dates are wrong but within the same calendar year.	Edit the pay period dates in the Review Paycheck window and create a memo in the check register.
An employee was overpaid.	Correct the overpayment on the next payroll (rather than reissue the paycheck).
An employee was underpaid.	Issue an unscheduled payroll check or correct the underpayment on the next payroll. (Before delaying payment to an employee, make sure you understand the payroll regulations in your jurisdiction.)
A paycheck item is incorrect, and the error doesn't affect the amount due.	Edit the paycheck information in Lock Net Pay mode.

Note! Depending on the type of payroll service you subscribe to, there may be limitations on how you will be able to correct certain payroll errors.

Correcting a Payroll Liability Payment

Paying a payroll liability with a regular check rather than a liability check will create issues for you behind the scenes. To set things right, you need to void the regular check and then process the payment through the Pay Payroll Liabilities feature.

 Employees→Enter/Void Paychecks

DEVELOP YOUR SKILLS 9-6

In this exercise, you will replace a lost paycheck for Stephen Johnston.

1. Click the **Check Register** task icon in the Banking area of the Home Page.
2. Click **OK** to choose 10100•Checking as the account to use.

3. Resize the window and scroll, if necessary, and then double-click anywhere within the **Stephen Johnston's paycheck #10084** transaction.

   The Paycheck – Checking window displays.

4. Write down the check number (10084) and net amount ($1,038.75) for future reference.

   Your net amount may be different due to updates to the tax tables.

5. Reprint the check:

   • Click the checkbox to select **Print Later**.

   • Click **Print** (the icon, not the drop-down arrow ▼).

   • Click **Yes** in the Recording Transaction window.

   • Click **OK** in the Print Paycheck window displaying the next check number (10085).

6. Ensure the correct printer is selected and click **Print**.

   If applicable, print to PDF, saving the file to your file storage location.

7. Click **OK** in the Print Checks Confirmation window.

   This is the check you will give Stephen.

8. Click **Save & Close** in the Paycheck - Checking window.

   Leave the 10110•Checking register window open; you'll use it to create and then void the lost check.

9. Choose **Banking→Write Checks**.

10. Ensure the check will not be printed later (the option is on the ribbon at the top of the window).

11. Create a check matching the one that was lost:

Check No.	**10084**
Date	**122924**
Payee	**Stephen Johnston** (click **Not Now** in the Warning)
$ (Amount)	**1038.75**
Memo (on check and the Expense tab)	**Lost paycheck, reissued as #10085**
Account	**62700•Payroll Expenses**

12. Click **Save & Close**; close the Set Check Reminder window, if necessary.

    The 10110•Checking register window should be displayed.

13. Locate the check you just created (10084) in the 10110•Checking window, scrolling as necessary.

14. Right-click anywhere within the two lines of the check 10084 transaction and choose **Void Check**.

    You will see VOID: *preceding the memo you entered into the check; the dollar amount is zero.*

15. Click **Record**; click **Yes** to record the transaction.

16. Click **No, Just Void the Check**, close the Set Check Reminder window (if necessary), and then close the Checking register window.

Payroll Forms and Reports

The forms you can produce through QuickBooks depend on the payroll option selected. Let's look at a few basic payroll forms used in the United States and how QuickBooks supports each of them. If you live in Canada, check out quickbooks.ca to learn about payroll solutions and Intuit products available for the Canadian market.

W-2s and W-3s

W-2s are provided to each employee. They summarize earnings and deductions for the year. A W-3 form is what you prepare and submit to the government; it summarizes the W-2 information you provided to employees.

> **Note!** If you subscribe to one of the Enhanced payroll services, you can print W-2s and W-3s on blank paper right from QuickBooks. If you subscribe to the Full Service, QuickBooks provides the completed forms for you.

940 and 941

Form 941 is the Employer's Quarterly Federal Tax Return. QuickBooks will fill in the appropriate amounts. You can edit the amounts if the IRS rules instruct you to do so. Form 940 is the Employer's Annual Federal Unemployment (FUTA) Tax Return. QuickBooks stores forms for only one year at a time. You will need to subscribe to a payroll service to download the correct year's form. QuickBooks will fill in the appropriate amounts, which you can edit if necessary.

1099-MISC and 1096

When you have vendors to whom you subcontract work, you will report their earnings on and provide to them form 1099-MISC. The 1096 form is something you prepare for the federal government; it summarizes the 1099 information you provided to subcontractors. Before you can run 1099-MISC forms, you must turn on the preference and properly set up your 1099 vendors. A wizard will walk you through 1099 and 1096 form preparation and filing.

> **Note!** You can print 1099-MISC forms for your subcontractors right from QuickBooks. If you subscribe to the Full Service, Intuit will prepare the 1099-MISC forms for you.

Other Payroll Reports

In addition to the payroll reports you've already seen, QuickBooks provides a variety of additional reports, including some that can be run in Excel. All of these reports can be found in the Employees & Payroll category in the Report Center.

> **Note!** You can track changes to employee pay rates with the Employee Pay Adjustments History report.

> ↱ Employees→Payroll Tax Forms & W-2s→Process Payroll Forms

> ↱ Vendors→Print/E-file 1099s

> ↱ Reports→Employees & Payroll

In this exercise, you will create three payroll reports, including one in Excel.

1. Choose **Reports→Employees & Payroll→Employee Earnings Summary**.

   The default date range for this report is the current calendar quarter. Note that it displays values for all payroll items for October–December 2024.

2. Close the Employee Earnings Summary report.

3. Choose **Reports→Employees & Payroll→Workers Comp Summary**.

   If you have set the preference, QuickBooks tracks Workers Compensation data for you, which you can easily display on reports.

4. Close the Workers Compensation Summary report.

Run a Payroll Report in Excel

The rest of this exercise assumes Excel is installed on your computer. If you don't have Excel, move on to the next topic.

5. Choose **Reports→Employees & Payroll→More Payroll Reports in Excel→Payroll Summary by Tax Tracking Type**.

   Excel will launch. If you have not enabled macros, you will be prompted to do so. You will then see the QuickBooks Payroll Tax Tracking Reports Workbook window.

6. Follow these steps to summon the correct QuickBooks data for the report:

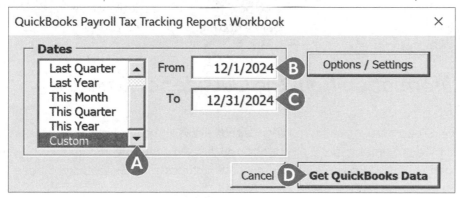

   Ⓐ Scroll down and click **Custom**.

   Ⓑ Delete the existing From date and type: **120124**

   Ⓒ Delete the existing To date and type: **123124**

   Ⓓ Click **Get QuickBooks Data**.

7. Click **OK** in the QuickBooks Payroll Tax Tracking Reports Workbook – Updated window after reading the information.

   Notice the QuickBooks tab at the top of the Excel window and that there are two worksheets in your workbook (the tabs at the bottom of the window allow you to switch between them).

8. Explore the data on both worksheets and then close Excel.

Outside Payroll Services

Many companies use an outside payroll service. If this is your case, you still must enter the information into QuickBooks so you can create meaningful financial statements. The level of information you track in QuickBooks does not have to be as detailed when you use an outside service because much of the information is tracked for you.

Information to Track

You need not worry about setting up QuickBooks for payroll or using the payroll features of the software because you are not tracking specific withholdings and deductions. Your intent when working with an outside service is to track expenses, cash flow, and balances being held in liability accounts so your balance sheet, profit & loss, and cash flow reports are accurate.

 Warning! DON'T turn on the QuickBooks payroll features if you track payroll from an outside source.

Employees, Expenses, and Liabilities

Enter your employees into the Employees List in QuickBooks. You will not need to enter information on the Payroll Info tab, though, as that will be tracked by the service. To account for the company's payroll expenses, you set up an expense account, such as Payroll Expenses, and appropriate subaccounts for each type of payroll expense. Examples of subaccounts are Gross Wages, Company-Paid Benefits, and Company-Paid Taxes. You will still be holding deductions and withdrawals from employees that have to be paid to the appropriate agency in the future. To do so requires you set up an Other Current Liability account, such as Payroll Liabilities, to track this information.

Entering Information from the Outside Service into QuickBooks

When you receive a report from the payroll service that shows the payroll activity for your company, you will need to enter it into QuickBooks. You will see payments going to employees and out to the agencies for which you are currently holding funds in the Payroll Liabilities account.

Employee Paychecks

Employee paychecks are entered in the Write Checks window. You enter gross wages on the first line of the Expenses tab. All deductions are entered on the second line as a negative amount and will flow into the Payroll Liabilities account.

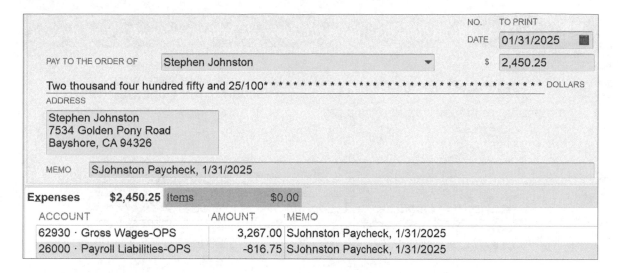

Tax and Benefit Payments

When using an outside payroll service, you also use the Write Checks window to enter payments when you pay the payroll liabilities. On the Expense tab, you enter the employee-paid taxes and deductions being held in Payroll Liabilities. Company-paid taxes and benefits are entered on separate lines using the appropriate Payroll Expenses subaccounts.

Warning! What we are talking about here applies *only* when a company is using an outside payroll service! *Never* use the Write Checks window for payroll transactions if you are completing payroll using QuickBooks' Payroll feature!

Reporting on an Outside Payroll Service

The payroll reports provided in QuickBooks are designed to be used with the QuickBooks payroll features. To display data regarding outside payroll service transactions, you will need to use the "regular" reports and modify them to display this information.

Rock Castle Construction - Chapter 9
Employee Paychecks
As of January 31, 2025

Type	Date	Num	Name	Memo	Split	Amount
10100 · Checking						
Check	01/31/2025	10090	Samuel Hakala	SHakala Pa...	-SPLIT-	-3,337.46 ◄
Check	01/31/2025	10091	Stephen Johnston	SJohnston ...	-SPLIT-	-2,450.25
Total 10100 · Checking						-5,787.71
TOTAL						**-5,787.71**

In order to show paychecks produced based on an outside payroll service, you can run a checking account QuickReport and filter it to show only employees. The report title can be changed.

BEHIND THE SCENES: *Outside Payroll Service*

62930•Gross Wages-OPS	10100•Checking 26000•Payroll Liabilities-OPS
INCREASE to Expenses	*DECREASE to Assets* *INCREASE to Liabilities*

→ *Equity*

$$Assets = Liabilities + (Capital + Revenue - Expenses)$$

$$-\$5{,}787.71 = \$1{,}929.29 + \$0.00 + \$0.00 - \$7{,}717.00$$

62930•Gross Wages-OPS

Debit	Credit
$7,717.00	

10100•Checking

Debit	Credit
	$5,787.71

26000•Payroll Liabilities-OPS

Debit	Credit
	$1,929.29

Edit→Preferences : Payroll & Employees→Company Preferences tab

Banking→Write Checks

File→Print Forms→Checks

DEVELOP YOUR SKILLS 9-8

In this exercise, you will enter information from an outside payroll service for January 2025 (employees are paid on the last day of each month). To begin, you will turn off payroll in QuickBooks.

1. Choose **Edit→Preferences** and then click the **Payroll & Employees** category and the **Company Preferences** tab.

2. Choose **No Payroll** to turn off the QuickBooks payroll features and click **OK**; click **OK** in the Warning window.

   Now you will set up the expense and liability accounts.

3. Choose **Company→Home Page** and then click the **Chart of Accounts** task icon in the Company area of the Home Page.

Chart of Accounts

As you know from previous exercises in this chapter, subaccounts are set up for Payroll Liabilities and being used with the sample payroll subscription. You will create a second set of payroll liability accounts to track the liabilities you'll be collecting when working with an outside payroll service. You will also create a new payroll expense account and subaccounts to track this data.

4. Click the **Account** drop-down arrow ▾ and choose **New**.

5. Choose **Other Current Liability** from the Other Account Types drop-down list and click **Continue**.

6. Type **26000** as the account number and **Payroll Liabilities-OPS** as the account name; click **Save & New**.

7. Choose **Expense** as the account type.

You must *use the correct account type, or you will have a disaster behind the scenes!*

8. Create the new expense account and subaccounts, clicking **Save & New** after the first three and **Save & Close** after the last:

Account Number	Account Name	Subaccount of
62900	**Payroll Expenses-OPS**	None; this is the parent account.
62910	**Company-Paid Benefits**	**62900·Payroll Expenses-OPS**
62920	**Company-Paid Taxes**	**62900·Payroll Expenses-OPS**
62930	**Gross Wages-OPS**	**62900·Payroll Expenses-OPS**

9. Close the Chart of Accounts window.

Create Paychecks Using Data from an Outside Service

You will now enter data received from an outside payroll service into QuickBooks for Samuel and Stephen. Here is the statement received from the payroll service:

ROCK CASTLE CONSTRUCTION JANUARY 2025 PAYROLL						
Employee	Gross Wages	Employee Fed Taxes W/H	Employee State Taxes W/H	Net Pay	Company Fed Taxes Owed	Company Benefits Owed
Samuel Hakala	$4,450.00	$890.04	$222.50	$3,337.46	$333.75	$895.00
Stephen Johnston	$3,267.00	$653.40	$163.35	$2,450.25	$245.03	$895.00
Totals, 1/31/2025	$7,717.00	$1,543.44	$385.85	$5,787.71	$578.78	$1,790.00

In this example, all employee federal taxes, withholding and FICA, are combined.

10. Click the **Write Checks** task icon in the Banking area of the Home Page.

Write Checks

11. Create the two paychecks, where each is dated **1/31/2025**, will be printed later, and draws from **10100·Checking**. Click **Save & New** after each check.

Pay to the Order of	Samuel Hakala	Stephen Johnston
Amount	3337.46	2450.25
Memo (all)	SHakala Paycheck, 1/31/2025	SJohnston Paycheck, 1/31/2025
Account / Amount	(first row) **62930·Gross Wages-OPS** / 4450 (second row) **26000·Payroll Liabilities-OPS** / −1112.54	(first row) **62930·Gross Wages-OPS** / 3267 (second row) **26000·Payroll Liabilities-OPS** / −816.75

Expenses $3,337.46	Items	$0.00
ACCOUNT	**AMOUNT**	**MEMO**
62930 · Gross Wages-OPS	4,450.00	SHakala Paycheck, 1/31/2025
26000 · Payroll Liabilities-OPS	-1,112.54	SHakala Paycheck, 1/31/2025

Hint: Type the account numbers in the Account column to fill in the proper accounts more efficiently.

Once you enter the gross wages, the payroll liabilities amount automatically calculates. It's a negative number because the accounts on the Expenses tab are debited, and you want to credit 26000·Payroll Liabilities-OPS. And, basic arithmetic tells us that $3,337.46 = $4,450.00 − $1,112.54! Leave the Write Checks window open.

BEHIND THE SCENES BRIEF

62930·Gross Wages-OPS DR 7,717.00; **10100·Checking CR 5,787.71 |** **26000·Payroll Liabilities-OPS CR 1,929.29**

62930·Gross Wages-OPS has **increased**; 10100·Checking has **decreased |** 26000·Payroll Liabilities-OPS has **increased**

Check Figure: Checking $28,302.97

Warning! Remember, you use the Write Checks window to create paychecks only if you use an outside payroll service. *Never* use it if you're running payroll through QuickBooks!

Pay Payroll Liabilities

Now you will use the monthly payroll statement to create a payroll liability check and a benefits check for January 31, 2025. The state taxes are due quarterly, so you will not remit them at this time.

12. Create the two liability checks, each dated **1/31/2025**, to be printed later, and drawing from **10100·Checking**. The check for the U.S. Treasury is for all federal taxes owed (including the amount held in Payroll Liabilities and the amount owed by the company). Click **Save & New** after the first check and Quick Add any new vendors.

Pay to the Order of	U.S. Treasury	Health Solutions, Inc.
Amount	2122.22	1790
Memo (all)	Payroll Taxes, Jan 2025	Employee Benefits, Jan 2025
Account / Amount	(first row) **62920•Company-Paid Taxes** / 578.78 (second row) **26000•Payroll Liabilities-OPS** / 1543.44	(first row) **62910•Company-Paid Benefits** / 1790 (no second row)

BEHIND THE SCENES BRIEF

26000•Payroll Liabilities-OPS DR 1,543.44 | 62910•Company-Paid Benefits DR 1,790.00 | 62920•Company-Paid Taxes DR 578.78; **10100·Checking CR 3,912.22**

26000•Payroll Liabilities-OPS has **decreased** | 62910•Company-Paid Benefits has **increased** | 62920•Company-Paid Taxes has **increased**; 10100·Checking has **decreased**

Check Figure: Checking $24,390.75

Print Paychecks and Liability Checks

The final step is to print the paycheck and liability checks. Because you have additional checks in the queue, you will print them as well.

13. Click the **Print Checks** task icon in the Banking area of the Home Page.

14. Ensure the bank account is **10100·Checking** and the first check number is **10086**; click **OK**.

Print Checks

15. Choose the option that allows you to print/save to a PDF file and click **Print**, navigate to your file storage location, and click **Save**.

16. Close the PDF file and then click **OK** in the Print Checks - Confirmation window.

Run a Payroll Report for an Outside Payroll Service

You can't use the preset payroll reports in QuickBooks to view data for payroll transactions dealing with an outside payroll service. So, you will create a QuickReport based on 10100·Checking and set it to only show employees.

17. Click the **Chart of Accounts** task icon in the Company area of the Home Page.

18. Right-click **10100·Checking** and choose **QuickReport : 10100·Checking**.

19. Set the date range to **01/01/2025** to **01/31/2025** and refresh the report.

20. Follow these steps to filter the report to show only employees:

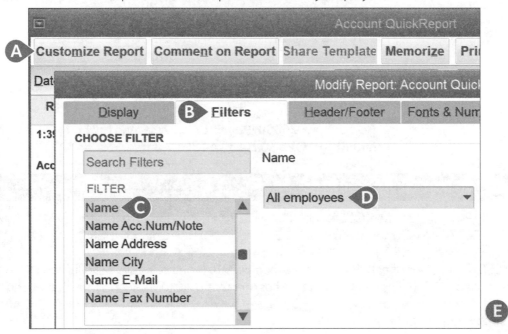

Ⓐ Click **Customize Report**.

Ⓑ Click the **Filters** tab.

Ⓒ Scroll down and click **Name**.

Ⓓ Click the drop-down arrow ▼ and choose **All Employees**.

Ⓔ Click **OK**.

You will see all checks written to employees in the month of January displayed.

21. Close the Account QuickReport and the Chart of Accounts windows.

Tackle the Tasks

Now is your chance to work a little more with Rock Castle Construction and apply the skills you've just learned to accomplish additional tasks. Continue with the same company file you've been using in this chapter so far.

Set the Payroll Preference	Set QuickBooks to run full payroll
Add an Employee	Tammy Reagan; SS# 333-22-1111; Female; DOB 06/17/1969; 14896 Highridge Estates, Bayshore, CA 94326; (415) 555-4004; Marital Status: Divorced; U.S. Citizen: Yes; Ethnicity: White; Disabled: No; I-9 Form: On file; U.S. Veteran: No
	(Payroll Info tab) Payroll Schedule: Biweekly; Earnings Items: Regular Pay, Hourly Rate $20; Overtime Rate, Hourly Rate $30; Deductions: 401k -6%; Charity Donation $35; Health Insurance $500; 401k Co. Match -2.5%
	(Tax information) Federal Filing Status: Single; Form W-4: 2020 and Later; Deductions: 1; State: CA; State Worked: CA; State Subject to Withholding: CA, single with one allowance
Pay the Employee	Use the Start Unscheduled Payroll button in the Employee Center: Payroll Center window to create a paycheck for Tammy for the pay period ending 12/29/2024; date the paycheck 12/29/2024 for 80 regular pay hours and 7 overtime hours
Print a Paycheck and Pay Stub	Print the paycheck you just created for Tammy as a PDF file using the next check number (10095); prepare a pay stub to go with it
Pay Liabilities	On 01/15/2025, pay the five payroll liabilities due based on Tammy's paycheck (change the date of each check)
Run Reports	Create a report showing all employees and their withholding information
	Create a report showing a payroll summary for 12/29/2024

Self-Assessment

Check your knowledge of this chapter's key concepts and skills using the Self-Assessment quiz here, in your ebook, or in your eLab course.

1. Most payroll mistakes are due to payroll items being set up incorrectly. *True   False*

2. Subcontractors are entered in the Employees List. *True   False*

3. Only those transactions entered via QuickBooks' payroll features affect payroll reporting. *True   False*

4. You should set up employee defaults before you set up your employees. *True   False*

5. Workers' compensation can be tracked within QuickBooks Payroll. *True   False*

6. Payroll schedules allow you to set how often you pay employees. *True   False*

7. To pay the payroll liabilities while running full payroll in QuickBooks, use the Write Checks window. *True   False*

8. When you use an outside payroll service, you should set up QuickBooks to track full payroll. *True   False*

9. In QuickBooks, an employee is someone to whom you issue a W-2 or 1099-MISC. *True   False*

10. If you discover that an employee was overpaid after you've issued the paycheck, void the paycheck and create a new one with the correct amount. *True   False*

11. Which is NOT a payroll item?
    A. Federal withholding
    B. Hours worked
    C. Vacation hourly
    D. Health insurance

12. When you create paychecks, which account is credited?
    A. Gross Wages
    B. Payroll Expenses
    C. Payroll Liabilities
    D. Accounts Payable

13. In which account do you keep the taxes you withhold from your employees?
    A. Sales Tax Payable
    B. Payroll Liabilities
    C. Checking
    D. Payroll Assets

14. Which payroll form do you provide to subcontractors at the end of the year?
    A. W-2
    B. 940
    C. 1099-MISC
    D. 1096

Reinforce Your Skills

Just as you used a sample company file for the Develop Your Skills exercises in this chapter, so will you for the Reinforce Your Skills section. This time you will work with the company file for Quality-Built Construction.

REINFORCE YOUR SKILLS 9-1

Turn on Payroll and Enter a New Employee

In this exercise, you will add a new employee who was just hired.

1. Choose **File→Open or Restore Company**.
2. Open **RYS_Chapter09 (Company)** *or* restore **RYS_Chapter09 (Portable)** and save it as: **RYS_Chapter09 Quality Built Construction**
3. Click **OK** to acknowledge you are opening a QuickBooks Desktop sample file.
4. Choose **Edit→Preferences** and then click the **Payroll & Employees** category and the **Company Preferences** tab.
5. Confirm the Full Payroll function is turned on and click **OK**.

Enter a New Employee

6. Choose **Employees→Employee Center**.

   The Employee Center will display with seven employees.

7. Click the **New Employee** button and set up the new employee:

Name	**Ms. Aiyana Harrison**	U.S. Veteran	**Yes**
SSN	**999-88-6666**	Status	**Reserve**
Gender	**Female**	Address	**503 Birch Hill Road, Woodcrest, CA 92504**
Date of Birth	**04/13/1986**	Main Phone	**(951) 555-2134**
Marital Status	**Single**	Item Name (Payroll Info tab, Earnings box)	**9891-Office** (delete the other items added by default)
U.S. Citizen	**Yes**	Hourly Rate	**20.00**
Ethnicity	**Black**	Form W-4	**2020 and Later**
Disabled	**No**	Filing Status and Deductions	**Single, 0**
I-9 Form	**On File**	State Worked and State Subject to Withholding / Allowances	**CA, 0**

8. Click **OK** four times and then click **Leave As Is** and close the Employee Center window.

Create Paychecks for Employees

In this exercise, you will create paychecks for Aiyana Harrison and Young-Kyu Yoo for the period of 12/16/2019–12/31/2019. No scheduled payrolls have been set up for this company, so there's no Unscheduled Payroll button; instead, there is the Pay Employees button.

1. Choose **Employees→Pay Employees**.
2. Set the check date and pay period ending dates to **12/31/2019**. If the Pay Period Change window opens, click **No**.
3. Select **Print Paychecks on Check Stock** under Check Options.
4. Add checkmarks next to **Aiyana Harrison** and **Young-Kyu Yoo** and then enter **80** in the **9891-Office** column for Aiyana.
5. Change the number of hours for Young-Kyu to: **80**

Create and Print Paychecks

You will now review the information entered for Aiyana and Young-Kyu and then create the paychecks.

6. Click **Continue**.

   The Review and Create Paychecks window displays.

7. Click **Create Paychecks**.

   The Confirmation and Next Steps window appears, showing a summary of how many paychecks were created as well as providing you with a shortcut to printing paychecks and pay stubs.

8. Click **Print Paychecks** and type **497** as the first check number.
9. Click **OK** in the Select Paychecks to Print window, choose to print to PDF, and click **OK** in the Print Checks Confirmation window.
10. Click the **Print Pay Stubs** button and set the date range (if necessary):
    - From: **123119**
    - To: **123119**
11. Click **Preview** to view how the pay stubs will print and then close the Print Preview window.
12. Close the Select Pay Stubs and Confirmation and Next Steps windows.
13. Close the Payroll Center.

Pay the Payroll Liabilities

In this exercise, you will pay the payroll liabilities due in January 2020.

1. Choose **Employees→Payroll Taxes and Liabilities→Pay Scheduled Liabilities**.

2. Add checkmarks to the left of all liability payments due in January.

3. Click the **View/Pay** button in the Pay Scheduled Liabilities area of the Payroll Center.

   A Liability Payment – Checking Account window for the first payment appears.

4. Change the date to **011420** and choose **U.S. Treasury** as the vendor; click **Save & Next** to view the next payment.

5. Change the dates of all checks to: **011420**

6. Click **Save & Next** to record each liability check; click **Save & Close** when finished.

7. Close the Payment Summary window and then close the company file.

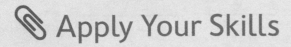

Apply Your Skills

Wet Noses Veterinary Clinic is expanding and must hire a new employee to keep up with demand. The clinic uses an outside payroll service and you will pay employees and payroll liabilities, as well as review reports to help analyze the business spending. The password for all files unless otherwise stated is Password1.

APPLY YOUR SKILLS 9-1 QG

Set Up QuickBooks to Track Payroll from an Outside Service

Dr. James has been using an outside payroll service at Wet Noses. In this exercise, you will verify that the correct accounts are set up to properly track expenses and liabilities. Then you will enter a new employee. You will need to have accounts set up in your Chart of Accounts to track your payroll expenses and liabilities.

Note! The QuickBooks payroll features should *not* be turned on when entering payroll from an outside source.

1. Choose **File→Open or Restore Company**.
2. Open **AYS_Chapter09 (Company)** *or* restore **AYS_Chapter09 (Portable)** and save it as: **AYS_Chapter09 Wet Noses Clinic**
3. Open the **Chart of Accounts** and verify that Payroll Liabilities is set up as an Other Current Liability.
4. Scroll down and verify that Payroll Expenses is set up as an Expense account.

   Dr. James has learned that she should set up subaccounts for the Payroll Expenses account. You will help her do this now.

5. Set up three subaccounts for Payroll Expenses:
   • 66010•Gross Wages
   • 66020•Company-Paid Taxes
   • 66030•Company-Paid Benefits

Enter a New Employee

When entering a new employee and using an outside payroll service, you do not need to set up tax information.

6. Create a new employee for Wet Noses:

Name	Mr. Viho Locklear
SSN	000-33-5555
Gender	**Male**
Date of Birth	04/24/1983
Address	2611 Lake Road, Kirkland, WA 98034
Main Phone	(425) 555-1066

7. Run an **Employee Contact List** report to show the details for each employee.

8. Notice that the phone numbers for three employees are missing. Using QuickZoom, add the phone numbers to the employee records and then return to the report:

- Bently Batson: (206) 555-8789
- Carrie Jones: (425) 555-2052
- Samantha Reese: (425) 555-1742

9. Click the **Excel** button and export this report to a new workbook saved as: `CH9_A1 Employee Contact List`

10. Close the Excel window and the Employee Center.

APPLY YOUR SKILLS 9-2 QG

Create Paychecks Using Information from an Outside Payroll Service

Dr. James received a statement from the payroll service showing the amount to pay each employee and the amount that has been deducted. In this exercise, you will help her create the paychecks for the employees.

WET NOSES VETERINARY CLINIC JUNE 2023 PAYROLL					
Employee	**Gross Wages**	**Employee Federal Taxes Withheld**	**Net Pay**	**Company Federal Taxes Owed**	**Company Benefits Owed**
Bently Batson	$1,500.00	$234.62	$1,265.38	$114.75	$450.00
Carrie Jones	$2,166.00	$395.72	$1,770.28	$165.70	$450.00
Samantha Reese	$2,166.00	$324.21	$1,841.79	$165.70	$450.00
Viho Locklear	$1,000.00	$119.48	$880.52	$76.50	$225.00
Totals	$6,832.00	$1,074.03	$5,757.97	$522.65	$1,575.00

1. Using the Write Check window, create paychecks dated 06/30/2023 for the employees listed above; they are to be printed later.

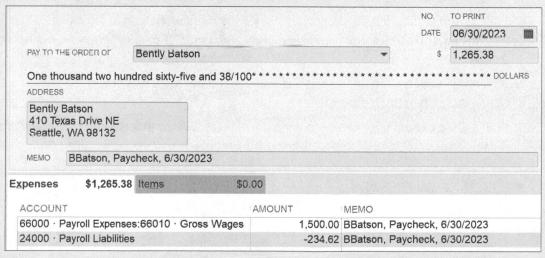

Warning! Remember, use the Write Checks window to create paychecks only if you use an outside payroll service. *Never* use it if you're running payroll through QuickBooks!

2. Run a **QuickReport** from 06/30/2023 to 06/30/2023 on the **Payroll Liabilities** account to show the transaction detail for this account.

3. Click the **Excel** button and export this report to a new workbook saved as:
CH9_A2 Payroll Liabilities

4. Close the QuickReport and Chart of Accounts windows.

APPLY YOUR SKILLS 9-3 QG

Pay the Payroll Liabilities and Print Checks

In this exercise, you will use the information from the table in Apply Your Skills 9-2 to create payroll liability checks for June 2023.

1. Open the **Write Checks** window and set the date to 07/01/2023.

2. Create a liability check to the U.S. Treasury (Quick Add the new vendor) for all federal taxes owed.

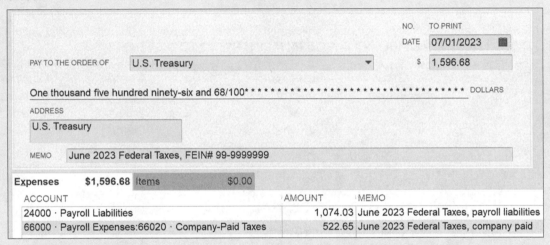

3. Create a second check dated 07/01/2023 for $1,575 made payable to Kellerman Insurance for the company-paid medical benefits owed, entering June 2023 Medical/Dental Insurance for Employees as the memo and **66030•Company-Paid Benefits** as the account.

4. Choose to print all checks in the queue waiting to be printed, using 1444 as the first check number.

5. Run a **Check Detail** report from the Banking section of the Report Center for checks dated from 06/30/2023 to 07/01/2023.

6. Click the **Excel** button and export this report to a new workbook saved as:
CH9_A3 Check Detail

7. Run a **QuickReport** for the Checking account; click **Customize Report** and choose the **Filters** tab and filter by **Name**, choosing **All Employees**, to see how much has been paid in payroll.

8. Click the **Excel** button and export this report to a new workbook saved as:
CH9_A3 Employee Payroll

9. Close the company file.

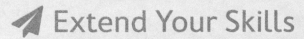

Extend Your Skills

Before You Begin: Open **EYS_Chapter09 (Company)** *or* restore **EYS_Chapter09 (Portable)**. The password is *Password1*.

You've been hired by Arlaine Cervantes to help her with her organization's books. She is the founder of Niños del Lago, a nonprofit organization that provides impoverished Guatemalan children with an engaging educational camp experience. You just sat down at your desk and opened a large envelope from Arlaine that contains a variety of documents; you also have several emails from her. It's your job to sort through the papers and emails and make sense of what you find, entering information into QuickBooks as appropriate and answering any questions in a word-processing document saved as: CH09_EYS_[LastnameFirstinitial]

Remember, you're dealing with random papers dumped out of an envelope and various emails, so part of your challenge is determining the order in which to complete the tasks.

- Sticky note from Arlaine: Hired two part-time employees to work at the U.S. office to raise funds and sell inventory on 8/15/2020. Will use an outside payroll service. How will we enter payroll information into QuickBooks? (Explain your answer.)

- Completed W-4 and I-9: Chelsea Sathrum; 8213 NW College Ct., Salem, OR, 97304; 503-555-2003; SS# 999-22-3333; Female; DOB 05/21/1988.

- Sticky note from Arlaine: Please prepare a check to pay all federal payroll liabilities owed. The amount in Payroll Liabilities that is owed to the U.S. Treasury is $66.55, but don't forget to pay the company's share!

- Note from accountant: Enter the accounts and subaccounts necessary to track an outside payroll service in QuickBooks.

- Create paychecks; statement from payroll service, dated 8/31/2020:

Employee	Gross Wages	Employee Federal & State Taxes W/H	Net Pay	Company Federal Taxes Owed	Company Unemployment Owed
Jose Martinez	$450.00	$78.00	$372.00	$34.42	$16.28
Chelsea Sathrum	$420.00	$48.71	$371.29	$32.13	$15.35

- Completed W-4 and I-9: Jose Martinez; 16932 SE Freedom Way, Salem, OR 97306; SS# 999-22-1111; Male; DOB 07/04/1987.

- Scribbled note from Arlaine: Can you produce a report for me that shows how much has been paid in payroll for each employee?

10 | Job Costing, Creating Estimates, and Time Tracking

QuickBooks lets you create estimates for your jobs (or for your customers, if you don't have jobs assigned to them). Once you're awarded a job based on an estimate, QuickBooks makes it easy to convert the estimate to an invoice, so you don't have to reenter the information. Job costing is an important aspect for many businesses. In this chapter, you will use jobs in QuickBooks to track profitability by those jobs. You will also use progress invoicing and deal with customer deposits. You will explore the time-tracking feature, which allows you to track time spent by employees on each job, resulting in more accurate payroll expenses for job costing. Finally, you'll look at a QuickBooks app that aids you in time tracking and employee scheduling, TSheets.

LEARNING OBJECTIVES

▸ Create an estimate for a job or customer and convert it to a progress invoice

▸ Apply the time tracking feature and create a paycheck based on tracked time

▸ Enter customer deposits on account

▸ Assign finance charges to overdue accounts

▸ Run appropriate job-related reports for estimates and time tracking

Project: Rock Castle Construction

We'll continue to work with the QuickBooks sample company file used for payroll in the previous chapter, Rock Castle Construction, as this will enable you to use the time tracking features to run payroll.

Job costing is used a lot in the construction industry, and you'll begin by creating an estimate for a job you're bidding on. When the job is awarded, you'll convert the estimate to an invoice and bill the customer as portions of the job are completed using QuickBooks' progress invoicing feature. You will receive a payment and handle customer deposits for unearned income. In addition, you'll use time tracking to monitor employee time on a job and create a paycheck using that time data. You will assess finance charges for customers, too. You'll then run job reports for analyzing this and other jobs, estimates, and time tracking data for the company. Finally, you will explore the possibility of using TSheets to track employee time more precisely.

Job Costing

To keep track of the income and expenses involved in this and all the jobs Rock Castle Construction does, individual jobs are created for each customer. When applied via sales and purchase forms, job costing provides a method for determining the profitability of each job and will help in planning for the future.

Job information is stored with the customer data in the Customers & Jobs List, which is a component of the Customer Center. If you have multiple projects for an individual customer, you can create separate jobs for that customer. If you'll complete just one job for a customer, you can track that information in the customer's record on the Job Info tab. As you create your estimates and invoices or incur any expenses for that job, you enter them for the job and not the customer directly.

When customers have a job associated with them, you *must* choose a job on a form, not just the customer. The time tracking feature allows a company to track employee time and to create paychecks and invoices based on the data collected. You can also charge employees' time to jobs.

Job Profitability

For companies that deal with jobs, especially businesses such as construction companies, it's important to be able to determine the profitability of each job. To conduct job costing in QuickBooks, you need to take three basic steps:

1. Set up your data in the Customers & Jobs List.

2. Enter all job revenues and expenses.

3. Use QuickBooks reports to analyze job data.

The first two steps are covered if you set up your customers and jobs correctly and then enter them properly on sales and purchase forms. We'll look at the QuickBooks job costing reports later in this chapter.

Creating an Estimate for a Job

QuickBooks creates a non-posting account when you create an estimate, which allows you to track outstanding estimates (just as it does for purchase and sales orders). This account is displayed at the bottom of your Chart of Accounts. The non-posting account is created because estimates, like purchase orders, don't affect anything behind the scenes and, therefore, don't affect actual QuickBooks accounts.

You can create estimates for customers or, if using jobs, for each job you do for a customer. You can also create multiple estimates for a customer or a job. If a customer doesn't have jobs created for it, you will see a Job Info tab in the Edit Customer window; however, if even one job has been created for a customer, that Job Info tab will not be available, and you will work with the individual jobs created for the customer. Estimates must be turned on via the Company tab of the Preferences window.

> ### FLASHBACK TO GAAP: MATCHING
>
> Remember that expenses need to be matched with revenues. A sink bought for a bathroom remodel should be a job cost for that remodel. This principle allows for a better evaluation of the profitability and performance.

Change Orders

A change order occurs after an estimate has been entered. If a customer wants a change to an estimate (and you're using the Contractor or Accountant's version of QuickBooks Desktop), when you make that change, you will be asked if you want to add it as a change order to the estimate. Changes are listed under the original estimate. If you're using a different version of QuickBooks, you can still make changes to estimates, but they won't be called out as change orders.

The change order feature details the amount of each change, exactly what changed, and the net change to the amount of the estimate. It also documents the change order for you in the description field of the estimate window.

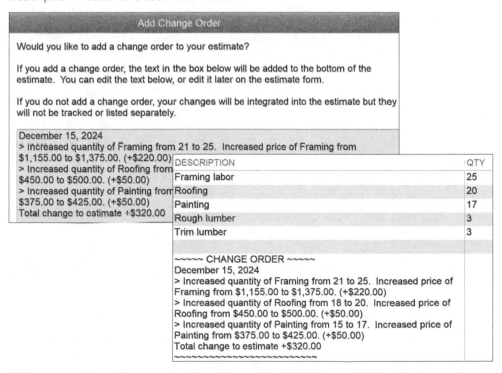

When you make a change to an estimate, the Add Change Order window appears so you can add a change order. The change order is displayed in the description column below the last item.

↱ Customers→Customer Center : [choose customer]→New Customers & Jobs button→Add Job

↱ Edit→Preferences : Jobs & Estimates→Company Preferences tab

↱ Customers→Create Estimates

DEVELOP YOUR SKILLS 10-1

In this exercise, you will turn on the preferences for estimates and progress invoicing and create an estimate for a new customer. You will be using a QuickBooks sample company file, which sets the date to 12/15/2024 when opening the company or a new window. Leave the company file open unless otherwise instructed.

1. Start QuickBooks 2020.
2. Open **DYS_Chapter10 (Company)** *or* restore **DYS_Chapter10 (Portable)** and save it as: **DYS_Chapter10 Rock Castle Construction**
3. Click **OK** to acknowledge you're using a sample company file.
4. Choose **Edit→Preferences** and then click the **Jobs & Estimates** category and the **Company Preferences** tab.
5. Choose **Yes** under both *Do you create estimates?* and *Do you do Progress Invoicing?* and then click **OK**; click **OK** in the Warning window.

   QuickBooks needs to close all open windows to activate these preferences.

6. Choose **Company→Home Page**.

   Notice the new Estimates task icon in the Company area of the Home Page as well as the lines connecting it to Create Invoices and Sales Orders.

Create a New Customer

The City of Danville is not yet set up as a customer, so you will create a new customer and job for the City of Danville.

7. Click the **Customers** [CUSTOMERS] button in the Customers area of the Home Page.
8. Press [Ctrl]+[n] to open a New Customer window.
9. Create the new customer:

Company/Customer Name	**City of Danville**
Full Name	**Ms. Cam Brennan**
Main Phone	**(415) 555-2496**
Address (also use in Ship To field)	**1706 Duck Pond Lane, Danville, CA 94526**
Terms	**1% 10 Net 30**
Sales Tax Code	**Non**

10. Click **OK**.

    You will see your new customer selected on the Customer & Jobs list.

Create a New Job for the Customer

11. Click the **New Customer & Job** button and choose **Add Job**.

12. Type **Picnic Structures** in the Job Name field.

13. Click the **Job Info** tab and enter information about the new job, clicking **OK** when finished:

    • Job Description: **3 picnic shelters in city park**

    • Job Type: **New Construction**

    • Job Status: **Pending**

Create an Estimate for a Job

The newly created job now appears indented under City of Danville in the Customers & Jobs List. It's selected, and now you're ready to create a new transaction for that job.

14. Click the **New Transactions** button and choose **Estimates**.

    The Create Estimates window opens with the Picnic Structures project job already filled in.

15. Follow these steps to complete the estimate (the date and estimate number will fill in automatically):

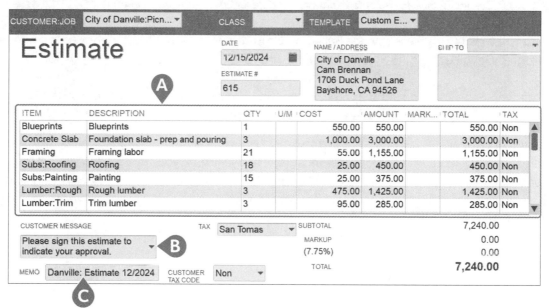

Ⓐ Enter these rows by first choosing the item and then entering the quantity and cost.

   The Description column will populate and the amounts in the Total column will calculate automatically.

Ⓑ Click the drop-down arrow ▾ and choose: **Please sign this estimate to indicate your approval.**

Ⓒ Tap ⌷Tab⌷ and type: **Danville: Estimate 12/2024**

16. Click **Save & Close**.

    The estimate is created. Remember that nothing happens behind the scenes here! If the job doesn't come through, you can choose to mark it as inactive.

Progress Invoicing

If you have a job that will span weeks or months, progress invoicing allows you to submit invoices based on parts of the work completed (stages or phases) as you go through the job. You start by creating an estimate for the entire job and then create an invoice based on it, choosing one of these three options:

- Create an invoice for the entire estimate (100%).

- Create an invoice for a percentage of the entire estimate.

- Create an invoice for selected items or for different percentages of each item.

You can create an invoice by opening the existing estimate or using the Create Invoices window and selecting the customer.

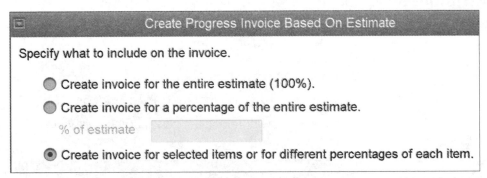

Use the Create Progress Invoice Based on Estimate window to choose what to include on a progress invoice.

After you've selected one of the three options and chosen how much to include on the invoice, QuickBooks will display the Progress Invoice template.

There will be several new columns on the progress invoice template, depending on the option selected (such as Est Amt, Prior Amt, and Total %). Every time you create a subsequent invoice for that customer (or customer:job), it will reflect the prior amount(s) and/or percentages. It's an easy way to bill your customer as you work through the job and for your customer to see what's already been done.

BEHIND THE SCENES: *Progress Invoice*

11000•Accounts Receivable
INCREASE to Assets

40110•Design Income 40140•Materials Income
INCREASE to Revenue

→ *Equity*

Assets	=	Liabilities	+	Capital	+	Revenue	−	Expenses
$2,260.00	=	$0.00	+	$0.00	+	$2,260.00	−	$0.00

11000•Accounts Receivable	
Debit	Credit
$2,260.00	

40110•Design Income	
Debit	Credit
	$550.00

40140•Materials Income	
Debit	Credit
	$1,710.00

↱ Customers→Create Invoices [and then choose the desired customer and estimate]

↱ Customers→Create Estimates : [find estimate]→Create Invoice button

DEVELOP YOUR SKILLS 10-2

Rock Castle was awarded the City of Danville Picnic Structures job and has begun work on it. In this exercise, you will edit the Customer:Job record to change the status and then use the job estimate created earlier to create the progress invoice. The first step is to open the Edit Job window for the Picnic Structures job and change the status on the Job Info tab.

Before You Begin: *The Customer Center should be displayed. If not, choose Customers→Customer Center.*

1. Double-click the **Picnic Structures** job for the City of Danville to open it for editing.

2. Click the **Job Info** tab and edit the job:

   • Job Status: **In progress**

   • Start Date: **122024**

   • Projected End Date: **011525**

3. Click **OK** to save the Job and then close the Customer Center window.

Create the Invoice

Now you will create a progress invoice based on the estimate. Rock Castle has completed the blueprints for the job, and the materials have been ordered.

Create Invoices

4. Click the **Create Invoices** task icon in the Customers area of the Home Page.

5. Choose the **City of Danville:Picnic Structures** job as the Customer:Job.

   The Available Estimates window appears, displaying all the available estimates for the job.

6. Click the **12/15/2024** estimate for $7,240.00 in the Available Estimates window and click **OK**.

   The Create Progress Invoice Based on Estimate window appears with three choices.

7. Click the circle to the left of **Create invoice for selected items or for different percentages of each item.** and then click **OK**.

   The Specify Invoice Amounts for Items on Estimate window appears.

8. Follow these steps to enter the invoice amounts:

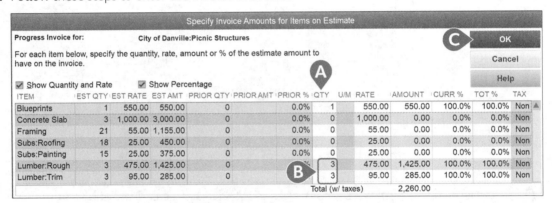

A Click in the **Blueprints Qty** field and type: **1**

B Click in the **Qty** field for both **Lumber:Rough** and **Lumber:Trim** and type **3** in each.

C Click **OK**.

The Create Invoices window displays using the Progress Invoice template. The full amounts for the blueprints and lumber are calculated for you. You can change the preference to not print items with zero amounts but don't delete the items on the invoice with zero amounts.

9. Follow these steps to complete the invoice:

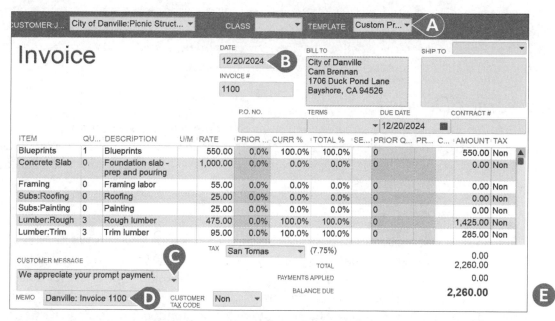

Ⓐ Click this drop-down arrow ▼ and choose the **Custom Progress Invoice** template.

Ⓑ Tap `Tab` and type **122024**.

Ⓒ Click this drop-down arrow ▼ and choose the **We appreciate your prompt payment.** message.

Ⓓ Tap `Tab` and type **Danville: Invoice 1100**

Ⓔ Click **Save & Close**.

The progress invoice is recorded. The next time you create an invoice based on the estimate for the Picnic Structures job, the amounts you just invoiced will show as a prior amount.

BEHIND THE SCENES BRIEF

11000•Accounts Receivable DR 2,260.00; **40110•Design Income CR 550.00 | 40140•Materials Income CR 1,710.00**

11000•Accounts Receivable has **increased**; 40110•Design Income has **increased** | 40140•Materials Income has **increased**

Check Figure: Accounts Receivable $95,267.93

Unearned Income

There will be some cases in which you require a deposit on a job or a customer prepayment. Funds received as a deposit or sold as a gift certificate are considered unearned income because no work has been performed and no product has been sold. You may also hear this called *unearned revenue* or *deferred revenue*. You shouldn't credit unearned income to an income account. The proper way to deal with it is to hold it in a liability account such as Customer Deposits or Unearned Revenues. After you deliver the goods or perform the service, you decrease the liability account and credit (or increase) the appropriate income account.

Customer Deposits

Customer deposits and gift certificates are tracked the same way in QuickBooks, with both requiring you to go through the three steps of setting up, collecting, and recording. We will deal specifically with customer deposits, but you can apply the same principles if you need to account for gift certificates.

Accounting for customer deposits is a three-step process:

1. **Set up to track customer deposits:** To begin, you set up an Other Current Liability account and two items (Other Charge and Payment type). The Other Current Liability account is necessary because, by accepting a customer deposit or a payment for a gift certificate, you're essentially accepting both as a liability. The deposit will eventually be turned into a payment and the gift certificate redeemed for goods or services. By setting up a liability account, you can show that you're holding the funds in a separate account until the income becomes "earned." The two new items are necessary for creating an invoice.

2. **Receive a customer deposit:** Next you use an invoice to record receipt of the deposit, selecting the new items and directing the funds to a liability account. You are "liable" for doing something in return for the funds received. You don't record the income until the service is performed, the product delivered, or the gift certificate redeemed. This won't affect an income account or Accounts Receivable because the balance owing on the invoice will be zero.

3. **Turn a deposit into a payment:** After you've delivered on your promise by trading goods or services for the deposit or gift certificate, you use an invoice to record the income. The invoice increases an income account and then reduces the liability account when the income becomes "earned" and you're no longer liable to perform or deliver.

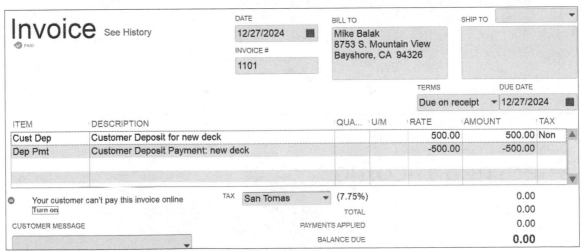

When you accept a customer deposit, the net amount of the invoice is zero because Accounts Receivable is not affected.

BEHIND THE SCENES: *Customer Deposit*

12000•Undeposited Funds
INCREASE to Assets

25000•Customer Deposits
INCREASE to Liabilities

→ **Equity**

Assets = Liabilities + (Capital + Revenue − Expenses)

$500.00 = $500.00 + $0.00 + $0.00 − $0.00

12000•Undeposited Funds	
Debit	*Credit*
$500.00	

25000•Customer Deposits	
Debit	*Credit*
	$500.00

Lists→Chart of Accounts : Account→New : Other Account Types→Other Current Liability account

Lists→Item List : Item→New : Other Charge *or* Payment

DEVELOP YOUR SKILLS 10-3

In this exercise, you will prepare to track customer deposits, receive a deposit for a customer, and turn the deposit into a payment. Before you can deal with unearned income, you must set up the proper account and items.

1. Click the **Chart of Accounts** task icon in the Company area of the Home Page.
2. Click the **Account** drop-down arrow ▼ and choose **New**.
3. Create the account:
   - Account Type: **Other Current Liability**

     Hint: First choose Other Account Types.
   - Number: **25000**
   - Account Name: **Customer Deposits**
4. Click **Save & Close** and then close the Chart of Accounts.

   Now you will create the services for the two items needed to track the deposit.

5. Click the **Items & Services** task icon in the Company area of the Home Page.

Items & Services

6. Click the **Item** drop-down arrow ▾, choose **New**, and then complete the first item:

Type	**Other Charge**
Item Name/Number	**Cust Dep**
Description	**Customer Deposit**
Tax Code	**Non**
Account	**25000•Customer Deposits**

The Amount field is left as 0.00; you will fill that in at the time of sale.

7. Click **Next** and create the second new item:

Type	**Payment**
Item Name/Number	**Dep Pmt**
Description	**Customer Deposit Payment**

8. Click **OK** and then close the Item List window.

Collect a Customer Deposit

Mike Balak just called and asked Rock Castle Construction to build a deck, including installing a gas BBQ. You will begin by entering a customer deposit and before recording this deposit, you'll create a new job for the customer.

9. Click the **Customers** [CUSTOMERS] button in the Customers area of the Home Page.

10. Right-click **Balak, Mike** and choose **Add Job**.

11. Type **Deck** as the Job Name and click **OK**.

   The Customer Center will still be open with the new job selected.

12. Click the **New Transactions** button and choose **Invoices**.

13. Complete the invoice:

Date	**122724**	
Invoice #	**1101**	
Terms	**Due on receipt**	
	First Item	**Second Item**
Item	**Cust Dep**	**Dep Pmt**
Description	**Customer Deposit for new deck**	**Customer Deposit Payment for new deck**
Rate	**500** (tap Tab to fill in the Amount field)	**−500** (tap Tab to fill in the Amount field)
Memo	**Balak: Deck Deposit 12/2024**	

The total due for the invoice should be 0.00 because the net effect to Accounts Receivable is 0.00. In other words, the customer doesn't owe anything as a result of the transaction. Behind the scenes, though, you collected the $500 deposit that debited Undeposited Funds and credited Customer Deposits, as the Cust Dep item is tied to the Other Liability Account: 25000•Customer Deposits.

BEHIND THE SCENES BRIEF
12000•Undeposited Funds DR 500.00; **25000•Customer Deposits CR 500.00**
12000•Undeposited Funds has **increased**; 25000•Customer Deposits has **increased**
Check Figure: Undeposited Funds $2,940.00

14. Click **Save & Close**.

15. Click **No** in the Information Changed window and then close the Customer Center.

You changed the terms to due on receipt *for this one transaction but want the default terms you have set for the customer to remain the same. The deposit is now recorded! You will apply it to an invoice in the next exercise.*

Passing on Expenses to Customers

When you enter a bill or make a purchase using cash or a credit card, you may be acquiring equipment or supplies whose costs you want to pass on to a customer. QuickBooks allows you to easily indicate which expenses are to be billed to a customer by providing a "Billable?" column in the Enter Bills window. When you make an item billable to a specific customer, the next time you invoice that customer, you will be asked if you'd like to add the outstanding billable time and costs to the invoice.

The expense or cost of goods sold account you debit when you make the purchase essentially functions as a "holding account," as you will credit it when you invoice the customer for the expense.

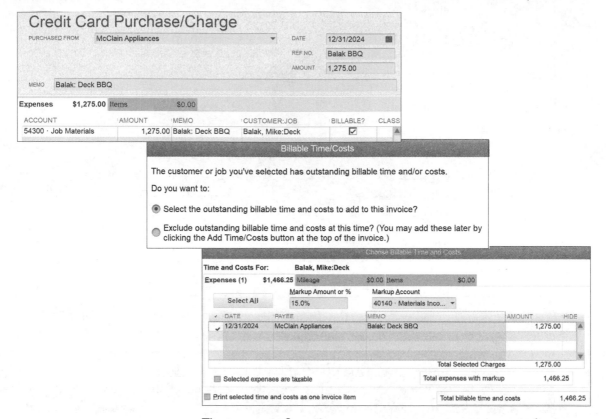

The process of passing an expense on to a customer: indicate the customer to pass it on to on the purchase form, select the outstanding billable costs, select the expense(s) to pass on, and enter any markup.

Markups

If you wish to increase the amount charged for a service or item, you can enter the amounts individually, set a default markup percentage, or use the price level feature to apply it. You can also apply a markup to billable time and costs. Typically, you don't show the markup amount on sales forms, though you can customize an estimate template to show it when printed for customers as well.

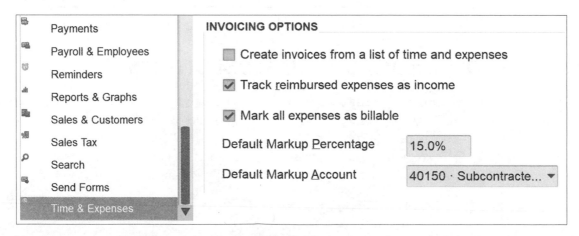

You can set up a default markup in the Time & Expenses preferences category.

BEHIND THE SCENES: *Pass an Expense to a Customer*

11000•Accounts Receivable 25000•Customer Deposits	54300•Job Materials 40140•Materials Income
INCREASE to Assets *DECREASE to Liabilities*	*DECREASE to Expenses* *INCREASE to Revenue*

Equity

$$Assets = Liabilities + (Capital + Revenue - Expenses)$$

$$\$966.25 = -\$500.00 + \$0.00 + \$191.25 - -\$1,275.00$$

11000•Accounts Receivable

Debit	Credit
$966.25	

54300•Job Materials

Debit	Credit
	$1,275.00

25000•Customer Deposits

Debit	Credit
$500.00	

40140•Materials Income

Debit	Credit
	$191.25

You are emptying out the amount being "held" in Job Materials.

DEVELOP YOUR SKILLS 10-4

You will be purchasing the gas BBQ for Mike Balak's Deck BBQ job. In this exercise, you will record the purchase, paying for it using a credit card and passing on the expense to Mike Balak's deck job.

1. Click the **Enter Credit Card Charges** task icon in the Banking area of the Home Page.

2. Choose **20500•QuickBooks Credit Card** as the credit card account.

Enter Credit Card Charges

3. Complete the charge that will be passed on to the customer:

Purchased From	**McClain Appliances**
Date	**123124**
Ref No.	**Balak BBQ**
Amount	**1,275**
Memo (use this text on the Expenses tab, too)	**Balak: Deck BBQ**
Account (Expenses tab)	**54300•Job Materials**
Customer:Job	**Balak, Mike:Deck**

4. Ensure the **Billable** checkbox is checked and then click **Save & Close**.

Create an Invoice with a Billable Cost

The final step is to turn the deposit into a payment. You will add the billable amount from the McClain Appliances purchase to Mike Balak's invoice.

5. Click the **Create Invoices** task icon in the Customers area of the Home Page.

6. Choose **Balak, Mike:Deck** as the Customer:Job.

The Billable Time/Costs window will appear, informing you that this customer has outstanding billable time and costs.

7. Ensure the option for **Select the outstanding billable time and costs to add to this invoice?** is selected and click **OK**.

Notice that you can put off billing for this cost and save this selection as a preference.

8. Follow these steps to select the expense and enter a markup:

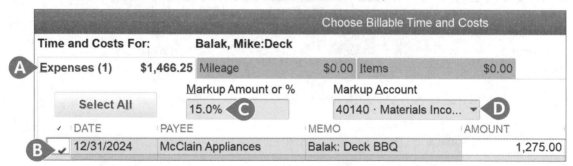

Ⓐ Click the **Expenses** tab.

Ⓑ Click the checkbox column to the left of **12/31/2024**.

Ⓒ Click in the **Markup Amount** field and type: **15%**

Ⓓ Click this drop-down arrow ▼ and choose **40140•Materials Income**.

The Expenses tab displays a number in parentheses indicating how many items are listed on it. Three tabs can contain billable costs or charges: Expenses, Mileage, and Items. When time tracking is turned on, a fourth tab, Time, is displayed as well. In this case, there's only one expense charge. Notice that you can enter a markup by amount or percentage. You can also print all selected time and costs as one invoice item so the breakdown doesn't show on the invoice.

9. Click **OK**.

The expense you are passing on and its markup appear on separate lines of the invoice.

Turn a Deposit into a Payment

You will now apply the $500 deposit you collected to the invoice.

10. Complete the invoice, entering the Cust Dep item below the second Time and materials line:

Date	**010325**
Terms	**Due on receipt**
Item / Rate	**Cust Dep / –500**
Customer Message	**We appreciate your prompt payment.**
Memo	**Balak: BBQ Invoice 1102**

It's up to you to type the amount of the deposit that will be applied to the invoice as a negative number. In this case, the invoice is greater than the deposit, so the customer still owes $966.25, and Accounts Receivable will be debited for this amount. If the deposit was for more than the total invoice amount, you would enter the amount from the customer deposit that covered the invoice; the rest would remain in the liability account.

BEHIND THE SCENES BRIEF

25000•Customer Deposits DR 500.00 | 11000•Accounts Receivable DR 966.25;
54300•Job Materials CR 1,275.00 | 40140•Materials Income CR 191.25

25000•Customer Deposits has **decreased** | 11000•Accounts Receivable has **increased**;
54300•Job Materials has **decreased** | 41040•Materials Income has **increased**

Check Figure: Accounts Receivable $96,234.18

11. Clear the **Email Later** checkbox and then click **Save & Close**.

12. Click **No** in the Information Changed window and add *Balak* and *BBQ* to the dictionary in the Check Spelling on Form window, if necessary.

The invoice is recorded. There are no longer funds on deposit in the liability account for this customer.

13. Click the **Chart of Accounts** task icon in the Company area of the Home Page.

Chart of Accounts

14. Double-click **25000•Customer Deposits** to see how the money increased and then decreased from that account.

Now you have a record of the deposit.

15. Close the register and the Chart of Accounts window.

Assessing Finance Charges and Producing Statements

If you're invoicing customers, you'll inevitably find that not all your customers pay their invoices on time. You may wish to assess finance charges. (In some states, the terms "late fee" or "service charge" may be used.)

Warning! Finance charge (lending) laws vary! Research your jurisdiction to know whether you can assess finance charges on overdue balances. Do *not* use the specifics in this book. Find out the laws that apply to your location and then apply them appropriately.

You can set several finance charge preferences in the Finance Charge category on the Company Preferences tab.

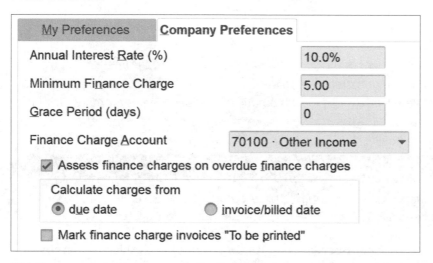

The finance charge account is an Other Income account as the income received is not the result of your normal business practices (unless you're a financial institution).

If assessing a finance charge, be sure to clearly note the payment terms on the invoice. Include such wording as "Accounts not paid within terms are subject to a ___% monthly finance charge and a $___ late fee. Grace period 5 days." (Provided for example only. Do your research for your own company.)

The Assess Finance Charges Window

The Assess Finance Charges window does more than provide you with a means to determine which customers are overdue and should be charged a finance charge. It also calculates the charge due (based on the preferences set) and gives you a quick way to view the preferences and customize the finance charge invoice template.

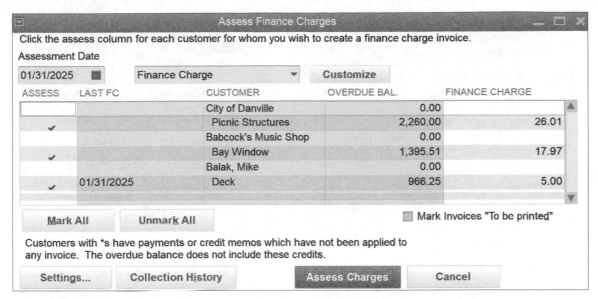

The Assess Finance Charges window gives you many options. If you need to view or make changes to the preferences for finance charges, click the Settings button.

The Assess Finance Charges window can also serve as a way to see customers that need collections calls or may need to have their balances written off as bad debt.

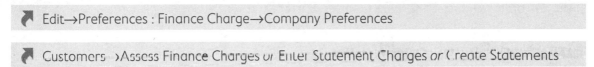

↗ Edit→Preferences : Finance Charge→Company Preferences

↗ Customers →Assess Finance Charges or Enter Statement Charges or Create Statements

Remove a Finance Charge

After applying finance charges, you may decide not to charge a specific customer a finance fee— especially if it's a good customer or one from whom you might expect to get a volume of work. You can use the Statement Charges window to remove a finance charge. Even if you remove it, you can still charge a finance fee to this customer in the future.

Creating Statements for Customers

There are many instances when you may wish to send your customer a statement rather than an invoice. You may have one customer for which you do multiple jobs within a billing period, and you wish to bill them with an itemized statement. Another example would be to create a statement to bill a customer for a finance charge. You can produce statements for an individual customer or in a batch for multiple customers.

> ✔ **Best Practice**
>
> The more common way to alert customers to finance charges they owe is to produce a statement that reflects the finance charge, outstanding invoices, and aging information.

 You can send an invoice reflecting assessed finance charges to your customers. Just check the "To be printed" checkbox in the Preferences window.

Statements can be printed for one or more customers, and there are a variety of ways you can go about selecting the customers to whom you will produce and send a statement. There are also options that will dictate how your statements will print.

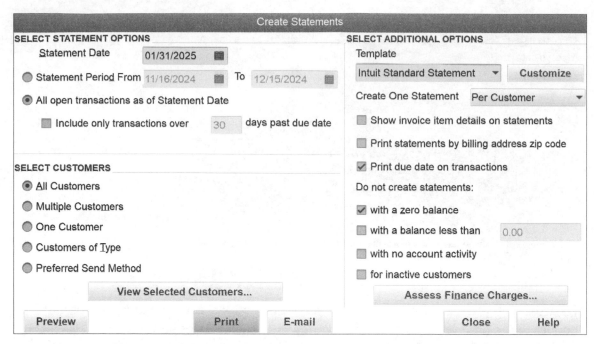

The Create Statements window provides many choices for creating a batch of statements for your customers.

➤ Customers→Enter Statement Charges *or* Create Statements

Emailing Forms and Reports

You can send more than just invoices from QuickBooks. In the Preferences window, you can set the default message for twelve types of forms and reports that you can easily send. You can also set which email service to use on the My Preferences tab of the Send Forms category.

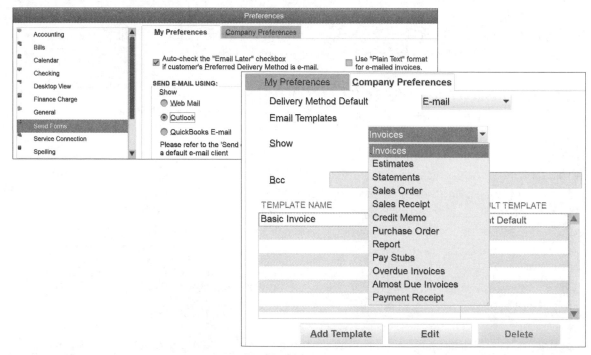

You will set the service with which you send emails on the My Preferences tab of the Send Forms category, while the company's email templates are set on the Company Preferences tab.

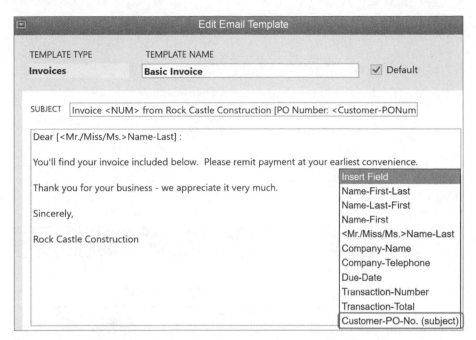

When editing the Invoice email template, you can insert the customer's purchase order number in the subject line of the email. Note the other fields that draw from your QuickBooks data that you can include in an email template as well.

 In QuickBooks 2020, you can easily include customer PO numbers in the subject line of your email.

Combining Forms to Send

 You may have multiple forms to send to a customer. Rather than sending each individually, QuickBooks allows you to combine all forms for a customer onto one email in the Send Forms window.

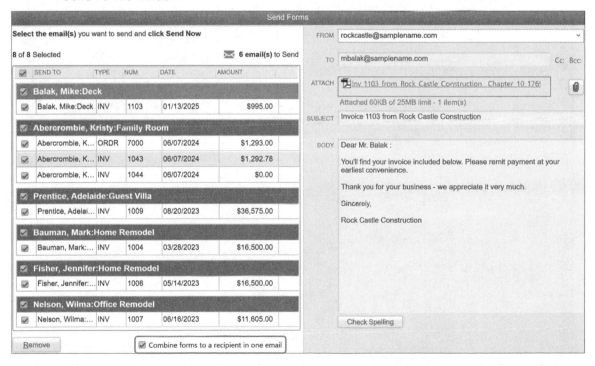

The Send Forms window allows you to choose the emails to send, combine the forms for a single recipient into one email message, and edit the email text.

File→Send Forms

Customer Payment Reminders

Many small businesses fail because they can't keep track of their receivables. QuickBooks now offers a powerful Payment Reminders feature that allows you to create mailing lists of customers, send payment reminders, and schedule reminders to be sent out in the future.

 QuickBooks 2020 makes it easy to send payment reminders to customers who have invoices due. You can view these reminders using the See History feature in the Create Invoices window.

BEHIND THE SCENES: *Assess Finance Charges*

11000•Accounts Receivable	70100•Other Income
INCREASE to Assets	*INCREASE to Revenue*

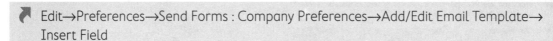

$$Assets = Liabilities + (Capital + Revenue - Expenses)$$

$$\$33.42 = \$0.00 + \$0.00 + \$33.42 - \$0.00$$

11000•Accounts Receivable		70100•Other Income	
Debit	*Credit*	*Debit*	*Credit*
$33.42			$33.42

 Customer→Payment Reminders→Manage Mailing Lists : New List

 Edit→Preferences→Send Forms : Company Preferences→Add/Edit Email Template→ Insert Field

File→Send Forms→Combine Forms to a Recipient in One Email

DEVELOP YOUR SKILLS 10-5

In this exercise, you will confirm the company preferences for finance charges are set up correctly and create statements.

1. Choose **Edit→Preferences** and then click the **Finance Charge** category and the **Company Preferences** tab.

   See that the company is set up to charge a 10 percent annual interest rate with a minimum finance charge of $5.00. The finance charges will be directed to the 70100•Other Income account as they are not income tied to Rock Castle Construction's type of business.

2. Click **Cancel**.

3. Click the **Finance Charges** task icon in the Customers area of the Home Page.

   The Assess Finance Charges window will be displayed.

Finance Charges

4. Type **013125** as the Assessment Date and tap ⌈Tab⌋.

   All customers with open invoices that are past due as of 01/31/2025 display, along with the calculated finance charge.

5. Click **Assess Charges** in the Assess Finance Charges window for all customers listed and then click **Yes**.

   The finance charges are now reflected in Accounts Receivable for each customer assessed. This Behind the Scenes Brief reflects the assessed finance charges for both customers.

BEHIND THE SCENES BRIEF
11000•Accounts Receivable DR 14.84; **70100•Other Income CR 14.84**
11000•Accounts Receivable has **increased**; 70100•Other Income has **increased**
Check Figure: Accounts Receivable $96,249.02

You're expecting a lot of additional business from the City of Danville, so you've decided to delete the finance charge. You'll do this through the customer's register.

6. Click the **Statement Charges** task icon in the Customers area of the Home Page.

Statement Charges

   When you enter a statement charge, you view the customer's Accounts Receivable register. Be sure to choose the correct customer. If there are multiple charges, you click the Customer:Job field drop-down arrow ▼ and choose the job.

7. Choose **City of Danville:Picnic Structures** as the Customer:Job.

8. Right-click anywhere within the two lines of the **01/31/2025 FC 122** finance charge transaction and choose **Delete Invoice** and then click **OK** in the Delete Transaction window.

BEHIND THE SCENES BRIEF

70100•Other Income DR 7.43; **11000•Accounts Receivable CR 7.43**

70100•Other Income has **decreased**; 11000•Accounts Receivable has **decreased**

Check Figure: Accounts Receivable $96,241.59

---

9. Close the City of Danville:Picnic Structures - Accounts Receivable window.

   Now you will create statements for all customers with a balance, including those with finance charges.

10. Click the **Statements** task icon in the Customers area of the Home Page.

Statements

11. Produce a batch of statements for all customers with a balance:

    • Statement Date: **013125**

    • Click the circle to the left of **All Open Transactions as of Statement Date**.

    • Choose **All Customers**, if necessary.

    • Click the **With a Zero Balance** checkbox.

12. Click **Preview** and then use the **Next Page** button to view the statements.

    You can now see what each statement will look like printed.

13. Click the **Close** button at the top of the Print Preview window.

    At this point, you could choose to print or email the statements by clicking the appropriate button at the bottom of the window.

14. Click **Close** in the Create Statements window.

Send Payment Reminders from QuickBooks

Rock Castle Construction has many customers who don't pay their invoices in a timely manner. You will create a mailing list of these customers and then set a schedule for when reminders to pay will be sent to them.

15. Choose **Customers→Payment Reminders→Manage Mailing List** and then click **New List**.

16. Follow these steps to set up the new list:

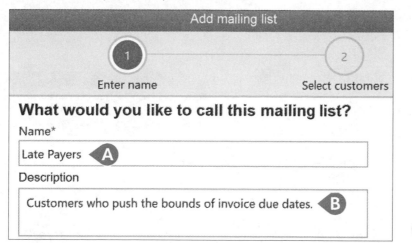

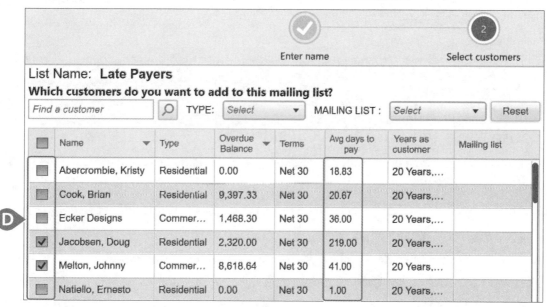

Ⓐ Type **Late Payers** in the **Name** box.

Ⓑ Tap ⎡Tab⎤ and type: **Customers who push the bounds of invoice due dates.**

Ⓒ Click **Next**.

Ⓓ Click to the left of each customer who takes 40 or more days to pay, scrolling down to find them all.

Look in the Avg days to pay *column to determine which customers to select. There are 17.*

17. Click **Save** and then click **Close** in the Manage Mailing List window.

18. Choose **Customers→Payment Reminders→Schedule Payment Reminders**.

19. Click **Get Started** and then follow these steps to set up the schedule:

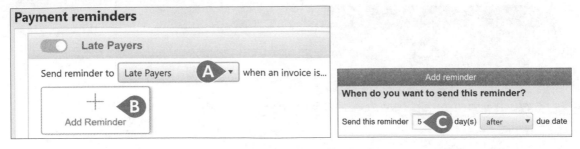

- Ⓐ Click the drop-down arrow ▼ and choose **Late Payers**.
- Ⓑ Click **Add Reminder**.
- Ⓒ Type: **5**

You will leave the default text of the email. Note the fields surrounded by square brackets [ ] that will be filled in with data from your QuickBooks file.

20. Click **OK**.

The Schedule payment reminders window will display with the 5 days after due date reminder scheduled.

21. Click **Save** and then click **Close**.

Choose to Send Forms from QuickBooks

Now you will send a batch of open invoices to customers, making sure to combine multiple forms for customers with more than one.

22. Choose **File→Send Forms**; click **No** in the Outlook Profile window, if necessary.

The Send Forms window displays.

23. Add a checkmark next to **Combine forms to a recipient in one email**.

If you don't have Outlook, this option will be grayed out so just move on.

Emails to be sent on the left side of the window are now grouped by customer. If you were working with your own company and had your email set up, you would click Send Now.

24. Click **Close** in the Send Forms window.

Tracking Time and Mileage

The Time Tracking feature allows you to create weekly timesheets so you can break down the hours by customer/job or record single activities for a customer/job. In addition to these payroll benefits, time tracking also allows you to:

- Invoice customers for number of hours worked
- Automatically fill in the hours worked on paychecks
- Track time for subcontractors by automatically filling in time data on bills and checks
- Track payroll costs by job, class, or type of work performed
- Track billable versus non-billable time

After you've used time data, you can run reports such as the Time by Job Summary to view how many hours were tracked for each job. Time tracking also allows you to allocate the appropriate payroll costs to a job, making your job costing reports more accurate and meaningful.

Methods of Entering Time

There are two methods by which you can enter time data in QuickBooks:

- **As a single activity when it occurs:** You can type the amount of time in the single activity window or use the built-in timer to record the exact amount of time.

- **On a weekly timesheet:** Use the weekly timesheet to enter time data for multiple customer/ jobs, service items, and payroll items for a single employee. You can use this information to create paychecks. You can use the "Billable" column on a timesheet to determine whether the time is billable. If a checkmark is in this field, the customer can be billed for the time. If an invoice icon appears, the time has already been invoiced.

Fields Available in Both Time Data Entry Windows

Whether you enter time as single activities or on a weekly timesheet, each window provides these same fields:

- **Customer:Job:** This information allows you to bill a customer for the time and to keep track of information required for accurate job costing.

- **Service Item:** This information allows you to track services performed.

- **Payroll Item:** This information allows you to choose the appropriate payroll item for your time data.

- **Billable:** Choose this field to make the information available to bill the customer for the time.

- **Notes:** This information displays in the Description field on reports and invoices.

> ↱ Employees→Enter Time→Use Weekly Timesheet *or* Time/Edit Single Activity

Batch Timesheets

Some businesses may have employees or vendors who work the same hours for a job—for instance, if you own a construction company with crews who work together on the same jobs each day. These businesses can create one timesheet for multiple payroll names (employees for whom you use time data to create paychecks) or multiple non-payroll names (such as subcontractors).

> *Tip!* When working with batch timesheets, all workers for whom you're creating a timesheet must have in common the job, number of hours worked per day, payroll item(s), and service item(s).

When setting up a weekly timesheet, the name field at the top of the window provides options to choose multiple payroll (employees) or multiple non-payroll names (such as subcontractors) in order to create billable time in a batch.

Tracking Mileage

The QuickBooks mileage tracking feature is used to track billable mileage for your business vehicle. Its purpose is not for reimbursing employees. The mileage data can be billed to customers as an expense or for tax reporting purposes. QuickBooks will calculate the mileage expense based on the approved rate on the specific day. You will need to ensure you have the latest IRS mileage reimbursement rates entered. To track mileage for a vehicle, you must first enter that vehicle into the Vehicle List.

To view the mileage information you've been tracking, QuickBooks provides mileage reports. You can choose to pass on the mileage expense to your customers and create reports to view the amount that has been billed.

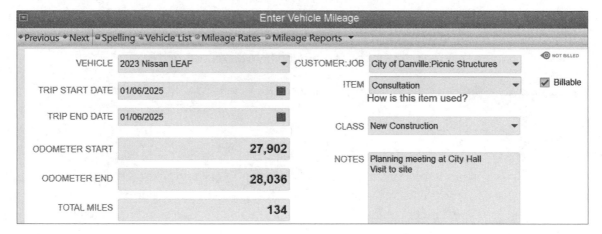

Billable vehicle mileage can be included on an invoice for this customer.

- Company→Enter Vehicle Mileage
- Lists→Customer & Vendor Profile Lists→Vehicle List : Vehicle→New
- Lists→Item List : Item→New
- Reports→Jobs, Time & Mileage | Reports→Report Center : Jobs, Time & Mileage

DEVELOP YOUR SKILLS 10-6

In this exercise, you will track time to be used to create paychecks for Rock Castle Construction, recording time spent on two jobs. You will begin by turning on the time tracking preference.

1. Choose **Edit→Preferences** and then click the **Time & Expenses** category and the **Company Preferences** tab.

2. Follow these steps to set the preferences:

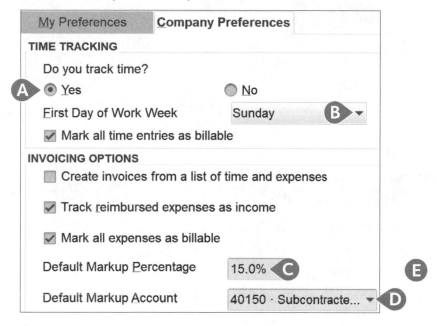

A Click to choose that **Yes**, you track time.

B Click this drop-down arrow ▼ and select **Sunday** as the first day of the work week.

C Type **15%** as the default markup percentage.

D Click this drop-down arrow ▼ and choose **40150·Subcontracted Labor Income** as the default markup account.

E Click **OK**.

3. Click **OK** in the Warning window and then choose **Company→Home Page**.

   Notice the new Enter Time task icon in the Employees area of the Home Page.

   Now you will enter the billable time.

4. Click the **Enter Time** task icon in the Employees area of the Home Page and then choose **Time/Enter Single Activity**.

5. Follow these steps to enter the employee's billable time:

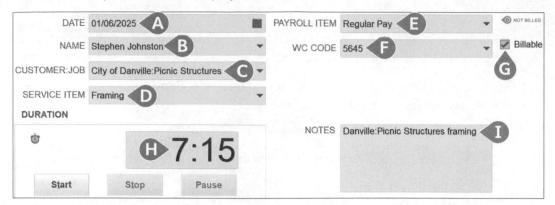

(A) Type the date as: **010625**

(B) Click this drop-down arrow ▾ and choose **Stephen Johnston (Employee)**, clicking **Yes** to set up the employee to use time data.

(C) Choose **City of Danville:Picnic Structures** as the Customer:Job.

(D) Choose **Framing** as the Service Item.

(E) Choose **Regular Pay** as the Payroll Item.

(F) Choose **5645 — Carpentry** as the WC Code.

(G) Ensure **Billable** is checked.

(H) Click and type **7:15** in the Duration field.

(I) Click in the **Notes** field and type: **Danville:Picnic Structures framing**

If you enter the duration with a colon, as you did here, the time is calculated in minutes and seconds. If you use a decimal instead of a colon, time will be calculated as a fraction of a minute.

6. Click **Save & Close**.

Enter Time Using a Weekly Timesheet

You will now enter the rest of Stephen's time for the week.

7. Click the **Enter Time** task icon in the Employees area of the Home Page and then choose **Use Weekly Timesheet**.

8. In the **Name** field, type **ste** and tap ⎡Tab⎤ to fill in *Stephen Johnston*.

9. Set the time frame for the timesheet:

- Click the **Calendar** 🔲 icon to the right of the Week Of date range.

- Use the right arrow button to the right of December 2024 to advance to **January 2025**.

- Click the **6** (Monday).

QuickBooks sets the week of Jan 5 to Jan 11, 2025, as the date range for the timesheet. Notice that the time data you just entered as a single activity appears on the weekly timesheet for Monday the 6th.

10. Complete the remainder of the time data for the week, noting that all items use the **Regular Pay** payroll item, **5645** as the WC Code, and are **Billable**:

Customer:Job	Service Item	Notes	TU	W	TH	F
City of Danville:Picnic Structures	**Framing**	`Danville:Picnic Structures framing`	8:00			
Balak, Mike:Deck	**Framing**	`Balak:Deck framing`		8:00	5:00	
Balak, Mike:Deck	**Installation**	`Balak:Deck BBQ Install`			3:00	5:00

Warning! Be careful! Tapping Enter will save what you've entered and display a new, blank timesheet. If this happens, repeat steps 8–9.

Total hours should be 36:15 on the Total row at bottom of the screen.

Timesheet

NAME Stephen Johnston   WEEK OF Jan 5 to Jan 11, 2025

CUSTOMER:JOB	SERVICE IT...	PAYROLL IT...	WC CO...	NOTES	SU 5	M 6	TU 7	W 8	TH 9	F 10	SA 11	TOTAL	BILLABLE?
City of Danville:Picnic...	Framing	Regular Pay	5645	Danville:Picnic Structures framing		7:15	8:00					15:15	☑
Balak, Mike:Deck	Framing	Regular Pay	5645	Balak:Deck framing				8:00	5:00			13:00	☑
Balak, Mike:Deck	Installation	Regular Pay	5645	Balak:Deck BBQ Install					3:00	5:00		8:00	☑
				Totals	0:00	7:15	8:00	8:00	8:00	5:00	0:00	36:15	

11. Click **Save & Close**.

Using Time Tracking Hours for Paychecks and Invoices

You can use time data for employees to create their paychecks and for vendors to create their bills by entering the time using the single or weekly timesheets. Using time data for either employees or vendors also allows you to invoice your customers for any billable time. Allocating time spent by employees or vendors on a job should help in producing more accurate job cost reports. By marking the time as Billable on the timesheets, the hours will automatically be imported when you create the paychecks or bills.

When you create an invoice, you can choose to pass billable time to customers, just as you can with expenses. You will be prompted that there is billable time, including billable mileage if you're tracking that. Regardless of which type of cost you're passing on to the customer, the process is almost the same—and you can even choose to specify a markup amount for the hours.

Invoice Using Billable Time

Just as you passed on the cost of the BBQ to Mike Balak for his deck job, you can also pass the actual time worked on the job to him. The process for passing on billable time uses the same Choose Billable Time and Costs window used to pass on expenses.

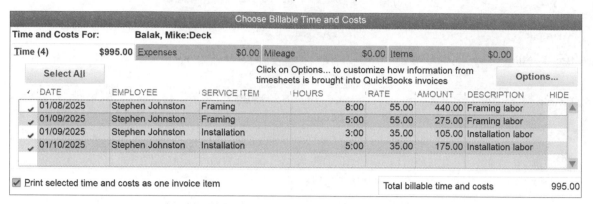

With the time tracking preference turned on, a fourth tab (Time) appears in the Choose Billable Time and Costs window. Use it to choose time on which to invoice a customer.

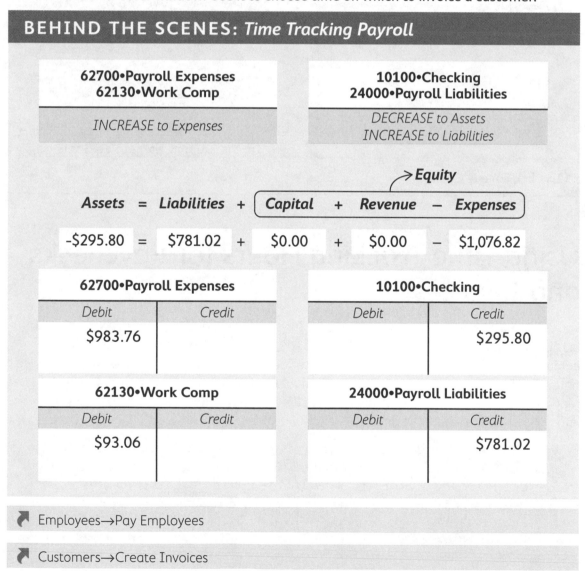

In this exercise, you will create a paycheck for Stephen based on the time data that was entered and then invoice Mike Balak.

1. Click the **Pay Employees** task icon in the Employees area of the Home Page.

Pay Employees

2. Click the **Start Unscheduled Payroll** button in the middle of the Employee Center: Payroll Center window.

   The Enter Payroll Information window displays. Look at the Regular Pay column for Stephen Johnston and notice that the amount is in blue, which indicates it's for billable time.

3. Set up the paycheck for Stephen Johnston:

   • Check Date: **011325**

   • Pay Period Ends: **011125**

   • Click **No** in the Pay Period Change window to update the Pay Period Ends date without updating the hours worked.

   • Click in the checkmark column to the left of **Stephen Johnston** to choose to pay him.

4. Click **Stephen's** name and then click **OK** in the Special Calculation Situation window.

5. Review the Preview Paycheck window:

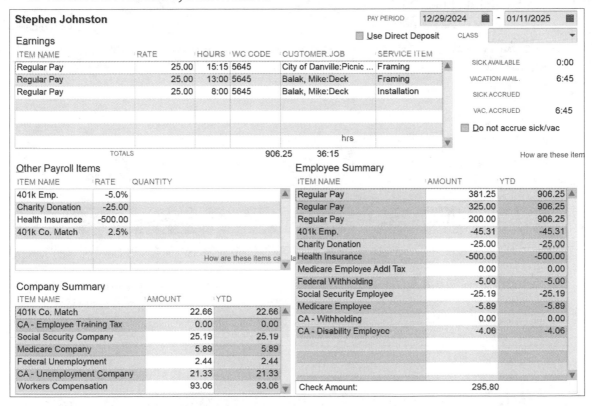

The entries in the Earning section match the time data you entered for Stephen. Your net Check Amount may differ from what shows here as a result of payroll tax table updates.

6. Click **Save & Close** and then click **Continue** to move to the Review and Create Paychecks window.

   This window lists the paychecks to be created. You can choose Finish Later if necessary.

7. Click **Create Paychecks** and then close the Confirmation and Next Steps window.

   The Payroll Center now indicates the paycheck status of To Print for the 01/13/2025 payroll.

   This Behind the Scenes Brief shows the parent accounts for Payroll Expenses and Payroll Liabilities, not the various subaccounts. Your figures may vary slightly due to payroll tax table updates.

BEHIND THE SCENES BRIEF
62700•Payroll Expenses DR 983.76	62130•Work Comp DR 93.06; **10100•Checking CR 295.80	24000•Payroll Liabilities CR 781.02**
62700•Payroll Expenses has **increased**	62130•Work Comp has **increased**; 10100•Checking has **decreased**	24000•Payroll Liabilities has **increased**
Check Figure: Checking $24,379.34

8. Close the Payroll Center.

Create an Invoice from Time Data

You will now create an invoice for Mike Balak that includes the time costs for the work completed.

9. Click the **Create Invoices** task icon in the Customers area of the Home Page.

10. Choose **Balak, Mike:Deck** as the Customer:Job and then click **OK** in the Billable Time/Costs window.

11. Click **Select All**, click to the left of **Print selected time and costs as one invoice item**, and click **OK**.

12. Complete the invoice:

    • Date: **011325**

    • Customer Message: **Thank you for your business.**

    • Memo: **Balak Deck: Billed Time 1/13/2025**

13. Click **Save & Close**.

BEHIND THE SCENES BRIEF
11000•Accounts Receivable DR 995.00; **40130•Labor Income CR 995.00**
11000•Accounts Receivable has **increased**; 40130•Labor Income has **increased**
Check Figure: Accounts Receivable $97,236.59

Tracking Reports (Jobs, Time & Mileage)

QuickBooks' job costing, estimating, and time tracking features include many preset reports that you can run to learn more about your business. Not all the Jobs, Time & Mileage reports are in all versions of QuickBooks. For instance, some reports are only available if you use a Premier version of QuickBooks that is specialized for your type of company. Like other reports, these standard reports can be customized.

Job Profitability Summary	Jobs, Time & Mileage
Job Profitability Detail	Vendors & Payables
Job Estimates vs. Actuals Summary	Purchases
Job Estimates vs. Actuals Detail	Inventory
Job Progress Invoices vs. Estimates	Employees & Payroll
Item Profitability	Banking
Item Estimates vs. Actuals	Accountant & Taxes
Profit & Loss by Job	Budgets & Forecasts
	List
Estimates by Job	Industry Specific
Unbilled Costs by Job	
Open Purchase Orders by Job	Contributed Reports
	Custom Reports
Time by Job Summary	QuickReport
Time by Job Detail	Transaction History
Time by Name	Transaction Journal
Time by Item	
Mileage by Vehicle Summary	
Mileage by Vehicle Detail	
Mileage by Job Summary	
Mileage by Job Detail	

QuickBooks provides you with many reports to track jobs, time, and mileage, which are broken down into four categories.

The Jobs Reports Column Collapsing Feature

The column collapsing feature available in certain reports, such as Profit & Loss by Job, allows you to easily show or hide the columns displaying jobs or classes so you can better view the totals for each job or class displayed. This means that in job reports, the details for specific jobs can collapse down to just display customer totals.

NEW! 2020 You can collapse columns horizontally with a click to better view totals.

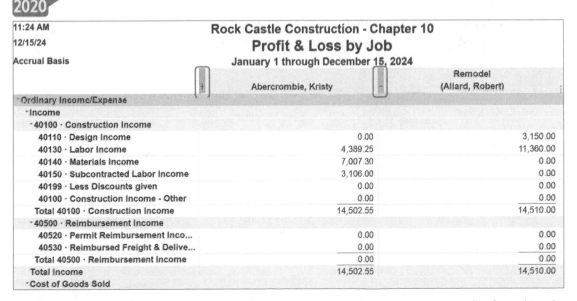

11:24 AM 12/15/24 Accrual Basis	Rock Castle Construction - Chapter 10 **Profit & Loss by Job** January 1 through December 15, 2024		
		Abercrombie, Kristy	Remodel (Allard, Robert)
▾ Ordinary Income/Expense			
▾ Income			
▾ 40100 · Construction Income			
40110 · Design Income		0.00	3,150.00
40130 · Labor Income		4,389.25	11,360.00
40140 · Materials Income		7,007.30	0.00
40150 · Subcontracted Labor Income		3,106.00	0.00
40199 · Less Discounts given		0.00	0.00
40100 · Construction Income - Other		0.00	0.00
Total 40100 · Construction Income		14,502.55	14,510.00
▾ 40500 · Reimbursement Income			
40520 · Permit Reimbursement Inco...		0.00	0.00
40530 · Reimbursed Freight & Delive...		0.00	0.00
Total 40500 · Reimbursement Income		0.00	0.00
Total Income		14,502.55	14,510.00
▾ Cost of Goods Sold			

The jobs for Kristy Abercrombie are collapsed, evidenced by the plus sign displayed to the left of her column. Conversely, the jobs for Robert Allard are not collapsed, so a minus sign displays to the left of the column displaying the data for his Remodel job. The plus and minus buttons toggle between showing and hiding the job columns.

DEVELOP YOUR SKILLS 10-8

In this exercise, you will produce a variety of job-related reports for Rock Castle Construction.

1. Choose **Reports→Jobs, Time & Mileage→Job Progress Invoices vs. Estimates**.
2. Set the date range as: **120124** to **123124**

Rock Castle Construction - Chapter 10
Job Progress Invoices vs. Estimates
December 2024

Type	Date	Num	Estimate Active	Estimate Total	Progress Invoice	% Progress
City of Danville						
Picnic Structures						
Estimate	12/15/2024	615	✓	7,560.00	2,260.00	29.89%
Abercrombie, Kristy						
Remodel Bathroom						
Estimate	12/12/2024	613		7,676.13	7,633.28	99.44%
Jacobsen, Doug						
Poolhouse						
Estimate	12/05/2024	612		6,323.50	0.00	0.0%
Natiello, Ernesto						
Kitchen						
Estimate	12/13/2024	614		14,595.25	13,560.39	92.91%

The Job Progress Invoices vs. Estimates report displays all the estimates and the amount that has been included on a progress invoice for December 2024.

3. Close the Job Progress Invoices vs. Estimates window.

The next report will show the time spent on each job.

4. Choose **Reports→Jobs, Time & Mileage→Time by Job Summary**.
5. Set the date range as: **010125** to **013125**

Rock Castle Construction - Chapter 10
Time by Job Summary
January 2025

	Jan 25
▼Balak, Mike:Deck	
Framing	13:00
Installation	8:00
Total Balak, Mike:Deck	21:00
▼City of Danville:Picnic Structures	
Framing	15:15
Total City of Danville:Picnic Structures	15:15
TOTAL	**36:15**

The Time by Job Summary report displays for January 2025. Notice the time for which you invoiced Mike Balak for the deck job.

6. Close the Time by Job Summary window.

The next report will show the profitability of each job.

7. Choose **Reports→Jobs, Time & Mileage→Job Profitability Summary**.

8. Set the date range as: **121624** to **013125**

Rock Castle Construction - Chapter 10 Job Profitability Summary December 16, 2024 through January 31, 2025	Act. Cost	Act. Revenue	($) Diff.
City of Danville			
Picnic Structures	443.47	2,260.00	1,816.53
Total City of Danville	443.47	2,260.00	1,816.53
Balak, Mike			
Deck	1,885.69	2,468.66	582.97
Total Balak, Mike	1,885.69	2,468.66	582.97
TOTAL	2,329.16	4,728.66	2,399.50

The Job Profitability Summary report displays the most profitable jobs for the date range specified. Note the profitability so far for both jobs you have worked on in this chapter.

9. Close the Job Profitability Summary window.

Create a Report on Profit & Loss by Job

The final report you will create is the Profit & Loss by Job. You will also use the collapse column feature on this report to better view the customer totals.

10. Choose **Reports→Jobs, Time & Mileage→Profit & Loss by Job**.

The report will be displayed with the default date range of 1/1/2024–12/15/2024. The first four columns display data for Kristy Abercrombie and her three jobs. You will now collapse the jobs for Kristy so that you can more easily view the totals for her.

11. Click the **minus sign** to the left of the Family Room job.

The job columns for Kristy Abercrombie will be collapsed, and the first column displayed in the report will show all her jobs combined.

12. Close the Profit & Loss by Job report.

Time Tracking with TSheets

You may find that the time tracking standard in QuickBooks Desktop doesn't meet your company's needs. No worries! Intuit now owns the TSheets app that works seamlessly with QuickBooks. There is an additional fee to use TSheets, but you may find that the cost is worth the benefits. Let's look at some of them.

Precision and Reduced Payroll Processing Time

Gone are the days of rounding up on timesheets! With TSheets, employees can clock in and out right from their mobile devices and receive reminders regarding breaks, overtime, and clocking in/out. They can choose to clock in for specific jobs as well, which makes it easier for you to invoice clients for the time spent on their jobs.

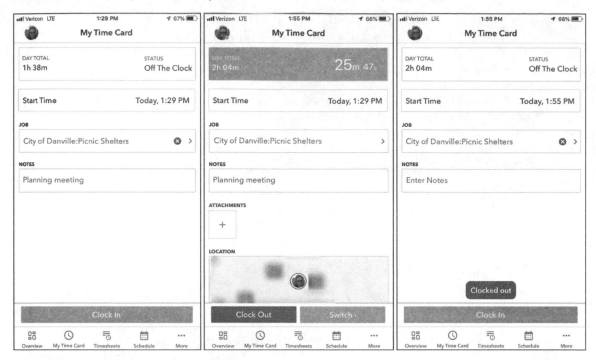

Here's what the TSheets My Time Card feature looks like on an iPhone when an employee is preparing to clock in (left), has clocked in and added a note about what the time is for (middle), and has clocked out (right). Note the precision of time tracked—this employee could have easily rounded up to a half-hour or even an hour!

Payroll specialists may be scared over the fact that payroll processing will become more efficient, but it can free them up to do less rote work and more innovative projects! With the days of handwritten time cards in the past, electronic timesheet approvals will leave you with more time available for activities that can boost both the bottom line and morale.

QuickBooks Integration

With just one click you can take all the data in TSheets and export it to QuickBooks. You can use the same customers, jobs, classes, items, etc., you use in QuickBooks, making it very easy to sync the two.

Scheduling and GPS

This app also provides scheduling capabilities so you can see who's working where and on what job easily. You can also track employee time on the job by GPS, providing another benefit to your clients and employees (it helps solve the "he said, she said" debate that may pop up from time to time regarding whether an employee was at a particular job site).

TSheets is just one of many apps available to QuickBooks users. As someone who is learning QuickBooks, it may be worth your while to spend some time with TSheets and other popular apps that integrate with QuickBooks. The time investment can make you more valuable to your employer or may help you make your own business more efficient. To learn about all the apps that work with QuickBooks, visit apps.com.

Tackle the Tasks

Now is your chance to work a little more with Rock Castle Construction and apply the skills you've just learned to accomplish additional tasks. Continue with the same company file you've been using in this chapter so far.

Create an Estimate for a New Job	Create a new job for Babcock's Music Shop called Bay Window (you'll be bidding on a job to install a bay window in her kitchen)
	Create an estimate for Babcock's Music Shop:Bay Window job on 01/14/2025 for Blueprints for $350; 9 hours of removal labor; 11 hours of framing labor; 7 hours of drywall installation; 6 hours of painting; $375 of rough lumber; $135 of trim lumber; and $600 for windows; use the memo Babcock: bay window estimate, 1/14/2025
Create a Progress Invoice Based on an Estimate	You were awarded the Bay Window job for Babcock's Music Shop, so edit the job to show this; the dates for the start and projected end date are 01/21/2025 and 01/31/2025, respectively; the job type is Remodel and its description is: Install bay window
	Create a progress invoice dated 01/21/2025 for 50% of the estimate; set the terms as Due on receipt (don't make it a permanent change); include an appropriate customer message and memo
Receive a Customer Deposit	Carr's Pie Shop wants you to remodel its restroom to meet ADA requirements; name the new job Restroom Remodel; you'll collect a deposit up front
	Receive the deposit from Carr's Pie Shop:Restroom Remodel on 01/25/2025 for $1,000; the account (25000•Customer Deposits) and items (Cust Dep and Dep Pmt) already exist; invoice item descriptions:
	• Cust Dep: Customer Deposit for Remodel • Payment: Payment of Deposit • Terms: Due on receipt (not permanent)
Apply a Customer Deposit as a Payment	Create a bill for Patton Hardware Supplies on 01/22/2025 for bathroom fixtures for $1,079.42, billable to Carr's Pie Shop:Restroom Remodel
	Create an invoice on 01/30/2025 for the Carr's Pie Shop:Restroom Remodel, selecting the outstanding billable time and costs to add to this invoice; markup amount 15%; markup account 40140•Materials Income
	Apply the $1,000 customer deposit to the invoice with terms of Net 15; include an appropriate customer message and memo
Create a Job Report	Run a Profit & Loss by Job report for January 2025 to see the net income from the two jobs

Self-Assessment

Check your knowledge of this chapter's key concepts and skills using the Self-Assessment quiz here, in your ebook, or in your eLab course.

1. You can only create estimates for jobs but not customers.   *True*   *False*

2. A progress invoice must be for a percentage of all items; you can't create one for selected items from the estimate.   *True*   *False*

3. You can enter time data as either a single activity or on a weekly timesheet.   *True*   *False*

4. When you pass on billable time to a customer, you select the cost for the time on the Expenses tab of the Choose Billable Time and Costs window.   *True*   *False*

5. QuickBooks allows users to track outstanding estimates using a non-posting account.   *True*   *False*

6. Unearned income refers to the funds being held in the Undeposited Funds account.   *True*   *False*

7. When you receive funds for a gift certificate, you hold them in an Other Current Liability account.   *True*   *False*

8. In QuickBooks, you can use the mileage tracking feature to track mileage to be reimbursed to employees for the use of their own cars.   *True*   *False*

9. The most common way to bill customers for finance charges is to create and send separate invoices.   *True*   *False*

10. Which report do you produce to find your most profitable job for a specific period of time?
    A. Job Profitability Detail
    B. Job Estimates vs. Actuals Summary
    C. Time by Job Summary
    D. Job Profitability Summary

11. What is NOT a step when conducting job costing in QuickBooks?
    A. Enter all job revenues and expenses.
    B. Create an estimate for the job.
    C. Use QuickBooks reports to analyze job data.
    D. Set up your data in the Customers & Jobs List.

12. To enter mileage for a vehicle in QuickBooks, you first:
    A. enter the current IRS mileage rate
    B. add the vehicle in the Vehicle List
    C. create a new non-inventory item in the Item List
    D. None of these options

13. What is NOT something you need to set up to track customer deposits in QuickBooks?
    A. Inventory-part item
    B. Other Current Liability account
    C. Other charge item
    D. Payment item

Reinforce Your Skills

Just as you used a sample company file for the Develop Your Skills exercises in this chapter, so will you for the Reinforce Your Skills section. Angela Stevens has hired you as a senior bookkeeper for Quality-Built Construction. You will be entering estimates, creating progress invoices, and performing other tasks such as receiving customer deposits and entering time tracking data to ensure proper billing and job costing.

Create a Job and an Estimate for a Customer

In this exercise, you will enter a new customer and a job for the customer, who has requested an estimate for a kitchen remodel. Preferences must be set before you can create estimates and conduct progress invoicing.

1. Choose **File→Open or Restore Company**.
2. Open **RYS_Chapter10 (Company)** *or restore* **RYS_Chapter10 (Portable)** and save it as: **RYS_Chapter10 Quality Built Construction**
3. Click **OK** to acknowledge you are opening a QuickBooks Desktop sample file.
4. Choose **Edit→Preferences** and then click the **Jobs & Estimates** category and the **Company Preferences** tab.
5. Ensure the Create Estimates and Progress Invoicing features are turned on and then click **OK**

   Next you will enter a new customer and job.
6. Choose **Customers→Customer Center**.
7. Click the **New Customer & Job** button and choose **New Customer**.
8. Type **Bates, Tania** as the Customer Name and click **OK**.

   Bates, Tania *should be selected.*
9. Click the **New Customer & Job** button and choose **Add Job**.
10. Type **Remodel Kitchen** as the Job Name.
11. Click the **Job Info** tab and enter the job information:
    - Job Description: **Complete kitchen remodel**
    - Job Type: **Remodel**
    - Job Status: **Pending**
12. Click **OK** to save the new job.

    The new job appears on the Customers:Jobs List and is selected.

Create an Estimate for a Job

Now that you have a job set up for the kitchen remodel, you will create an estimate for it. The Remodel Kitchen *job should still be selected.*

13. Click the **New Transactions** button and choose **Estimates**.
14. Type **010720** as the Date.
15. Type **20-0001** as the Estimate No.

16. Complete the estimate:

Hint: You will only need to enter data for the Item, Qty, and Estimate columns. The rest will fill in for you.

Item	Qty	Estimate		Item	Qty	Estimate
01 Plans & Permits:01.4 Remodel Plans	1	1200		18 Interior Walls	8	55
02 Site Work:02.10 Demo	8	55		20 Millwork & Trim	12	50
07 Wall Framing	5	60		23 Floor Coverings	8	45
13 Windows & Trim	6	65		24 Paint	9	50
14 Plumbing	5	75		25 Cleanup	10	45

The estimate should total $5,005.

17. Type **Bates: Kitchen remodel** in the Memo field.

18. Click **Save & Close** for the estimate and then close the Customer Center.

REINFORCE YOUR SKILLS 10-2

Create a Progress Invoice Based on an Estimate

In this exercise, you will create a progress invoice to charge for the remodel plans that have been completed.

1. Choose **Customers→Create Invoices** and then choose **Bates, Tania:Remodel Kitchen** as the Customer:Job.

2. Click the estimate for **01/07/2020** in the Available Estimates window and click **OK**.

3. Choose to create the invoice for **selected items or different percentages** and click **OK**.

4. Deselect the **Show Quantity and Rate** and **Show Percentage** checkboxes, if necessary.

5. Type **1200** in the **Amount** column for the first line (01.4 Remodel Plans) and click **OK**.

You can adjust the column widths by dragging the border between columns.

6. Click **OK** in the Zero Amount Items window.

Note that, after that selection is made, everything will fill into the Create Invoices window.

7. Choose **Due On Receipt** as the terms and set the date to: **012220**

8. Click **Save & Close** and choose to have the terms permanently changed.

Collect a Customer Deposit

In this exercise, you will help Angela collect a deposit from Tania Bates for $2,000 toward the remainder of the work. These funds will be held in a liability account until they're earned, at which time you will create a progress invoice to record the income. There is already a Customer Deposits account set up, so you will begin by creating the two items you will use for the actual deposit.

1. Choose **Lists→Item List**.

2. Create a new **Other Charge** item named: **Cust Dep**

3. Leave the Description blank so you can fill it in on each invoice, change the Tax Code to **Non** and direct it to the **2200•Customer Deposits** account, and click **Next**.

   The New Item window appears.

4. Create a new Payment item named: **Payment**

5. Type **Customer Payment** as the Description for the new item and click **OK**.

6. Close the Item List.

Collect the Deposit

7. Choose **Customers→Create Invoices** and then choose **Bates, Tania:Remodel Kitchen** as the Customer:Job.

8. Click **Cancel** in the Available Estimates window (you're not ready to invoice for the remaining work).

9. Ensure the date is set to **01/22/2020** and then enter the deposit and payment:

Item	Description	Rate
Cust Dep	**Customer Deposit: Remodel Kitchen**	2000
Payment	**Customer Payment**	−2000

10. Type **Bates: remodel $2,000 deposit** in the Memo field and then click **Save & New**.

Apply the Customer Deposit to a Progress Invoice

Angela has completed the kitchen remodel and will invoice Tania to record the earned income, using the deposit. The Create Invoices window should still be open. If not, choose Customers→Create Invoices.

11. Choose **Bates, Tania:Remodel Kitchen** as the Customer:Job.

12. Click the estimate for **01/07/2020** in the Available Estimates window and click **OK**.

13. Click **OK** to create an invoice for the remaining amounts of the estimate; click **OK** again.

14. Set the date of the invoice to **02/22/2020** and enter **02−1055** in the Invoice # field.

15. Scroll down in the item area of the invoice and then enter the customer deposit in the line below *25 Cleanup*, choosing **Cust Dep** as the Item.

16. Type **Customer Deposit Applied** for the Description and **-2000** in the Amount column.

    The Balance Due should be $1,805 after deducting the $2,000 deposit.

17. Click **Save & Close**.

REINFORCE YOUR SKILLS 10-4

Assess Finance Charges

In this exercise, you will assess finance charges for customers with overdue invoices. The finance charge preferences have already been set up for the company.

1. Choose **Customers→Assess Finance Charges**.

2. Type **013120** as the Assessment Date and tap ⌨Tab.

   Two invoices are selected to have finance charges assessed.

3. Click **Assess Charges**.

REINFORCE YOUR SKILLS 10-5

Enter Time Tracking Data and Produce a Paycheck

In this exercise, you will enter time spent on a job by Clark Mitchell and then create a paycheck for him.

1. Choose **Employees→Enter Time→Use Weekly Timesheet**.

2. Enter Clark Mitchell's time for the week of Jan 27 to Feb 2, 2020:

Customer:Job	Service Item	Payroll Item	M 27	TU 28	W 29	TH 30	F 31
Ramirez, Hector:New Home	06 Floor Framing	5646-Carpentry	8	8	8	8	8

3. Click **Save & New**.

4. Enter Clark's time for the week of Feb 3 to Feb 9, 2020:

Customer:Job	Service Item	Payroll Item	M 3	TU 4	W 5	TH 6	F 7
Ramirez, Hector:New Home	06 Floor Framing	5646-Carpentry	8	8	8	8	8

5. Click **Save & Close**.

6. Choose **Employees→Pay Employees**.

7. Use the calendar icon to change the Pay Period Ends date to **02/09/2020** and click **Yes** in the Pay Period Change window.

8. Change the Check Date to **02/11/2020**.

9. Click in the checkmark column to the left of **Mitchell, Clark** and then click **Continue**.

10. Review the paycheck you're about to create using time data and then click **Create Paychecks**.

11. Close the Confirmation and Next Steps window.

REINFORCE YOUR SKILLS 10-6

Display Reports for Estimates and Time Tracking

In this exercise, you will help Angela to create estimate and time tracking reports.

1. Choose **Lists→Chart of Accounts**.

2. Click in the **Look for Account Name or Number** field and type **Estimates** and then click **Search**.

3. Right-click the **Estimates** account and choose **QuickReport: 4•Estimates** from the bottom of the pop-up menu.

4. Set the date range to All.

   On the report, review the estimates that have been created; the one you entered is at the bottom.

5. Close the Account QuickReport and the Chart of Accounts windows.

   You will now run a report to show the percentage of the estimates that have been invoiced.

6. Choose **Reports→Jobs, Time & Mileage→Job Progress Invoices vs. Estimates**.

7. Type **a** to set the date range to All.

   Notice the estimate you created and the amount that has been invoiced.

8. Close the Job Progress vs. Estimates window, choosing not to memorize the report.

   Finally, you will create a report that shows time spent on Hector Ramirez's New Home job.

9. Choose **Reports→Jobs, Time & Mileage→Time by Job Summary**.

10. Type **a** to set the date range to All.

    Scroll down to view the time data for the new home job for Hector Ramirez. The image shows the detail for each job collapsed, except for the Ramirez, Hector:New Home *job.*

11. Close the Time by Job Summary report, choosing not to memorize the report; close the company file.

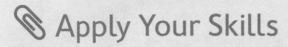

Apply Your Skills

You've decided that it's advantageous to do estimates and progress invoicing for Wet Noses Veterinary Clinic. Now you will take the necessary steps to start using these features. The password for all files unless otherwise stated is Password1.

APPLY YOUR SKILLS 10-1

Set the Preferences and Create a New Job

In this exercise, you will set the preferences to use QuickBooks' estimating and progress invoicing features. Then you will create a new job for Amy Ridgeway's new kitten, Autumn.

1. Choose **File→Open or Restore Company**.
2. Open **AYS_Chapter10 (Company)** *or* restore **AYS_Chapter10 (Portable)** and save it as: **AYS_Chapter10 Wet Noses Clinic**
3. Edit the preferences to create estimates and do progress invoicing for the company.

   Now that the preferences have been set, you will create the job for Amy's new kitten.

4. Create a new job for Amy Ridgeway called Cat-Autumn.

   Dr. James has decided that it's not important to track job status for her customers, so you'll leave the fields on the Job Info tab blank.

APPLY YOUR SKILLS 10-2 QG

Create an Estimate for a Job

Amy Ridgeway needs to bring in her new kitten to be spayed, tested for FIV and feline leukemia, and vaccinated, but she's concerned about the total cost and needs to budget the services. In this exercise, you will create an estimate for Amy so she can see the full cost for all the services.

1. Create an estimate on **071523** for **Amy Ridgeway:Cat-Autumn**. Each item has a quantity of one and is non-taxable

   Hint: Click OK in the Tax Codes window, if necessary.

   - New Patient
   - Vaccine
   - Pre-A Blood Work
   - Spay Cat
   - IV Fluids
   - Pain Meds
   - FIV/FeLV
   - F Leuk
   - Feline DHC
   - Rabies
   - Rev-Cat/Sm Dog

   Remember that all service and non-inventory items are not taxable; only inventory items are taxable.

2. Add an appropriate memo and then click **Save & Close**.
3. Run the **Estimates by Job** report for the dates **07/01/2023** to **07/31/2023**.
4. Click the **Excel** button and export this list to a new workbook saved as: **CH10_A2 Estimates by Job**
5. Close the report, choosing not to memorize it, and then close Excel.

Create a Billable Expense

In this exercise, you will create a bill to be charged back to Amy for the expense of the anesthesiologist hired for the spaying procedure on her kitten, Autumn. You've already informed Amy of this charge.

1. Create a bill for Samantha Peters (new vendor), using a new expense account numbered 66600 and named Medical Professionals and this information:

Date	071823
Ref. No.	Anes 01
Amount Due	250
Terms	**Net 30**
Memo (use on Expense tab, too)	Ridgeway, Cat-Autumn, Spay
Customer	**Ridgeway, Amy:Cat-Autumn**

2. Ensure the **Billable** column is checked.
3. Click **Save & Close** and **Yes** to accept the payment terms.

Create an Invoice from the Estimate

Amy has decided to get Autumn the care she needs in phases. Now you will create a progress invoice for the first set of items.

4. Create an invoice based on the **07/15/2023** estimate for Ridgeway, Amy:Cat-Autumn, choosing the option to determine which items to invoice.

5. In the Specify Invoice Amount for Items on Estimate window, click in the **Show Percentage** checkbox and type 100 in the Curr % column to include the items New Patient, Spay Cat, IV Fluids, Pain Meds, and Vaccine on the invoice.

    Tip! After you enter 100 in the Curr % column for the first item, you can use the down arrow key to move down the column to enter the percentages for the other four items.

6. Click **OK**.
7. Read the warning message; click **OK** in the Zero Amount Items window.

    The Billable Time/Costs window appears because the anesthesiologist was entered as billable against this job.

8. Click **OK** to select the outstanding billable time and costs to add to the invoice.
9. Click the **Expenses** tab, click in the checkmark column to the left of **07/18/2023** for Samantha Peters, and click **OK**.
10. Scroll down to see the entry on the last line of the invoice and then set the date to **07/19/2023** and the invoice # to **184**. Enter Ridgeway, Cat-Autumn, Inv. 184 as the memo.

11. Click **Save & Close** on the invoice.

    The invoice is created for the customer. The rest of the estimate will still be available, from which you can create future invoices.

12. Run the **Job Estimates vs. Actuals Detail** report for **Ridgeway, Amy:Cat-Autumn**.

13. Click the **Excel** button and export this list to a new workbook saved as:
    `CH10_A3 Job Estimates vs. Actuals`

14. Run the **Job Profitability Detail** report for Amy Ridgeway's cat, Autumn.

15. Click the **Excel** button and export this list to a new workbook saved as:
    `CH10_A3 Job Profitability`

16. Close Excel and the company file.

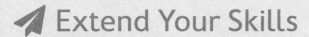

Extend Your Skills

Before You Begin: Open **EYS_Chapter10 (Company)** *or* restore **EYS_Chapter10 (Portable)**. The password is *Password1*.

You've been hired by Arlaine Cervantes to help her with her organization's books. She is the founder of Niños del Lago, a nonprofit organization that provides impoverished Guatemalan children with an engaging educational camp experience. You just sat down at your desk and opened a large envelope from Arlaine that contains a variety of documents; you also have several emails from her. It's your job to sort through the papers and emails and make sense of what you find, entering information into QuickBooks as appropriate and answering any questions in a word-processing document saved as: CH10_EYS_[LastnameFirstinitial]

Remember, you're dealing with random papers dumped out of an envelope and various emails, so part of your challenge is determining the order in which to complete the tasks.

- Handwritten receipt: Dated 9/19/2020 for a $500.00 donation from Matthew Drill to purchase food for a camp to be offered in December 2020. Sticky note from Arlaine on the receipt: Can you figure out a way to account for this donation since the food won't be purchased and consumed until December?

- Handwritten estimate for Expanding Opportunities Together: Dated 9/17/2020 for 50 scarves and 35 handbags. (Expanding Opportunities Together is another nonprofit that's looking to help us raise funds by purchasing and reselling the goods we get from the women in Guatemala.) Each product was on a separate line and both at 25% off regular retail.

- Message from Arlaine: "We should think about what we'll do if customers don't pay their bill on time…. Can we assess finance charges in QuickBooks? If so, please set it up so we charge 12% interest on overdue invoices. I think we need to have a nice grace period, though; set that at 30 days. Don't worry about charging a minimum finance charge or charging interest on overdue finance charges."

- Printed email: Received the contract from Expanding Opportunities Together. Could you please invoice them for 50% up front?

- Scribbled note from Arlaine: Is there a report you can create for me that will show how much of the estimate has been invoiced?

11 | Customizing and Integrating in QuickBooks

Finally, the artist in you gets to have some fun! It's time to learn about customizing QuickBooks forms and reports to look professional and work best for your company. In this chapter, you will customize reports to include pertinent information and make them look more attractive. You'll also create custom fields, explore price and billing rate levels, and create a custom invoice template. In addition, you'll see how well QuickBooks integrates with Microsoft Office to help you manage your company's data.

LEARNING OBJECTIVES

▸ Create and use custom fields

▸ Set up and use price and billing rate levels

▸ Customize reports and graphs

▸ Create custom templates

▸ Integrate with Microsoft Office

📁 **Project: Parrot's Paradise Resort**

You've grown tired of the standard QuickBooks look to the company's forms and reports and have decided to jazz them up! Jimmy asked you to show him how the lists and custom fields can be used for his business and is interested in using Word and Excel seamlessly with QuickBooks. In addition to adding some finesse to Parrot's Paradise Resort's reports and templates and helping Jimmy with Microsoft Office integration, you'll be setting price levels and markups for the services and products sold.

Custom Fields

You will work with many templates in QuickBooks, many of which will be sent to customers and vendors. QuickBooks provides many templates by default (such as invoice, purchase order, and sales receipt), but you can also create your own or customize those provided. To use a custom field on a template, you must create your own rather than using one provided with the software. You can also make a copy of a template and customize it.

Custom fields for names include customers/jobs, vendors, and employees and can be created in the same window, which is accessible from any of these three lists. Custom fields for items must be set through the Item List. All types of custom fields can be used on multiple forms once they're created. These fields can also be included on reports or just used to store additional information, such as favorite brand, which might be useful if you're a fashion retailer and want to produce a list of customers who all like the same brand for an event. Consistency in entries is the key to using these types of fields!

Adding Custom Fields

Before you can use custom fields in forms and reports, you must first set them up in the lists where they belong.

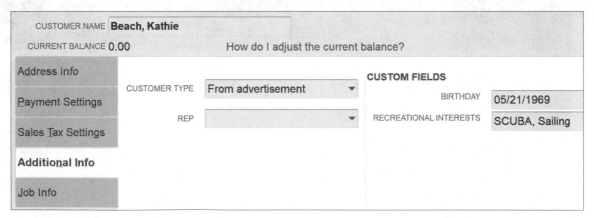

You can create custom fields for customers, vendors, and employees on the Additional Info tab of any list entry from these lists.

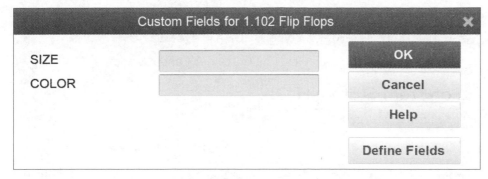

Custom fields for items are created for each individual item. In this case, the fields were not populated as they will be when a purchase is made.

> *Note!* Custom fields are available for all types of items except subtotals, sales tax items, and sales tax groups.

↗ Customers→Customer Center : [open customer record]→Additional Info→Define Fields

↗ Lists→Item List : [edit item]→Custom Fields

DEVELOP YOUR SKILLS 11-1

In this exercise, you will create custom fields to track additional information for future use on custom templates. The password for all files unless otherwise stated is Password1. *Leave the company file open unless otherwise instructed.*

1. Start QuickBooks 2020 and choose **File→Open or Restore Company**.
2. Open **DYS_Chapter11 (Company)** *or* restore **DYS_Chapter11 (Portable)** and save it as: **DYS_Chapter11 Parrot's Paradise Resort**
3. Click the **Customers** [CUSTOMERS] button in the Customers area of the Home Page.
4. Double-click **Beach, Kathie** in the Customers & Jobs List at the left.
5. Click the **Additional Info** tab and then click the **Define Fields** button in the Custom Fields section of the window.
6. Set up two custom fields:

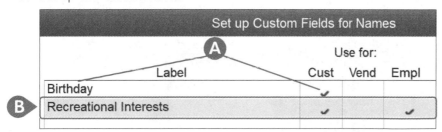

Ⓐ Type **Birthday** and then add a checkmark to use this for **Cust** (customers).

Ⓑ Click in the second row; type **Recreational Interests** and add a checkmark to use this for **Cust** and **Empl**.

7. Click **OK**; click **OK** again to acknowledge the prompt that you can use custom fields in templates, if necessary.

8. Click in the **Birthday** field and type **05/21/69** to enter Kathie Beach's date of birth.

9. Click in the Recreational Interests field and type: **SCUBA, Sailing**

10. Click **OK** to accept the changes and then close the Customer Center window.

Create and Fill an Item Custom Field

You will now add a custom field for an item.

11. Click the **Items & Services** task icon in the Company area of the Home Page.

12. Double-click **1.102 Flip Flops** to open the Edit Item window.

Items & Services

13. Click the **Custom Fields** button, click **OK**, and then click the **Define Fields** button in the Custom Fields for 1.102 Flip Flops window.

14. Add the custom fields:

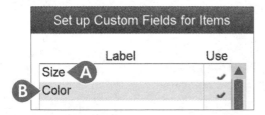

Ⓐ Type **Size** and check **Use**.

Ⓑ Type **Color** and check **Use**.

15. Click **OK** and then click **OK** two more times, closing the Information and Custom Fields for 1.102 Flip Flops windows.

You've created the custom fields but didn't add any data here because you'll add it to the individual forms instead. If you wish, you can type the custom field information into the Custom Fields for 1.102 Flip Flops window; it would then appear on each form or report you create that displays the field.

16. Click **OK** one last time to close the Edit Item window and then close the Item List.

Price Levels

There are many instances when a business may wish to charge different prices. Perhaps a customer is a dealer of your product or a high-volume customer to whom you wish to give a better price. Using price levels is a way to customize varying prices without having to manually type them on your sales forms. When a price level is set and associated with a customer or job, it will automatically fill in on forms or future transactions (you can manually change what fills in). A price level can also be set directly on the form without editing the customer's record. Price levels require that the items in the Item List have prices set. QuickBooks will calculate the price level according to the price already set.

With all versions of QuickBooks, the price level can be set by a fixed percentage. If you're working with a Premier or higher version of QuickBooks, you can also set price levels per item. Before setting up price levels, make sure the preference is turned on in QuickBooks.

Note! Although you can use a discount to reduce a price, price levels might be better because discounts are not linked to individual customers or jobs.

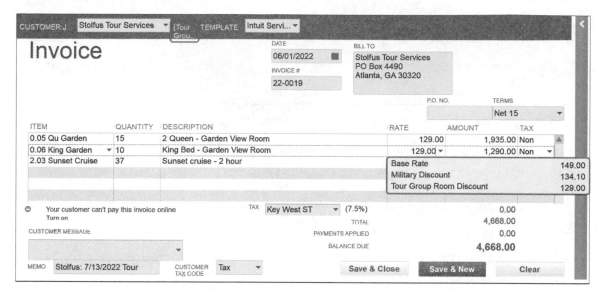

When price levels are set up, you can choose from them in the Rate field on sales forms. Note that the price level applied to a customer is displayed to the right of the Customer:Job field in brackets. When you click the drop-down arrow next to a price, you will see all of the price level options available to you.

Fixed Percentage Price Levels

The fixed percentage price level lets you decrease or increase the items being charged to a customer or job by a specific percentage amount. For instance, you may wish to decrease all items purchased by tour groups by 15 percent or military member purchases by 10 percent.

Per Item Price Levels

If you use the Premier version or higher option, you can create specific dollar amounts for items or groups of items that you can associate with selected customers or jobs. For instance, you may wish to charge Gator Tours $129 for garden view rooms rather than the standard $149 per day rate.

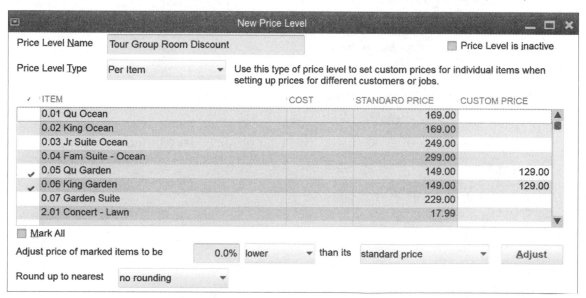

When creating a price level per item, you can choose individual items or all of them. You also have the option of setting a custom price or reducing it by a certain percentage.

↗ Edit→Preferences : Sales & Customers→Company Preferences tab

↗ Lists→Price Level List : Price Level→New

DEVELOP YOUR SKILLS 11-2

In this exercise, you will first create a fixed percentage price level of 10 percent less than the "normal" price as a military discount and then create a second one to provide a discounted room rate on garden rooms for tour companies. Next, you will assign a price level to Toni Martinez, as she is a retired Marine. Finally, you will create an invoice using the new price level on an invoice for Stolfus Tour Services.

1. Choose **Edit→Preferences** and then display the **Company Preferences** tab of the **Sales & Customers** category.

2. Click to select **Enable Price Levels** in the Custom Pricing area and then click **OK** twice.

3. Choose **Company→Home Page** and then **Lists→Price Level List**.

4. Click **Price Level** button at the bottom of the window and then click **New**.

5. Create a new price level:

- Ⓐ Type: `Military Discount`
- Ⓑ Click the drop-down arrow ▾ and choose **Fixed %**.
- Ⓒ Tap ⟦Tab⟧ twice and type: **10**

6. Click **OK**; click the **Price Level** button at the bottom of the window and choose **New**.

7. Create the per item price level:

    - Price Level Name: `Tour Group Room Discount`
    - Price Level Type: **Per Item**
    - Items (place a checkmark for each): **0.05 Qu Garden** and **0.06 King Garden**
    - Custom Price (for both items): **129**

    If you have questions about how to enter this information, take a quick peek in the concepts section!

8. Close the Price Level List.

Assign Price Levels to Customers

9. Click the **Customers** [CUSTOMERS] button in the Customers area of the Home Page.

10. Double-click **Martinez, Toni** and then click the **Payment Settings** tab.

11. Click the **Price Level** drop-down arrow ▼, choose **Military Discount**, and click **OK**.

Now every time you create an invoice for Toni Martinez, the military pricing will fill in. Don't worry, though; you can always change it if there's an item you don't want to discount!

12. Change the price levels for each of the four tour companies: **Gator Tours**, **Humboldt Tour Company**, **Sherwood Tours**, and **Stolfus Tour Services**.

Create an Invoice Using a Price Level

13. Select **Stolfus Tour Services** and then click the **New Transactions** button and choose **Invoices**.

14. Create the invoice:

Template	**Intuit Service Invoice**
Date	**060122**
Invoice #	**22-0019**
Item / Quantity	First: **0.05 Qu Garden** / **15** Second: **0.06 King Garden** / **10** Third: **2.03 Sunset Cruise** / **37**
Memo	**Stolfus: 7/13/2022 Tour**

The Tour Group Room Discount will automatically be applied to the first two lines since you have set this price level for the customer. The third line does not have a price level applied since you did not indicate this item when setting up the per-item price level.

BEHIND THE SCENES BRIEF

11000•Accounts Receivable DR 4,668.00; **40000•Lodging Sales CR 3,225.00 | 42000•Banquets and Events Income CR $1,443.00**

11000•Accounts Receivable has **increased**; 40000•Lodging Sales has **increased** | 42000•Banquets and Events Income has **increased**

Check Figure: Accounts Receivable $4,492.96

15. Click **Save & Close** to record the invoice and then close the Customer Center window.

Billing Rate Levels

Just as you can use price levels to provide variable prices for customers and jobs, you can use billing rate levels to differentiate the amount charged by different vendors and employees. Billing rate levels are used when you have employees or vendors performing the same job at different levels of expertise, and you want to bill accordingly. When you've set up the billing rate level, you will go to the specific employees or vendors and choose the appropriate level.

 Note! This feature is available only in the Premier and Enterprise editions of QuickBooks.

When setting up billing rates, you can either set a fixed hourly rate that would be used for all service items, employees, and vendors with this billing rate level or set a custom hourly rate for one or more service items. The service items must be set up as two-sided items. When used with a time sheet, the time can then be billed back to the customer at the adjusted hourly rate.

➤ Lists→Billing Rate Level List

DEVELOP YOUR SKILLS 11-3

The massage therapists at Parrot's Paradise Resort are subcontractors who charge different rates. In this exercise, you will create a new billing rate level for massage and assign it to a name.

1. Choose **Lists→Billing Rate Level List**.
2. Click the **Billing Rate Level** button and choose **New**.
3. Create a new billing rate level:

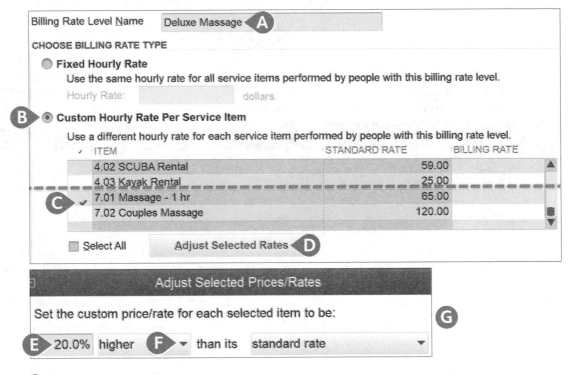

Ⓐ Type: **Deluxe Massage**

Ⓑ Click to choose **Custom Hourly Rate Per Service Item**.

Ⓒ Scroll down and click to the left of *7.01 Massage - 1 hr.*

Ⓓ Click **Adjust Selected Rates**.

Ⓔ Type: **20**

Ⓕ Click the drop-down arrow ▼ and choose **higher**.

Ⓖ Click **OK**.

The adjusted rate for 7.01 Massage - 1 hr is now displayed in the Billing Rate column as $78.

4. Click **OK** in the next window and then close the Billing Rate Level List.

Edit the Service Item

Before you can use a billing rate with a service item, you need to make sure the item is set up as a two-sided item.

5. Click the **Items & Services** task icon in the Company area of the Home Page.

6. Double-click **7.01 Massage – 1 hr** to open it for editing.

7. Click **This service is used in assemblies or is performed by a subcontractor or partner**.

8. Type **One-hour massage-by-the-sea** for the description.

9. Use **45** as the cost and **68000·Subcontractor Expense** as the expense account.

10. Click **OK** and then click **Yes** in the Account Change window. Close the Item List window.

Assign the Billing Rate Level to a Vendor

11. Click the **Vendors** [VENDORS] button in the Vendors area of the Home Page.

12. Tap ⌈Ctrl⌉+⌈n⌉ and create a new vendor named: **Clausen, Zander**

13. Click the **Payment Settings** tab, choose **Deluxe Massage** as the billing rate level, and click **OK**.

14. Close the Vendor Center.

Customizing Reports and Graphs

Customization takes place on many fronts, and the ability to customize the reports that you produce is important for business analysis. You may find yourself asking:

- Which accounts should I display?

- What information do I need to filter out?

- What header and footer information should I include?

- How do I want my fonts and numbers to look?

Clicking the Customize Report button at the top of the report window opens the Modify Report window, from where you can choose from four tabs to make formatting changes to your report: Display, Filters, Header/Footer, and Fonts & Numbers. The options available for modification on each tab are determined by the report. Just keep in mind that formatting deals with the *appearance* of the report; it has nothing to do with the data contained within it.

The Display Tab

The Display tab of the Modify Report window allows you to set the "bones" of your report. Essentially, it provides the skeleton on which the data will lay. In a profit & loss report, for example, the skeleton includes the dates the report represents, your reporting basis (cash or accrual), the columns to display, and subcolumn preferences.

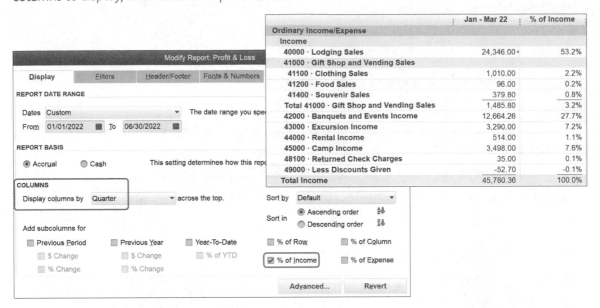

When you display columns by quarter and show subcolumns by % of Income, you get the report displayed. (Although not shown, the report includes columns for the second quarter and a total for the six months).

Report Date Range

Each preset report has a default date range when the report is first created. The date can either be:

- When the reporting period ends, such as a balance sheet report created "As of June 30, 2022."

- For a range of days, such as a profit & loss report created for January 1, 2022–June 30, 2022.

The date range is determined by the report type.

Report Basis

As you know, there are two methods of accounting from which you can choose for your company:

- Accrual Basis: Income is recorded when a sale is made, and expenses are recorded when incurred. This method is used often by firms and businesses with large inventories; it's required for publicly traded companies.

- Cash Basis: Income is recorded when cash is received, and expenses are recorded when cash is paid. This method is commonly used by small businesses and professionals.

You enter data into QuickBooks the same way regardless of the basis of accounting used. When you create your reports, you can easily switch between cash and accrual basis. When you first create a QuickBooks company, the default for reports is to use the accrual basis. You can set your company's default report basis in the report section of the Edit Preferences window.

If you operate using the cash basis, you don't need to display Accounts Receivable and Accounts Payable on your financial statements. They're displayed only when transactions have occurred, but cash has yet to change hands.

FLASHBACK TO GAAP: REVENUE & CONSISTENCY

Remember that publicly traded companies are required to use the accrual basis of accounting (revenue GAAP) and that companies need to use the same accounting principles and methods from year to year (consistency GAAP).

Columns and Subcolumns

Each preset report displays certain default columns. You can change the columns to make your report more useful. For instance, you can choose to display multiple months on a Profit & Loss report to compare income and expenses by month. Some reports allow you to add subcolumns to further analyze your data. The use of columns and subcolumns to stratify data can be a very valuable way to help you to analyze and scrutinize your company's financial data.

Header and Footer Options

All preset QuickBooks reports display the default headers and footers. You can accept the default or choose to hide any element. Any of the options that have a text box can be customized with your own wording. There is a standard page layout, or you can choose left, right, or centered alignment.

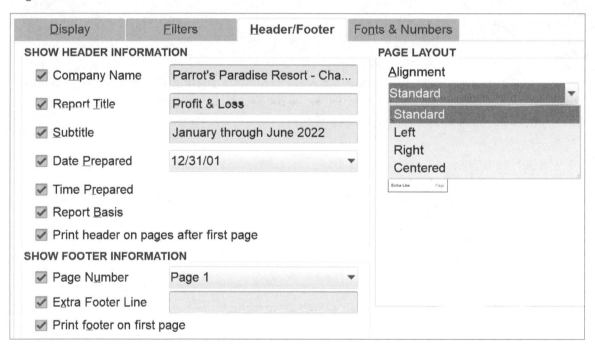

Font and Number Formatting

You can change the characteristics of the font and number style on QuickBooks reports much the same as you would in a word-processing program. For example, QuickBooks displays its preset reports in a default font. You can make many choices as to the characteristics of the font in your report, such as the font name, style, color, and size. You can also choose how QuickBooks will display all numbers in your report; for instance, you can display negative numbers with parentheses or a minus sign.

The Fonts & Numbers tab lets you select a report element, such as Column Labels, and then click the Change Font button to modify it. You can then apply the changes to all related fonts. Notice the preview of the new formatting above the Change Font button.

Edit→Preferences : Reports & Graphs→Company Preferences tab

Reports→Company & Financial→[select report] : Customize Report

DEVELOP YOUR SKILLS 11-4

In this exercise, you will create and begin to customize a Profit & Loss report to display the income for January–June 2022. You will run the preset Profit & Loss Standard report and make customizations.

1. Choose **Reports→Company & Financial→Profit & Loss Standard** and then click the **Customize Report** button on the report toolbar.

2. Follow these steps to set display options:

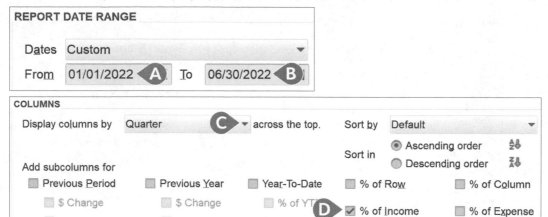

- **A** Type: **010122**
- **B** Tap ⌷Tab⌷ and type: **063022**
- **C** Click the drop-down arrow ▾ and choose **Quarter**.
- **D** Click the box for **% of Income**.

3. Click **OK** and then resize the report window to see all the data.

QuickBooks displays the report with the date range and column/subcolumn changes.

Modify the Header and Page Layout

4. Click the **Customize Report** button and then click the **Header/Footer** tab.

5. Follow these steps to make changes to the header and page layout:

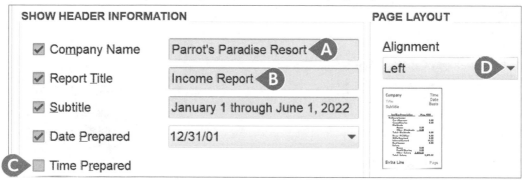

- **A** Tap ⌷Tab⌷ and type **Parrot's Paradise Resort** in the Company Name field.
- **B** Tap ⌷Tab⌷ twice and type: **Income Report**
- **C** Uncheck **Time Prepared**.
- **D** Click the drop-down arrow ▾ and choose **Left**.

6. Click **OK**.

Take a moment to look at the changes you made to the header and layout of your report.

Change the Font and Number Formatting

Now you will spruce up the report by changing the way the font and numbers appear.

7. Click the **Customize Report** button and then click the **Fonts & Numbers** tab.

8. Follow these steps to change the formatting:

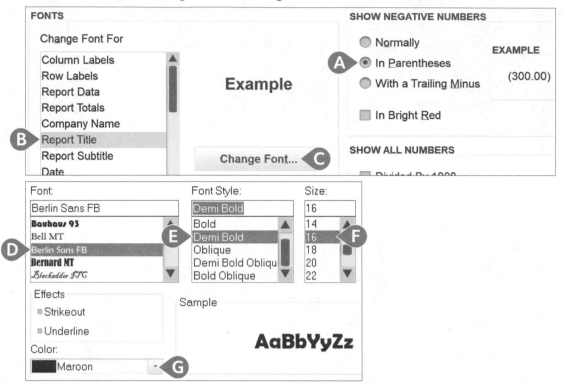

Ⓐ Click this circle to show negative numbers **In Parentheses**.

Ⓑ Click **Report Title**.

Ⓒ Click the **Change Font...** button.

Ⓓ Choose **Berlin Sans FB**.

Ⓔ Choose **Demi Bold**.

Ⓕ Choose **16**.

Ⓖ Click the **Color** drop-down arrow ▾ and choose **Maroon**.

9. Click **OK** in the Report Title window and click **Yes** to change all related fonts; click **OK**.

    Looking at the font formatting changes that you just made, you realize that formatting the report data in bold makes it hard to read, so you will change the formatting.

10. Click **Customize Report**, display the **Fonts & Numbers** tab, and change the font for **Report Data**:

    • Font: **Arial**

    • Font Style: **Narrow**

    • Size: **8**

    • Color: **Black**

11. Click **OK** in the Report Data window and click **No** to not change all related fonts; click **OK**.

    Leave the report open or you will have to recreate it before you can complete DYS 11-5.

Filtering and Sorting Reports

To hone in on specific data in your reports, you may wish to filter and/or sort your data. Sorting allows you to organize a column of choice in your report in ascending or descending order. Filtering allows you to choose what information to include, thereby "filtering out" the rest.

Filtering

Reports, unless customized, display all data for accounts, customers, or any other category. Filters can be applied to any report; the report type determines what information can be filtered. You can also filter for text contained in custom fields, if those fields are on the forms for transactions included in the report. And, interestingly, choosing a date range other than the default functions as a filter as well!

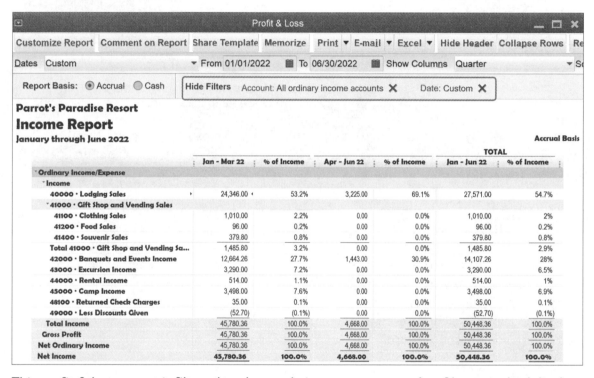

This profit & loss report is filtered to show only income accounts. Any filters applied display to the right of the Report Basis section when you choose to Show Filters.

Sorting

You choose the column to sort by using the drop-down list at the top of the window or on the Display tab of the Modify Report window. You can sort columns in ascending (alphabetically A to Z or numerically from lowest to highest) or descending order.

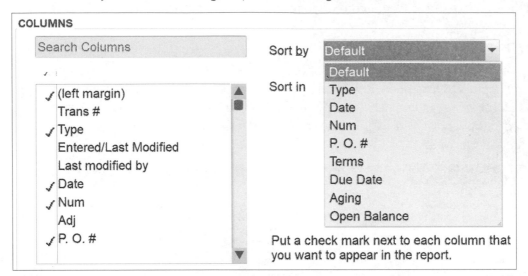

The fields to sort by will change according to the report displayed. On reports that have column headers, you can sort by the columns included on the report. This example is from the Open Invoices report.

Memorizing Reports

After you've created a report with your chosen settings, you may wish to save the report options so you can easily produce the same report again. The process of saving the settings of a report is called *memorizing* a report, and it's available for all reports. The memorizing feature memorizes the format of the report, not the data within it. This means that when you open a memorized report, it will contain all data, even that entered after it was memorized. To recall the memorized report, you can choose it from the Memorized Report List.

Memorized Report Groups

QuickBooks allows you to organize your memorized reports into groups. When you're ready to add your memorized report to a group, you can choose from one of the six preset groups (accountant, banking, company, customers, employees, and vendors) or create your own. A memorized report can be added to a group when it's memorized or later.

Batch Processing of Reports

If you have a group of reports that you run together on a regular basis, you may wish to process them as a batch to save time. The first step is to set the desired reports as a memorized report group; then you'll be able to process them all at once.

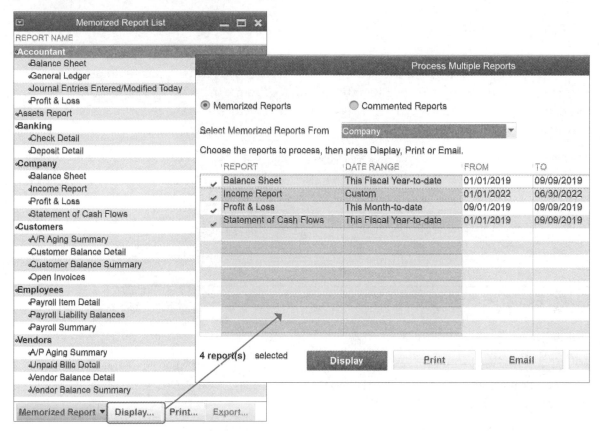

The Memorized Report List organizes your reports into six prepopulated groups (each is customizable). Clicking Display on the Memorized Report List window opens the Process Multiple Reports window, where you choose which group of reports to batch process. You can change the date range here, if necessary.

Specialized Reports

You can report on your transactional data and examine the health of your business in many ways within QuickBooks. Not only can you schedule reports to be sent to your email regularly, but you can also comment on reports and share them within your organization, as well as contribute and share reports across the QuickBooks community.

Scheduled Reports

As a business owner, it's important to continually monitor and analyze your company's financial data. QuickBooks facilitates this by allowing you to schedule reports to be sent regularly by email. You choose which reports to send and the frequency by which they are sent.

Note! To use the Schedule Reports feature, you must have Outlook open if you use it to email through QuickBooks. You must also close other company files and keep your computer on, with sleep mode turned off.

Commented Reports

You can view, add, or delete comments to any report, thus creating a commented report that you can save, print, or share. When you add comments to a report, QuickBooks saves a snapshot of the report at that time into the Commented Reports List.

Contributed Reports

You can customize or create your own reports to meet a specific need. If that report can be beneficial to others, you can add it to Contributed Reports by clicking Share Template on the report toolbar. It's a great way to help the QuickBooks community! It's free to share and free to use contributed reports. Note that you're sharing the template *only*; the report data doesn't get transmitted.

There are several industry-specific reports listed under the Contributed tab of the Report Center menu, including many job costing professional services reports, construction reports, and retail reports.

 Reports→Memorized Reports→Memorized Report List *or* Commented Reports *or* Process Multiple Reports

---

DEVELOP YOUR SKILLS 11-5

In this exercise, you will make additional customizations to the report and memorize the final product. You will then add comments to and save the report.

Before You Begin: *The Profit & Loss Standard report should still be open. If not, repeat Develop Your Skills 11-4 to produce the report.*

1. Click the **Customize Report** button on the report toolbar.
2. Follow these steps to apply a filter to show only income accounts on the report:

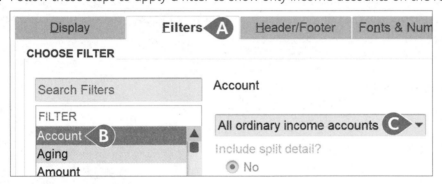

   Ⓐ Click the **Filters** tab.

   Ⓑ Ensure **Account** is chosen as what to filter by.

   Ⓒ Click this drop-down arrow ▼ and choose **All ordinary income accounts**.

3. Click **OK**.
4. Click the **Show Filters** button above the report.

   You will now see the report with no COGS or expense accounts shown and the filters applied displayed at the top.

Memorize a Report

Now that the report is the way you want it, you will memorize it for easy recall.

5. Click the **Memorize** button on the report toolbar.

6. Memorize the report and place it in a group:

- Name: `Income Report`
- Add a checkmark to: **Save in Memorized Report Group**
- Save in Memorized Report Group: **Company**

7. Click **OK** and then close the Income Report window.

Process Multiple Reports

You will now process a batch of reports from the Company group.

8. Choose **Reports→Memorized Reports→Memorized Report List**.

9. Click **Display** at the bottom of the window.

10. Click the **Select Memorized Reports From** drop-down arrow ▾ and choose **Company**.

You will see that the report you just memorized, Income Report, is included in this group.

11. Click **Display** to process the batch of reports.

QuickBooks will produce all the reports in the Company group for the date ranges displayed. If your report windows are maximized, you'll only see the topmost report. Restore the topmost window to see the rest of the report windows.

12. Choose **Window→Close All**.

Add a Comment to a Report

You will add a comment to your Income Report and then save it in the Commented Reports List.

13. Choose **Reports→Memorized Reports→Company→Income Report**.

14. Click the **Comment on Report** button on the report toolbar.

15. Follow these steps to create a commented report:

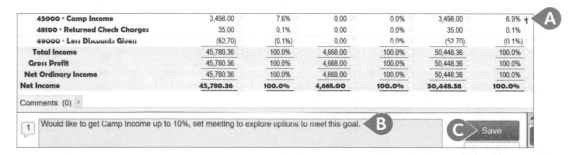

Ⓐ Click in the comment balloon for Camp Income.

Ⓑ Click and type: `Would like to get Camp Income up to 10%, set meeting to explore options to meet this goal.`

Ⓒ Click **Save**.

16. Click **Save** on the toolbar.

17. Enter `Camp Income Goal Setting` as the report name and click **OK**.

18. Click **OK** to acknowledge the commented report was saved and then close the report window; close the Income Report.

This saves your report in the Commented Reports List, which you can view from the Reports menu.

Sort a Report

Now you will run a report to see the customers that bring in the greatest sales amount.

19. Choose **Reports→Sales→Sales by Company Summary**.

20. Set the date range to **All** and then click the **Customize Report** button.

21. Choose to sort by **Total** in **Descending order** and click **OK**.

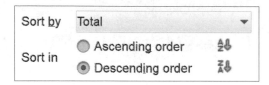

Your report will show the customers with the highest sales first, all the way down to the lowest. If you had chosen to sort in ascending order, this would be reversed.

22. Close the Sales by Summary report, choosing not to memorize it.

Custom Forms

Before you customize your forms, think about what you want them to do for you:

- Do you want to include custom fields?

- Do you want to include a company logo?

- What do you want the forms you'll be sending to stakeholders to say about your company?

- How much detail do you want to include?

- What size fields will you need?

Templates

A template is a specific form format (with no data) on which you can base future forms. Quick-Books provides several templates, but you can also create custom templates to meet the needs of your unique company or create templates for preprinted forms. All templates for a particular type of form are available from the drop-down list at the top of the form. Changing templates for a transaction that has already been entered will not change the information recorded in the transaction, even if the field is not visible on the new form.

Creating a Custom Template

When creating a custom template, you begin by specifying information in the Basic Customization window. This window also provides a preview of how the template looks as you make changes to the various fields and information.

You assign a name for your new template in the Manage Templates window. You can also access additional templates online from this window. When you click the Download Templates button, QuickBooks launches a web browser and displays the QuickBooks website, from which you can browse additional templates.

Adding a Company Logo

You can further personalize your templates by including your company logo. When you add a logo to your template, the image file is stored in the folder where your company file is located. And this folder must be located on the computer's hard drive or on a shared server. It will not work if your company file is located on a flash drive.

Using Custom Fields in Forms and Reports

You need to create your own custom form template to use the custom fields you set up earlier in this chapter. You can add the custom field information for names on the Header tab of the Additional Customization window. To add the custom fields for items, you must use the Columns tab. It's up to you to determine whether the various fields will be displayed on the screen, on the printed form, on both, or not at all.

The Order column on the Columns tab shows how the columns will be displayed from left to right.

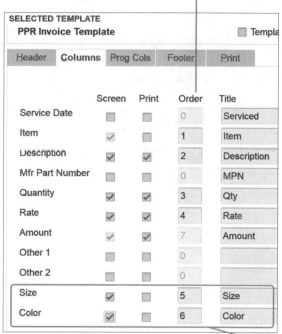

The custom fields created earlier are available to be included in a custom template.

The Additional Customization window organizes customization options on five tabs.

The Layout Designer Window

QuickBooks allows you to determine not only what is included on a template, but also where it will be placed. You can move fields and labels around your template and change the size of fields in the Layout Designer window. Each element on the template is termed an "object" in the Layout Designer window, and you can use some standard techniques to select, move, and resize all objects. The Snap to Grid feature ensures that all objects line up to a grid for which you can specify the spacing. In addition, you will see two shadows where the standard envelope windows are located so you can make sure to line up the addressees and return addresses properly.

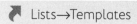 Lists→Templates

In this exercise, you will create an invoice template for the company.

1. Choose **Lists→Templates**.
2. Click the **Templates** drop-down arrow ▼ and choose **New**.
3. Ensure **Invoice** is the template type selected and click **OK**.
4. Click the **Manage Templates** button in the Basic Customization window.
5. Replace the default template name at the top right with **PPR Invoice Template** and click **OK** to return to the Basic Customization window.

Add Some Color to the Template

6. Change the color scheme and add a logo:

- Ⓐ Choose the **Blue** color scheme.
- Ⓑ Click the **Apply Color Scheme** button.
- Ⓒ Click to check **Use logo** and open the Select Image dialog box.

  You can see the new color in the preview area on the right side of the window.
- Ⓓ Navigate to your file storage location.
- Ⓔ Double-click **PPR Logo**.

7. Click **OK** in the Warning window.

Modify Header and Column Fields

Now it's time to decide which fields to include in the header and columns of the new template.

8. Click the **Additional Customization** button at the bottom of the window.
9. Click the checkbox for **Due Date** in the Print column.

   A Layout Designer window appears to guide you through making changes to how the new field will be laid out on the template. You don't need to make any changes at this time.

10. Click the checkbox for **Do not display this message in the future** and tap ⏎ Enter .
11. Customize your template using custom fields:
    - Header tab: In the Screen column, check **Birthday** and **Recreational Interests** (scroll down if necessary).
    - Columns tab: In the Screen column, check **Size** and **Color**.
12. Click **OK** in the Additional Customization window.
13. Feel free to customize your template further, including using the Layout Designer. When you're finished customizing, click **OK** in the Basic Customization window and close the Templates window.

Integrating with Microsoft Office

QuickBooks works very well with a variety of Microsoft Office Suite programs. For instance, you can import and export lists from Outlook, export reports to Excel, import list entries from Excel, and merge data from QuickBooks with a Word document to produce letters.

Sending Letters with Word

There are many letter templates provided in QuickBooks to use with Word, or you can customize your own. After you have prepared your letter, QuickBooks will launch Word and merge your QuickBooks data into the letter for you.

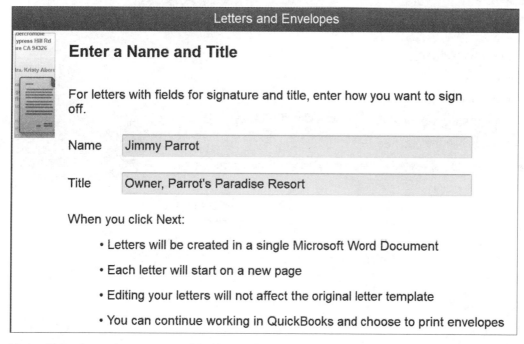

You will set how the signature block will look in Word in the Letters and Envelopes window. Your letters will appear as a single Word document with each letter starting on a new page. You can edit the letters as you like in Word.

Exporting QuickBooks Reports to Excel

While there are many reports provided for you in QuickBooks, you may want more control over how you manage and display your data. To analyze your data more effectively, you can export it to Microsoft Excel, a spreadsheet program, so you can use the advanced features available in Excel. QuickBooks makes it very easy to export and update a report.

You can easily export a report or update an existing spreadsheet via the Excel button on a report's toolbar.

Updating Excel Reports

You can update reports exported to Excel without having to reformat all the data each time a new entry has been made in QuickBooks. The formatting changes that you make to your Quick-Books data will be memorized in Excel, so when you export that same report in the future, you can update an existing worksheet. Use this process to avoid going in and changing all the formatting each time you export the report. Some of the formatting options that will be memorized for you are report titles, new formulas, row and column headers (both font changes and new header names), and inserted columns and rows. You initiate the updating of an exported report from the report window in QuickBooks or from the Excel window while viewing the report.

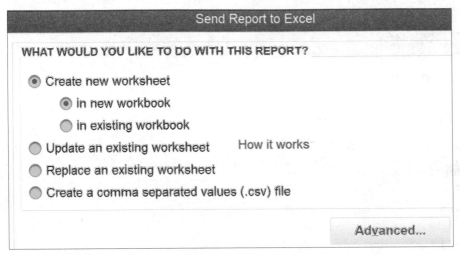

When you send a report to Excel, you have options as to how the program will handle it. Clicking the Advanced button launches a window where you can set Excel, QuickBooks, and printing options.

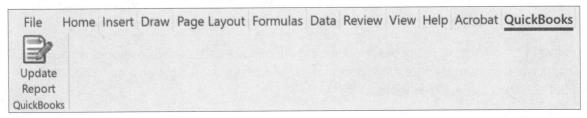

When working with a QuickBooks report in Excel, you can update it using the QuickBooks tab from within Excel.

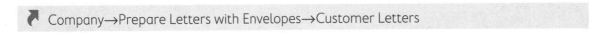

Company→Prepare Letters with Envelopes→Customer Letters

Using Excel to Import Multiple List Entries into QuickBooks

Another valuable role that Excel can play with your QuickBooks work is that it can be used to help you import multiple list entries. Be sure to start with an Excel worksheet that is set up with the correct fields, so the import process goes smoothly.

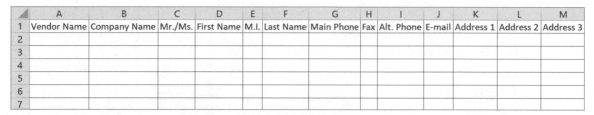

	A	B	C	D	E	F	G	H	I	J	K	L	M
1	Vendor Name	Company Name	Mr./Ms.	First Name	M.I.	Last Name	Main Phone	Fax	Alt. Phone	E-mail	Address 1	Address 2	Address 3
2													
3													
4													
5													
6													
7													

This example shows how to set up the Excel spreadsheet to import multiple vendors seamlessly into QuickBooks.

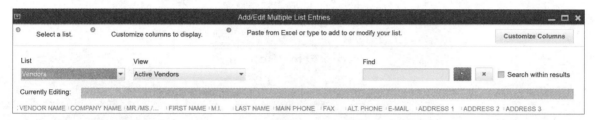

Notice how the column names (the fields) in the QuickBooks Add/Edit Multiple List Entries window match those in the Excel worksheet shown above.

You can add multiple list entries from an Excel worksheet to six of the lists within QuickBooks:

- Customers
- Vendors
- Service Items
- Inventory Parts
- Non-Inventory Parts
- Inventory Assemblies

 Lists→Add/Edit Multiple List Entries

DEVELOP YOUR SKILLS 11-7

In this exercise, you will produce letters for your tour company customers to let them know about your special garden room pricing for tour groups!

To complete this exercise, Microsoft Word must be installed on your computer. If you don't have Word, skip this exercise and continue to the next topic.

1. Choose **Company→Prepare Letters with Envelopes→Customer Letters**.

2. Click **Copy** to place a copy of the QuickBooks letter templates in your company file folder, if necessary.

The Letters and Envelopes window will appear, asking you to choose the recipients. By default, all customers are selected.

3. Follow these steps to select the tour company customers:

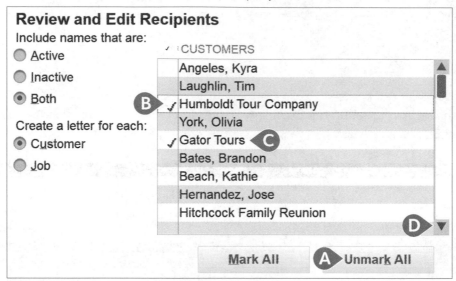

Ⓐ Click **Unmark All**.

Ⓑ Click to the left of **Humboldt Tour Company**.

Ⓒ Click to the left of **Gator Tours**.

Ⓓ Scroll down and add checkmarks to left of **Sherwood Tours** and **Stolfus Tour Services**; click **Next**.

You now have the chance to choose from a template or create or edit your own template. You'll use a template.

4. Scroll down in the list of letter templates, click **Thanks for business (service)**, and click **Next**.

5. Set how you want to sign the letters:

   • Name: **Jimmy Parrot**

   • Title: **Owner, Parrot's Paradise Resort**

6. Click **Next** and then click the **Word** task icon at the bottom of your computer screen.

QuickBooks will create the letters and launch Microsoft Word. You may have to switch to Microsoft Word to see the letters. If required information was missing from your customer record(s), the QuickBooks Information Is Missing window would appear to help you resolve the issue.

7. Use this image to edit the letters for the tour companies (don't worry about the spacing). If you feel adventurous, try inserting the logo into the letters!

Parrot's Paradise Resort
730 Panama Street
Key West, FL 33040

[Current Date]

Humboldt Tour Company
James McDonald
575 Industrial Way
Eureka, CA 95501

Dear Mr. James McDonald,

Thank you for choosing to do business with us. As a special thank you, we are offering a special on Garden View rooms for tour companies. The price per room, per night is $129, compared to our $149 regular price.

Our goal is to serve clients to the best of our ability. If we ever disappoint you, we hope you let us know; we'll do everything we can to make things right.

Thank you again for selecting us. It is our privilege to work with you.

Sincerely,

Jimmy Parrot
Owner, Parrot's Paradise Resort

---

8. Close Word without saving the changes and then switch back to QuickBooks; read the information regarding how to print the letters and envelopes and click **Next**.

9. Click **Cancel** in the Envelope Options window and then click **Cancel** in the QuickBooks Letters and Envelopes window.

Add Multiple Vendor List Entries

Now you will use the Add/Edit Multiple List Entries method to enter vendors into QuickBooks. This method can be used with the other five lists that allow multiple entries to be imported into QuickBooks as well.

To complete this part of the exercise, Excel must be installed on your computer and you should have a basic knowledge of how Excel works. If you don't have both of these, move on to Tackle the Tasks or close QuickBooks.

10. Choose **Lists→Add/Edit Multiple List Entries**.

11. Choose **Vendors** as the list to add additional entries to.

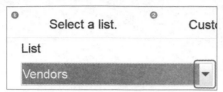

12. Navigate to your file storage location and double-click **Vendor List.xlsx** to open it in Excel. Click the button at the top of the Excel window to enable editing, if necessary.

13. Select the **range A2:O9** and then press [Ctrl]+[C] to copy the information.

    Make sure to select only the data, not the column headers, in Excel.

14. Switch back to QuickBooks, scroll to the bottom of the **Vendors List**, and click the line directly below **Williams Party Rentals**.

15. Tap [Ctrl]+[V] to paste the information from Excel into QuickBooks.

16. Click **Save Changes** and then click **OK** in the Record(s) Saved window.

17. Close the Add/Edit Multiple List Entries window and then close Excel.

Tackle the Tasks

Now is your chance to work a little more with Parrot's Paradise Resort and apply the skills you've just learned to accomplish additional tasks. Continue with the same company file you've been using in this chapter so far. If you need to reopen the company file, the password is *Password1*.

Create Custom Fields	Create an Anniversary custom field for customers; enter these anniversary dates: Kathie Beach, Nov. 10; Brandon Bates, June 18; Toni Martinez, May 21
Set a Price Level	Create a new fixed percentage price level that gives a 15% discount to local customers
Customize a Report	Create a Balance Sheet Standard report that displays only assets, customizing it as you like and using the date June 30, 2022; memorize it as Assets Report
Create a Custom Template	Create a new template for sales receipts named PPR Cash Sale; customize it as you see fit
Create a Letter	Create letters for Kyra Angeles and Tim Laughlin to let them know about the new discount for local customers

Self-Assessment

Check your knowledge of this chapter's key concepts and skills using the Self-Assessment quiz here, in your ebook, or in your eLab course.

1. Before you can use custom fields for items in reports, you must set them up in the Item List.   *True   False*

2. Formatting deals with the appearance of the report, not the data contained within it.   *True   False*

3. You can customize your own Word template to use with your QuickBooks data.   *True   False*

4. After you set your company's default report basis, you can't change it on individual reports.   *True   False*

5. You can filter to display only income accounts on a report.   *True   False*

6. Memorizing a report memorizes the data along with the formatting.   *True   False*

7. Price levels are set up to be used with employees.   *True   False*

8. You must create your own form template to display custom fields.   *True   False*

9. You must memorize a report before you can process it with a batch of reports.   *True   False*

10. Which attribute will NOT be the same each time you recall a memorized report?
     A. The company name in bold
     B. The accounts displayed
     C. The accounting basis of the report
     D. The balance of the accounts on the report

11. For which type of item can a custom field be set up?
     A. Sales tax group
     B. Subtotal
     C. Service
     D. Sales tax item

12. If you're using the cash basis of accounting, which account is NOT displayed on the balance sheet?
     A. Accounts Receivable
     B. Prepaid Rent
     C. Company Checking Account
     D. American Express Credit Card

13. What are billing rates used for?
     A. To differentiate the amount charged to different customers
     B. To customize varying prices on forms
     C. To differentiate the amount charged by different vendors and employees
     D. To set the amount the company pays to vendors for different items

📌 Reinforce Your Skills

Colleen is ready to have you help her spruce up Donnell Construction's reports and estimate template. In addition, you will create custom fields and set a price level. The password for all files unless otherwise stated is Password1.

REINFORCE YOUR SKILLS 11-1

Create and Populate Custom Fields

In this exercise, you will create and populate a custom field.

1. Choose **File→Open or Restore Company**.
2. Open **RYS_Chapter11 (Company)** *or* restore **RYS_Chapter11 (Portable)** and save it as: **RYS_Chapter11 Donnell Construction**
3. Choose **Customers→Customer Center** and then double-click to open **Burning Sparrow Tattoo** for editing.
4. Click the **Additional Info** tab and then click the **Define Fields** button.
5. Type **Birthday** as a label and then place checkmarks in the **Cust** and **Vend** columns to the right of the label.
6. Type **Anniversary** as a label and then place checkmarks in the **Cust** and **Empl** columns to the right of the label.
7. Click **OK** twice to accept the new custom fields.
8. Click in the **Birthday** custom field for Burning Sparrow Tattoo and then type **2/28/1979** and click **OK**.
9. Click in the **Anniversary** custom field for Burning Sparrow Tattoo and then type **8/25/2001** and click **OK**.
10. Click **OK** and then close the Customer Center.

REINFORCE YOUR SKILLS 11-2

Create a New Fixed Percentage Price Level

In this exercise, you will turn on the Price Levels function and create a new fixed percentage price level.

1. Choose **Edit→Preferences**.
2. Click the **Sales & Customers** category and then the **Company Preferences** tab.
3. Ensure **Enable Price Levels** is selected and click **OK**; click **OK** again, allowing QuickBooks to close any open windows, if necessary.
4. Choose **Lists→Price Level List**.
5. Click the **Price Level** drop-down arrow ▼ and click **New**.
6. Name the fixed percentage price level **Military Discount** and choose to decrease item prices by **10** percent.
7. Click **OK** to save the new price level and then close the Price Level List.

Create an Invoice for a Military Customer

Donnell Construction has a new customer, Zoe Minch, who is a captain in the Marine Corps Reserve. She's contracted with you to build a new house for her. While she was in the office, she saw your solid oak wine cart and purchased one. You will create an invoice for her using the military price level.

8. Choose **Customers→Customer Center** and create the new customer: `Minch, Zoe`

9. On the **Payment Settings** tab, set Zoe's price level to **Military Discount** and then click **OK**.

   Now you will create an invoice for Zoe's purchase.

10. Choose **Customers→Create Invoices** and then choose **Minch, Zoe** as the Customer:Job.

11. Fill in the invoice:

    • Date: **06142022**

    • Invoice number: **22-007**

    • Item: **Wine Cart**

12. Click the **Rate** column drop-down arrow ▼ and verify that **Military Discount** is the rate for Zoe; click **Save & Close** and then close the Customer Center window.

REINFORCE YOUR SKILLS 11-3

Customize a Profit & Loss Report and Export It to Excel

In this exercise, you will create a customized Profit & Loss report for Donnell Construction and export it to Excel.

1. Choose **Reports→Company & Financial→Profit & Loss Standard**.

2. Set the dates from **010122** to **063022** and then click **Refresh** on the report toolbar; resize the window to view the report data.

   You will now display the columns by quarter across the top of the report.

3. Click the **Customize Report** button on the toolbar and then click the **Display** tab, if necessary.

4. In the Columns section of the window, choose to display the columns across the top by **Month** and then click **OK**.

   This report will allow you to compare the income and expenses from month to month. You will now customize the report formatting.

5. Click the **Customize Report** button on the toolbar and display the **Header/Footer** tab.

6. Customize the report:

   • Report title: `Profit & Loss by Month`

   • Alignment: **Left**

   • Display the **Fonts & Numbers** tab and make any changes you like.

7. Click **OK** to save your changes.

8. Memorize the report, naming it `Profit & Loss by Month` and saving it in the **Company** group.

9. Click the **Excel** button and export this report to a new workbook saved as: `CH11_R3 Profit and Loss by Month 2022`

10. Close Excel and then close the Profit & Loss by Month report in QuickBooks.

Modify the Custom Estimate Template

In this exercise, you will create an appealing estimate template for Donnell Construction. You can make changes to a template directly from an open form, and that's the approach you'll use to modify the estimate template.

1. Choose **Customers→Create Estimates** and ensure the **Custom Estimate** template is displayed.

2. Click the **Formatting** tab on the ribbon and then click **Manage Templates**. Click **OK** in the Manage Templates window.

   The Basic Customization window displays.

3. In the Company & Transaction area of the window, choose to include the **Phone Number**.

4. Click **OK** in the Layout Designer window, choosing to not have it appear again.

5. Choose to include the **Web Site Address**.

6. Change the font and color scheme of the template to your liking.

7. Click the **Additional Customization** button and, on the Footer tab, add a plain text message that is to be printed:

   `We stand behind all work that we do. Please let us know if you are not fully satisfied so that we can have a chance to make you happy.`

Use Layout Designer

Finally, you will open the form in Layout Designer and make a few more changes.

8. Click the **Layout Designer** button.

> **Note!** As of printing, the Layout Designer is not displaying properly. If this is the case for you, do your best to work with it or skip this exercise.

9. Scroll down; select and move the **Phone #** and **Web Site** objects to the top of the form.

   Hint: Hold `Shift` to select multiple objects and move them simultaneously.

10. Move and adjust these and any other objects as you see fit and, when you have the template just right, click **OK** to save your changes.

11. Click **OK** in the Additional Customization window and then click **Print Preview** to see how the customized estimate looks. Close the Print Preview and Basic Customization windows to save the changes to the template.

12. Close the Create Estimates window and then close your file.

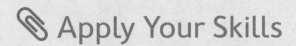 Apply Your Skills

Dr. James is ready to spruce up her company's QuickBooks image and has asked you to customize the forms and reports that are used regularly. You will be creating custom fields and a custom template for Wet Noses Veterinary Clinic as well as a customized profit & loss report. The password for all files unless otherwise stated is Password1.

APPLY YOUR SKILLS 11-1

Create Custom Fields

In this exercise, you will create a custom field and populate it for a customer.

1. Choose **File→Open or Restore Company**.

2. Open **AYS_Chapter11 (Company)** *or* restore **AYS_Chapter11 (Portable)** and save it as:
   `AYS_Chapter11 Wet Noses Clinic`

3. Open the customer record for **Becky Karakash:Dog-Spencer** and then click the **Additional Info** tab and the **Define Fields** button.

4. Add these labels for Cust (customers): Species, Breed, Color, and Gender

5. Click **OK** twice to add the new custom fields.

6. Fill in the custom fields for Spencer:

   • Species: Canine

   • Breed: Golden Retriever

   • Color: Light Brown

   • Gender: Male

7. Click **OK** to close the Edit Job window and then close the Customer Center.

APPLY YOUR SKILLS 11-2 QG

Set a Price Level and Create an Invoice

In this exercise, you will set a price level and then create an invoice using that new price level.

1. Ensure price levels are enabled in the Preferences window.

2. Choose **Lists→Price Level List** and choose to create a new price level.

3. Name the fixed percentage price level Educator Discount and decrease item prices by 10 percent.

4. Click **OK** to save the new price level and then close the Price Level List.

Create an Invoice for an Educator

Emily Dallas and Rita Lance are teachers at the school that Dr. James' kids go to. You will first assign the discount to them and then use the discount on invoices.

5. Choose **Customers→Customer Center**.

6. Double-click **Dallas, Emily**, scrolling as needed. On the **Payment Settings** tab, set the price level and click **OK**. Complete these steps for both of Emily's jobs as well.

7. Set the price level for both **Lance, Rita** and her job to **Educator Discount**.

   Now you will create an invoice for Emily Dallas's cat, Maverick.

8. Click on **Dallas, Emily:Cat-Maverick** and then choose **New Transactions→Invoices**.

9. Set the date as 7/21/2023 and the invoice number as 184 and then choose **Exam**, **Dental**, and **Ears**.

10. Click the **Rate** column drop-down arrow ▼ and verify that **Educator Discount** is the rate for Emily and then click **Save & New**.

11. Choose **Lance, Rita:Dog-Sam** as the Customer:Job.

12. Set the date as 7/24/2023 and the invoice number as 185 and then choose **Annual Exam** and **Cat Collar**.

13. Click the **Rate** column drop-down arrow ▼ and verify that **Educator Discount** is the rate for Rita; click **Save & Close** and then close the Customer Center window.

14. Choose to create an **Open Invoices** report and set the date to **All**.

15. Click the **Excel** button and export this report to a new workbook saved as:
    `CH11_A2 Open Invoices`

16. Close Excel and the QuickBooks report.

APPLY YOUR SKILLS 11-3 QG

Customize a Profit & Loss Report

In this exercise, you will help Sadie create a customized Profit & Loss report.

1. Choose **Reports→Company & Financial→Profit & Loss Standard**.

2. Set the date range from 050123 to 053123 and click **Refresh**.

   You will now display the columns by week across the top of the report.

3. Click the **Customize Report** button on the toolbar and then click the **Display** tab, if necessary.

4. In the Columns section, display the columns across the top by week and click **OK**.

   This report will allow you to compare the income and expenses from week to week.

   Sadie doesn't like the look of the default header, and she needs your help to get it just right.

5. Click the **Customize Report** button on the toolbar and then display the **Header/Footer** tab.

6. Change the report title to Profit & Loss by Week and left-align it.

7. On the **Fonts & Numbers** tab, make any desired changes to the formatting of the fonts and numbers and then click **OK** to save.

8. Memorize the report into the **Company** group as Profit & Loss by Week.

9. Click the **Excel** button and export this report to a new workbook saved as:
   `CH11_A3 Profit and Loss by Week`

10. Close Excel and the QuickBooks report.

Modify the Custom Sales Receipt

In this exercise, you will create an appealing sales receipt for Wet Noses.

1. Choose **Customers→Enter Sales Receipts**.

2. On the **Formatting** tab, click **Manage Templates** and click **OK**.

3. In the Company & Transaction Information area of the window, choose to add the options for printing the company phone and fax numbers.

   Close the Layout Designer window, choosing to not have it appear again in the future.

4. Change the font and color scheme of the template to your liking.

5. Click the **Additional Customization** button and, on the Footer tab, add a long text that is to be printed:

   We care about your pets! Please let us know if you see anything out of the ordinary for your pet so that we may help as early as possible.

Use Layout Designer

Finally, you will open the form in Layout Designer and make a few more changes.

6. Click the **Layout Designer** button and move the **Phone #** and **Fax #** objects to the top of the form.

7. Move any other objects around as you see fit, clicking **OK** when you have the template as you like it.

8. Click **OK** in the Additional Customization and Basic Customization windows.

9. On the Main tab, click the **Save** drop-down arrow ▾ and choose **Save as PDF**, saving the file to your file storage location as: **CH11_A4 Sales Receipt**

10. Close all windows and the company file.

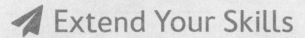

Extend Your Skills

Before You Begin: Open **EYS_Chapter11 (Company)** *or* restore **EYS_Chapter11 (Portable)**. The password is *Password1*.

You've been hired by Arlaine Cervantes to help her with her organization's books. She is the founder of Niños del Lago, a nonprofit organization that provides impoverished Guatemalan children with an engaging educational camp experience. You just sat down at your desk and opened a large envelope from Arlaine that contains a variety of documents; you also have several emails from her. It's your job to sort through the papers and emails and make sense of what you find, entering information into QuickBooks as appropriate and answering questions in a word-processing document saved as: CH11_EYS_[LastnameFirstinitial]

Remember, you're dealing with random papers dumped out of an envelope and various emails, so part of your challenge is determining the order in which to complete the tasks.

- Note: The invoice that we send out looks so boring.... Please fancy it up a bit! Add a picture (as a logo) that relates to Guatemalan culture and make it more colorful. Also, please include our U.S. office phone number on the invoice.

- Printed copy of the Balance Sheet report: A note on the report reads, "Please change the font and make the title align to the right. Make the heading color match the color on the new invoice template. Memorize it or something so it will be easy to run it next time with the same look."

- Note from Arlaine: Send letters to all our donors, thanking them for their support during the year and inviting them down to visit the camp.

- Note from Arlaine: I'd like to indicate the color of the scarves that we sell on our sales forms. Is there a way to add this information? Can you make it appear on the new invoice template that you created?

12 Bringing It All Together: Merchandising Project

You've now encountered and used the main QuickBooks tasks. You should be feeling pretty comfortable working in the program at this point! In this chapter, you will further hone your skills in working with inventory transactions, setting up other balance sheet accounts, dealing with payroll and time tracking, and customizing a QuickBooks file.

Project: Skortis Landscaping

Justin Skortis owns a landscaping company, Skortis Landscaping, that offers planning, installation, and monthly landscape maintenance services. Justin began using QuickBooks last month (January 2022), and you're his bookkeeper.

In this project, you will be entering transactions for February 2022. In addition, Skortis Landscaping has started carrying certain inventory items, so you'll be setting up the company to track inventory and sales tax. Justin will be purchasing a new Ford F-150 truck with a loan, so you will create the necessary accounts to track it. And since he'll be using an outside payroll service for his employees, you'll need to account for this in QuickBooks. Finally, you will help Justin to spruce up the appearance of the reports and templates his company uses.

Note! This project is broken down into sessions. At the end of each session, you'll produce deliverables for evaluation. You will not be given specifics in many cases, just as you will not be given specifics when working with your own company. You may need to add new customers, vendors, or other information "on the fly" and use your own problem-solving and reasoning skills. Use QuickBooks' help and search features as needed. Now, let's get started!

Session 1: Lists

Before You Begin: Restore **Chapter12 (Portable)** from your file storage location, saving it as CH12_Skortis Landscaping.

In this session, you will set up the company to track inventory, fixed assets, and payroll from an outside service.

EMPLOYEES		
Name	Shannon Clausen	Caleb Coon
Address	1706 Palsgraf Lane, Poway, CA 92064	4508 Willamette Drive, San Diego, CA 92128
Phone	(858) 555-5438	(858) 555-9441
SSN	123-45-6789	234-56-7890
Gender	Female	Male
DOB	10/31/1987	12/25/1990
Marital Status	Married	Single
U.S. Citizen	Yes	Yes
Ethnicity	American Indian	White
Disabled	Yes	No
I-9	Yes	Yes
Military Service	Yes, Reserves	No

Add the required vendors, payroll expense (Gross Wages, Company-Paid Benefits, and Company-Paid Taxes), and payroll liability accounts.

PAYROLL INFORMATION

- Federal taxes are to be paid to U.S. Treasury, 2020 Lucille Lane, Washington DC 20039
- State taxes are to be paid to CA Tax Authority (already set up)
- Payment for employee benefits are to be paid to Sunrise Insurance Co., 3011 Abernathy Circle, Hampton, VA 23661

Note! Do NOT use this information when completing payroll for your own company, as it's provided only as a learning tool. Find the information that applies to your company based on its location.

FINANCE CHARGE INFORMATION

- Annual interest rate: 12%
- Minimum finance charge: $1.00
- Grace period: 30 days
- Finance charge account: Finance Charge Income
- Do not assess on overdue finance charges
- Calculate charges from due date

SALES TAX INFORMATION

- San Diego County sales tax is 9.25%, payable to CA Tax Authority.
- Make all non-inventory parts nontaxable and all inventory parts taxable. All services are nontaxable and all customers are taxable. Verify that the correct tax rate is applied for each sale.
- You will need to go into the Item List to mark all service items as nontaxable.

All fixed assets were purchased new prior to Justin's QuickBooks start date. Set up all fixed assets as fixed asset items. Enter the cost in the appropriate fixed asset cost account and long-term liability loan account (if it has an associated loan). Set up all fixed asset loans as long-term, regardless of the remaining balance.

Because these purchases were made before 1/1/2022, they will affect Opening Balance Equity when entered. You'll be entering the balance as of 12/31/2021, the day before your QuickBooks company started.

Create a new fixed asset account with cost and accumulated depreciation subaccounts for each item. Delete the three fixed asset accounts that were set up automatically when you created the company file (Accumulated Depreciation, Furniture and Equipment, and Landscaping Equipment) because you're using the book value method of fixed asset tracking.

FIXED ASSETS AND LIABILITIES

Fixed Asset Name	Purchase Date	Description	Cost	Associated Long-Term Liability?	Loan Account Vendor/ Balance (as of 12/31/2021)
JD Riding Mower	5/21/2018	John Deere riding mower	2,599	No	
2017 F-150	11/9/2019	2017 Ford F-150 SuperCrew XLT	34,790	Yes	Ford Loan – 1/ $17,489
PW Landscape Trailer	11/10/2018	Pac West Tandem Landscape Trailer, 16'	5,792	Yes	Trailer Loan – 1/ $2,609

Create a new account, Product Sales, to record the income from the sale of inventory items. These fields will be the same for all items: COGS Account: Cost of Goods Sold; Income Account: Product Sales; Asset Account: Inventory Asset; Sales Tax: SD County. (Hint: You can copy down this information for Product Sales if you're using the Add/Edit Multiple List Entries method.)

PRODUCTS FOR SALE					
Item Name	Description	Cost	Preferred Vendor	Sales Price	Reorder Point
Birdbath	Wrought iron birdbath	37.45	Temecula Iron Works 34220 Zinfandel Way Temecula, CA 92591	159.00	5
Trellis	Wrought iron trellis	29.85	Temecula Iron Works	105.00	10
Bench	Cedar bench	32.50	Bill's Woodworking 19002 Tinie Place Fallbrook, CA 92028	125.00	8
Screen	Ornate cedar screen	23.65	Bill's Woodworking	85.00	15

Deliverables

Justin has asked you the following questions. For your response, you'll provide him with certain reports. (Hint: Display the Report Center in list view.)

> **Note!** If your class is using Quick Grader, be sure to export the report to Excel, including the identifiers (e.g., "CH12-1") in the filenames.

QG **CH12-1:** What are the names of each of my company's accounts?

QG **CH12-2:** What is the detailed information about each inventory item?

QG **CH12-3:** What is the contact information and Social Security number for each employee?

QG **CH12-4:** For my company's fixed assets, what are the purchase date, description, and original cost of each asset?

Session 2: Transactions

Enter the transactions for Skortis Landscaping for February 2022. Create relevant memos for each transaction and Quick Add any new list entries.

WEEK 1	
2/1/2022	Create purchase orders for 8 birdbaths, 15 trellises, 10 benches, and 20 screens.
2/2/2022	Enter a bill for $741.62 payable to Bates Bank to make a payment on the Visa-0319 account.

(cont.)

WEEK 1 (cont.)

2/3/2022	Create a custom invoice template for Skortis Landscaping, named SL Invoice. Let your creativity flow and customize it as you see fit. You will use this invoice template for all invoice transactions in this chapter.
2/4/2022	Receive all the inventory you ordered with the bills. Add a $45 shipping charge to the invoice for Temecula Iron Works and a $53 shipping charge to the Bill's Woodworking invoice.
2/5/2022	Enter an invoice for Nathaniel Jones for 2 hours of design work, 4 hours of installation, 4 hours of yard care, a birdbath, and 2 screens.

 CHECK FIGURE *Checking $45,424.13 • A/R $3,319.43 • A/P $2,328.82 • Visa-0319 $0.00*

WEEK 2

2/7/2022	Purchase a new 2022 Ford F-150 truck for $42,679. Set up the fixed asset account (2022 Ford F-150), subaccounts, and fixed asset item. Write a check to Poway Ford for $10,000 as a down payment, to be printed later, and fund the rest of the purchase with a long term loan (Ford Loan – 2).
2/8/2022	Create an estimate for Jurassic Ventures for 12 hours of design work, 24 hours of installation, 2 benches, and a birdbath.
2/9/2022	Enter an invoice for Victoria Martusheff for 2 hours of installation, 4 hours of yard care, a trellis, and 2 screens.
2/10/2022	Enter a sale for Maddy Gessford, paid for by check #842, for 2 hours of installation, 5 hours of yard care, a bench, and a birdbath.
2/11/2022	Receive payments for the full amount due from Mariner's Park, Inc. (Visa 4321 4321 4321 4321, exp. 12/2023) and Twin Peaks Realty (check #2009).
2/12/2022	Pay all bills due by 2/12/2022 (checks to be printed), print all checks in the queue (first check number: 1898), and deposit all funds being held in Undeposited Funds to Checking.

 CHECK FIGURE *Checking $37,782.78 • A/R $1,539.87 • A/P $1,587.20 • Visa-0319 $0.00*

WEEK 3

2/14/2022	Create an invoice from the estimate for Jurassic Ventures for 50 percent of the total amount.
2/15/2022	Enter an invoice for Twin Peaks Realty for 5 hours of design work, 14 hours of installation, 8 hours of maintenance, 2 benches, and 3 trellises.
2/16/2022	Enter a cash sale for Irie Spaeth for 2 hours of installation, 4 hours of yard care, and a birdbath.
2/17/2022	Transfer $175.55 from PayPal to Checking.
2/18/2022	Enter an invoice for Mariner's Park, Inc. for 6 hours of design work, 13 hours of installation, 8 hours of maintenance, 4 benches, and a birdbath.
2/19/2022	Pay all bills due by 2/19/2022 (checks to be printed), print all checks in the queue (first check number is 1900), and deposit all funds being held in Undeposited Funds to Checking.

 CHECK FIGURE *Checking $36,818.69 • A/R $7,440.51 • A/P $-56.15 • Visa-0319 $0.00*

13 | The Accounting Cycle and Using Classes

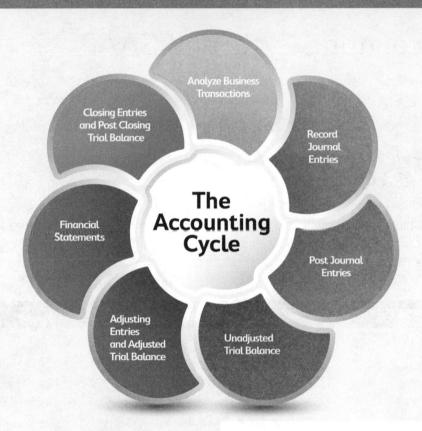

The Accounting Cycle

- Analyze Business Transactions
- Record Journal Entries
- Post Journal Entries
- Unadjusted Trial Balance
- Adjusting Entries and Adjusted Trial Balance
- Financial Statements
- Closing Entries and Post Closing Trial Balance

I n this chapter, you will learn about the accounting cycle and review Generally Accepted Accounting Principles (GAAP) through a QuickBooks lens. Throughout this chapter, you will work in depth on the first three steps of the accounting cycle while exploring how classes can help with the process. Using classes in QuickBooks allows you to classify transactions, giving you more data with which to manage your business. Wrapping up this chapter, you will learn about and produce a Statement of Cash Flows.

LEARNING OBJECTIVES

▸ Work with the accounting cycle and GAAP

▸ Use class tracking in transactions and reports

▸ Create a Statement of Cash Flows

Project: Parrot's Paradise Resort

In this chapter, you will continue working with Parrot's Paradise Resort as you go a step past "behind the scenes" and look at the steps of the accounting cycle. There are seven accounting cycle steps, and you will work closely with the first three steps as well as with classes in this chapter. Finally, you will examine the cash flow for the business and the profit & loss by class by producing Statement of Cash Flows and Profit & Loss by Class reports.

The Accounting Cycle and GAAP

Now we will dive deeper into what occurs behind the scenes in QuickBooks. So far, you've had a glimpse of this through the Behind the Scenes and Flashback to GAAP features of this book. Next, we will look at how the accounting cycle and GAAP apply to QuickBooks users.

Time to Review Generally Accepted Accounting Principles (GAAP)

Every industry follows standards and best practices for that industry. When it comes to accounting principles, the best practices are the same across industries. GAAP are rules used to prepare, present, and report financial statements for a variety of entities and must be followed by publicly traded companies. As GAAP attempt to achieve basic objectives, they have several assumptions, principles, and constraints.

GENERALLY ACCEPTED ACCOUNTING PRINCIPLES (GAAP)	
Principle	**Description**
Business entity principle	The business is separate from the owners and from other businesses. Business revenues and expenses should be kept separate from the business owner's personal expenses.
The assumption of the going concern	The business will be in operation indefinitely.
Monetary unit principle	A stable currency is going to be the unit of record.
Time-period principle	The activities of the business can be divided into time periods.
Cost principle	When a company purchases assets, it should record them at cost. An item worth $750 bought for $100 is recorded at $100.
Revenue principle	Publicly traded companies must record when the revenue is realized and earned (accrual basis of accounting), not when cash is received (cash basis of accounting).
Matching principle	Expenses are matched with revenues during the same accounting period. This allows for better evaluation of profitability and performance (how much did you spend to earn the revenue?).
Objectivity principle	A company's statements should be based on objectivity.

(cont.)

GENERALLY ACCEPTED ACCOUNTING PRINCIPLES (cont.)	
Materiality principle	When an item is reported, its significance is considered. An item is considered significant when it would affect the decision made regarding its use.
Consistency principle	The company uses the same accounting principles and methods from year to year.
Prudence principle	When choosing between two solutions, the one that is least likely to overstate assets and income should be selected.

The Accounting Cycle and Fiscal Period

Accounting records are kept and used to produce financial information. The records are kept for a period of time called a *fiscal period,* which can be any length of time. It may be a month or even a quarter of the year. Most businesses use a year as their fiscal period. A business doesn't have to use the dates January 1 through December 31 as its fiscal period. Many businesses start their fiscal period in February and end in January. Local government and educational institutions often use a fiscal period that begins July 1 and ends June 30.

The accounting cycle is a series of steps that help the business properly keep its accounting records during the fiscal period. Prior to the steps outlined here, you should make sure to collect source documents and verify the financial information (which is sometimes considered a first step).

The Steps of the Accounting Cycle

1. Analyze the business transactions.

2. Record the business transactions (both debit and credit parts) in a journal.

3. Post each journal entry to the ledger accounts.

4. Prepare the unadjusted trial balance.

5. Prepare adjusting entries and run an adjusted trial balance.

6. Generate the financial statements.

7. Prepare closing entries and the post-closing trial balance.

This information is used by business owners, of course. Banks also use it as part of their analysis before lending money to a business owner; they need to know how the business is doing financially. And, finally, when assessing taxes, the government needs to know how much revenue a business is generating, so they use this information as well.

QuickBooks takes care of a lot of the steps behind the scenes. But you'll need to exercise some common sense to avoid possible future trouble. Throughout this chapter, we'll look at the first three steps of the accounting cycle and how you and QuickBooks can work as a team to ensure your books accurately document your company's financial scenario.

Collecting and Verifying Source Documents

To complete the first step in the accounting cycle and analyze transactions, you must first ensure the information on source documents is recorded correctly in QuickBooks. Source documents take many forms. Whether you're dealing with a receipt, check stub, utility bill, memo documenting the transaction, or another document, it's up to you to verify the information on it. The Doc Center makes it easy for you to keep track of source documents.

The QuickBooks Doc Center

The Doc Center stores your source documents electronically, attaching them to the transactions or list entries to which they belong. You can enter documents into the Doc Center in several ways, including:

- Via the drag-and-drop method from Windows or Outlook

- From a scanner

- From another storage location accessible by your computer

While it's convenient and affordable to use the Doc Center, the files contained within it are not secure, so you need to take additional precautions when storing documents with sensitive information. You may wish to consider a third-party secure document management service (guess what...there's an app for that!) that interfaces well with the QuickBooks Doc Center and provides security features to protect sensitive information if that's a concern.

You can search for a document using keywords, customer names, and other information.

You can attach documents from a storage location or scanner.

You can attach documents directly to a source form.

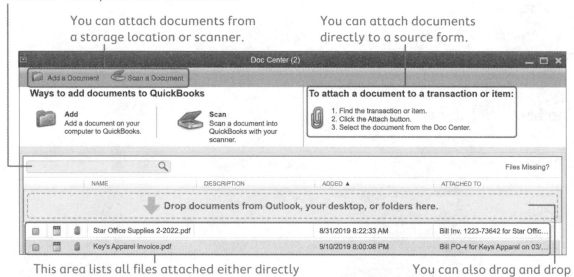

This area lists all files attached either directly through the Doc Center or through the source forms.

You can also drag and drop your files into this area.

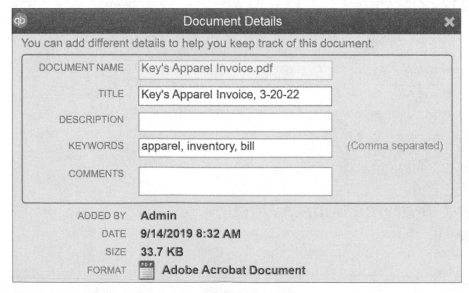

You can add additional details regarding the file, as well as view the date/time stamp of when it was added.

DEVELOP YOUR SKILLS 13-1

In this exercise, you will add a document to the Doc Center and then attach it to a QuickBooks transaction. The password for all files unless otherwise stated is Password1. *Leave the company file open unless otherwise instructed.*

1. Start QuickBooks 2020 and choose **File→Open or Restore Company**.
2. Open **DYS_Chapter13 (Company)** *or* restore **DYS_Chapter13 (Portable)** and save it as: **DYS_Chapter13 Parrot's Paradise Resort**

   You will begin by adding a file to the Doc Center.
3. Choose **Company→Documents→Doc Center** and then resize the window if necessary.
4. Click **Add a Document** at the top of the window and then browse to your file storage location and double-click **Key's Apparel Invoice.pdf**.
5. Click the **Key's Apparel Invoice.pdf** checkbox, click the **View Details** button, and enter the title and keywords:
   - Title: **Key's Apparel Invoice, 3-20-22**
   - Keywords: **apparel**, **inventory**, **bill**
6. Click **Save & Close** and then close the Doc Center.

Attach the File to a Transaction

7. Click the **Enter Bills** task icon in the Vendors area of the Home Page.

8. Click the **Previous** ◀ button until you see the 3/20/2022 bill from Key's Apparel displayed.
9. Click the **Attach File** button on the ribbon and choose to attach from the **Doc Center**.

   The Select Doc Center Documents window will appear.

10. Resize the **Select Doc Center Documents** window so you can see the Attach button in the bottom-right corner, click the **Key's Apparel Invoice** checkbox, and click **Attach**.
11. Close the Attachments window and then click **Save & Close**.

    Before closing the Enter Bills window, notice that the Attach File button now has a small indicator on it with a "1" signifying there is one attachment for the bill.

> **Note!** When you attach a document, QuickBooks creates an Attach folder with subfolders for the added documents. Don't delete these folders unless you've removed the documents from the Doc Center first.

Cycle Step 1: Analyze Business Transactions

After you've compiled and verified the source documents (receipts, bills, etc.), you're ready to analyze the transactions QuickBooks style. When you perform this analysis, you'll need to answer these questions from the perspective of *your business*:

- Which accounts are involved and what type are they?

- Is each account increased or decreased?

- Which account(s) is/are debited and for what amount?

- Which account(s) is/are credited and for what amount?

- What does the completed entry look like?

The good news here is that in the Behind the Scenes feature throughout this book, you have been seeing this analysis in action. You will now perform it for yourself!

DEVELOP YOUR SKILLS 13-2

In this exercise, you will analyze a variety of transactions.

1. Complete this table.

    You can download Analyze Business Transactions.pdf from your file storage location if you don't want to write in the book.

	Invoice #22-0019	Sales Receipt #10	Bill for Star Office Supplies dated 2/25/2022	Payment received, invoice 22-0011, dated 3/12/2022	Deposit to checking, 3/27/2022
Which accounts are involved and what type is each?					
Is each account increased or decreased?					
Which accounts are debited and by how much?					
Which accounts are credited and by how much?					

The last question of "What does the completed entry look like?" is not included because you're using the completed entry to answer the other questions!

Classes

Classes and subclasses provide an additional way to track information about transactions. They allow you to keep an eye on particular segments of your business (such as new construction vs. remodel), tracking income and expenses for each. This way, if you want to evaluate which segment of the business was most profitable, it will be easy because transactions containing class information can easily be displayed on reports. Class tracking is a tool for you to use with your unique business based on what you want to see on your reports. Classes can help you during the accounting cycle by providing another level of analysis.

When the class tracking preference is enabled, QuickBooks adds class fields to many forms and registers such as the Create Invoices form, Enter Bills form, and reports. You can also run specific class reports such as the Profit & Loss by Class. Similar to other lists such as the Vendor Type List, you can't delete a class that's been used in any transaction. Classes can be edited in much the same way you edit other list entries.

A Class Example

Jimmy just opened a new venue in town that will allow him to host larger events. He'll be selling merchandise at this location as well. To track his profit at each location, he will be using classes in QuickBooks. You will set up three classes for Jimmy: Resort, Amphitheatre, and Overhead. Any purchase or sale that is not for one location will be coded with the Overhead class as a "catch-all."

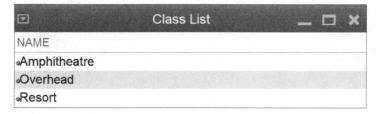

The classes for Parrot's Paradise Resort will allow Jimmy to track profit and loss by location.

Planning for Class Tracking

Just as when you create a new company in QuickBooks and you take time to plan what you need the company to do for you, you need to do the same before you begin to track classes in QuickBooks. Think about what type of reporting you need for your company and exactly what information you need to display on your reports. Classes should be used to track just one aspect of your business or the data will be meaningless. Additionally, you should not use class tracking for an aspect of your business that is already tracked, such as a customer or vendor type, and you must be able to apply the class to all transactions involving income and expense accounts.

When setting up classes for your own company, also create a class for any type of transaction that doesn't apply to one of your named classes (such as "Overhead" or "Administrative"). This is important because you want to make sure you apply a class to every transaction involving an income and/or expense once you set up your company to track classes.

Using Classes for Profit Center Reporting

Many businesses use classes for profit center reporting. A profit center is a sector of a business for which income and expenses are tracked separately so its individual profitability can be determined. One type of business that often relies on profit center reporting, to ensure that the entire business is operating efficiently, is farming.

Subclasses

Even though you are allowed to use classes to track only a single aspect of your business, you can use subclasses to classify your data further. For instance, a restaurant can set up "main" classes to track income and expenses by location and then list food, bar, and catering as subclasses under each location (main class).

 Tip! Don't use classes to track more than one aspect of your business. If you need additional tracking, use subclasses. If you use classes to track more than one aspect, it will render the class data meaningless.

DEVELOP YOUR SKILLS 13-3

In this exercise, you will verify class tracking is turned on and then set up the class list for Parrot's Paradise Resort.

1. Choose **Edit→Preferences**.

2. Turn on the class tracking preference, clicking **OK** when done:
   - Category: **Accounting**
   - Tab: **Company Preferences**
   - Use class tracking for transactions: **Yes**

   Once you turn on the preference, QuickBooks adds class fields to many forms and registers such as the Create Invoices and Enter Bills forms. You can also run reports such as the Profit & Loss by Class.

3. Choose **Lists→Class List**.

4. Click the **Class** button and choose **New**.

5. Type **Resort** as the Class Name and click **Next**.

6. Type **Amphitheatre** as the Class Name and click **Next**.

7. Type **Overhead** as the Class Name, click **OK**, and then close the Class List.

Applying Classes to Transactions

If you decide to use classes, apply them to all transactions involving an income and/or expense account. This can be done through most forms, registers, or journal entries. QuickBooks provides several class tracking reports, and you can customize many other reports by adding the class field; you can create budgets based on them. You can also apply classes to payroll transactions—either to a whole paycheck or individual earning items.

You find the class field in sales forms, such as Create Invoices and Create Purchase Orders, and on expense forms, such as Pay Bills.

 Note! Customer deposits don't need to have a class assigned to them because they don't affect the income statement.

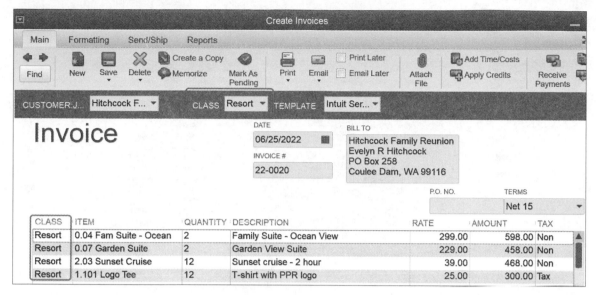

Once class tracking is turned on, you will see fields on forms in which to enter the class data. When you enter a class at the top of the form, it will automatically apply it to each line, although you can change it if needed.

Consistent Class Applications

When you begin using class tracking, it's important to consistently apply a class to every transaction that deals with income and expense accounts so your data, and therefore reporting, is meaningful. If you apply classes to only some transactions and then create a report to show the profitability by class, the information will be skewed. This is why it's important to have a class for transactions that don't fit one of your main classes (like Overhead).

Cycle Step 2: Record Journal Entries

When you enter a transaction in a QuickBooks form (invoice, bill, etc.), QuickBooks performs the work behind the scenes by including the necessary general journal information. In other words, it uses the correct accounts and moves the money accordingly along with the memos and other information that you've entered into the form. When entering any transaction, be sure to follow GAAP. If you were doing this by hand, you would need to enter:

- The date of the transaction

- The account names and amounts of each of the debit and credit parts

- A reference to the source document or a brief explanation

In QuickBooks, ensure your items are set up properly (i.e., routed to the right accounts) so the proper accounts are debited and credited in the journal that is kept behind the scenes for you.

Parrot's Paradise Resort - Chapter 13
Journal
January through June 2022

Trans #	Type	Date	Num	Adj	Name	Memo	Account	Class	Debit	Credit
139	Invoice	06/25/2022	22-0020		Hitchcock Family Reunion	Hitchcock: ...	11000 · Accounts Receivable	Resort	1,846.50	
					Hitchcock Family Reunion	-MULTIPLE-	40000 · Lodging Sales	Resort		1,056.00
					Hitchcock Family Reunion	Sunset crui...	42000 · Banquets and Events I...	Resort		468.00
					Hitchcock Family Reunion	T-shirt with...	41100 · Clothing Sales	Resort		300.00
					Hitchcock Family Reunion	T-shirt with...	12100 · Inventory Asset	Resort		76.68
					Hitchcock Family Reunion	T-shirt with...	52900 · Purchases - Resale Ite...	Resort	76.68	
					Florida Department of Reve...	-MULTIPLE-	25500 · Sales Tax Payable	Resort		22.50
									1,923.18	1,923.18
140	Invoice	06/27/2022	22-0021		Angeles, Kyra	Angeles: C...	11000 · Accounts Receivable	Amphit...	473.05	
					Angeles, Kyra	Concert on...	42000 · Banquets and Events I...	Amphit...		200.00
					Angeles, Kyra	-MULTIPLE-	41100 · Clothing Sales	Amphit...		200.00
					Angeles, Kyra	-MULTIPLE-	12100 · Inventory Asset	Amphit...		58.24
					Angeles, Kyra	-MULTIPLE-	52900 · Purchases - Resale Ite...	Amphit...	58.24	
					Angeles, Kyra	Reef-safe 3...	41500 · Sundry Sales	Amphit...		54.00
					Florida Department of Reve...	-MULTIPLE-	25500 · Sales Tax Payable	Amphit...		19.05
									531.29	531.29
141	Bill	06/23/2022	HBTB ...		Handyman by the Bay	Installation ...	20000 · Accounts Payable			237.50
					Handyman by the Bay	Installation ...	67200 · Repairs and Maintenan...	Resort	237.50	
									237.50	237.50
142	Bill	06/28/2022	AmpR...		Williams Party Rentals	Rentals for...	20000 · Accounts Payable			675.00
					Williams Party Rentals	Rentals for...	63000 · Event Rentals	Amphit...	675.00	
									675.00	675.00
TOTAL									**501,665.86**	**501,665.86**

QuickBooks keeps a journal for you as you enter each transaction. Note the last four transactions that you just entered and the class field that has been added to the Journal report.

Cycle Step 3: Post Journal Entries

In the third step of the accounting cycle, you find the entries that were entered into the general journal posted to the individual ledger accounts. This step is done entirely behind the scenes for you (thank you, QuickBooks!). If using the Premier Accounting version of QuickBooks, you can run a General Ledger report that shows the balance of each account and the transactions that affect it, broken down by debits and credits, for the stated time period.

Parrot's Paradise Resort - Chapter 13
General Ledger
As of June 30, 2022

Type	Date	Num	Adj	Name	Memo	Split	Debit	Credit	Balance
40000 · Lodging Sales									0.00
Invoice	01/03/2022	22-0001		Martinez, Toni	King Bed - Oc...	11000 · Accounts Rec...		507.00	-507.00
Invoice	01/10/2022	22-0002		Bates, Brandon	Junior Suite - O...	11000 · Accounts Rec...		996.00	-1,503.00
Invoice	01/13/2022	22-0003		Beach, Kathie	2 Queen - Ove...	11000 · Accounts Rec...		845.00	-2,348.00
Invoice	01/21/2022	22-0004		Park, Ginny	King Bed - Ga...	11000 · Accounts Rec...		596.00	-2,944.00
Invoice	01/25/2022	22-0005		Hernandez, Jose	Family Suite - ...	11000 · Accounts Rec...		1,794.00	-4,738.00
Invoice	01/25/2022	22-0006		Stolfus Tour Services	-MULTIPLE-	11000 · Accounts Rec...		8,050.00	-12,788.00
Invoice	02/04/2022	22-0008		Gator Tours	-MULTIPLE-	11000 · Accounts Rec...		3,209.00	-15,997.00
Invoice	02/14/2022	22-0009		Gator Tours	-MULTIPLE-	11000 · Accounts Rec...		3,507.00	-19,504.00
Invoice	02/26/2022	22-0011		Humboldt Tour Comp...	-MULTIPLE-	11000 · Accounts Rec...		2,773.00	-22,277.00
Invoice	03/11/2022	22-0014		Sherwood Tours:29M...	King Bed - Oc...	11000 · Accounts Rec...		2,366.00	-24,643.00
Credit Memo	03/21/2022	CR1		Park, Ginny	King Bed - Ga...	11000 · Accounts Rec...	596.00		-24,047.00
Invoice	03/22/2022	22-0017		Park, Ginny	Family Suite - ...	11000 · Accounts Rec...		299.00	-24,346.00
Invoice	06/01/2022	22-0019		Stolfus Tour Services	-MULTIPLE-	11000 · Accounts Rec...		3,225.00	-27,571.00
Invoice	06/25/2022	22-0020		Hitchcock Family Reu...	-MULTIPLE-	11000 · Accounts Rec...		1,056.00	-28,627.00
Total 40000 · Lodging Sales							596.00	29,223.00	-28,627.00
41000 · Gift Shop and Vending Sales									0.00
41100 · Clothing Sales									0.00
Invoice	03/11/2022	22-0014		Sherwood Tours:29M	T-shirt with PP...	11000 · Accounts Rec...		500.00	-500.00
Invoice	03/15/2022	22-0015		Angeles, Kyra	T-shirt with PP...	11000 · Accounts Rec...		5.00	-505.00
Invoice	03/15/2022	22-0016		Laughlin, Tim	T-shirt with PP...	11000 · Accounts Rec...		5.00	-510.00
Invoice	03/22/2022	22-0018		Gator Tours	PPR logo flip f...	11000 · Accounts Rec...		500.00	-1,010.00
Invoice	06/25/2022	22-0020		Hitchcock Family Reu...	T-shirt with PP...	11000 · Accounts Rec...		300.00	-1,310.00
Invoice	06/27/2022	22-0021		Angeles, Kyra	-MULTIPLE-	11000 · Accounts Rec...		200.00	-1,510.00
Total 41100 · Clothing Sales							0.00	1,510.00	-1,510.00
41200 · Food Sales									0.00
Invoice	03/11/2022	22-0014		Sherwood Tours:29M...	Basket of grah...	11000 · Accounts Rec...		96.00	-96.00
Total 41200 · Food Sales							0.00	96.00	-96.00

This general ledger shows accounts and the transactions that make up their balances for the period January–June 2022.

DEVELOP YOUR SKILLS 13-4

In this exercise, you will create two invoices and two bills, applying classes to each. You will also produce journal and general ledger reports.

1. Click the **Create Invoices** task icon in the Customers area of the Home Page.

2. Create the invoices, clicking **Save & New** after the first one:

Create Invoices

	First Invoice	**Second Invoice**
Customer:Job	**Hitchcock Family Reunion**	**Angeles, Kyra**
Class	**Resort**	**Amphitheatre**
Date	**062522**	**062722**
Item / Qty	(first line) **0.04 Fam Suite – Ocean / 2** (second line) **0.07 Garden Suite / 2** (third line) **2.03 Sunset Cruise / 12** (fourth line) **1.101 Logo Tee / 12**	(first line) **2.02 Concert – VIP / 4** (second line) **1.101 Logo Tee / 4** (third line) **1.501 Sunscreen / 4** (fourth line) **1.102 Flip Flops / 4**
Memo	`Hitchcock: 7/2022 reunion`	`Angeles: Concert 6/2022`

Selecting the class from the top of the form will apply that class to all items on the invoice.

3. Click **Save & Close**.

The following Behind the Scenes Brief is for both invoices:

BEHIND THE SCENES BRIEF

11000•Accounts Receivable DR 2,319.55; **40000•Lodging Sales CR 1,056.00 | 42000•Banquets and Events Income CR 668.00 | 41100•Clothing Sales CR 500.00 | 41500•Sundry Sales CR 54.00 | 25500•Sales Tax Payable CR 41.55**

11000•Accounts Receivable has **increased**; 40000•Lodging Sales has **increased** | 42000•Banquets and Events Income has **increased** | 41100•Clothing Sales has **increased** | 41500•Sundry Sales has **increased** | 25500•Sales Tax Payable has **increased**

Check Figure: Accounts Receivable $6,812.51

You will now enter two bills for Parrot's Paradise Resort

4. Click the **Enter Bills** task icon in the Banking area of the Home Page.

Enter Bills

5. Enter the bills, clicking **Save & New** after the first one, and make sure to enter the expense accounts on the Expenses tab:

	First Bill	Second Bill
Vendor	**Handyman by the Bay**	**Williams Party Rentals**
Date	`062322`	`062822`
Ref. No.	`HBTB 6/22`	`AmpRent 6/27`
Amount Due	`237.50`	`675`
Memo	`Installation work, 6/2022`	`Rentals for concert, 6/27/2022`
Account	**67200·Repairs and Maintenance**	**63000·Event Rentals**
Class	**Resort**	**Amphitheatre**

The following Behind the Scenes Brief is for both invoices:

BEHIND THE SCENES BRIEF

63000·Event Rentals DR 675.00 | 67200·Repairs and Maintenance DR 237.50; **Accounts Payable CR 912.50**

63000·Event Rentals has **increased** | 67200·Repairs and Maintenance has **increased**; Accounts Payable has **increased**

Check Figure: Accounts Payable $1,381.20

6. Click **Save & Close**.

Run Journal and General Ledger Reports

7. Choose **Reports→Accountant & Taxes→Journal** and then click **OK** in the Collapsing and Expanding Transactions window.

8. Set the date range to **All**.

   Scroll through the report to see how all the different transactions are displayed.

9. Close the report, choosing not to memorize it.

10. Choose **Reports→Accountant & Taxes→General Ledger** and then click **OK** in the Collapsing and Expanding Transactions window.

11. Set the date range to **All**.

   Scroll through the report to see how the general ledge is set up.

12. Close the report, choosing not to memorize it.

Running Class Reports

The goal of using class tracking is to produce reports that focus on the areas of the business you are tracking. They will help you determine profitability in those classes and could assist you in making decisions on the future direction of the company.

Profit & Loss Unclassified

This report displays any transaction amount that is not associated with a class. Running this report periodically can help ensure you don't miss any transactions. It's then easy to use the QuickZoom feature to drill to the unclassified transactions (source documents) and assign a class to them.

Profit & Loss by Class

When you've applied classes to all your transactions, running this report displays the net income (loss) by class, broken down by income and expenses and categorized by class. If there are unclassified transactions, you'll have a column before the Total column displaying the total amount that has not been classified for each account. You can drill down to the source documents through this report so you can assign classes to the transactions.

Parrot's Paradise Resort - Chapter 13
Profit & Loss by Class
June 2022

	Amphitheatre	Resort	TOTAL
Ordinary Income/Expense			
Income			
40000 · Lodging Sales	0.00	4,281.00	4,281.00
41000 · Gift Shop and Vending Sales			
41100 · Clothing Sales	200.00	300.00	500.00
41500 · Sundry Sales	54.00	0.00	54.00
Total 41000 · Gift Shop and Vending Sales	254.00	300.00	554.00
42000 · Banquets and Events Income	200.00	1,911.00	2,111.00
Total Income	454.00	6,492.00	6,946.00
Cost of Goods Sold			
52900 · Purchases - Resale Items	58.24	76.68	134.92
Total COGS	58.24	76.68	134.92
Gross Profit	395.76	6,415.32	6,811.08
Expense			
63000 · Event Rentals	675.00	0.00	675.00
63700 · Landscaping and Groundskeeping	0.00	175.00	175.00
67200 · Repairs and Maintenance	0.00	237.50	237.50
Total Expense	675.00	412.50	1,087.50
Net Ordinary Income	-279.24	6,002.82	5,723.58
Net Income	-279.24	6,002.82	5,723.58

The Profit & Loss by Class report shows net income by each class as well as overall for the company. We've only entered a handful of transactions for June 2022, so you should realize that this report will be much more extensive once all transactions for the month are entered.

The Balance Sheet by Class Report

The Balance Sheet by Class report is available in the Premier and Enterprise versions of QuickBooks. In this report, each class appears as a column. This is not a basic report for novice users, as it may display unexpected results at times, and the ability to understand and fix these anomalies requires a solid accounting background.

 Reports→Company & Financial→Profit & Loss Unclassified

 Reports→Company & Financial→Profit & Loss by Class

DEVELOP YOUR SKILLS 13-5

In this exercise, you will run the Profit & Loss Unclassified report and apply a class to a transaction. Then, you will run the Profit & Loss by Class report to show Jimmy exactly how class tracking will benefit him.

1. Choose **Reports→Company & Financial→Profit & Loss Unclassified**.

2. Change the date range to be from **060122** to **063022** and click **Refresh**, resizing the window as necessary to view the data.

   This report lists unclassified transactions. You will use QuickZoom to drill down to an invoice and add the class.

3. Mouse over the 40000•Lodging Sales amount (**3,225.00**) and then double-click using the **QuickZoom** tool.

   The Transaction Detail by Account report appears, displaying the transaction for this account and listing the invoice number.

4. Double-click with the **QuickZoom** pointer on the invoice for **Stolfus Tour Services** to drill down to the source document (invoice).

   You must assign the class on the line items because you can't do it for the entire transaction after it's been saved for the first time.

5. For each of the three lines, choose **Resort** in the Class field for the item.

ITEM	QUANTITY	DESCRIPTION	RATE	AMOUNT	CLASS	TAX
0.05 Qu Garden	15	2 Queen - Garden View Room	129.00	1,935.00	Resort	Non
0.06 King Garden	10	King Bed - Garden View Room	129.00	1,290.00	Resort	Non
2.03 Sunset Cruise	37	Sunset cruise - 2 hour	39.00	1,443.00	Resort	Non

6. Click **Save & Close** and then click **Yes** to record the transaction. Close the Transaction Detail by Account window.

   The invoice transaction will no longer be displayed on the report.

7. Mouse over the 63700•Landscaping and Groundskeeping amount (**175.00**) and then double-click using the **QuickZoom** tool.

   The Transaction Detail by Account report appears, displaying the transaction for this account.

8. Double-click with the **QuickZoom** pointer on general journal transaction number **5** dated **06/01/2022** to drill down to the source (13200•Prepaid Pool Service account register).

9. Click within the **06/01/2022** transaction and choose **Edit→Edit General Journal**; choose to not display the message again and click **OK** in the Assigning Numbers to Journal Entries window.

You can't apply a class in the register window, so you have to make the edit in the general journal.

10. Choose **Resort** in the Class column for the expense line in the transaction.

Remember that we don't need to apply classes to the balance sheet accounts.

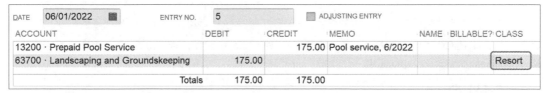

11. Click **Save & Close**, click **Yes**, and, finally, click **Save Anyway**.

12. Close the 13200•Prepaid Pool Service and Transaction Detail by Account windows.

There will no longer be anything displayed on the Profit & Loss Unclassified report.

13. Close the Profit & Loss Unclassified report, choosing not to memorize it.

Create a Profit & Loss Report with Class Data

14. Choose **Reports→Company & Financial→Profit & Loss by Class**.

15. Change the date range to be from **060122** to **063022** and click **Refresh** on the toolbar.

The income from the Stolfus Tour Services invoice is now listed in the Resort column. If you still had unclassified transactions for this time period, there would also be an Unclassified column.

16. Close the Profit & Loss by Class report, choosing not to memorize it.

Including Classes on Reports

Many reports can be customized to have the class included on them. On some reports, you can also use the class as a filter to focus on one or more classes at a time.

Parrot's Paradise Resort - Chapter 13
Sales by Customer Detail
June 2022

Type	Date	Num	Memo	Name	Item	Class	Qty	Sales Price	Amount	Balance
Hitchcock Family Reunion										
Invoice	06/25/2022	22-0020	Family Suit...	Hitchcock Family R...	0.04 Fam Suite...	Resort	2	299.00	598.00	598.00
Invoice	06/25/2022	22-0020	Garden Vie...	Hitchcock Family R...	0.07 Garden Su...	Resort	2	229.00	458.00	1,056.00
Invoice	06/25/2022	22-0020	Sunset crui...	Hitchcock Family R...	2.03 Sunset Cr...	Resort	12	39.00	468.00	1,524.00
Invoice	06/25/2022	22-0020	T-shirt with...	Hitchcock Family R...	1.101 Logo Tee...	Resort	12	25.00	300.00	1,824.00
Total Hitchcock Family Reunion							28		1,824.00	1,824.00
Stolfus Tour Services										
Invoice	06/01/2022	22-0019	2 Queen - G...	Stolfus Tour Services	0.05 Qu Gardo...	Resort	15	129.00	1,935.00	1,935.00
Invoice	06/01/2022	22-0019	King Bed - ...	Stolfus Tour Services	0.06 King Gard...	Resort	10	129.00	1,290.00	3,225.00
Invoice	06/01/2022	22-0019	Sunset crui...	Stolfus Tour Services	2.03 Sunset Cr...	Resort	37	39.00	1,443.00	4,668.00
Total Stolfus Tour Services							62		4,668.00	4,668.00
TOTAL							90		6,492.00	6,492.00

After filtering by the Resort class, the Sales by Customer Detail report shows only those transactions within the date range (June 2022) that have been assigned that class.

In this exercise, you will run a sales report and add the class field to the report. You will also use the Class field as a filter on the report.

1. Choose **Reports→Sales→ Sales by Customer Detail**.

2. Use the date range **060122** to **063022** and then refresh the report, resizing the window to view the report data.

   The report shows the three sales you have entered for June 2022, broken down by customer.

3. Click the **Customize Report** button, scroll down in the Search Columns field and choose **Class**, and then click **OK**.

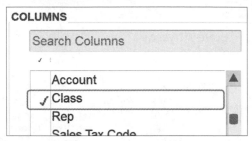

   The Class field is now displayed on the report. You could also type class (or even just "cl"!) in the Search Columns field to locate the field.

4. Click the **Customize Report** button and then the **Filters** tab.

5. Follow these steps to filter the report by the Resort class:

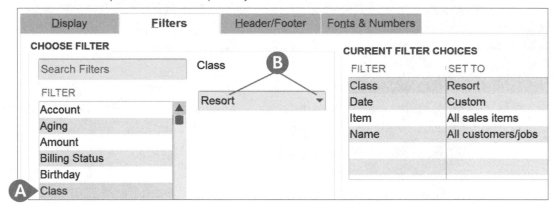

   Ⓐ Click **Class** in the Filter list.

   Class will now appear as the field to be filtered by (to the right of the Search Filters field).

   Ⓑ Click the **Class** drop-down arrow ▾ and choose **Resort**.

   The Current Filter Choices section displays all filters applied to this report. Note that some are based on the report you chose to run (Name and Item) and two are based on your customization of the report (Date and Class).

   Tip! You can filter by more than one class by selecting Multiple Classes from the Class list.

6. Click **OK**.

   You are viewing only transactions for June 2022 that have been assigned the class Resort. You can see why it's important to assign classes to all transactions if you decide to use class tracking.

7. Close the Sales by Customer Detail report, choosing not to memorize it.

Producing a Statement of Cash Flows

The Statement of Cash Flows is a financial report that's been required under GAAP since 1987. It plays an important part in showing how viable a company is in the short term. This helps stakeholders determine whether the company will be able to pay its bills, payroll, and other expenses. It also indicates the financial health of the company.

While the Profit & Loss report looks at the total amount of income coming in and the expenses going out, the Statement of Cash Flows specifically looks at the cash inflows and outflows during a period of time. Per GAAP, corporations are required to use the accrual basis of accounting that records when income and expenses are accrued rather than when cash is exchanged. The Statement of Cash Flows essentially translates the company's data from accrual to cash basis so an understanding of how the company is operating and how cash is being handled can be reached.

FLASHBACK TO GAAP: REVENUE PRINCIPLE

Remember that publicly traded companies must record when revenue is realized and earned (accrual basis of accounting), not when cash is received (cash basis).

Method of Reporting

QuickBooks uses the indirect method when creating a Statement of Cash Flows. This means net income is the starting point for the report, and you adjust for noncash transactions from there. Basically, you take a net income generated using the accrual basis of accounting and convert it to the cash basis by adding increases to current liability accounts and subtracting increases to current asset accounts.

FLASHBACK TO GAAP: CONSISTENCY

Remember that "consistency" means the company uses the same accounting principles and methods from year to year.

Sections of the Statement of Cash Flows Report

There are three sections of the Statement of Cash Flows that organize your company's financial information:

- **Operating section:** You take the activities that result from the normal business operation and convert them to the cash basis. These activities may include such things as sales receipts, production costs, advertising, payroll, and expenses for services performed.

- **Investing section:** You account for fixed assets bought or sold, loans you have issued, and other payments unrelated to normal business operation (e.g., payments related to a merger).

- **Financing section:** You take into account such items as cash from investors (company stock and bond transactions) and dividends that are paid.

> **Note!** Ensuring the accuracy of the Statement of Cash Flows is critical. All transactions to receive payments, pay bills, and deposit funds should be performed before running the report.

Parrot's Paradise Resort - Chapter 13
Statement of Cash Flows
January through June 2022

	Jan - Jun 22
OPERATING ACTIVITIES	
Net Income	▸ 45,228.20 ◂
Adjustments to reconcile Net Income	
to net cash provided by operations:	
11000 · Accounts Receivable	-6,812.51
12100 · Inventory Asset	-1,019.80
13100 · Prepaid Insurance	-1,180.00
13200 · Prepaid Pool Service	-1,750.00
20000 · Accounts Payable	1,381.20
21400 · Visa-4545	227.20
25500 · Sales Tax Payable	41.55
Net cash provided by Operating Activit...	36,115.84
INVESTING ACTIVITIES	
16110 · Cost	-179,000.00
16210 · Cost	-3,995.00
16310 · Cost	-22,639.00
Net cash provided by Investing Activities	-205,634.00
FINANCING ACTIVITIES	
26000 · Loan - Everglades Boat	161,100.00
27000 · Loan - Furniture (Office)	17,639.00
31400 · Shareholder Distributions	-20,000.00
Net cash provided by Financing Activit...	158,739.00
Net cash increase for period	-10,779.16
Cash at beginning of period	549,860.32
Cash at end of period	**539,081.16**

The Statement of Cash Flows shows the company financials as if you were using the cash basis of accounting. It helps determine the "liquidity" of your company.

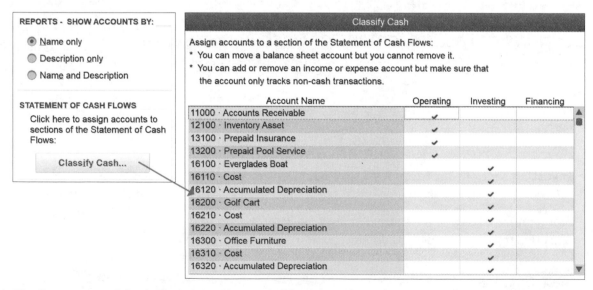

The Statement of Cash Flows section on the Company Preferences tab (Reports & Graphs category) holds the Classify Cash... button, which allows you to assign accounts to different sections of the report.

Forecasting Cash Flow

The Cash Flow Forecast report is important because it's one of the main financial statements used to get approved for a loan, attract shareholders, or demonstrate the financial health of your company. You can also use it internally to help guide decisions that you have to make for your company by giving you a tool by which you can forecast the cash that is and will be flowing into and out of your company. The date range for this report will be in the immediate future.

Parrot's Paradise Resort - Chapter 13 Cash Flow Forecast July 2022					
	Accnts Receivable	Accnts Payable	Bank Accnts	Net Inflows	Proj Balance
Beginning Balance	4,492.96	706.20	539,081.16		542,867.92
Jul 1 - 2, 22	0.00	0.00	0.00	0.00	542,867.92
Week of Jul 3, 22	0.00	0.00	0.00	0.00	542,867.92
Week of Jul 10, 22	2,319.55	675.00	0.00	1,644.55	544,512.47
Week of Jul 17, 22	0.00	0.00	0.00	0.00	544,512.47
Week of Jul 24, 22	0.00	0.00	0.00	0.00	544,512.47
Jul 31, 22	0.00	0.00	0.00	0.00	544,512.47
Jul 22	2,319.55	675.00	0.00	1,644.55	
Ending Balance	6,812.51	1,381.20	539,081.16		544,512.47

The Cash Flow Forecast report gives you a glimpse of what you can expect your cash flow to look like in the near future based on the data in your company file now.

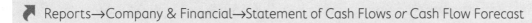 Reports→Company & Financial→Statement of Cash Flows *or* Cash Flow Forecast

Edit→Preferences : Reports & Graphs→Company Preferences tab

DEVELOP YOUR SKILLS 13-7

In this exercise, you will produce the Statement of Cash Flows and create a report to be used internally to make some decisions for the company. Payments received, deposits made, and most outstanding bills have already been recorded for this exercise. There will still be some outstanding transactions, as is normal for most businesses.

1. Choose **Reports→Company & Financial→Statement of Cash Flows**.

   QuickBooks displays the Statement of Cash Flows report with a default date range of This Fiscal Year-to-date.

2. Enter the date range **010122** to **063022** and then refresh the report.

   Notice the three main sections of the report: Operating Activities, Investing Activities, and Financing Activities.

3. Close the report window, choosing not to memorize it.

   The next report will look at the cash flow forecast for the immediate future.

4. Choose **Reports→Company & Financial→Cash Flow Forecast**.

   QuickBooks displays the Cash Flow Forecast report with a default date range of Next 4 Weeks.

5. Use the date range **070122** to **073122** and then refresh the report.

6. Close the report window, choosing not to memorize it.

The Accounting Cycle in Practice

In theory, there are particular things you should be doing on a daily, weekly, monthly, and quarterly basis in your business. These practices help with report accuracy and ensure you aren't missing anything. By coming up with a routine, you will also be more aware of potential cash flow problems. These are some tasks you should stay on top of to make QuickBooks work best for you.

- Know what's in your bank accounts at the start of every business day.

- Record all transactions, including cash sales, bills paid, checks deposited, and orders placed. Run payroll on time and scan any related documents, such as receipts, into the Doc Center.

- Run reports such as the Unpaid Bills Detail, Open Invoices, A/R Aging Detail, Unbilled Costs by Job, and any other that will aid in pointing you to a potential issue.

- Depending on what these reports tell you, take action by paying your vendors, making collection calls, or sending statements. Don't forget your tax bill!

- Try to estimate your cash flow for the near future. What will you need to spend? Can you make payroll?

- Reconcile your bank and credit card accounts on a monthly basis. It's a good idea to run a trial balance on a monthly basis.

- If you're maintaining inventory, make sure it's accurate. Cash flow is important. Stocking too much can hurt your cash flow; not having enough to sell can hurt your bottom line.

- Run the Profit & Loss and Balance Sheet reports fairly often. They tell the bigger picture.

Tackle the Tasks

Now is your chance to work a little more with Parrot's Paradise Resort and apply the skills you've just learned to accomplish additional tasks. Continue with the same company file you've been using in this chapter so far. If you need to reopen the company file, the password is *Password1*.

Analyze Transactions	Answer these questions about invoice #22-0021 and the Williams Party Rentals bill dated 6/28/2022, which you produced in this chapter, using **CH13_TTT_Analyze Business Transactions** • Which accounts are involved and what type is each? • Is each account increased or decreased? • Which accounts are debited and by how much? • Which accounts are credited and by how much?
Apply Classes to Transactions	Use the Visa card to purchase 5 lifejackets from Ahmed Marine on 6/29/2022 for $276.43; use 67500•Service Supplies as the account and the memo as Ahmed: Life Jackets, 6/2022; assign Resort as the class Create a sales receipt for Tim Laughlin for 4 lawn seating concert tickets and 4 logo t-shirts on 6/30/2022; he paid in cash; use Amphitheatre as the class, and the memo is Laughlin: concert 7/4/2022
Produce a Class Report	Produce a Profit & Loss Unclassified report for May 2022 and then use it to apply a class to three unclassified accounts by using QuickZoom; add the following classes to the appropriate expenses: 63300•Insurance Expense: Overhead 63700•Landscaping and Groundskeeping: Resort 63900•Meals and Entertainment: Overhead Run a Profit & Loss by Class report for May 2022
Create a Statement of Cash Flows	Use the date range of 3/1/2022 through 6/30/2022

Self-Assessment

Check your knowledge of this chapter's key concepts and skills using the Self-Assessment in your ebook or eLab course.

1. Class tracking in QuickBooks should be used to track different types of customers. *True* *False*

2. The accounting cycle is a series of steps that helps a business keep its accounting records properly during the fiscal period. *True* *False*

3. Classes should be used to track multiple aspects of your business. *True* *False*

4. Classes can be used by companies to track multiple profit centers. *True* *False*

5. The QuickBooks Doc Center is encrypted, providing a secure storage location for your documents containing sensitive information. *True* *False*

6. You can customize a report to add the Class field or filter by class. *True* *False*

7. A Statement of Cash Flows essentially translates a company's data from accrual to cash basis. *True* *False*

8. You find company stock transactions in the operating section of the Statement of Cash Flows report. *True* *False*

9. The GAAP are rules used to prepare, present, and report financial statements. *True* *False*

10. The Cash Flow Forecast report shows cash flow for prior quarters. *True* *False*

11. Classes are most efficiently used to:
    A. Track types of customers
    B. Track additional information for one purpose
    C. Assign accounts to customers
    D. Record information about one customer

12. Which report do you run to easily apply classes to unclassified transactions?
    A. Profit & Loss by Class
    B. Balance Sheet by Class
    C. Class Change
    D. Profit & Loss Unclassified

13. Which is NOT a question you ask when analyzing business transactions in the first step of the accounting cycle?
    A. What account is credited and by how much?
    B. What is the source document for the transaction?
    C. Is each account increased or decreased?
    D. What does the completed entry look like?

14. Which is an element you would find in the Financing section of the Statement of Cash Flows report?
    A. Dividends that are paid
    B. Production costs
    C. Assets that the company bought
    D. Payroll costs

⚲ Reinforce Your Skills

Colleen Donnell is beginning to review the end-of-quarter reports. She's also decided to start using class tracking for Donnell Construction to track the projects by location. You will be assisting Colleen by running the appropriate reports and setting up class tracking. The password for all files unless otherwise stated is Password1.

REINFORCE YOUR SKILLS 13-1

Analyze Transactions

In this exercise, you will analyze transactions to help you understand the accounting concepts "behind the scenes." Remember that you can run the Journal report to see all transactions.

1. Start QuickBooks 2020 and choose **File→Open or Restore Company**.
2. Open **RYS_Chapter13 (Company)** *or* restore **RYS_Chapter13 (Portable)** and save it as: **RYS_Chapter13 Donnell Construction**
3. Open **CH13_RYS_Analyze Business Transactions.pdf** from your file storage location and complete the analysis of transactions.

REINFORCE YOUR SKILLS 13-2

Track and Use Classes

In this exercise, you will turn on class tracking and set up the classes to track where Donnell Construction's jobs are located.

1. Choose **Edit→Preferences**.
2. Click the **Accounting** category and the **Company Preferences** tab.
3. Click the **Use Class Tracking for Transactions** checkbox and click **OK**.
4. Choose **Lists→Class List**.
5. Set up these classes:
   - **Oak Park & West Suburbs**
   - **Chicago**
   - **Northwest Suburbs**
   - **South Suburbs**
   - **Northwest Indiana**
   - **Overhead**
6. Click **OK** and close the Class List window.

Use Classes in Transactions

With class tracking turned on, you can now use classes in all transactions. Make sure to enter the correct class for each transaction and choose Save & Close after entering the details of each.

7. Enter these transactions, using the appropriate class for each (Quick Add new names to the correct list):
   - On **040322** you purchased office supplies for **$98.64** at **Priceco** and paid with your **Visa-7220** card. (Hint: Choose **Banking→Enter Credit Card Charges**.) Enter

the memo **Office Supplies** for the charge and the expense and use the **64900•Office Supplies** account and **Overhead** class.

- On **041022** you received a bill from **Four Brothers Hardware** for **$1,349** for **50400•Construction Materials Cost** for a kitchen renovation job for Archive Coffee & Wine. Assign a reference number; the terms for the bill are **Net 15**. Use **Chicago** for the class. The memo for both the bill and expense is **Archive: kitchen reno supplies, 4/2022** (Hint: Choose **Vendors→Enter Bills**.)

- On **041622**, **Oceans, Peggy** submitted an invoice for **$3,200** (she's a new drywall subcontractor). Assign a reference number; the terms for the bill are **Net 15**. The account is **53600•Subcontractors Expense**. Use **Oak Park & West Suburbs** for the class. The memo for both the bill and expense is **Oceans: Drywall installation** (Hint: Choose **Vendors→Enter Bills**.)

- On **042022 Gigi Rodriguez** hired you for **$2,670** to do a cleanup and restoration job (**25 Cleanup**) resulting from storm damage. Use invoice number **22-0007** and assign **Oak Park & West Suburbs** as the class. Enter **Rodriguez: Restoration 4/2022** as the memo. (Hint: Choose **Customers→Create Invoices**.)

REINFORCE YOUR SKILLS 13-3

Classify Transactions Using a Report

In this exercise, you will run a Profit & Loss Unclassified report for April 2022 and use it to drill down and add classes to two transactions.

1. Choose **Reports→Company & Financial→Profit & Loss Unclassified**; set the dates from 04/01/2022 to 04/30/2022.

2. Double-click the amount for **66500•Postage and Delivery** and then double-click the Check transaction.

3. Choose **Overhead** as the class in the Write Checks – Petty Cash window; **Save & Close** the transaction. Click **OK** and then close the Transaction Detail by Account window.

4. Double-click the amount for **67100•Rent Expense** and then double-click the Check transaction.

5. Choose **Overhead** as the class for the **67100•Rent Expense** amount (the other line refers to a balance sheet account, so you do not need to add a class) in the Write Checks – Petty Cash window; **Save & Close** the transaction. Click **Yes** twice and then close the Transaction Detail by Account window.

6. Close the Profit & Loss Unclassified report, choosing not to memorize it.

Create a Statement of Cash Flows Report

Now you will look at how the company's cash flow has been for January–March 2022.

7. Choose **Reports→Company & Financial→Statement of Cash Flows**.

8. Use the date range: **010122** to **033122**

9. Review the cash flow for Donnell Construction for the period and then close the Statement of Cash Flows window, choosing to not memorize the report.

10. Close the company file.

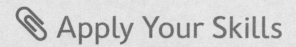
Apply Your Skills

Dr. James has asked you to take control over analyzing and entering transactions. She's also asked you to set up class tracking and produce reports based on class, jobs, and forecasting. She is looking to you as the lead in helping her determine the health of the company. The password for all files unless otherwise stated is Password1.

APPLY YOUR SKILLS 13-1

Analyze Transactions

In this exercise, you will analyze a variety of transactions.

1. Start QuickBooks 2020 and choose **File→Open or Restore Company**.

2. Open **AYS_Chapter13 (Company)** *or* restore **AYS_Chapter13 (Portable)** and save it as:
   `AYS_Chapter13 Wet Noses Clinic`

3. Open **CH13_AYS_Analyze Business Transactions.pdf** from your file storage location and complete the worksheet.

APPLY YOUR SKILLS 13-2 [QG]

Use Classes to Track Why Customers Visit

Dr. James wants to know more about what brings her customers through her doors. In this exercise, you will help her to use classes to track this aspect of her business by creating classes and applying them to transactions.

1. Turn on the class tracking preference.

2. Set up four new classes: Routine/Scheduled, Emergency, Product Sales, and Overhead.

3. Choose the appropriate QuickBooks window to record these transactions, making sure to apply the classes you've created:

   • On 07/01/2023, enter a bill for the monthly rent for $2,300 payable to Oberg Property Management.

   • On 07/01/2023, Chris Lorenzo brought in his cat, Jaguar, who was having a hard time breathing. Create invoice #186 for the visit and charge him for an Exam, a Venipuncture, and a CBC Chem.

   • On 07/02/2023, you received bill #77-9-57 from Seattle Vet Supply for $3,787.49 ($1,946.72 for medical supplies, $994.22 for medicines, and $846.55 for vaccines). The terms for the bill are Net 15. All these items are used in the practice for a variety of procedures and ailments.

   • On 07/02/2023, Teresa Martinez brought in her cat, Pinkie, for her annual exam, a rabies shot, and one Revolution Cat/Small Dog. She paid the same day with check number 2627.

   • On 07/05/2023, you received a bill from Brian's Pet Taxi for $56 for transporting Steve Gaines' injured dog Jasper to your office (you will need to create a new expense account called Pet Transportation using 64500 as the number). You will pass this expense to the dog's owner.

   • On 07/05/2023, Toni Wagner brought in her dog, Arizona, for a routine exam and paid in cash.

4. Run the **Profit & Loss by Class** report for 07/01/2023 to 07/10/2023.

5. Click the **Excel** button and export this list to a new workbook saved as:
   `CH13_A2 Profit and Loss by Class`

APPLY YOUR SKILLS 13-3 QG

Customize a Report and Run a Report to Display Transactions Without Classes

Now that you've been using classes, you will run some reports to see how you can better determine where the company's profits and/or losses are coming from. In this exercise, you will classify a transaction that was missed. You will also customize a report by adding class information and look at the future cash flow for the upcoming months August and September.

1. Run the **Profit & Loss Unclassified** report for the date range 07/01/2023 to 07/31/2023.

2. Add the **Overhead** class to the **60000•Advertising and Promotion** transaction in the amount of $135. Refresh the report after recording the transaction, after which the 60000•Advertising and Promotion account should no longer be displayed. Close the Profit & Loss Unclassified report, choosing to not save the changes.

3. Run the **Item Profitability** report in the **Jobs, Time & Mileage** category, from 07/01/2023 to 08/31/2023.

4. Customize the report to filter by **Class**, choosing **Routine/Scheduled** as the filter to apply.

5. Click the **Excel** button and export this report to a new workbook saved as:
   `CH13_A3 Item Profitability by Class`

6. Run the **Cash Flow Forecast** report for the date range 08/01/2023 to 08/31/2023 and displayed in one-week periods.

7. Click the **Excel** button and export this report to a new workbook saved as:
   `CH13_A3 August Forecast Cash Flow`

8. Close the company file.

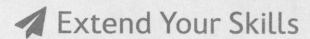

Extend Your Skills

Before You Begin: Open **EYS_Chapter13 (Company)** *or* restore **EYS_Chapter13 (Portable)**. The password is *Password1*.

You've been hired by Arlaine Cervantes to help her with her organization's books. She is the founder of Niños del Lago, a nonprofit organization that provides impoverished Guatemalan children with an engaging educational camp experience. You just sat down at your desk and opened a large envelope from Arlaine that contains a variety of documents; you also have several emails from her. It's your job to sort through the papers and emails and make sense of what you find, entering information into QuickBooks as appropriate and answering any questions in a word-processing document saved as: CH13_EYS_[LastnameFirstinitial]

Remember, you're dealing with random papers dumped out of an envelope and various emails, so part of your challenge is determining the order in which to complete the tasks.

- Credit card receipt: From Crafters Supply Warehouse, dated 9/2/2020 in the amount of $1,200 for the purchase of supplies for the camp

- Message from Arlaine: "Can you set up a way for us to easily give a 25 percent discount to resale customers on a fixed percentage basis?"

- Note from the accountant: "Please develop a system to keep better track of source documents. You can do it electronically or physically, but we need the backup documentation organized."

- Scribbled on a scrap of paper: Can we keep track of the funds that come in and go out for different purposes? Is there a feature that tracks income and expense by, say, Food-Camp, Building-Camp, Supplies-Camp, General Use, Administrative Costs?

- Handwritten donation receipt dated 9/5/2020: For camp supplies in the amount of $775 from Sharona Duke; make sure to indicate on the sales receipt that this is for camp supplies

- Scribbled note from Arlaine: "I'd like to see what our cash flow is for July. Is there a report that will show this? What if I want to see a prediction of cash flow for September 2020? Is there an easy way to do that in QuickBooks?"

QUICKBOOKS DESKTOP 2020

14 | Reporting, Adjusting Entries, and Closing the Books

It's now time to wrap up all you've learned and finish out the accounting cycle. In this chapter, you will work through the last four steps of the cycle as you close out the fiscal period. You will dive in and look a bit more closely at what's behind the scenes by making general journal entries as well as inventory adjusting entries. You will also produce the major end-of-period financial reports—Trial Balance, worksheet, Income Statement, Statement of Owner's Equity, and Balance Sheet. Finally, you will learn how QuickBooks closes the books for you and how to set a closing date.

LEARNING OBJECTIVES

▸ Prepare a Trial Balance report
▸ Make general journal entries
▸ Adjust inventory
▸ Create financial statements
▸ Close the books in QuickBooks

Project: Parrot's Paradise Resort

We've fast forwarded in time to December 2022, and Jimmy has asked you to close Parrot's Paradise Resort's books for the year. You will begin by creating a Trial Balance report, which will tell you whether the debits and credits are equal and display the balances of each account. Then it'll be time to look at what a "pen-and-paper" worksheet includes and how the information flows from column to column through it. Next, you will look behind the scenes at the Make General Journal Entries window, where you will enter adjusting entries for depreciation and the Opening Balance Equity account. Any necessary inventory adjustments will also be made before creating the end-of-year financial reports.

Closing the Books in QuickBooks

The last four steps of the accounting cycle deal with closing the books at the end of a fiscal period. At the end of the fiscal year, QuickBooks uses the fiscal year information based on what you entered when you first created your company. You can view this information through the My Company window, accessed from the Company menu.

You can set a closing date in QuickBooks, although QuickBooks will perform year-end adjustments automatically based on your fiscal year. You will learn how to set a closing date in QuickBooks at the end of this chapter, after you've explored the rest of the accounting cycle.

The Final Steps of the Accounting Cycle

The final steps result in your company books being closed for the past fiscal period and prepared for the next one. For many companies, the last steps of the accounting cycle are carried out by an accountant. A company needs to decide whether it will use an accountant to close the books or if it's something it will take on independently.

So far in your path through the accounting cycle, you have ensured that source documents are available and organized before analyzing and recording transactions (QuickBooks posted them in a journal and to ledger accounts behind the scenes). Now you will prepare reports to show how your company performed for the fiscal period and close out temporary accounts. As you explore these final steps, you will see how QuickBooks addresses each.

Permanent Accounts

Accounts for which the ending balance for one fiscal period is the opening balance for the next are called permanent accounts, also called the Balance Sheet accounts. Similar to your personal checking account, you wouldn't zero out your account at the end of each year; it continues on from one accounting period to the next.

Temporary (aka Nominal) Accounts

Not all accounts are permanent! Called temporary, or nominal, the income and expense accounts are zeroed out at the end of each fiscal period, with the amounts moving into an equity account as either a net income (if income was greater than expenses) or a net loss (if expenses exceeded income for the period). An example of a temporary account is a sales account.

The Income Summary Account

If you were doing paper-based accounting, you would use an Income Summary account to "clear out" the temporary account balances and move the lump sum to an equity account. QuickBooks doesn't create an Income Summary account, but it takes the net income or loss resulting from the balances in your income and expense accounts and moves it to the capital/equity account for you. You will learn more about this temporary account as we progress through this chapter.

QuickBooks' Automatic Year-End Adjustments

Specific tasks are performed automatically behind the scenes at the end of your fiscal year, such as:

- Closing out temporary accounts by moving the balances to a "virtual" income summary account

- Determining a net income or loss for the company to be displayed on the balance sheet for the last day of the fiscal year, after transferring the balances from the temporary accounts

- Automatically transferring the net income or loss from the last day of the fiscal period to the Retained Earnings account on the first day of the new fiscal period

The result of this behind-the-scenes action is that you will start off the new fiscal year with a net income of zero (and a zero balance in each of the temporary accounts).

 Company ›My Company : Edit ›Report Information

DEVELOP YOUR SKILLS 14-1

In this exercise, you will verify that the correct month is set as the first month of the fiscal period for Parrot's Paradise Resort. The password for all files unless otherwise stated is Password1. *Leave the company file open unless otherwise instructed.*

1. Start QuickBooks 2020 and choose **File→Open or Restore Company**.
2. Open **DYS_Chapter14 (Company)** *or* restore **DYS_Chapter14 (Portable)** and save it as: **DYS_Chapter14 Parrot's Paradise Resort**
3. Choose **Company→My Company**.
4. Click the **Edit** 🖉 button at the top-right corner of the My Company window.
5. Click **Report Information** and verify that *January* is displayed as the company's first month of the fiscal year.

6. Click **OK** in the Company Information window and then close the My Company window.

Preparing a Worksheet

In pen-and-paper accounting, a worksheet is a report you create to assist yourself when preparing year-end financial statements. The worksheet has five sets of debit and credit columns that represent these sections (displayed from left to right):

• Trial Balance

• Adjustments

• Adjusted Trial Balance

• Income Statement

• Balance Sheet

The information from the Trial Balance report is, unsurprisingly, displayed in the Trial Balance section. You work across the worksheet as adjustments are made and then recorded in the Adjusted Trial Balance section. Finally, the amounts from the Adjusted Trial Balance are transferred to the Income Statement and Balance Sheet sections, based on which accounts are found on each. Because QuickBooks does this behind the scenes, there is no worksheet for you to physically produce.

 Reports→Accountant & Taxes→Trial Balance

DEVELOP YOUR SKILLS 14-2

In this exercise, you will create the Trial Balance report for Parrot's Paradise Report for January–June 2022.

1. Choose **Reports→Accountant & Taxes→Trial Balance**.

2. Set the date range from **010122** to **123122** and then refresh the report.

   This report displays all accounts in your Chart of Accounts and the current balance for each. The debits and credits are in balance.

3. Close the Trial Balance report, choosing not to memorize it.

Digging In Behind the Scenes with Adjusting Entries

QuickBooks has been performing journal entries all along as you enter transactions, whether you're depositing funds or paying bills. Still, there may be times when you have to make your own adjusting journal entries, especially before closing the books for a period.

The Accounting Cardinal Rule: Debits and Credits Must Always Be Equal

When you venture into the General Journal Entry window, you will see a Debit column and a Credit column. As you create your journal entries, you must make sure that the debits equal the credits. (Don't worry! QuickBooks won't let you record a transaction until this equation is in line.)

Note! Depending on your version of QuickBooks, the Make General Journal Entries window may look a bit different. The images in this text show the Premier Accountant version.

Journal Entries

If you're familiar with manual accounting, you'll notice that the Journal report shows the entries as they would appear in the pen-and-paper journal used in manual accounting. You run the Journal report to see all transactions made within a certain period. It can also be useful in locating problems.

Parrot's Paradise Resort - Chapter 14
Journal
December 2022

Trans #	Type	Date	Num	Memo	Account	Debit	Credit
162	Inventory Adjust	12/31/2022	1	Gift Basket: YMCA A...	60000 · Advertising and Prom...	24.35	
				-MULTIPLE-	12100 · Inventory Asset		24.35
						24.35	24.35
163	Inventory Adjust	12/31/2022	1	Inventory Adjustmen...	63500 · Inventory Adjustment	3.78	
				1.501 Sunscreen Inv...	12100 · Inventory Asset		3.78
						3.78	3.78
164	General Journal	12/31/2022	23	Boat depreciation 20...	62400 · Depreciation Expense	5,500.00	
				Boat depreciation 20...	16120 · Accumulated Deprec...		5,500.00
						5,500.00	5,500.00
165	General Journal	12/31/2022	24	Golf cart depreciation	62400 · Depreciation Expense	549.00	
				Golf cart depreciation	16220 · Accumulated Deprec...		549.00
						549.00	549.00
166	General Journal	12/31/2022	25	Op Bal Equity Transfer	30000 · Opening Balance Eq...	549,860.32	
				Op Bal Equity Transfer	30100 · Capital Stock		549,860.32
						549,860.32	549,860.32

The Journal report shows all transactions made in QuickBooks, including adjusting entries made through the Make General Journal Entries window. This illustration displays adjusting entries from December 2022.

General journal entries are not to be taken lightly. They're used to balance the books and for the reasons listed in Cycle Step 5 (below) only when there is no other way to fix the issue. When making a general journal entry, at least two lines are used. Debit entries are listed first, followed by credit entries.

Cycle Step 5: Adjusting Entries and Adjusted Trial Balance

Adjusting entries are made at the end of an accounting period to bring some of the general journal account balances up to date so they're correct on the financial statements. Examples of adjusting entries that are often made include:

- Updating the book value of fixed assets by recording depreciation for the fiscal period

- Updating prepaid accounts (other current assets) by transferring the amount used in the fiscal period to an expense account

- Transferring balances out of the Opening Balance Equity account to their correct "resting place"

After the adjusting entries have been made, an adjusted trial balance is prepared.

Adjusting Inventory Quantity/Value on Hand

There may be times when you have inventory that is no longer in sellable condition. These items should be removed from inventory and the amount expensed. Other times you may need to adjust the value of your inventory due to obsolescence or another reason. Or, you may need to adjust both the quantity and the value of your inventory.

Adjusting the Quantity of Your Inventory

You can either enter the new quantity on hand, which might be the best choice if you have just conducted an annual inventory, or the quantity difference, which works well if you know how many items you have to remove. If you enter the quantity difference, make sure to enter a minus sign in front of the number to show a decrease in the number of items.

Choose the type of adjustment, date, and account to be charged.

Assign a class or customer.

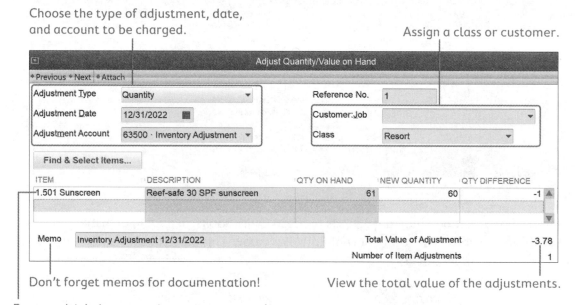

Don't forget memos for documentation!

View the total value of the adjustments.

Enter multiple inventory items on separate lines.

Adjusting the Value of Your Inventory

If you don't need to adjust the quantity of your inventory but rather need to adjust its *value*, you can use the same window. QuickBooks Desktop uses the average cost method of inventory valuation. You can adjust the average cost per inventory item by adjusting the total value of the inventory. Obsolescence or an incorrect beginning cost for inventory may require you to take this step.

BEHIND THE SCENES: *Inventory Adjusting Entry*

63500•Inventory Adjustment	12100•Inventory Asset
INCREASE to Expenses	*DECREASE to Assets*

→ **Equity**

Assets	**=**	**Liabilities**	**+**	**Capital**	**+**	**Revenue**	**−**	**Expenses**
-$3.78	=	0	+	0	+	0	−	$3.78

63500•Inventory Adjustment

Debit	Credit
$3.78	

12100•Inventory Asset

Debit	Credit
	$3.78

➤ Vendors→Inventory Activities→Adjust Quantity/Value on Hand

➤ Company→Make General Journal Entries

➤ Reports→Inventory→Physical Inventory Worksheet

DEVELOP YOUR SKILLS 14-3

You've completed a physical inventory count and need to make sure the items on hand match the count in QuickBooks. In this exercise, you will make necessary inventory adjustments. You will begin by creating an inventory report to assist you with your physical inventory count.

1. Choose **Reports→Inventory→Physical Inventory Worksheet**.

   At this time, you would normally print the worksheet and manually enter the inventory count.

   ### Parrot's Paradise Resort - Chapter 14
   ### Physical Inventory Worksheet

Item	Description	Preferred Vendor	Quantity On Hand	Physical Count
▸ 1.101 Logo Tee	T-shirt with PPR logo	Keys Apparel	8	8
1.102 Flip Flops	PPR logo flip flops	Keys Apparel	26	25
1.201 Smores Pack	Basket of graham crackers, ...	Creola Catering	37	35
1.301 Beach Hat	Floppy beach hat	Keys Apparel	40	40
1.401 Water Bottle	32oz. logo water bottle	Carolina Coast Wholesale	30	29
1.501 Sunscreen	Reef-safe 30 SPF sunscreen	Carolina Coast Wholesale	61	60

   You will now use information from the physical inventory count to adjust Parrot's Paradise Resort's inventory.

2. Close the Physical Inventory Worksheet window, choosing not to memorize the report, if necessary.

Adjust the Inventory

Back in July, Jimmy provided a basket for the local YMCA fundraising auction, hoping to help promote the new amphitheater venue. In addition to two VIP concert tickets, the basket included flip-flops, two smores packs, and a water bottle, so you need to adjust those items out of inventory. In addition, you need to adjust for a bottle of sunscreen that was damaged.

3. Click the **Chart of Accounts** task icon in the Company area of the Home Page and then choose **Account→New**.

4. Create a new account:
   • Account Type: **Expense** (click **Continue**)
   • Account Number: **63500**
   • Account Name: **Inventory Adjustment**

5. Click **Save & Close** and close the Chart of Accounts.

6. Click the **Inventory Activities** task icon drop-down arrow ▼ in the Company area of the Home Page and then choose **Adjust Quantity/Value On Hand**.

7. Make the two **Quantity** inventory adjustments dated **12/31/2022**, clicking **Save & New** after the first:

Adjustment Account	**60000·Advertising and Promotion**	**63500·Inventory Adjustment**
Class	**Amphitheatre**	**Resort**
Item / New Quantity	(first line) **1.102 Flip Flops / 25** (second line) **1.201 Smores Pack / 35** (third line) **1.401 Water Bottle / 29**	(first line) **1.501 Sunscreen / 60**
Memo	**Gift Basket: YMCA Auction 7/2022**	**Inventory Adjustment 12/31/2022**

You could also type -1 in the Qty Difference column, and then the New Quantity would automatically adjust.

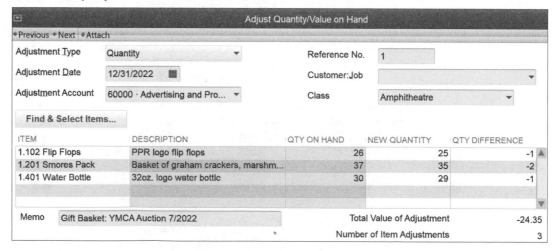

The following Behind the Scenes Brief accounts for both inventory adjustments:

BEHIND THE SCENES BRIEF

60000•Advertising and Promotion DR 24.35 | 63500•Inventory Adjustment DR 3.78; **12100•Inventory Asset CR 28.13**

60000•Advertising and Promotion has **increased** | 63500•Inventory Adjustment has **increased**; 12100•Inventory Asset has **decreased**

Check Figure: Inventory Asset $966.11

8. Click **Save & Close**.

9. Choose **Reports→Inventory→Inventory Stock Status by Item** and then show all dates and view the updated report.

10. Close the report, choosing not to memorize it.

Accounting for Depreciation

Fixed assets are not expensed when purchased but rather over the life of the asset. Therefore, you need to enter a depreciation transaction for your fixed assets for every fiscal period in which you produce financial statements. For small businesses, this is typically at the end of a fiscal year.

The depreciation adjusting entries are made in the Make General Journal Entries window. They affect the expense account that tracks depreciation and the accumulated depreciation fixed asset contra accounts for each asset. When you make this transfer, the current book value of your fixed assets will be updated, by subtracting the credit amount in the accumulated depreciation subaccount from the debit balance of the cost subaccount.

NAME	TYPE	BALANCE TOTAL
◇16100 · Everglades Boat	Fixed Asset	173,500.00 ←
◇16110 · Cost	Fixed Asset	179,000.00
◇16120 · Accumulated Depreciation	Fixed Asset	-5,500.00
◇16200 · Golf Cart	Fixed Asset	3,446.00 ←
◇16210 · Cost	Fixed Asset	3,995.00
◇16220 · Accumulated Depreciation	Fixed Asset	-549.00

Entering the depreciation for the accounting period subtracts from the cost of the fixed asset because Accumulated Depreciation is a contra account. The result is the current book value of the asset displayed in the parent account.

Note! After entering the adjusting entries, you can create the Adjusted Trial Balance report, which shows the beginning balance, adjustments, and ending balance for each account. These ending balances are used in financial statements. This report represents one of the workbook sections for the fifth step of the accounting cycle.

BEHIND THE SCENES: *Depreciation Adjusting Entry*

62400•Depreciation Expense
INCREASE to Expenses

16120•Accumulated Depreciation
DECREASE to Assets

> Equity

$$Assets = Liabilities + (Capital + Revenue - Expenses)$$

$$-\$5,500.00 = 0 + 0 + 0 - \$5,500.00$$

62400•Depreciation Expense		16120•Accumulated Depreciation	
Debit	Credit	Debit	Credit
$5,500.00			$5,500.00

DEVELOP YOUR SKILLS 14-4

In this exercise, you will record the depreciation and memorize the depreciation transaction for the boat and golf cart for 2022. The Everglades boat cost was $179,000 and will depreciate over 20 years, the expected amount of time you will use it. After twenty years, it will be worth $69,000. Thus, the boat will depreciate $5,500 per year for 20 years. This is using the straight-line method of depreciation ($179,000 – $69,000 = $110,000). A total of $110,000 is what will depreciate over the next 20 years ($110,000 / 20 = $5,500 per year for 20 years). The golf cart cost $3,995 and will depreciate over five years. After five years it will be worth $1,250. Thus, the golf cart will depreciate $549 per year for five years.

Warning! Contact your accountant to determine the depreciation method and amount that are best for your company.

1. Choose **Company→Make General Journal Entries**.
2. Click the **Previous** ◀ button a few times to view how transactions that you've entered are displayed in the general journal and then choose **Edit→New General Journal** to start a new entry.

3. Enter the Everglades boat depreciation transaction:

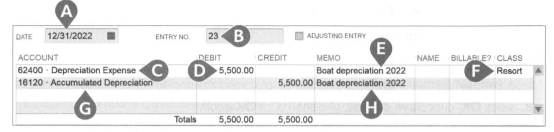

A Type **123122** in the Date field.

B Tap `Tab` and type: **23**

C Click the drop-down arrow ▾ and choose **62400•Depreciation Expense**.

D Tap `Tab` and type: **5500**

E Tap `Tab` twice and type: **Boat depreciation 2022**

F Choose **Resort** as the Class.

G Click the drop-down arrow ▾ and choose **16120•Accumulated Depreciation**.

H Tap `Tab` three times and type: **Boat depreciation 2022**

Note! Be sure to choose the correct Accumulated Depreciation account!

4. Click **Memorize** on the ribbon and then memorize the transaction:

- Name: **Boat depr, annual**
- Select **Automate Transaction Entry**
- How Often: **Annually**
- Next Date: **123123**
- Number Remaining: **19**

5. Click **OK**, click **Save & New**, and then click **OK** again.

6. Enter the golf cart depreciation transaction for 2022 on **12/31/2022**:

First Account Line	**62400•Depreciation Expense**
Debit	**549**
Memo	**Golf cart depreciation**
Class	**Resort**
Second Account Line	**16220•Accumulated Depreciation**
Credit	**549**
Memo	**Golf cart depreciation**

7. Click **Memorize** on the ribbon and then memorize the transaction:

The Balance Sheet

The Balance Sheet displays the permanent accounts, which make up the elements of the accounting equation (Assets = Liabilities + Equity). It reflects the financial condition of a business on a particular date. In pen-and-paper accounting, the values for the Balance Sheet come from the Balance Sheet section of the worksheet.

> **FLASHBACK TO GAAP: TIME PERIOD**
>
> Remember that the activities of the business can be divided into time periods.

Just as the Income Statement is not a perfect tool for analyzing a business, the Balance Sheet is not always the right tool. It can, though, be useful for looking at:

- Ratios to measure profitability, liquidity, and financial strength in the long run (current ratio, quick ratio, return on assets, and return on equity)

- Comparison of assets to liabilities over time

- Working capital (current assets less current liabilities)

- Leverage (debt/worth)

The Statement of Owner's Equity

The Statement of Owner's Equity shows the capital at the beginning of the fiscal period, any additional investments as well as draws by the owner, the net income or loss, and the ending amount. Amounts on the Statement of Owner's Equity come from two sections of the pen-and-paper worksheet. The net income or loss comes from the Income Statement section, while the beginning capital, investments, and draws come from the Balance Sheet section.

QuickBooks does not provide this as a report for you. One way to look at the change in owner's equity from one fiscal period to another is to customize a Balance Sheet Previous Year Comparison report by filtering it to show only equity accounts.

Reports That Compare Data from Previous Fiscal Periods

QuickBooks provides ready-made reports to help you compare company financial information from the current and previous fiscal periods. The Profit & Loss Previous Year Comparison and Balance Sheet Previous Year Comparison reports show the dollar values for each year and detail the change in amount and percentage. In addition to the preset reports, you can customize summary reports to show the same previous period information.

Financial Statement Headers

Report headers are laid out in a specific way in accounting reports. The first line is the company's legal name, the second line is the report name, and the third line is the report time period. Headers for reports that provide a snapshot in time, like the Balance Sheet, show a specific date, such as *December 31, 2022*. Reports for a period of time, like the Income Statement, show a header date that references a range, such as *For the year ended December 31, 2022*. QuickBooks provides default report headers for you, but these can be edited.

Parrot's Paradise Resort, Inc. **Balance Sheet** As of December 31, 2022	Parrot's Paradise Resort, Inc. **Income Statement** For the year ended December 31, 2022

The Balance Sheet report displays the date the "snapshot" was taken, whereas the Income Statement shows the date range from which the data is drawn.

 Reports→Company & Financial→Profit & Loss Standard *or* Balance Sheet Standard *or* Balance Sheet Prev Year Comparison

DEVELOP YOUR SKILLS 14-5

In this exercise, you will create financial statements for Parrot's Paradise Resort. In each report, you will change the company name to reflect the legal name (rather than the name given to the QuickBooks company file), Parrot's Paradise Resort, Inc. You will begin by creating the Income Statement for the period.

1. Choose **Reports→Company & Financial→Profit & Loss Standard**.

2. Set the date range from **010122** to **123122** and then refresh the report, resizing the window as needed to view the data.

3. Click the **Customize Report** button on the toolbar and then click the **Header/Footer** tab.

4. Edit the header:
   - Company Name: **Parrot's Paradise Resort, Inc.**
   - Report Title: **Income Statement**
   - Subtitle: **For the year ended December 31, 2022**

5. Click **OK**.

   Notice the Depreciation Expense of $6,049.00 in the Expense section and the new Inventory Adjustment expense account with the adjustment for the sunscreen.

6. Close the Profit & Loss report, choosing not to memorize it.

Run a Balance Sheet Report

Now you will produce the Balance Sheet report for the period ending December 31, 2022.

7. Choose **Reports→Company & Financial→Balance Sheet Standard**.

8. Set the As of date to **123122** and then refresh the report, resizing the window to view the data.

9. Click the **Customize Report** button on the toolbar, click the **Header/Footer** tab, and then change the company name to: **Parrot's Paradise Resort, Inc.**

   For this report you do not need to change the report title or time frame.

10. Click **OK**.

    Notice how the book value of the fixed assets is displayed on the Balance Sheet and that Opening Balance Equity is no longer displayed on the report as the balance is zero.

11. Close the Balance Sheet report, choosing not to memorize it.

Show Equity Account Information from Two Periods

Next, you will create a report that shows the change in equity information from one period to the next. This is what will simulate the Statement of Owner's Equity report.

12. Choose **Reports→Company & Financial→Balance Sheet Prev Year Comparison**.

13. Click the **Customize Report** button.

14. Run the report from **123121** to **123122**.

15. Follow these steps to modify the report to show the change in equity accounts:

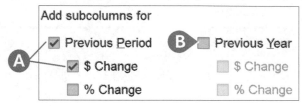

  Ⓐ Select **Previous Period** and **$ Change**.

  Ⓑ Deselect **Previous Year**.

16. Click the **Filters** tab and ensure the **Account** filter is selected and then choose **All Equity Accounts**.

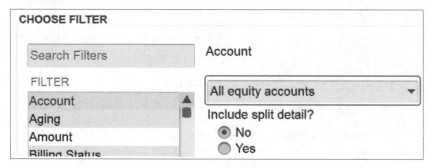

17. Click the **Header/Footer** tab and make these changes:

  • Company Name: `Parrot's Paradise Resort, Inc.`

  • Report Title: `Statement of Owner's Equity`

  • Subtitle: `As of December 31, 2022`

18. Click **OK**.

   The report displays the balances for the equity accounts on 12/30/2021 (you entered 12/31/2021 as the date, but the report will show one day prior) and 12/31/2022 as well as the dollar change. In this scenario, the company was not operating on 12/30/2021, but it still shows the change in equity from one year to the next!

19. Close the Balance Sheet Prev Year Comparison report window, choosing not to memorize the report.

Wrapping Up the Accounting Cycle and Closing the Books

To wrap up the accounting cycle, you need to "zero out" the temporary accounts and move the resulting net income or net loss to a permanent account (specifically an equity account) to begin the next fiscal year. You also need to zero out the account that tracks owner's draw or shareholder distributions.

Cycle Step 7: Closing Entries and the Post-Closing Trial Balance

In pen-and-paper accounting, there are five tasks involved in the final step of the accounting cycle:

1. Transfer the ending amounts from all income accounts to the Income Summary account.

2. Transfer the ending amounts from all expense accounts to the Income Summary account.

3. Transfer the amount in the Income Summary account to the capital account.

4. Transfer the amount in the owner's draw account to the capital account (Retained Earnings).

5. Create a post-closing trial balance report.

Each task results in journal transactions that close out the temporary accounts and move the amounts to Income Summary. Then a transaction is recorded that transfers the amount from Income Summary to the capital account. Take note:

- If the Income Summary account balance is a credit, you debit that account and credit the capital account. This signifies that the company has experienced a net income.

- If the Income Summary account balance is a debit, you credit that account and debit the capital account. This signifies that the company has experienced a net loss.

When you close the books in QuickBooks, all of this is done for you behind the scenes. This step will result in either an increase or decrease in the capital account balance based on whether the company saw a net income or a net loss and the amount of funds the owner(s) drew from the company.

The final report that you will create is a post-closing Trial Balance that shows all temporary accounts with a zero balance. It also lets you check one last time that debits and credits are equal. Only permanent accounts display in the post-closing Trial Balance.

If you choose not to close the books, these year-end adjustments will be made automatically:

- Income and expense accounts are zeroed out.

- Net income is adjusted so the Equity section of the Balance Sheet displays a line for net income the same as it was on the last day of the prior year.

- Retained Earnings is increased by the prior year's net income and then decreased by the same amount (so you start with a net income of zero for the new period.)

Setting a Closing Date

As you know, you're not required to close the books in QuickBooks. When you close the books by setting a closing date, QuickBooks automatically transfers the net income or net loss to Retained Earnings and restricts access to transactions prior to the closing date by requiring a password. After closing the books, you can run the Condense Data Utility, which cleans up your data.

Only the company file administrator can set a closing date and allow or restrict access to prior-period transactions by user.

SETTING A CLOSING DATE IN QUICKBOOKS	
Pros	**Cons**
• You can restrict access to prior-period transactions by setting a password. • You can create a closing date exception report that displays modified transactions dated on or before the closing date. • Transactions can't be changed without your knowledge. Users would need the closing date password and permissions.	• You can't easily access all the details from previous-period transactions. • You can't create reports that compare transaction data from prior periods.

 Company→Set Closing Date

DEVELOP YOUR SKILLS 14-6

In this exercise, you will set a closing date and password for the Parrot's Paradise Resort QuickBooks company file.

1. Choose **Company→Set Closing Date** and then click the **Set Date/Password** button in the Preferences window.

   The Set Closing Date and Password window appears.

2. Set the closing date and password:

   • Click the checkbox to **Exclude estimates, sales orders, and purchase orders from closing date restrictions**.

   • Closing Date: **123122**

   • Closing Date Password: **123**

   When closing the books, you can exclude transactions that don't affect what happens behind the scenes by keeping out estimates, sales orders, and purchase orders. If you're not sure what to do for your own company, consult an accountant. Also, remember to set a strong password for the company file. The simple one used here is just for practice.

3. Click **OK** in the Set Closing Date and Password window and then close the Preferences window.

Working with a Company File After Closing

After you've set a closing date, there's one additional step to the accounting cycle. It has to do with creating another Trial Balance report. You also may choose to clean up your company's data after you close the books by condensing the company file.

DEVELOP YOUR SKILLS 14-7

In this exercise, you will run the Trial Balance for 2022 and then again for the first day of 2023. In the report for 2022, you will see the entries you made for Accumulated Depreciation, Owners Equity, and Inventory Adjustment. In the report for 2023, you will see how QuickBooks has closed the books for you at the end of your fiscal period.

1. Choose **Reports→Accountant & Taxes→Trial Balance**.
2. Set the dates as from **010122** to **123122** and then refresh the report.

   Notice the amounts in Accumulated Depreciation, Owners Equity, and Inventory Adjustment.

3. Change the dates to from **010123** to **010123** and then refresh the report.

   See that QuickBooks has closed out all the temporary accounts and transferred the net income to Owners Equity.

4. Close the Trial Balance report, choosing not to memorize it.

Correcting Transactions from a Closed Period

After setting a password for a closed period, you'll need to enter it in order to change or add a transaction in the prior period. You can produce the Closing Date Exception report that shows any transactions dated on or before the closing date that were entered after you set the closing date.

The Audit Trail

The audit trail feature of QuickBooks allows you to track every entry, modification, or deletion to transactions in your file. The audit trail feature is always on to make sure an accurate record of your QuickBooks data is kept. The audit trail does not track changes to lists, only to transactions. This can help you research transaction history and determine whether certain types of fraudulent activity are occurring. To view the audit trail, run the Audit Trail account, which is available from the Accountant & Taxes category of the Report Center.

Condensing the Company File

After you've closed the books, you may decide to condense your company file. Condensing the file is a way of reducing a large company file that has accumulated a lot of data over the years. This process also gives you choices to replace transactions from before the company closing date that are no longer needed with "summary" transactions. Transactions that will not be summarized include:

- Those with open balances or that are linked to others with open balances
- Any that have not been reconciled or cleared
- Any that are marked "To be printed"

QuickBooks will not remove any payroll transactions for the current calendar year because of payroll tax reporting requirements.

> **Warning!** Condensing your company data has huge implications, so make sure you understand what you're doing before you perform this operation.

After you've decided what to clean up during the condensing process, QuickBooks will create a copy of the company file, which will be in its original state prior to the condensing process. The name of the file will include the date and the word "copy" appended to the end. The location of the copy will also be displayed. QuickBooks will also verify the integrity of your company file.

Remember that transactions dated after your company closing date will not be affected by the clean-up process. During the process you will be asked:

- The date to use to remove transactions

- How you want inventory to be handled (summarized or with details)

- Which transactions to remove, such as uncleared bank and credit card transactions and time and mileage activities to name a few

- Which list entries to remove, if any, such as accounts, classes, and completed To Do notes

An advantage to condensing the company file is that it removes list entries that haven't been used since the prior period. When all the transactions for a list entry have been deleted or summarized, you can then delete the list entry.

You can reduce your company size without removing any data through data file optimization. Essentially, QuickBooks removes the information in the audit trail from a previous period, which decreases the company file size and may help your company run more smoothly as a result. Don't worry, though; QuickBooks will prompt you to save a copy of your file with the audit trail intact before this process so you can go back and view it later, if needed.

> **Tip!** Make sure you have completed all year-end activities, such as producing W-2s, W-3s, and 1099-MISC forms, before cleaning up your company file.

 File→Utilities→Condense Data

Working with an Accountant's Copy

If your accountant needs to adjust your QuickBooks file, but you don't want to lose access to it while it's in use, you can create an accountant's copy. Your accountant can make the needed adjustments, and you can at least keep up with your daily transactions. There are some tasks you *cannot* do while your accountant is working on your file, such as:

- Edit or delete accounts

- Add, edit, or delete transactions dated on or before the dividing date

- Reconcile an account

Just as with setting a closing date, only the company file administrator can create an accountant's copy. When the accountant's copy is created, QuickBooks appends the date and time the file was created to the filename (e.g., *QuickBooks2020 Acct Transfer Dec 04,2020 08 20 PM*). The extension will be *.QBX*.

The Dividing Date

When you create an accountant's copy, you must set a dividing date. The dividing date determines the fiscal period that the accountant will be working on. The accountant will be able to work on transactions prior to that date, and you will be able to continue to work entering transactions after that date. Be careful when setting this date to ensure that your accountant will have the access needed and that you will still be able to modify recent transactions, if necessary. If your accountant is making adjusting entries, it makes sense to set the dividing date as the last day of the previous fiscal year.

 **Best Practice**

It's generally best to set the dividing date about two weeks after the last day of the fiscal period you need. Typically, it will be the end of a quarter. This way the accountant can move transactions between the two periods, if needed.

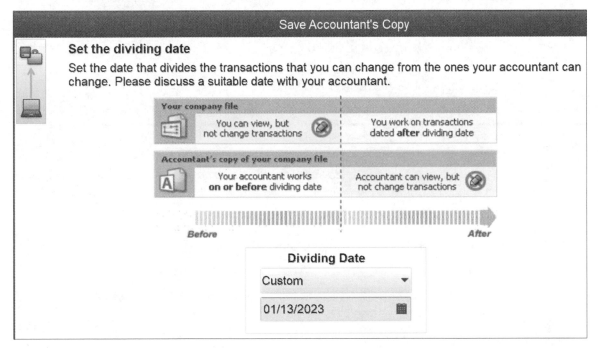

The dividing date determines the date from which your accountant can make changes to your company file. It also dictates your own access to your company file while the accountant is working.

Managing Accountant's Copies

You will encounter four tasks when working with accountant's copies: saving, sending, importing, and removing restrictions. All of these are accessible through the File option on the menu.

- **Saving an accountant's copy of the file:** You have two options. The first is to create an accountant's copy; you and the accountant can work independently, and you later import the accountant's changes. The second is to create a portable or backup file if the accountant needs to set up the books, do daily bookkeeping, or work on payroll. You won't be able to work on the file until the accountant is finished.

- **Sending the file:** You can email the file or save it to a CD or other storage media to provide to your accountant. Or, use the Accountant's Copy File Transfer service (File→Send Company File→Accountant's Copy→Send to Accountant). It requires Internet access, as the file will be uploaded to Intuit's web server. Your accountant will receive an email with a link to download the file.

> **Warning!** If you use the Accountant's Copy File Transfer service, the company file will not be available during the process of creating and uploading the file. The file will show "(Accountant's Changes Pending)" on the title bar. You must wait for the process to be finished.

- **Importing the file:** When you receive the file back from your accountant, you must import any changes into your company file. When you do this, you'll be prompted to create a backup copy of your file. This is important in case the import is not successful—you will still have a workable copy of your company file. During the import process, it's up to you to accept all or none of the changes into your company file and to view any notes left by your accountant.

- **Removing restrictions on your file:** To cancel an accountant's copy, you must choose to remove restrictions. If you do this, though, you won't be able to import the accountant's copy changes. On the other hand, if you accidentally create an accountant's copy file, just cancel it to work with your file in normal mode.

> Reports→Accountant & Taxes→Audit Trail

> File→Send Company File→Accountant's Copy

DEVELOP YOUR SKILLS 14-8

Jimmy realized that invoice #22-0019, dated 06/01/2022, should have been dated 05/31/2022. In this exercise, you will correct a transaction from a closed period and produce an Audit Trail report.

1. Choose **Edit→Find** and then click the **Simple** tab, if necessary.
2. Type **22-0019** in the Invoice # field and click **Find**.
3. Click the **Go To** button.

   Invoice #22-009 was already selected, so when you clicked Go To, QuickBooks opened the Create Invoices window with it displayed.

4. Change the date to: **053122**
5. Click **Save & Close** to record the new date for the invoice and click **Yes** to make the change to the transaction.

   A QuickBooks window appears, letting you know that you're changing a transaction from a closed period. To bypass this window and make the change, you need to enter the closing date password.

6. Type **123** and click **OK**; close the Find window.

Create an Audit Trail Report

You will now look at the Audit Trail report, which will show the change you just made to invoice #22-0019.

7. Choose **Reports→Accountant & Taxes→Audit Trail**.
8. Ensure the Date Entered/Last Modified is set to **Today**.

9. Click the **Customize Report** button and then set the report date range as from **053122** to **053122** and click **OK**.

Parrot's Paradise Resort - Chapter 14
Audit Trail
Entered/Last Modified September 15, 2019

Num	Entered/Last Modified	Last modified by	State	Date	Name	Memo	Account	Split
Transactions entered or modified by Admin								
Invoice 22-0019								
22-0019	09/15/2019 13:15:58	Admin	Latest	*05/31/2022*	Stolfus Tour Serv...	Stolfus: 7/1...	11000 · Accounts...	-SPLIT-
					Stolfus Tour Serv...	2 Queen - G...	40000 · Lodging ...	11000 · Acc...
					Stolfus Tour Serv...	King Bed - ...	40000 · Lodging ...	11000 · Acc...
					Stolfus Tour Serv...	Sunset crui...	42000 · Banquets...	11000 · Acc...
					Stolfus Tour Serv...	Key West S...		11000 · Acc...
					Florida Departme...	Florida Sta...	25500 · Sales Ta...	11000 · Acc...
					Florida Departme...	Key West L...	25500 · Sales Ta...	11000 · Acc...

The Audit Trail report displays the transaction you just modified and shows the prior and most current versions of a transaction. The entry date will differ from yours.

10. Close the Audit Trail report window, choosing not to memorize it.

Tackle the Tasks

Now is your chance to work a little more with Parrot's Paradise Resort and apply the skills you've just learned to accomplish additional tasks. Continue with the same company file you've been using in this chapter so far. If you need to reopen the company file, the password is *Password1*. Use **CH14_TTT_Worksheet Answers** to record your work.

CREATE A BALANCE SHEET REPORT AS OF 12/31/2022	
Calculation	**Answer**
Quick ratio: (current assets – inventory)/ current liabilities	
Return on assets: net income/total assets	
Working capital: current assets – current liabilities	

CREATE AN INCOME STATEMENT FOR THE PERIOD 01/01/2022–12/31/2022	
Calculation	**Answer**
Gross profit margin: (revenue – COGS)/ revenue	
Operating profit margin: revenue – expenses related to day-to-day operations of the business	
Net profit margin: net income/revenue	

Self-Assessment

Check your knowledge of this chapter's key concepts and skills using the Self-Assessment quiz here, in your ebook, or in your eLab course.

1. An example of an adjusting entry is one that updates the value of a fixed asset.   *True*   *False*

2. An Income Summary account is used to clear out permanent account balances.   *True*   *False*

3. QuickBooks won't allow you to record a transaction for which debits do not equal credits.   *True*   *False*

4. QuickBooks provides a worksheet to use when preparing financial statements.   *True*   *False*

5. When accounting for depreciation, you credit the Accumulated Depreciation account.   *True*   *False*

6. A permanent account is one for which the ending balance for one fiscal period is the opening balance for the next.   *True*   *False*

7. The Income Statement shows the balance of permanent accounts as of a certain date.   *True*   *False*

8. Analyzing the Balance Sheet allows you to calculate the gross margin percentage.   *True*   *False*

9. The Income Statement is a financial report that displays income and expenses over a specific period.   *True*   *False*

10. An advantage of closing the books in QuickBooks is that you can restrict access to prior-period transactions by setting a password.   *True*   *False*

11. Which of the following is a permanent account?
    A. Boat Loan
    B. Bank Service Charges
    C. Cost of Goods Sold
    D. Product Sales

12. An adjusting entry may allow you to _____.
    A. enter a bill from a vendor
    B. record depreciation for a fiscal period
    C. create a sales receipt to record the daily sales
    D. record a deposit into the Checking account

13. Which report lets you track every entry, modification, or deletion to transactions in your file?
    A. Closing Date Exception
    B. Post-Closing Trial Balance
    C. Accountant's Copy
    D. Audit Trail

14. What does QuickBooks NOT do for you automatically at the end of the fiscal year?
    A. Transfer net income or net loss to Retained Earnings
    B. Ensure you start the new fiscal year with zero balances for the permanent accounts
    C. Close out temporary accounts
    D. Allow you to start the new fiscal year with a net income of zero

Reinforce Your Skills

Colleen Donnell from Donnell Construction has asked you to prepare her company's books for closing by running the end-of-period financial reports and making adjusting entries. You will also close the books. The password for all files unless otherwise stated is Password1.

REINFORCE YOUR SKILLS 14-1

Work with the Trial Balance Report

In this exercise, you will create a Trial Balance report for Donnell Construction.

1. Start QuickBooks 2020 and choose **File→Open or Restore Company**.
2. Open **RYS_Chapter14 (Company)** *or* restore **RYS_Chapter14 (Portable)** and save it as:
   RYS_Chapter14 Donnell Construction
3. Choose **Report→Accountant & Taxes→Trial Balance**.
4. Set the date range as **010122** to **123122** and then refresh the report.

   The Trial Balance report for the fiscal year displays.
5. Close the Trial Balance report, choosing not to memorize it.

REINFORCE YOUR SKILLS 14-2

Create an Adjusting Entry and Inventory Adjustment

In this exercise, you will make an adjusting entry to record depreciation for 2022. Then you will record an inventory adjustment to account for a hall mirror that was damaged.

For this exercise, depreciation is calculated using the straight-line method. The cost of the Ford F-150 was $34,269, and it has a 10-year life. The salvage value after 10 years is $12,380, so the amount to be depreciated over 10 years is $21,889. The annual depreciation that you enter will be $2,188.90.

1. Choose **Company→Make General Journal Entries** and then click **OK** in the Assigning Numbers to Journal Entries window.
2. Type **123122** as the date.
3. Enter the depreciation transaction:
   - Debit **62400·Depreciation Expense** for **2188.90**
   - Memo: **F-150 Depreciation**
   - Class: **Overhead**
   - Credit **17000·Accumulated Depreciation** for **2188.90**
   - Memo: **F-150 Depreciation**

4. Choose **Edit→Memorize General Journal** and enter the memorized transaction:
   - Name: `Truck depr, annual`
   - Choose to **Automate Transaction Entry**
   - How Often: **Annually**
   - Next Date: **123123**
   - Number Remaining: **9**

5. Click **OK**, click **Save & Close**, and then click **OK** again.

Make an Inventory Adjustment

Next you will create an inventory adjustment to deduct the damaged Hall Mirror from inventory.

6. Choose **Vendors→Inventory Activities→Adjust Quantity/Value on Hand**.

7. Type **123122** as the Adjustment Date and tap Tab.

8. Type `Inventory Adjustment` in the Adjustment Account field, tap Tab, and click **Set Up**.

9. Set the account type as **Expense** and the number as **63600** and then click **Save & Close**.

10. Choose **Overhead** as the class.

11. Reduce the number of Hall Mirrors in inventory by **−1** in the Qty Difference column, enter `Inv. Adjustment, damaged hall mirror, 12/31/2022` as the memo, and then click **Save & Close**.

REINFORCE YOUR SKILLS 14-3

Produce Financial Statements

In this exercise, you will produce an Income Statement and Balance Sheet for Donnell Construction.

1. Choose **Reports→Company & Financial→Profit & Loss Standard**.

2. Set the date range as from **010122** to **123122** and then refresh the report.

   The Profit & Loss report displays for 2022. You will now change the report title.

3. Click the **Customize Report** button and then click the **Header/Footer** tab.

4. Modify the header:
   - Company Name: `Donnell Construction, LLC`
   - Report Title: `Income Statement`
   - Subtitle: `For the year ended December 31, 2022`

5. Click **OK** and then click the **Memorize** button on the toolbar.

6. Type `Income Statement 2022` as the report name and click **OK**; close the report window.

Create a Balance Sheet Report

7. Choose **Reports→Company & Financial→Balance Sheet Standard**.

8. Change the As of date to **123122** and then refresh the report.

9. Click the **Customize Report** button and then click the **Header/Footer** tab and modify the company name to: **Donnell Construction, LLC**

10. Click **OK** and then click the **Memorize** button on the toolbar.

11. Type **Balance Sheet 2022** as the report name and click **OK**; close the report window.

REINFORCE YOUR SKILLS 14-4

Close the Books

In this exercise, you will set a closing date for Donnell Construction's QuickBooks company file.

1. Choose **Company→Set Closing Date**.

2. Click the **Set Date/Password** button on the Company Preferences tab of the Accounting section.

   The Set Closing Date and Password window appears.

3. Click in the checkbox to **Exclude estimates, sales orders, and purchase orders from closing date restrictions**.

4. Complete the Set Closing Date and Password window:

   • Closing Date: **123122**

   • Closing Date Password: **789**

5. Click **OK** to set the closing date and password and then click **OK** in the Preferences window.

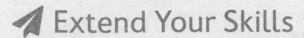# Extend Your Skills

Before You Begin: Open **EYS_Chapter14 (Company)** *or* restore **EYS_Chapter14 (Portable)**. The password is *Password1*.

You've been hired by Arlaine Cervantes to help her with her organization's books. She is the founder of Niños del Lago, a nonprofit organization that provides impoverished Guatemalan children with an engaging educational camp experience. You just sat down at your desk and opened a large envelope from Arlaine with a variety of documents; you also have several emails from her. It's your job to sort through the papers and emails and make sense of what you find, entering information into QuickBooks as appropriate and answering questions in a word-processing document saved as: CH14_EYS_[LastnameFirstinitial]

Remember, you're dealing with random papers dumped out of an envelope and various emails, so part of your challenge is determining the correct order in which to complete the tasks.

- Note from Arlaine: I know the end-of-period accounting for not-for-profits is a bit different from what's done for "regular" for-profit businesses. Will you please research the differences for me and report back?

- Scribbled note from Arlaine: Please create the Balance Sheet report as of 8/31/2020, using the name *Statement of Financial Position*. Export it to Excel, too, saving that file as: SFP, 8-31-20

A | Need-To-Know Accounting

Even though QuickBooks does the accounting work for you "behind the scenes," you should still have a basic understanding of what's happening to your books. In this appendix, you will learn about the basic financial statements important to any business and the accounts that appear on these reports. You will also learn about the double-entry accounting system and that debits and credits must always be equal.

Financial Statements

There are two main reports a company produces periodically to illustrate its financial well-being. Familiarizing yourself with the accounts that make up each of these reports is key to understanding your company's books.

- The *balance sheet* report displays all company holdings and debts as of a particular date.

- The *income statement* (aka profit & loss report) displays the income and expenses for a specified period.

The Accounting Equation and the Balance Sheet

When it comes to accounting, the first equation to internalize is the accounting equation:

$$\textbf{Assets = Liabilities + Equity}$$

This means if you take all your company's debt (liabilities) and add any investments (equity), you will have a value equal to all the assets your company owns. The balance sheet displays all asset, liability, and equity accounts (the balance sheet accounts).

Parrot's Paradise Resort - Chapter 14
Balance Sheet
All Transactions

	Jun 30, 22
ASSETS	
Current Assets	
Checking/Savings	
10100 · Money Market	37,382.35
10200 · Payroll Checking	100,000.00
10300 · Sailors Bank Checking	54,389.56
10400 · Sailors Bank Savings	347,091.49
10900 · Petty Cash	217.76
Total Checking/Savings	539,081.16
Accounts Receivable	
11000 · Accounts Receivable	6,812.51
Total Accounts Receivable	6,812.51
Other Current Assets	
12000 · Undeposited Funds	179.46
12100 · Inventory Asset	966.11
13100 · Prepaid Insurance	1,180.00
13200 · Prepaid Pool Service	1,750.00
Total Other Current Assets	4,075.57
Total Current Assets	549,969.24
Fixed Assets	
16100 · Everglades Boat	
16110 · Cost	179,000.00
16120 · Accumulated Depreciat...	-2,750.00
Total 16100 · Everglades Boat	176,250.00
16200 · Golf Cart	
16210 · Cost	3,995.00
16220 · Accumulated Depreciat...	-274.50
Total 16200 · Golf Cart	3,720.50
16300 · Office Furniture	
16310 · Cost	22,639.00
Total 16300 · Office Furniture	22,639.00
Total Fixed Assets	202,609.50
TOTAL ASSETS	**752,578.74**

	Jun 30, 22
LIABILITIES & EQUITY	
Liabilities	
Current Liabilities	
Accounts Payable	
20000 · Accounts Payable	1,381.20
Total Accounts Payable	1,381.20
Credit Cards	
21400 · Visa-4545	503.63
Total Credit Cards	503.63
Other Current Liabilities	
25500 · Sales Tax Payable	49.05
Total Other Current Liabilities	49.05
Total Current Liabilities	1,933.88
Long Term Liabilities	
26000 · Loan - Everglades Boat	161,100.00
27000 · Loan - Furniture (Office)	17,639.00
Total Long Term Liabilities	178,739.00
Total Liabilities	180,672.88
Equity	
30100 · Capital Stock	549,860.32
31400 · Shareholder Distributions	-20,000.00
Net Income	42,045.54
Total Equity	571,905.86
TOTAL LIABILITIES & EQUITY	**752,578.74**

In the balance sheet, the first section (Assets) represents the left side of the accounting equation, displaying all assets. The second section (Liabilities & Equity) represents the right side of the accounting equation, displaying all liabilities and equity accounts. Notice that total assets equal total of liabilities plus equity ($725,578.74).

The Income Statement (aka Profit & Loss Report)

The income and expense accounts are included on the income statement (or profit & loss report).

Parrot's Paradise Resort
Profit & Loss
June 2022

	Jun 22
Ordinary Income/Expense	
Income	
40000 · Lodging Sales	4,281.00
41000 · Gift Shop and Vending Sales	
41100 · Clothing Sales	600.00
41500 · Sundry Sales	54.00
Total 41000 · Gift Shop and Vending Sa...	654.00
42000 · Banquets and Events Income	2,182.96
Total Income	7,117.96
Cost of Goods Sold	
52900 · Purchases - Resale Items	160.48
Total COGS	160.48
Gross Profit	6,957.48
Expense	
60000 · Advertising and Promotion	24.35
62400 · Depreciation Expense	3,024.50
63000 · Event Rentals	675.00
63500 · Inventory Adjustment	3.78
63700 · Landscaping and Groundskeep...	175.00
67200 · Repairs and Maintenance	237.50
67500 · Service Supplies	276.43
Total Expense	4,416.56
Net Ordinary Income	2,540.92
Net Income	**2,540.92**

The total of all income accounts less COGS accounts is the gross profit.

Total expense is shown in this section.

The difference between gross profit and total expense is the net income (or net loss, if expenses exceed gross profit).

Debits and Credits: The Double-Entry Accounting System

There is another equation in accounting that is paramount to keep in mind:

Debits must always equal credits!

Accounts are often displayed in a "T" format in accounting (which you see in the Behind the Scenes sections). In a T-account, enter the account name on the top, account debits on the left side, and account credits on the right side. The debit (left) side across all T-accounts *must always equal* the credit (right) side across all T-accounts. The term *double entry* refers to the fact that there has to be at least one account debited and one account credited for each transaction.

Account Name	
Debit Side	Credit Side

B | The QBCU Exam Objectives and This Text

The QuickBooks Certified User (QBCU) certification can be an important credential for those in accounting and bookkeeping roles. To obtain certification, you must pass a comprehensive exam that focuses on QuickBooks program topics as well as accounting topics. This appendix includes a table that shows you where each of the exam objectives is covered in this book.

QBCU Exam Objectives

In this table, each exam objective (left column) is associated with a reference to the most prominent location(s) in this text that deal with that objective (right column). You might use this table as you prepare for the QBCU exam. Be sure to also check out the exam study guide presented by Certiport, the company that delivers the certification: https://certiport.pearsonvue.com/Certifications/QuickBooks/Certified-User/Overview

OBJECTIVE		TEXT LOCATION
1	**QuickBooks Setup**	
1.1	What information is required before setting up a QuickBooks file	pp. 28–32 Planning and Creating a Company File
1.2	How to start a new company data file in QuickBooks (EasyStep Interview)	pp. 28–32 Planning and Creating a Company File
1.3	How to keep the lists and preferences from an old file while removing old transactions	p. 29 Using an Existing QuickBooks File as a Template for a New File
1.4	How to customize the Home Page	p. 14 The Insights Tab
1.5	How to set up lists (customers, vendors, items, etc.); this includes understanding which names and items should appear on which lists	pp. 44–46 Customer & Vendor Profile Lists
2	**QuickBooks Utilities and General Product Knowledge**	
2.1	How to navigate or move around QuickBooks (use Home Page, menus, icon bar, etc.)	pp. 12–15 The QuickBooks Window
2.2	How to back up and restore a data file	p. 8 Opening and Restoring QuickBooks Files; pp. 16–17 Backing Up and Updating Your Company File
2.3	How to determine the release number and how to update QuickBooks	p. 17 Determining the Release Number
2.4	How to use QuickBooks in a single-user and multi-user mode	pp. 51–52 Working with QuickBooks in a Multi-User Environment
2.5	What versions and editions of QuickBooks are available for a specific year (Desktop version)	pp. 2–3 Editions of QuickBooks; p. 17 Determining the Release Number
2.6	How to password protect QuickBooks	pp. 51–52 Passwords
2.7	How and why to use preferences	pp. 37–38 Company vs. Personal Preferences
3	**List Management**	
3.1	How to manage lists (customers, vendors, items, etc.); list management includes:	
	3.1.1 Adding new entries	pp. 116–121 The Vendor Center
	3.1.2 Deleting entries	pp. 116–121 The Vendor Center
	3.1.3 Editing entries	pp. 116–121 The Vendor Center
	3.1.4 Merging entries	pp. 116–121 The Vendor Center

Glossary

accountant's copy A special copy of your QuickBooks file that allows your accountant to make adjustments while you retain limited access to your company data

accounting cycle A series of steps designed to help a business keep its accounting records properly during the fiscal period

accrual basis An accounting method wherein income is recorded when a sale is made and expenses are recorded when they're accrued; often used by firms or businesses with large inventories

activities Tasks that affect what happens behind the scenes; can be easily entered on forms, such as invoices or bills

Adjusted Trial Balance A listing of all company accounts contained in the general ledger that is prepared after adjusting entries are posted for an accounting period; it shows that debits equal credits

amortization The process of a balance decreasing over time

assets Anything owned by a company or owed to a company, such as a checking account, a building, a prepaid insurance account, or accounts receivable

audit trail Allows you to track every entry, modification, and deletion to transactions in your file; accessed via the Report Center (Accounting category) or Report (menu bar)

average cost method A way to determine the value of inventory; divides the total value of the inventory by the total number of inventory items

bad debt Funds owed to a company that are uncollectable and need to be written off

Balance Sheet A report that displays all assets, liabilities, and equity as of a specific date

balance sheet accounts The asset, liability, and equity accounts, such as bank, credit card, current liabilities (sales tax payable and payroll liabilities), accounts receivable, accounts payable, and retained earnings

Balance Sheet by Class report A balance sheet report in which each class shows in a separate column; designed for expert users

batch A group of customers that a user can create similar invoices for at one time

batch timesheets A feature that allows you to create timesheets for multiple employees who work the same hours on the same jobs and using the same payroll item(s)

behind the scenes The accounting that QuickBooks performs for you when you enter transactions

billing rate level A QuickBooks feature that allows you to differentiate the amount charged for services provided by different vendors or employees; can be used when you have employees or vendors who perform the same service at differing levels of expertise

bounced checks Checks returned by the bank due to insufficient funds; also called "NSF" checks

budget Defined by QuickBooks as "a detailed financial outline of what the business thinks will happen over a period of time financially"; usually based on a fiscal year

cash basis An accounting method wherein income is recorded when cash is received and expenses are recorded when cash is paid; commonly used by small businesses and professionals

Cash Flow Forecast A report that tells you the anticipated income and expenses over the next few weeks resulting from collecting receivables, paying bills, and banking tasks

Cash Flow Projector A report that predicts a company's cash flow for the near future based on current data in the company file

centers Areas in QuickBooks that allow you to view lists (Customers & Jobs, Employee, and Vendor), access QuickBooks reports, and view snapshots of information for individual records (customers, vendors, and employees); there are four centers: Customer, Employee, Report, and Vendor; a fifth center is available when the inventory preference is turned on

change order When a customer wants to make a change to an estimate, a change order can be added to the estimate detailing the amount of the change(s), exactly what changed, and the net change to the amount of the estimate; only available in QuickBooks Desktop Premier Contractor or Accountant versions

Chart of Accounts A list that displays every account set up for your company; accounts are displayed in a specific order: assets, liabilities, equity, income, cost of goods sold, expense, other income, and other expense

classes Provide an additional way to track information about a company's transactions; allow you to analyze a particular segment of your business; can be entered via forms such as Create Invoices and Enter Bills when creating or editing transactions

company setup A task that takes you through the steps of setting up a new company in QuickBooks

Company Snapshot A window that offers a quick view of your company's bottom line in one convenient place

condense A way to reduce the size of a large company file by summarizing old transactions (entered before the company's closing date); an advantage to condensing your company file is that you can remove old list entries that are no longer used

contributed reports Reports submitted by other users for general use; where you can share your custom reports

cost of goods sold (COGS) Expenses directly related to the manufacture or acquisition of products or services that the company sells

Customer & Vendor Profile Lists The lists generated upon company setup that store customizable information used when working with customers and vendors; examples are the Vendor Type List, Payment Method List, and the Sales Rep List; can be modified after company setup through the Lists menu

customer Defined by QuickBooks as "any person, business, or group that buys or pays for the services or products that your business or organization sells or provides"

depreciation A way to match income to expenses; a fixed asset is used to produce income over a period of time, and depreciation allows you to record the appropriate expense for the same period; many small businesses record depreciation transactions annually, but it can be done monthly or quarterly if the business produces financial statements for those periods

Doc Center A feature in QuickBooks where you can electronically store your source documents; the documents can be attached to the transactions or list entries that are based on them

draw An owner's withdrawal of funds from the company

edition Intuit creates a multitude of editions (versions) of QuickBooks to choose from: QuickBooks Pro, QuickBooks Premier, and QuickBooks Enterprise; *see also* version

employee Defined by QuickBooks as "someone to whom you issue a W-2 at the end of the year"; they are entered on the Employee List; subcontractors are not employees

equity accounts Reflect the owner's investment in the company and have a credit normal balance; in a sole proprietorship, equity is what the owner has invested in the company, and in a corporation, it's what shareholders have invested

FIFO (First In, First Out) An inventory valuation method wherein the value of the first inventory brought in is used to determine the COGS, whereas the value of the inventory sold is based on the inventory purchased last (which more closely resembles the actual replacement cost)

filtering How to include only your essential data in a report; filter out data such as accounts, dollar amounts, and types of customers; allows you to closely examine and report on a specific group of data

fixed asset An asset you don't plan to use or turn into cash within the next year; examples are vehicles, buildings, and equipment

fonts Typeface variations; QuickBooks displays preset reports in a default font that you can modify in terms of name (Arial, Times New Roman), style (bold, italic), color, and size

forecast A prediction for the business; forecasts can be created based on actual figures from the past year or from scratch

general journal A record of a company's transactions that is organized by date; information from it is posted to the general ledger

general ledger Shows the balance of each account and the transactions affecting them

Generally Accepted Accounting Principles (GAAP) Rules used to prepare, present, and report financial statements for a wide variety of entities

header and footer Information that appears at the top (header) or bottom (footer) of a report; you can change the default header/footer in preset reports along with how it's formatted via the Additional Customization window (Header and Footer tabs)

I-9 An IRS form used when hiring employees to verify identity and employment eligibility

Income Statement (aka Profit & Loss report) A financial report that reflects all transactions that affected income and expense accounts for a specified time period; found in the Company & Financial category of the Report Center window

Item List A list of products and services a company buys, sells, or resells; items must be created in the Item List as services, non-inventory parts, inventory parts, or other charges before being used in transactions

job costing Used to determine the profitability of each job for a customer by tracking the associated revenues and expenses

Layout Designer A window that provides rulers to line up objects and toolbar buttons to help manipulate template objects

Lead Center A feature used to track information about potential customers

liabilities Anything owed by the company, such as loans, expenses, or accounts payable

LIFO (Last In, First Out) Inventory valuation method wherein the value of the last inventory brought in is used to determine the COGS, and the total inventory value is based on inventory purchased earlier in the year

lists Where you store information about customers, vendors, employees, and other data important to your business

Loan Manager A QuickBooks tool that tracks your loans; also provides a "what if" tool to help you explore multiple loan scenarios

logo An image that represents your company; you can personalize your templates by adding a company logo

Long Term Liability account An account that tracks a liability (loan) you don't plan to pay off within the next year

normal balance Each account type has a normal balance that is either a debit or a credit, and the normal balance is the side that increases the account; assets and expenses have a debit normal balance, while liabilities, equity, and income have a credit normal balance

notes payable Promissory notes, or loans, you owe to other entities

notes receivable An account that tracks promissory notes, or loans, that you have issued to another individual or organization

online backup An app offered by QuickBooks for a monthly or annual fee as an online backup option called Intuit Data Protect

Opening Balance Equity account An equity account created by QuickBooks when you create your company, providing an accurate balance sheet from the start

outside payroll service A service that runs a company's payroll outside of QuickBooks; the company inputs the information into QuickBooks without using the payroll features

Payment reminders Feature that helps you manage receivables by creating mailing lists of customers, sending payment reminders, and scheduling reminders to be sent out in the future

Payroll Liabilities The account in which you hold payroll taxes and other deductions until you're required to pay them

Payroll Options Variety of methods by which to run payroll for your company; current options are found on Intuit's website

permanent account An account for which the ending balance for one fiscal period is the opening balance for the next; also known as a balance sheet account

petty cash Cash kept by businesses for small expenditures; in QuickBooks, Petty Cash is set up as a bank account in the Chart of Accounts

GREYSCALE

BIN TRAVELER FORM

Cut By _Michael A Huerta_ Qty _26_ Date _7-30_

Scanned By _Martin_ Qty _____ Date _7-31_

Scanned Batch IDs

_510175409_ _____ _____

Notes / Exception

_____

_____

_____

_____

_____

Daily Book Scanning Log

Name:_____ Date:_____ # of Scanners:_____

BIN #	BOOKS COMPLETED	# OF PAGES	NOTES / EXCEPTIONS
Bin 1	10		
Bin 2			
Bin 3			
Bin 4			
Bin 5			
Bin 6			
Bin 7			
Bin 8			
Bin 9			
Bin 10			
Bin 11			
Bin 12			
Bin 13			
Bin 14			
Bin 15			
Bin 16			
Bin 17			
Bin 18			
Bin 19			
Bin 20			
Bin 21			
Bin 22			
Bin 23			
Bin 24			
Bin 25			
Bin 26			
Bin 27			
Bin 28			
Bin 29			
Bin 30			
Bin 31			
Bin 32			
Bin 33			
Bin 34			
Bin 35			
Bin 36			
Bin 37			
Bin 38			
Bin 39			
Bin 40			

(BOOKS / LIBROS) TOTAL:_____**/ 600**

(PAGES/PAGINAS) TOTAL:_____

SHIFT:_____ **STATION #:**_____